CUSTOMER SERVICE OPERATIONS

Warren Blanding

CUSTOMER SERVICE OPERATIONS

The Complete Guide

amacom
American Management Association

This publication is designed to provide accurate and authorita-
tive information in regard to the subject matter covered. It is
sold with the understanding that the publisher is not engaged
in rendering legal, accounting, or other professional service. If
legal advice or other expert assistance is required, the services
of a competent professional person should be sought.

Library of Congress Cataloging-in-Publication Data
Blanding, Warren
      Customer service operations : the complete guide / Warren
   Blanding
         p.   cm.
      Includes index.
      ISBN 0-8144-5004-0 (hardcover)
      1. Customer service.   I. Title.
HF5415.5.B529   1991
658.8'12—dc20   90-56408
                                                               CIP

Printing number

10   9   8   7

Contents

Preface

This book of practical ideas and action plans is a complete guide to customer service operations in the momentous decade of the 1990s. It shows you how to start a customer service department from scratch, where to have it report, whether to centralize or decentralize, where to recruit the best people, and how to hang on to them when the stress begins to get to them. It explains the choices available to you in telecommunications and the different ways you can get management support for your department. It shows you how to cut costs and increase efficiency, how to make a measurable contribution to the bottom line, and how to measure that contribution and make it understandable to others.

But, most of all, this book shows you how to manage the best customer service department in your industry — how to keep it competitive, how to make it cost-effective and profit-oriented, and how to keep it on target with your customers' needs and expectations. You'll also learn how to keep your own career on a fast track as you move up to senior management levels, because as a customer service manager in the 1990s, you are faced with a rare opportunity to truly make a difference in your company.

That opportunity is the result of five historic changes that have been taking place in customer service since my book *Practical Handbook of Distribution Customer Service* (Van Nostrand Reinhold) was originally published in the mid-1980s:

1. *The accelerated march of automation and computerization* and its dramatically increased acceptance by a public that becomes more sophisticated daily. Few parts of the business have as many potential applications as customer service operations, as many opportunities for improving service and actually getting closer to customers than was possible in the depersonalized, early stages of automation characteristic of the 1970s and 1980s.

2. *The growing recognition by management that attracting and keeping a competent customer service work force will require considerably more accommodation* in the future than the traditional wages-and-benefits packages and the "clerical" label that have characterized customer service department staffing practices up until now.

3. *The transition of customer service from an after-sales-service mode, generally lumped under the heading of "operations," to a cornerstone of the corporate market-*

ing effort. Instead of an operating cost—fair game for a company's cost-reduction efforts—customer service is now recognized as a marketing strategy—an investment with measurable returns.

4. *The realization that the principles of customer service apply equally to businesses and to nonprofit and governmental bodies outside the business sphere.* Hospitals and educational institutions have made great strides in this direction. The 1989 service industries winner of the prestigious Award of Excellence of the International Customer Service Association was a hospital—Good Samaritan Hospital of Cincinnati—which competed head-to-head with a number of highly rated commercial organizations. In the governmental sphere, citizens in some jurisdictions have seen remarkable improvements in such commonplace areas as trash collection, motor vehicle inspection, and jury duty. (Many have a long way to go, but the discussion of queueing will help!)

5. Perhaps most important to readers of this book is *the increase in senior management positions with broad customer service responsibilities:* vice-president of customer service, senior vice-president of customer service, and even presidents of customer service divisions. As the 1980s were coming to an end, we began to hear about customer service reps who later became managers and finally ended up as presidents of their companies.

This book documents the actual customer service operations needed to make these new customer service strategies work, from setting standards and measuring performance to creating a customer service culture throughout the organization. It not only tells you the best way to write a statement of mission, but provides a series of actual examples you can adapt for your own use.

Besides these broad changes in the customer service environment, there have been many changes in the organizations, management techniques and technologies in customer service since my earlier book. There have been significant changes in telecommunications, the way standards are set and performance is measured, the way complaints are handled, the way return on investment (ROI) is calculated, the way customer service reps are trained, cross trained, and career-pathed. And there have been important changes in the ways the customer service department influences corporate policies and strategies.

This book has been written to help you understand those changes and apply them for the greatest benefit in your own organization. It differs from most books in the field in that it is highly specific to *management of customer service department operations:* how to develop and manage a profit-oriented, customer-oriented department in a profit-oriented, customer-oriented company.

Much of this book has been written from the point of view of line managers in customer service, often in companies very much like your own. There's a good reason for this. The book records what I have learned from working with several thousand customer service managers and again as many of their front-line customer service reps, from companies of all types and sizes in the United States, Canada, and Japan.

At home and abroad, these friends have been more than generous in sharing their experiences and knowledge with me. There is no end to their enthusiasm for what they are doing, nor to their dedication to customer service as a professional management discipline. All the ideas in this book that work for you (and most will) are theirs. The greatest compliment you can pay your fellow professionals who have contributed so heavily to this book is to document your own achievements and share them with others, as they have done through this book and the newsletters I edit.

My associates at Customer Service Institute have, as always, been supportive of my efforts and tolerant of the frequently unreasonable demands I place on them. Without them—particularly Leslie Harps, president and operating head of our company—this book could not have been written. Eva Weiss at AMACOM Books convinced me that the effort would be worthwhile and kept me convinced when I faltered. And, although our family has sadly decreased by one in the interim, this book, like my previous book, is dedicated to all my girls, and Albert, too.

Warren Blanding
Washington, D.C.

Section I

Overview of Key Customer Service Issues

Introduction

Many of the most essential elements of perfect customer service, or quality or excellent customer service as it's sometimes referred to here, are transparent or invisible to the customer. This doesn't make them any less important than the perfect service customers actually receive in tangible form. In fact, they make it possible.

As customer service manager, you need to understand—and you need to get others to understand—that perfect customer service is customer service that most nearly meets the combined needs of your customers and your own organization, with profits or benefits to both sides. In short, perfect customer service is real and measurable.

Ideally, perfect customer service is a systematized activity that involves your entire organization. In the private sector, customer service is organized to ensure maximum profitability from the customer base: a form of asset management where the results are measurable in highly favorable ROI (return on investment). In the public or nonprofit sectors, perfect customer service shows excellent cost-benefit ratios and has a favorable impact on public opinion as well.*

But many organizations have yet to develop this kind of awareness of customer service as a marketing strategy, investment, or cost-benefit issue. Even managers who have recognized the potential of customer service for increasing profits and market share often put all their emphasis on training service givers when they should pay equal attention to improving all ten of the elements that comprise the total customer service system, as listed below:

1. *Financial commitment by management.* Although it's desirable that top management have a philosophical commitment to customer service, the mark of a genuine customer service *system* is management's readiness to commit resources as well as moral support to customer service for a practical reason: its contribution to the bottom line.

---

*To avoid unnecessary duplication and repetition, the principles and applications described in this book should be considered as applying generally to customer service management in nonprofit or public sectors as well as to the for-profit businesses mainly used as examples.

Because of a long-standing tradition of treating customer service expenses as reducible operating costs rather than marketing investments like sales promotion and advertising, one of your most important jobs as customer service manager is to justify budgets that enable the systems and staffing support needed to provide genuinely excellent customer service that meets but does not exceed customer needs.

Chapter 14 explains in detail a number of practical cost justification methods, ready to be put into practice to increase acceptance of your own budgetary requests.

2. *Measurable and practical customer service standards.* Correct customer service standards reflect an understanding of what customers need and want and are willing to pay for—and what the competition is offering.

To have any meaning, standards must be stated in numbers and measurable in numbers. Words such as *excellent* and *superior* are good as motivators but need to be translated into specifics to which people can relate their performance (or the system's performance). For example:

"Ninety-five percent of incoming calls will be answered by a customer service representative within 15 seconds."

"Ninety-eight percent of customer inquiries will be answered live and on-line within 2 minutes."

"Credits will be posted to customer accounts within 3 days."

"Complaints involving $500 or less will be resolved within 5 working days or less."

"Ninety-five percent of orders will be shipped complete within 2 working days of receipt."

The complete step-by-step procedure for setting standards discussed in Chapter 7 is a valuable tool for achieving measurable excellence in customer service.

3. *Ongoing service monitoring.* Excellent customer service—excellent by your company's standards—requires that you as manager know at any time exactly how well the company is performing in meeting its standards. Waiting for customers to complain or periodically surveying their satisfaction levels cannot substitute for daily and sometimes hourly or continuous measurement of performance. The actual methods for measuring service performance vary considerably from industry to industry.

A good measure that can be applied in most customer service situations concerns the length and duration of the queue: the number of customers waiting for service at any given time and how long they have to wait. Understanding queueing applications is critical to efficient and acceptable customer service operations and is explained in nonacademic terms in Chapter 11.

You will find practical ways for measuring the queue and other key elements of customer service performance and productivity in Chapter 9, plus proven methods for using your findings to gain top management support for your customer service improvement proposals.

4. *A self-correcting stance by management.* As part of its willingness to commit resources to customer service, management must have in place the mecha-

nisms to correct quickly any failure to meet the company's customer service standards.

In practical terms, this means having contingency plans and decision rules that can be put into motion at the lowest practical level of the organization, in most cases by front-line personnel. Common examples include the airlines' lost baggage recovery and denied boarding (overbooking) compensation programs. Other familiar examples include product recalls, contingency plans for hazardous materials spills, and backup or emergency response systems in general. Increasingly, customer service contingency planning is embracing response to emergency situations at customer sites.

Apart from natural disasters, just-in-time practices have generated a need for formal standby plans of various types, and sound overall contingency planning is winning recognition for customer service managers in companies of all types. Chapter 12 explains how they have done so and how you can benefit from their experience.

Other types of self-correction, that is, the different ways of overcoming ongoing customer dissatisfaction, are covered in Chapter 8, which shows you how to use their feedback to improve the system and at the same time increase the customer service contribution to the bottom line.

5. *Policies that streamline rather than complicate customer service.* "Good" customer service policies are based on a combination of trust and economics: trust in the sense that the large majority of customers act in good faith and are not out to cheat their vendors; economics in the sense that even if there are some dishonest customers, honor systems and no-fault policies are often far less costly than traditional policies requiring in-depth investigations and multiple sign-offs on claims and complaints. As one manager put it, "My concern is with customers' profitability, not their honesty. I'm a businessperson, not a reformer!"

Chapter 5 explains in detail how you can write customer service policies that enhance service and at the same time are equitable to customers as well as to the company.

6. *An organization where service goals have priority over efficiency.* Efficiency and effective customer service aren't necessarily mutually exclusive, but the popular headcount approach, that is, structuring the customer service organization for productivity, inevitably subordinates the quality of customer service to the numbers of units of work performed. For example, a supermarket where all fifteen checkout lanes have lines of at least five customers waiting reflects maximum productivity but not necessarily optimum customer service. Similarly, an incoming call center with customers constantly in queue for an average of 2 minutes each is highly efficient from a headcount point of view because all agents are constantly busy, but it is unacceptable to many of the customers who are waiting.

By contrast, in a genuinely customer-oriented organization, headcount is driven by determining the kind of staffing required to meet the service quality standards the firm has set for itself, for example, assigning the number of agents needed to make the wait no longer than 1 minute.

But the problem of balancing efficiency with service to customers goes well beyond headcount and is compounded when some departments are held

responsible for meeting service goals and others for meeting financial goals—
and the two aren't always compatible. A standard that calls for prompt shipment of orders can easily be defeated by a policy restricting investment in
inventory or one prohibiting overtime in the warehouse or shipping department. The different ways you can overcome these roadblocks to excellent customer service are set forth in Chapters 5, 7, and 12.

7. *System.* In customer-driven companies, management recognizes that
effective customer service is a matter of logistics or system, not a single-
department responsibility, and everybody else in the organization realizes that
he or she is part of that system, not an independent operator.

Although it has become popular to talk of "teamwork" and "team spirit"
in customer service, the reality in business is that the way the system is
designed—the interfaces or meshing among the diverse departments in the
company—is what creates the sense of team, not vice versa. The most critical
aspect of system design is establishing internal standards and interdepartmental accountability, a process that in most cases must be initiated by the customer service manager. Chapters 5, 7, and 16 help prepare you for this
important mission.

8. *Customer-oriented, state-of-the-art technology.* There's a difference
between technology whose main function is to reduce the headcount and technology that actually improves service to customers. For example, an ACD
(automatic call distributor) system that sequences calls to the next available rep
maximizes productivity and minimizes headcount, but it doesn't necessarily
provide a level of service comparable to assignment of customer service reps
by account or territory. What works well in an application such as airline reservations, for example, may be completely inappropriate in customized software or engineering applications.

Yet well-designed ACD systems and other technological innovations such
as bar-code scanning, voice response units (VRU), and automatic teller
machines often improve the quality of customer service as well as the efficiency, provided always that the levels of automation are acceptable to customers or that there are reasonable alternatives or defaults to conventional systems.
Chapter 6 on departmental organization and Chapter 10 on inbound communications will guide you quickly through this complex and fast-moving area.

9. *Trained personnel.* For better or for worse, companies are most often
judged by the performance and perceived attitude of their front-line personnel.
There's a tendency to blame poor service on poor training, although in reality
it's often attributable to a poor system or poor support; what's perceived as a
poor attitude on the part of the service giver is more likely to be the service
giver's frustration at an inability to perform the job through lack of cooperation
in the organization or, more accurately, poor system design.

Managements in genuinely customer-oriented companies recognize that
continuing training is an essential part of good system design. But they also
recognize that it's the final step in customer service system design: the key-
stone that holds it all together. Chapter 6 on organization and Chapters 16 and
17 on training, morale, and motivation provide examples of how other managers are successfully handling these issues.

10. *Internal corporate culture.* Companies that treat their employees well also treat their customers well. In customer-driven companies this is not so much a matter of philosophy or morality as it is of sound business sense: recognizing that employees will never treat customers any better than they themselves are treated by their managements. There's no mystique or quasi-religious fervor associated with a genuine customer service culture; it's just good business sense. Chapter 9 describes a method for vetting your own organization to determine the extent to which a corporate culture exists and what steps can be taken to improve and fine-tune it.

A pervasive characteristic of customer-driven customer service is that customer-driven companies are perceived by their customers as easy to do business with. Yet there is likely to be considerable confusion about who the customer actually is and what he or she expects in the way of service. Chapters 1 and 2 address these issues in detail.

1

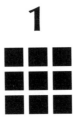

Who Is This Customer You Keep Talking About?

It's popular to generalize about customers and their importance to the company. "The customer puts bread on my table." "The customer signs my paycheck." These expressions show appreciation, but not necessarily understanding.

As a customer service manager growing in your job, you must be considerably more sophisticated in the way you define your customers. You need to develop a keen sensitivity to your customers, both as individuals and as members of specific markets or channels, and particularly as the main assets of your organization and the principal source of its revenues and profits.

In perfect customer service as we've defined it, the importance of customers is taken for granted. And it begins with the following seven specific assumptions about your company's relationship with its customers:

1. *The customer service activity focuses mainly on existing customers.* The primary mission of perfect customer service is repeat business and increased business—and more profitable business—from present customers. This goal requires specific knowledge about who those customers are, why they buy, how they buy and, particularly, what causes them to rebuy and to increase their purchases over time.

As customer service manager, you may have to compete for budget and other resources with marketing personnel whose primary mission is to acquire customers, not keep them. Your best ammunition is to demonstrate the profit contribution—in repeat business, account growth, and increased profitability—by your department. Chapter 14 explains three ways you can do just that and, as a special bonus, lists forty-five ways you can make a further profit by cutting costs and increasing margins.

2. *Some customers are more important than others.* This idea isn't always easy to accept, but it's usually true. Customers who make a bigger contribution to profit, or represent greater growth potential, are more important than customers who make a smaller contribution or reflect mature or declining markets. The concept of perfect customer service doesn't require that all customers get equal service, only that the different *classes* of customer get service commensurate with their contribution or potential contribution to profits.

Fifteen Versions of
The Customer As an Individual

1. An individual buying for himself or herself.

2. An individual buying for relatives or friends.

3. An individual buying as an agent for others.

4. An individual who receives the service or product but does not order it or pay for it.

5. An individual who orders or pays for the service or product but does not receive it.

6. An individual who specifies product or service characteristics or standards but does not specify the source.

7. An intermediate buyer who buys a service or product for resale as-is, for example, wholesaler, retailer, travel agent.

8. A buyer who buys the product or service for incorporation into other services or products: components for finished products, ingredients for prepared foods, music for productions, and so forth.

9. An individual involved in the intermediate handling or processing of services and products en route to final customers: third party trucker, communications company, typesetter.

10. A consultant who recommends services or products to clients but does not necessarily act in their behalf in the actual buying.

11. An individual who is a noncustomer but whose informal advice is sought by family, friends, and acquaintances.

12. A point-of-sale salesperson who recommends one product over another.

13. Internal customers within the seller organization are individuals dependent on others in the organization to complete certain tasks of their own. For the performance of many of their duties, customer service reps are effectively the internal customers of manufacturing, shipping, credit, and other departments.

14. A recipient of government services (wanted or unwanted), a patient at a health care facility, a member of a trade, professional, or social organization, a member of a political constituency.

15. A buyer, purchasing agent, traffic manager, materials manager, or other person with a job description spelling out his or her responsibilities—and who will be judged for promotion, compensation, and job tenure on the basis of how well he or she performs that job. This category includes everyone who reports to that particular person and is judged by similar criteria.

The Inconsistency of Customers

The popular concept that customer needs, wants, and expectations are constant and unchanging is just as fallacious as the assumption that all customers are alike and react to service offerings in the same way. Satisfaction levels almost always vary with circumstances; a customer who will tolerate a late delivery on Monday, when he is ordering for stock, will complain bitterly at a late delivery on Thursday, when he has ordered for production.

Wise investors learn as much about their investment assets as they can. Successful companies do the same in respect to their customers. Because people change, successful companies never lose touch with their customers as rebuy influences and particularly as human beings.

---

3. *Within a single customer base, customers of equal importance are likely to have significantly different service requirements.* For example, if you sell to the original equipment market as well as through dealers or distributors, you will find that each channel has highly specific and different service requirements. The same is true of companies selling to hospitals as well as distributors, institutions as well as fast-food outlets, yuppies as well as senior citizens, and so forth. Some examples of those differences in service requirements by channel are illustrated in Figure 1-1.

4. *The customer is someone who can be sold directly or indirectly by the customer service department.* Even though the department's main focus is on keeping the existing customers sold, occasionally you may get involved in direct selling to prospective rather than actual customers. For example, you may be called on to develop customer service features that meet specific needs of accounts targeted by your sales department. The so-called *kanban* or JIT (just-in-time) parts delivery arrangements that the Big Three automakers require of their suppliers are examples. Major retail chains and hospital chains often impose similar requirements on their suppliers. The vendor-customer relationship described as "partnershipping" is a comparable relationship in the service industries. Partnershipping is discussed further in Chapter 2. Of course both existing and prospective customers can be sold directly by the customer service department in other areas, including order enhancement, inquiry conversion, lead screening, and direct telemarketing. These are covered in detail in Chapter 13.

As an indirect selling tool, customer service often attracts new customers by simple word-of-mouth advertising. Many companies expand their customer base simply by asking their satisfied customers for referrals. It can also work the other way, that is, prospective customers asking for the names of some of your present customers whom they can contact. The customer service department plays an important role by ensuring that such customers do in fact exist. You can often help sales by having lists of such customers readily available as references, and you have the advantage of knowing who will give you an extra good reference because of something extra good your department did for them.

5. *Customers are assets.* An investment, often a substantial one, has been made in acquiring the customer. It's an integral part of the customer service

Figure 1-1. Diversity of customer service requirements in typical businesses or channels

Product or Service	Channel	Customer Service Requirements
Consumer goods	Retail store	Sales clerk, cashier, warehouse
Consumer goods	Mail order	Order, customer service personnel
Insurance	Agency, direct through employer	Adjusters, customer service Processed by doctor or hospital
Banking, financial	High end markets	Account execs, CSRs
Health care	Hospitals	Doctors, hospital personnel
Health care products	Hospitals Wholesalers Retailers	For critical care, urgent Varies Varies
Manufacturers	Retailers	For ads, promo, urgent
Manufacturers	Distributors	Usually routine
Food manufacturers	Distributors Indirect/ direct	Often a voluntary co-op Pooling through public warehouse
Custom manufacturers	Direct	Engineering, training, postinstallation service
Original equipment manufacturer suppliers	Direct to manufacturer	Just-in-time, kanban
Personal sales (Avon, Mary Kay, Tupperware)	Through agent to consumer	Great stress on service to agent to maintain motivation to sell
Commodities, generics	Various	High levels of service to make products/services stand out from competitive offerings
Books, publications specialized information	Various	Speed and accuracy often critical; facsimile and EDI (electronic data interchange) on increase
Captive suppliers	Direct	Service often perceived as not being as good as it actually is

Source: Customer Service Newsletter

Figure 1-2. Sample chart for profiling rebuy influences

Customer Needs	Weight	Customer Category (including percentage of total rebuy influence)				
		Purchasing Director (20%)	Buyer (30%)	Specifier (40%)	Other (7%)	Other (3%)
Total order or service cycle						
Service reliability and consistency						
Order completeness and/or accuracy						
Handling changes in orders or instructions						
Product/service order status information						
Documentation/ billing accuracy and clarity						
Response to technical and other inquiries						
Complaint resolution						
Issuing refunds, posting credits						
(Other)						
(Other)						

Source: Customer Service Newsletter

mission to protect that asset and maximize the return on the investment, which means creating a customer service environment and comfort level that effectively keeps the customer in and the competition out. You will want to constantly monitor your performance and your customers' perceptions of your service versus the competition. You will find four practical ways of doing just that in Chapter 9.

Some customers represent better investments than others, and, just as you would review a portfolio of investments, it's only logical to review your portfolio of customers. It may rub your marketing people the wrong way to degrade service to less profitable accounts—or in some cases demarket them altogether—but it may be your best bet in terms of providing the high levels of service demanded by your most remunerative accounts.

6. *The buying influences at whom presale marketing efforts are aimed are not necessarily the same individuals as the rebuying influences at whom the customer service effort is directed, or by whom it is actually received.* In a business-to-business market, for example, a customer company may include six or seven or even more rebuying influences: the original specifier, the end user, the purchasing agent, the buyer, the receiving clerk, the warehouse manager, operations or maintenance personnel, accounts payable, human resources, and more.

If you haven't already done so, you will find it very helpful to develop profiles of your key accounts and the different kinds of relationships you need to form. Figure 1-2 shows one way to list the rebuy influences in a customer organization to show the relative weight or importance of each and the service features most important to each. Note that the percentages assigned here are hypothetical and should be replaced by your own figures in your computations.

As one example of this type of directed service effort, the customer service manager in a grocery products company concentrates his efforts on the warehouse manager rather than the buyer in the customer's purchasing department. He has found that it is more productive to work on the actual logistics of delivery because that's actually the key to meeting the buyer's needs.

7. *The customer is always an individual.* Although an account may be a composite of many individuals, customer service people always deal with those individuals one-on-one. And they need to recognize that each of these individuals has *personal* aspirations quite apart from those of the account as an account—aspirations to keep their jobs, to look good to their associates and management, to progress in their careers, to educate their children, and so forth. Interfering with these aspirations could very well be more damaging to the vendor than an actual customer service failure.

Therefore, training your personnel in interpersonal relationships, and continually monitoring their performance against high standards, is one of the most important elements of your job as customer service manager. When you protect individual customers and maintain their self-esteem, you also go a long way toward protecting the account from even the fiercest competitors.

2

■■■
■■■
■■■

The Visible Elements of Perfect Customer Service

This chapter describes customer service applications in a select few industries or activities from the wide variety listed in Figure 2-1. (Note that service giver/ service receiver relationships exist even where there is no direct payment for the product or service by the customer.) Even though many of these industries and channels are likely to be quite different from your own, it is worthwhile to go through the entire list to determine whether there may be parallels to your own business in seemingly different enterprises. Some of your best ideas for customer service improvements may already be at work in a completely unrelated line of business!

For virtually all customer service activities, billing accuracy, speed of response to complaints and adjustment requests, and courtesy and accessibility of personnel are prime components—givens—of excellent customer service from the customer's viewpoint. Beyond these universal service components, individual industries and service-giving groups naturally have their own unique service elements that have developed largely in response to marketplace pressures.

To give you an idea of the diversity of ways that perfect or excellent customer service is defined in different industries or activities, a representative sample follows:

■ *In the retail business.* A customer-oriented retail organization has a wide variety of merchandise within its field, convenient hours, parking, reasonable policies on returns and exchanges, and ready availability of trained and courteous sales and service personnel. If it sells furniture, appliances, and other equipment, the customer-oriented retailer provides delivery suited to the customer's convenience, prompt attention to warranty repairs and adjustments, general maintainability of products, and ready availability of parts and/or supplies.

The quality of customer service, or the lack of it, is typically determined by management, not by sales personnel as is commonly thought. In one well-known retail organization, sales personnel are trained only in cash register operation, which drives the inventory management system, and in general they are penalized only for cash register errors but not customer service shortfalls,

Figure 2-1. Examples of customer service applications

Consumer		Business		Public/Institutional*	
Products	Services	Products	Services	Products	Services
Retail, general	Insurance	Manufacturing to inventory	Transportation	Infrastructure	Defense
Retail, special	Banking, financial	Manufacturing to order	Warehousing	Currency/stamps	Education
Mail order	Travel	Commodities	Insurance	Publications	Licensing, regulation
Do-it-yourself	Health care	Finished goods	Financial	Power/light	Police protection
Home delivery	Real estate	Hi-tech/low-tech	Factoring	Museums, parks	Health
Party sales	Domestic help	Bulk/packaged	Engineering	Sheltered workshops	Information
Door-to-door	Lawn, yard care	Consumer/industrial	Environmental	Research spinoff	Postal service
In-home demos	Bridal counseling	Original equipment manufacturers/distributors	Computer services	Surplus goods	Subsidies
Auctions	Catering	Direct/indirect	Security services	Timberlands	Taxes
Estate/yard sales	Riding, sports	Consignment	Consulting	Oil, minerals	Lotteries
Equipment rental	Recreation	Site delivery	Leasing		Agriculture department
Subscriptions	Entertainment	On-site construction	Waste management		Disaster relief
Negative options	Beauty				Standards
	Diet plans				Export/import
	Child care				Social services
	Education				Fire department
	Consulting				Waste management

*Products and services offered by associations and nonprofit organizations would also fall in this category.
Source: Customer Service Newsletter

which are rarely monitored. As a result, the company has no way of knowing what quality of service it is actually offering its customers and what impact this is having on sales and profits.

■ *In the consumer direct marketing or mail order business.* The nature of this business requires a high degree of trust on the part of customers and centers on ready availability of advertised products, prompt delivery, a liberal exchange and return policy, and hassle-free dealings in general.

Also, because the industry is closely watched by both the postal service and the Federal Trade Commission, it has a considerable incentive to represent products accurately in its catalogs and to bend over backward to avoid any semblance of unfair dealings.

Direct marketing is also a highly competitive business in upscale markets, and one of the marks of truly customer-oriented customer service in a company is that it's a few points ahead of its main competitors, a sure sign that management has been carefully monitoring the customer service performance of those competitors.

■ *In the manufacturing business.* This example is composed mainly of business-to-business companies where customers are mainly concerned with fast turnaround and completeness of orders, appropriate levels of technical support, forewarning about problems or inability to deliver on time, and an ability to respond to emergency situations.

In business-to-business dealings, a truly customer-oriented customer service organization recognizes that its primary obligation is to *help the customer make money.* And it recognizes a strong secondary obligation, as discussed in Chapter 1, to protect the individual buyer or specifier in his or her own company. If either of these service components is missing, all the courtesy and interpersonal skills in the world won't keep the customer on board.

Manufacturing for stock, as in the consumer goods business, is often characterized by highly competitive levels of customer service driven by marketplace forces. In manufacturing to order, or custom manufacturing, customers place less emphasis on delivery and stock availability and much more on specific skills on the part of customer service personnel: ability to estimate accurately, technical expertise in planning production for least cost consistent with quality standards, engineering support where needed, and reasonable schedules and commitments that are kept.

■ *In the banking and financial services business.* This area comprises many different types of businesses, commercial and retail, with a common denominator of being in business to help customers make or manage money. A high level of trust is implicit and is even more critical in the wake of the savings and loan scandals of the 1980s.

The retail banking industry has found that its historic image of aloofness, a management posture that was often imitated at the service giver level, was badly in need of humanizing and that an easy-to-do-business-with perception by customers was as important to banking as to retailing in general.

Of all industries, retail banking has shown the greatest advances in customer service, perhaps because it was far behind to begin with. Automatic teller machines, effective and interactive phone systems for handling account queries, increased availability and higher skill levels of customer service personnel, faster turnaround on loans, and quick resolution problems—all are signs of a customer-oriented retail banking organization.

On the commercial side, all of these features plus careful attention to making customers' money work its hardest would be considered major components of proactive customer service.

Not surprisingly, the industry is finding at all levels that the speed with which an institution responds to and resolves complaints and other problems creates high levels of loyalty and acceptance of new products and services introduced by that institution. Many of these same customer service features are characteristic of the insurance business as well.

In the transportation industry. This industry has two main sectors, passenger and freight. It's already been noted that the airline industry has demonstrated customer-oriented customer service for some time, although measures by the Federal Aviation Agency of individual airlines' performance show a wide margin in service quality between the best performers, in terms of customer service, and the worst. As might be expected, quality of service also varies with the amount of competition in different markets.

Although airlines tend to emphasize amenities and personnel in their advertising along with special discount fares aimed primarily at recreational travelers, regular business travelers—the backbone of the business—tend to select carriers in terms of a combination of routes, schedules, and the particular frequent flyer clubs they belong to.

Because travelers come in contact with so many different categories of service givers in the course of a typical trip—telephone personnel, ticket agents and ground crews at the airport, and flight crews aloft—highly trained and interpersonally sensitive personnel are essential to customer-oriented customer service. Beyond this, the elements of excellent customer service would also include on-time performance (not always under the individual airline's control, although maintenance practices and spare parts inventory policies may play a significant role in flight delays or cancellations resulting from mechanical problems). Overbooking or bumping rates and denied boarding compensation practices are another measure of customer service quality, as is the individual airline's record on lost, delayed, and damaged baggage and the speed with which it recovers lost baggage or resolves claims.

The industry is not without its critics, primarily among business travelers who feel that deregulation of passenger service has permitted airlines to charge unreasonably high rates in markets where they have near or complete monopolies.

After four decades of general inattention to its customers, the intercity rail passenger transportation business has adopted many of the customer service practices innovated by the airlines in the 1940s and 1950s as a means of attracting passengers to the "new" means of travel. Even so, it's doubtful that rail passenger service of any kind could survive without large federal subsidies. The main marketplace is concerned more with getting places fast than it is with seeing the scenery en route.

In the freight transportation industries, a field that was under federal economic regulation for some three-quarters of a century, deregulation and the subsequent increase in competition brought about an almost immediate improvement in customer service offerings.

In the small package business, speed of service, multilevel service, contract rates and on-line tracing and expediting are the standards of proactive customer service. Next-morning and second-morning delivery nationwide are taken for granted. In conventional rail and truck transportation, customer-oriented carriers have begun to develop the close working relationships with their customers often known as "partnershipping," even to the extent of exchanging personnel.

Surprising to some, there is pressure within the trucking industry for some measure of re-regulation. According to a 1990 press release from the Regular Common Carrier Conference of the American Trucking Associations, "Substantial discounts are bleeding many LTL [less-than-truckload] carriers to death, and keeping the industry generally on the precipice of failure." Although not all in the field would agree, this may illustrate the downside of customer service: providing the levels of customer service the customers need and want but are *not* willing to pay for.

In the lodging and food service industries. Customer service is a principal ingredient of the so-called hospitality industry. Yet one of the paradoxes is that the best service is usually invisible—the customer is not aware that it is happening. The customer is not aware that check-in at a hotel or motel or service in a restaurant is fast, is not aware that premises are neat and clean, that bills are accurate and personnel are responsive.

The hospitality industry aims to minimize the likelihood that guests will notice customer service because it is *bad*, and, at the other extreme, adds special services that are so unusual that guests can't help but notice them. The diversity of the hospitality industry makes it difficult to generalize about customer service quality, but certainly good logistics or system—"good" meaning transparent—and highly trained personnel are essential.

Visitors to the various Disney enterprises invariably comment about the quality of training reflected by Disney personnel; they almost never comment on the excellence of underlying systems and logistics that support the personnel. In other words, the systems and logistics are invisible and the personnel are visible in a positive way, which is the way quality customer service should be in the hospitality industry.

In education, health care, and institutional services. Perhaps the most significant development in this area has been the realization that the users of these services are de facto customers, not captives of "the system."

This development has been particularly notable in hospital administration, where patients are increasingly being called "guests" and service givers at all levels are being trained in guest relations. Hospital operations are being geared to the convenience of patients and their families with such amenities as free or low cost parking, cafeterias, comfortable waiting rooms, and, in some cases, hostesses whose primary function is to help patients' families deal with professional and business personnel at the hospital. There have been similar advances in institutional treatment of addiction, where it is the custom to refer to individuals in detoxification, recovery, or rehabilitation as "clients."

In education, institutions have started using student-friendly systems to facilitate such traditionally time-consuming and inefficient activities as registration. Increasing accommodation of disabled persons in the educational system as elsewhere is another service enhancement and one that is incidentally providing an excellent pool of workers for a wide range of customer service jobs.

In the public utility industry. Although public utilities have historically been monopolies, in recent years consumerism and regulatory bodies have forced them to become more responsive to their customers. Although the most visible improvement has been in the area of billing practices, shutoffs, and general customer relations, the most significant improvements have often been in improved system reliability along with improved dispatch and repair services.

Utilities have also had a good response to consumer centers they have set up in shopping malls to make it more convenient for customers to pay their bills and handle other transactions. They have also invested heavily in training contact personnel, recognizing that, even though their customers are captive, those same customers are taxpayers and voters and can have a direct influence on the regulatory process.

In the public sector: government services. Excellent customer service in the public sector is similarly characterized by the realization that citizens using public sector services are not captives but customers in every sense of the word. This applies as much to visitors to national parks as it does to welfare recipients and even inmates in prisons and taxpayers dealing with the Internal Revenue Service.

People who are well treated by the government process are more cooperative with it, which in turn reduces administrative costs. In the case of the IRS, the premise is that more revenue is collected simply by making the agency easier to deal with and changing the perception of its personnel from policemen to service givers.

Government agencies that were historically bogged down in red tape and delays have introduced such innovations as 800 numbers and appointments and explanations written in basic English and other languages. Saturday and evening hours—even free parking—help create the perception that public agencies do in fact belong to the public and not the bureaucrats. There is still plenty of room for improvement, but the fact that the effort is being made is a testimony to the effectiveness of the democratic process supported by a free press.

The transition to customer-driven customer service in these sectors is far from complete, of course. But two major characteristics can be taken for granted in any truly customer-driven organization: (1) it subscribes to the idea that customer service must make an organization easy to buy from or deal with; and (2) it depends on system and organization, not speeches and slogans, to see that its service fits the customer's needs—and at a price the customer is willing to pay.

Most of what you have read in this chapter will seem quite logical to you. But as customer service manager you must be *extremely* wary of senior managers in your company who profess to be strong believers in customer service excellence and often cap their remarks with, "After all, I always say good customer service is just plain common sense!" When the chips are down and you later turn to these same managers for support on your new project, it often develops that their notion of common sense and yours are light years apart!

You should avoid the popular admonitions to "think of the customer as yourself" or "put yourself in the customer's place." Doing so can lead you to a thousand and one opinions on what your customer service "mix" should be, none of them necessarily correct. The only way you can fully define and meet customer needs is to *think of the customer as the customer*, quite apart from your own biases, likes, dislikes, wants, and needs and to research the customer's true needs and how well you are meeting them, as described in Chapter 9.

Then you'll be making real progress toward perfect customer service!

3

The Seven Most Common Obstacles to Perfect Customer Service

The previous chapters have given you a working knowledge of the basic principles of perfect customer service. Before you start putting that knowledge into practice, you need to know how to deal with some of the most common problems that arise in typical dealings with customers. This chapter explains those problems and their causes and solutions so that when you start writing a mission statement and supporting policies for your department (see Chapters 4 and 5), you'll be well versed in the safeguards to include.

Unless you have just arrived from outer space, you don't need to be told that in the real world, customer service is often far from perfect. In 1987, *Harper's Index Book* reported that one in five Americans said that they would rather have a tooth pulled than take their car in for repairs. Similar views were being expressed in feature articles—often cover stories—in virtually every major U.S. newsmagazine, tradepaper, and metropolitan newspaper about the abominable state of customer service in general.

Most of this coverage was relatively superficial and consisted largely of "war stories." Many were inaccurate and showed little understanding of the complex mechanisms required to deliver consistently good service. Many of the stories left the impression that the fault for the majority of customer service "atrocities" recorded lay with the frontline service givers' lack of training and motivation, when in reality these valuable personnel are rarely the real cause of customer service problems of major consequence.

For, as you'll see in the review of typical customer service problems that follows, the fault lies most often with the system deficiencies or with the policies and procedures that are determined sometimes by you, sometimes by those further up the line, and sometimes by the supervisor or team leader reporting to you.

Many of the problems bear a strong resemblance to hassles you have experienced. That's understandable, because I've rounded up the seven most common problems that are also the most irritating to customers and costly to the company in terms of goodwill as well as administrative costs. When you get to Chapter 5, dealing with policies and procedures, you will want to refer back to this brief chapter as a reminder of what you *don't* want to have happen when you pick up your policy-making pen and set out to prove that it's mightier than the sword.

Many of the obstacles to perfect service described here reflect policies and procedures that originate in the marketing or financial sectors of a typical company. They represent good-faith efforts to protect the company and save money, but in practice they usually alienate customers and often cost more money to administer than they actually save, to say nothing of their potential cost in lost business:

1. *Problem: credits and adjustments.* In most companies, close to 90 percent of adjustments are issued or made in accordance with customer requests, but only after putting customers through an administrative process that costs the company more than the amount of money involved. The administrative cost of investigating a claim in the banking industry is currently more than $50. In manufacturing, the costs may be even higher; for bookkeeping purposes, one company uses standard costs of $450 on up per investigation of a claim resulting from a customer service failure.

There's often a comparable cost in terms of damage to the customer relationship: the customer's perception of bad faith on the company's part. Some companies delay posting credits for as long as 6 months, which understandably riles customers; the problem can become acute when the credit department starts collection procedures on unpaid invoices, which, in theory, are in the process of being adjusted.

The impact on future sales to that particular customer—and the damage to the firm's image in the marketplace—can be, and often is, considerable. If the product or service that's being sold tends to be generic or parity, the result can be loss of the customer's account or a reduction in the amount of business it does with the vendor.

The solution. Much of the problem could be avoided by adopting a no-fault policy on credits and setting an automatic adjustment level based on economics. For example, if the company spends $50 to investigate each claim or complaint and in the end pays out 90 percent of all claims under $500, it would come out as well simply paying out all claims under $500 *without* investigating. The mathematics are simple. To investigate ten $500 claims at an investigative cost of $50 each costs $500; to pay out 9 of those claims, or 90 percent, costs $4,500. Adding the $500 investigative cost and the $4,500 payout cost totals $5,000—the exact amount that would have been paid out on a no-fault, automatic adjustment basis, but without the delay or hassle factor.

As a general rule, a company can automatically approve any request for credits up to ten times the administrative costs that would otherwise be involved and still come out ahead. You won't find it easy to sell this concept because management will argue that once customers learn of your policy they'll start taking advantage of it. So, you'll have to prove not only the economics but also that you have a system in place for preventing abuses.

The financial department tends to oppose automatic credits because they are perceived as an avoidable or reducible expense and a logical target for cost reduction. Sales personnel also resist easy credits because they represent a reversal of sales and therefore a loss of their commissions. Yet if your management is serious about excellence in customer service, there's no better place to start than by eliminating the red tape and hassles involved in credits and adjustments. At the same time you'll be making a significant profit contribution by reducing administrative costs and keeping the customers in a buying frame of mind.

2. *Problem: returns and exchanges.* These are another dimension of the credits and adjustments problem, often driven by a similar mistrust of customers. Even though the mistake is theirs, some companies often will not reship the correct product to the customer until the misshipment has been shipped back and checked by the vendor.

The procedure is even more complicated when goods are shipped FOB shipping point, where the title passes to the buyer when the goods are loaded aboard the truck or other freight vehicle at the seller's plant, warehouse, or store. Then if the goods are damaged in transit, it becomes the customer's responsibility to file a claim with the freight carrier. This procedure can be tedious and drawn-out because the end or ultimate customer usually is the vendor's customer, not the carrier's, and has little clout with the carrier.

The returns and exchanges problem has other dimensions, too. Customers are sometimes motivated to overbuy in order to have backup stock on hand if sales of a particular item take off unexpectantly. Or they are induced to over-order as the result of a sales promotion campaign or premium offer. If customers have difficulty returning their overages in the future they will probably *under*buy.

There are parallels in the service industries, where customers contract for services to be delivered over a period of time—rent is a common example—and then find it very difficult to get out of the contract, even when their reasons are sound and plausible.

The solution. Since the problem is repetitive, an important part of the solution is simply to eliminate as many as possible of the reasons for returns and exchanges, that is, incorrect product descriptions in ads and in catalogs, errors in order entry or selection in the warehouse, improper packing leading to damage.

As statistical process control becomes increasingly used in customer service applications, you will find it relatively easy to bring problems such as these under control. Yet there are other reasons for returning or exchanging goods, and part of the mission of the customer service department should be to make the process as smooth and painless and fast as possible.

When the vendor assists customers with freight claims, as some do, the whole process is usually speeded up because the vendor is likely to be an important customer of the carrier's. Some vendors offer the customer a discount if they have damaged freight repaired locally rather than return the shipment. And some have honor-system policies and authorize customers to dispose of badly damaged merchandise locally and receive full credit.

Some vendors are gradually moving toward more liberal policies and away from traditional "punitive" procedures involving strict time limits, preapproval, and restocking charges. Although there's such a thing as being too liberal in returns and exchanges policies, companies with restrictive policies usually inhibit customers from purchasing more than what they need or in advance of the time they need it.

In business-to-business sales, this inhibition creates emergency situations when the customers' original forecasts turn out to have been low. If the original vendor can't meet the emergency, then the door is opened for a competitor who can. A more liberal returns policy would have encouraged the customer to order over estimates, which would have avoided the emergency situation altogether and resulted in more revenue for the seller as well.

3. *Problem: approvals.* Closely related is the matter of approvals, a process that is often as stressful internally as it is on customers. There are companies where simple credits or refunds of as little as $5 require the signature of as many as five company individuals, inevitably creating bottlenecks and delays and annoying the customers, who in turn vent their irritation on customer service reps who have no control over the situation.

The economics of multiple approvals of this order is alarming. For a customer service rep to handle a routine transaction costs about $6. For a supervisor or a manager to do so costs two or three times that. Five signoffs on a credit probably costs $50–$75, over and above a $50 research cost at the operating level. As many as 80 percent of approvals can probably be handled with a single approval through the use of decision rules reflecting corporate policies. Of course all these added costs are ultimately passed along to the customers — or subtracted from the firm's profits. And the irritation to customers caused by the inevitable delays is a good way to drive them into the arms of your competitors.

The solution. This situation is another where you need to demonstrate the economics to your financial people and document the feedback from angry customers for your sales and marketing departments and top management. But you also must offer an alternative to the multiple signoffs, which usually is a graduated scale similar to the following, using dollar amounts:

Signoffs by customer service rep:	Up to $25
Signoffs by supervisors:	Up to $100
Signoffs by manager:	Up to $500
Signoffs by director:	Up to $1,000
Signoffs over $1,000 approved by the vice-presidents of finance and sales	

These figures are hypothetical, of course, and limits may be higher because of the nature of your services or products. Similar sentiments are incorporated in some company mission statements (see Figure 4-2). The value of this approach is that it not only speeds up the process but also sets a level of authority commensurate with the amount involved; also, valuable managerial time is not being spent on matters that can be handled on the front line.

4. *Problem: accountability.* Although the phrase "that's not my department" isn't heard as often as it used to be, the mentality underlying it still prevails in many organizations. As a result, the customer service department is often perceived as the only department directly responsible to customers. There are seldom any standards of performance for other departments whose actions, or

lack of them, directly affect the customer service department's ability to meet its commitments to customers.

Other departments are rarely held accountable for service failures that they in fact cause by failing to perform. The customer service department is frequently blamed for problems over which it has no control, and customer service reps' frustration is likely to spill over on to customers. Trying to get some kind of response to problems as well as unmet commitments forces customers to view the entire process as at best a runaround and at worse a highly disorganized and demoralized company.

The solution. The accountability problem is usually a reflection of the company's lack of internal as well as external standards: external standards reflecting the company's best judgment of the service levels customers want and need; internal standards representing the levels at which the different departments must perform and/or produce in order for those external standards or commitments to be met.

Clearly, no system of this type can function unless performance is monitored across the board and individual departments, not just the customer service department, are held accountable for any failure to meet the standards. Chapter 7 explains why you need to involve top management in the standard-setting process, how to do it, and how it will result in a vastly improved system of accountability.

5. *Problem: information and getting answers.* Here, the problem has four main dimensions: (1) It's difficult for customers who telephone because of busy signals or long waits; (2) Nobody knows who has the appropriate information and calls are transferred several times; (3) Individuals who supposedly have the information are poorly informed or deliver the information in a disorganized and hardly credible manner; and (4) Different people in the company give different answers to the same question.

These problems can have serious consequences. Customers who consider the process a hassle may skip it altogether and cause costly problems, even liability situations, by acting without proper information or safety warnings. Customers who are misinformed may misapply the products or services, with a similar costly outcome. And there is always the possibility of turning to other vendors where information is easier to obtain.

The solution. The information problem results from a number of individual procedural problems. The first such problem is the lack of an organized information resource with a workable access system. Sometimes you can cure this simply by creating an alphabetical subject directory enabling customers or switchboard operators to quickly locate the proper department or individual. Sometimes it's a more complex problem of reconstructing and enlarging the database to permit on-line response to a higher proportion of inquiries.

The problem of getting through on the telephone often reflects an inadequate phone system and/or inadequate staffing. Another possibility is that workers are taking so long to answer other questions that calls back up and delays lengthen. A further problem reflected in getting different answers from different people is the lack of scripts for responding to repetitive inquiries.

Quite often, misinformation problems stem from a very simple cause: work overload on the telephone. This problem can often be corrected by an automated interactive phone system to handle routine inquiries and to free personnel for more complex questions.

These issues are as central to customer service operations as anything else you do. And yet you don't want to become too preoccupied with the attended telephone as the primary instrument of information and communications in customer service. Its cost is so high and its efficiency so low—and skilled and motivated people are getting so hard to find—that you will want to start looking for alternatives that enable you to use attended telephones for situations where the live contact and human skills represent the *only* way to handle things.

You can find a number of specific ways to deal with the information problems in Chapters 10, 12, and 16.

6. *Problem: availability of personnel.* Many of the problems listed in this chapter are compounded by the nonavailability of the particular individual needed to provide certain information or authorization or to review or update materials. This hassle worsens when the individual fails to return calls or follow up on commitments.

The solution. You need to overcome the underlying problem of organization and delegation and sometimes to remedy the shortcomings in certain job descriptions. If personnel have conflicting priorities, for example, servicing customer requests for technical information versus supervising bench repairs, it is almost certain that customer requests will be subordinated to the bench repair activity where the individual's performance is most likely to be measured.

The availability problem is most prevalent in companies that don't use decision rules enough to permit delegating authority to frontline personnel. You can alleviate this problem by a graduated signoff system, as described previously. But your problem can also be a simple matter of understaffing or of burdening personnel with excessive and unnecessary procedures in unimportant matters.

Possibly you can solve the problem with a different type of organization, for example, a system of account teams with primary and backup personnel for each account, personnel who *are* available and are also responsible for servicing the account. Chapter 6 gives a number of suggestions on this subject.

7. *Problem: availability of resources.* This common problem occurs when customers have been sold a service or a product, have made their plans accordingly, and then are told the service or product is not available. It's perhaps the most nearly universal problem, and certainly one of the most annoying to customers, and even more so when the news of nonavailability comes without forewarning and customers have little or no time to change their plans to compensate.

Nonavailability occurs as frequently in service industries as elsewhere: overbooking by airlines and hotels, doctors who schedule too many patients and are then called away by emergencies, late deliveries, field service engineers who arrive late to make critical repairs, banks and government offices where the lines are too long, and more.

The solution. The four principal reasons behind the nonavailability of resources are:

1. Poor forecasting of sales, reflecting a degree of indifference to the customer service consequences.
2. Overbooking or making commitments that cannot be met for lack of capacity or inventory.
3. Lack of an early warning system enabling you to alert customers to possible delays or shortages, unavailability of personnel, or whatever, in ample time to make alternative plans.
4. Unwillingness of management to commit funds enabling the necessary capacity or inventory level of goods, skills, or personnel.

8. Not all problems will be eliminated when your management decides to commit more resources to customer service. In fact, better results might be realized if you could persuade your management to commit the resources to improved forecasting, scheduling, or inventory management. Equally valuable is a system of accountability whereby each department is required to inform the customer service department when situations have arisen that compromise the original commitment to the customer.

The process of setting standards covered in Chapter 7 will help you develop a logical plan for remedying the resources problem — a particularly critical one, and the techniques of cost justification outlined in Chapter 14 will help you get support for it throughout the organization.

The problems and obstacles to perfect customer service described here are hardly ever the fault of frontline individuals, although these people are often blamed for them. What customers often perceive as a poor attitude on the service givers' part is in reality unverbalized stress and frustration at the inadequacies of the system of rules, regulations, equipment, and resources they're forced to work with.

It is important that you as a manager know how to solve the underlying problems, which in turn allows personnel to function far more effectively, avoid most of the seven problems, and deal more effectively and creatively with the few that are genuinely unavoidable.

Section II

How to Organize an Excellent Customer Service Department

4

Developing a Statement of Mission

Customer service departments come in a variety of shapes and sizes. What yours does, and how it does it, are largely functions of the kind of business you're in, the kind of markets you serve, and the way your company defines the customer service mission. Your organization may have never written down its specific customer service mission in black and white; very few U.S. companies have. But to be effective in your job as customer service manager, you will need such a statement of mission as a foundation for your operations. You should write it yourself for three reasons:

1. To clarify in your own mind the goals you intend your department to achieve and how it will achieve them
2. To be sure that those goals are expressed in clear and straightforward language that will be understood and supported by your employees
3. To see that those goals are expressed with the kind of logic and enthusiasm that will virtually guarantee buy-in by your management and other departments

Your statement of mission should be written in language that is inspirational as well as informative. It should reflect corporate policy and objectives as well as provide a road map showing how the department plans to reach those objectives. It should state what the department is expected to contribute to the company's overall goals and define the operations that will enable it to do so.

Your statement must avoid any intimation of "empire building" for the department and focus on the objectives that are acceptable to management and other departments. When you submit it for their comments and/or approval, it may be the first time that they have had to think of customer service as a corporate strategy. Getting them to face up to the real contribution of the department to corporate success will be a major achievement in itself. At the same time you will be creating, possibly for the first time, a real sense of identity and status for the department and its personnel.

Five Steps Toward a Statement of Mission

To help you develop a customer service statement of mission, this chapter contains several model statements of mission, a model statement of implementation, and a number of excerpts from the mission statements of different companies. You'll find a great deal here to draw from in shaping your own company's customer service mission statement. But first of all you'll want to make sure that the statement you ultimately develop accurately reflects positive goals that senior management will accept and support. Here's how to get started:

1. *Force managers in other departments as well as senior management to think positively about customer service.* In spite of all the attention customer service has received in recent years, many managers still regard it as primarily a clerical function concerned with complaint handling, returns, exchanges, credits, and the like. Many don't pay much attention to customer service, and when they do it's usually in a negative context.

Changing this way of thinking is an important first step in preparing your statement of mission. It's not as difficult as it might seem. Most customer service departments issue some type of departmental newsletter or bulletin to keep other departments (and sometimes customers) informed of changes in policies and procedures. You can use your departmental newsletter in much the same way as customer service managers in companies as different as Du Pont and Parker Pen have used theirs to initiate positive thinking about customer service. Here's how:

Select a cross-section of company personnel, including key managers, and ask each one to give you a statement of fifty to one-hundred words on "How I define customer service" for publication in your newsletter. Since these definitions will appear in print over the individual's names, it's highly unlikely that their comments will be negative. Some will find themselves in the position of having to think positively about customer service for the first time. And some will actually change their thinking, reinforced by endorsements of the others. Suggestion: Print their photos along with their statements. That will cause even more thought to go into these statements.

2. *Find out what's important to key managers.* The way to get managerial support for customer service—and for your mission statement—is to undertake the improvements management wants, not those that you consider important. One customer service manager sent a questionnaire to key managers asking them to rank a number of different projects. He formatted their responses in a matrix like Figure 4-1.

The most "popular" of these projects were incorporated into the manager's draft of the statement of mission. Not surprisingly, the statement received widespread support from these same managers.

3. *Research customer needs.* Customer research is an integral part of customer service management and is covered in detail in Chapter 9. As applied to your statement of mission, your research will be directed mainly to customer practices: how customers do things as an index to what you must do to make it easier for them to buy from your company than from others. For example,

Figure 4-1. Sample chart for ranking manager priorities

Rank 1 = High Priority, 2 = Medium Priority, 3 = Low Priority

Project Under Consideration	Ranking by Managers			
	Mgr. A	*Mgr. B*	*Mgr. C*	*Mgr. D*
Improve inquiry response to 90 percent on-line	____	____	____	____
Reduce minimum orders for service/product	____	____	____	____
Process 50 percent of orders on electronic data interchange	____	____	____	____
Reduce average order cycle time to 72 hours	____	____	____	____
Resolve claims under $500 within 2 weeks or less	____	____	____	____
Increase mean time between failures (MTBF) by 5 percent	____	____	____	____
Institute profitability analysis by account/ channel	____	____	____	____
Develop internal customers training programs	____	____	____	____
Improve customer training, technical/ software support	____	____	____	____

one manager's research revealed that a number of customers were using inefficient and outmoded purchasing methods. He made it part of his mission to develop self-training courses for them in such areas as forecasting, economic order quantities, inventory management, and similar topics. Both company and customers benefited from the improvement in purchasing practices. Because it became easier for customers to buy from this particular company, the competition was effectively shut out.

4. *Complete your draft and circulate for additions and deletions.* Put the emphasis on what the company, rather than the customer service department,

(text continues on page 39)

Figure 4-2. Sample Statements of mission

Sample Statement of Mission 1

The customer service mission of this organization is to:

- Be recognized by our customers as the best in the business in terms of quality of both product and service and, of course, personnel.
- Develop a customer focus throughout the organization.
- Develop high levels of service and positive relationships with our customers to insulate them from competitive offerings.
- Develop specific strategies to stimulate account growth as the result of high levels of customer satisfaction.
- Target key accounts to designate our organization as a prime, preferred, or exclusive supplier because of the quality of our service.
- Strengthen our company's public image through the excellence of its service, the quality of its personnel, and its actions as a responsible member of the business community and the local communities where it maintains offices and facilities.
- Develop a complaint handling strategy that enables us to capitalize on the tendency of satisfied complainers to "buy up" at a much higher rate than noncomplainers.
- Establish a system of standards that will ensure the correct levels of service for our targeted markets and a system of measures that will warn us immediately of any deviation from those standards.
- Develop recovery plans for emergency situations, including natural disasters, strikes, illness, and other problems at our own sites as well as at customer locations.
- Increase the firm's market share and its profits.

The customer service department will strive toward these goals by developing effective procedures and by providing resources— personnel, skills, systems, and communications—and participating in forward planning and other cooperative activity with management and concerned departments throughout the organization.

Sample Statement of Mission 2

These are our goals:

1. Helping customers make money, or in the case of consumers, derive social, psychological, and material benefits from the relationship
2. Giving customers reason to increase purchases and/or designate this company as a preferred or sole source supplier

3. Solving problems in such a way that customers will perceive the company as different from, and superior to, its competitors
4. Helping the individual customer in his or her career, peer group, or family setting
5. Managing complaints with the primary objective of keeping the account and increasing its volume of purchases
6. Bridging the gap between what customers expect and what the company can realistically provide
7. Developing acceptable alternatives when the customer's need cannot be fully met
8. Building personal relationships that will create loyalty to the individual as well as to the company
9. Controlling costs within the company
10. Creating and maintaining a constantly upbeat image of the company and a sense of teamwork among its personnel

It is understood that these goals will be met by all members of this organization in a thoroughly professional manner, through skilled, accurate workmanship in job performance, personal integrity, and a great sense of concern for customers as well as loyalty to the company.

How a Service Organization Says It

Since its "product" is a service itself, a service organization's mission statement is likely to differ from a comparable statement prepared by a manufacturing or retail organization. Here is an example from the Terminal Corporation, a Maryland public warehousing company:

Customer Service Policy

1. We promise we will be your best warehouse and transportation service company.
2. Everyone in our company will treat everyone in your company with respect, fairness, and honesty.
3. We promise to ship the right products to the right place at the right time.
4. We will handle any problem or complaint courteously and effectively until *you* the customer are fully satisfied with the results.
5. All of our equipment and facilities will be neat, clean, and orderly to guarantee your confidence in our storage and materials handling abilities.

(continues)

Figure 4-2. (continued)

6. We will respond to your emergencies. We will be accessible 24 hours a day, 7 days a week. All warehouses have 24-hour answering machines and we have an emergency service phone number during our nonbusiness hours.
7. Only properly trained employees will be permitted to handle your products.
8. We assure you that all our truck drivers will be neatly groomed, courteous, and eager to serve you.
9. All inventory reporting and billing will be accurate and timely.
10. If you are not getting exactly what you want as the customer, please call any of the company's key managers day or night. [Gives office and home phone numbers for chairman, president, and two vice-presidents.]

A Combined Service/Product Company's Statement

Rodale Press, in Emmaus, Pennsylvania, combines service in the form of information and products in the form of the magazines, newsletters, and books in which the information appears. Here's how Rodale describes the customer service mission:

1. We are committed to improving our understanding of our customers, including what they purchase from us and their motivation. We will develop quantifiable techniques to monitor customers' long-term relationship with us.
2. We are committed to developing, maintaining, and marketing high quality customer service with long-term strategies to retain and cultivate customers, increase sales, enlarge and protect market share, and perpetuate an identity that sets Rodale Press apart from its competition by:
   a. The best order fulfillment services in our industry
   b. Clear and easy methods of communication between us and our customers
   c. Swiftly responsive and efficient systems to ensure prompt and complete satisfaction to customer complaints

Sample Statement: Customer Services Company

Here is a straightforward, plain-language customer service mission statement by Clark-O'Neill, a New Jersey marketing services company providing customized mailing, fulfillment, and similar services for clients in the health care manufacturing industries.

Clark-O'Neill's Principles of Good Service

1. Tell the truth.
2. Keep promises.
3. If we mess up, we fix it. We'll replace our services—without questions.
4. The client should need to contact only two people at Clark-O'Neill—the outside salesperson or inside service rep. These two people are responsible for client service.
5. Our most serious errors are the "hidden" errors. We won't hide problems.
6. We've got to invoice clients as soon as their job is done. Invoices must be sent to the right person and show all the information needed for the client to process them easily.
7. Controversies between Clark-O'Neill and the client will be resolved promptly.
8. Clark-O'Neill information will be organized so that the client's most common questions are always answered quickly.
9. Clients want to know when their jobs are completed—so we'll tell them—every time.
10. We'll sell what we can do and do what we sell.
11. The outside sales person or inside service representative will approve the content and appearance of all reports sent to clients.
12. Ninety percent of our client contact is over the telephone, so we'll have superb telephone manners and skills.
13. We must make it easy for clients to adjust their systems so they fit into ours.
14. Our services will be organized to solve our *clients'* problems and answer *their* needs.
15. We'll make each client feel he or she is our most important customer.
16. Every 6 months we'll hold a service-satisfaction review with the major accounts in each submarket.

Mission Statement of Consumer Goods Manufacturer

Here's another very straightforward mission statement that speaks directly to customer service representatives with the immediate responsibility of servicing customers. It was developed by Gene Spilker, director of customer service of Brown Shoe Co., St. Louis, Missouri:

1. We want to make it easy for our customers to buy from us and for them to have confidence in our ability to serve them well.

(continues)

Figure 4-2. (continued)

2. We want our customers to feel good about doing business with us and to make it a pleasant experience.
3. We want to keep our existing customers and to grow by helping them grow.
4. We want our existing customers to increase their purchases from us and for them to become more profitable.
5. We want to attract new customers because of our reputation throughout the shoe industry for excellence in customer service.
6. We want to give our customers prompt, friendly, courteous, accurate, and honest answers to their problems and inquiries.
7. We want to closely follow, adhere to, and conform to these six principles of business conduct in all our dealings with our customers in order for Brown Shoe Co. to grow, prosper, and become more profitable.

Composite Statement: Implementation of Mission

When the statement of customer service mission is general in nature, it is usually followed by a description of the specific functions that will be performed by the customer service department in carrying out that mission. Here is a composite statement that describes almost every type of function a customer service department can be involved in. You can select those that fit your situation and rewrite them as necessary.

The customer service department will implement this mission through the development of an appropriate organization, policies, and procedures of such quality as to meet customer requirements within reasonable cost constraints.

The customer service department will provide the resources to carry out specific functions and responsibilities among the following that relate to its mission:

- Design and maintain state-of-the-art telecommunications and management information systems to ensure optimum accessibility to customers and optimum availability of information.
- Compile and maintain a complete and accurate database of accounts, account personnel, and account requirements and transactions profiles.
- Train personnel to the levels of expertise required to maintain these systems as well as to advise and instruct customers in the proper use of services and products.
- Staff the department in such a way as to ensure ready availability of competent personnel to handle customers' needs.
- Respond to inquiries about the company's services or products, including applications and technology as necessary, as well as policies, procedures, and terms of sale.

- Enter orders for the company's services or products and arrange for the furnishing or delivery of those services or products at the time and place and under the conditions specified by the customer.
- Issue in timely fashion correct invoices and other documentation associated with such orders.
- Inform and coordinate with all other departments and any third party providers associated with the furnishing or delivery of services and products to customers.
- Educate customers in the most beneficial use of the company's services and products.
- Provide a support staff to assist customers overcome unexpected problems and emergencies.
- Provide an early warning system to notify customers of any delays or problems affecting service commitments that have been made to them.
- Develop a complaint management system that will promptly and fairly resolve complaints and at the same time enable improved quality control to avoid recurrences.
- Handle returns, exchanges, deductions, and credits in an equitable and timely fashion.
- Conduct research on service quality, competitive offerings, and customer satisfaction.
- Monitor performance of all the elements involved to ensure that quality standards are maintained throughout.
- Provide management with timely reports on sales statistics and trends, including sales forecasting and resource planning.
- Provide timely reports on key account status and prepare a regular "endangered customers" list.
- Develop cost controls and cost reduction measures consistent with quality service.
- Furnish partnership support to field sales personnel, independent reps, brokers, and others engaged in sales and marketing.
- Build sound and lasting relationships with customers through onsite visitations, participation in trade shows, and a positive, helpful, and friendly attitude in daily dealings.

will do. Keep your statement fairly general; the less detail, the fewer objections your draft is likely to meet. But accept revisions from others gracefully. Your main objective is to provide an accepted reference point for developing sound and workable customer service policies and procedures.

5. *Prepare final version and get approval.* One of the statements that appear in Figure 4-2 starting on page 34 may be suitable for that version, but it should, of course, be modified to reflect the actual business environment of the company.

After writing a practical mission statement that reflects your company's customer service goals, your next big task is to write down the specific policies and procedures that will be used as working tools in day-to-day operations to achieve those goals. Translating mission statements into workable policies and procedures is the subject of Chapter 5.

5

**Developing Proactive
Policies and Procedures**

In customer service, the words *policies* and *procedures* are often used inter-changeably to describe the way customer service transactions are handled. Cus-tomer service policies are guidelines or decision rules developed to ensure consistency in dealings with customers in the spirit of the company's basic philosophy and statement of mission. Procedures are step-by-step instructions that detail how those dealings and policies are carried out in practice.

Policies are also similar in many respects to the "terms and conditions of sale" that are often printed on the back of order acknowledgments and may be made available to customers in abbreviated form. Figure 5-1 shows how an agricultural company's main customer service policies might be summarized.

While the policies in Figure 5-1 obviously relate to specific practices in one industry, excerpts from the policies of a company in another industry are more generic and are listed under the following headings:

- Acceptance of orders, conditions
- Accounts, major
- Adjustments, invoices under
- Change orders
- Communications with customers
- Competitive objective
- Complaints and adjustments
- Credit
- Customer inquiries
- Customer service
- Customers, communications with
- Customers, new
- Damage claims
- Delivery
- Etiquette, telephone
- Inquiries
- Inventory policy

- Invoicing
- New customers
- Objective, competitive
- Order cycle times
- Order editing
- Order entry
- Order status reporting
- Order writing
- Orders, change
- Orders, conditions
- Orders for future delivery
- Post entry review
- Proof transmittals
- Purchase order review
- Quotations
- Rush service
- Sales force training
- Ship-by dates
- Traffic

Figure 5-1. Customer service policies from an agricultural products company

1. We will fulfill dealers' orders on a timely basis and will ship corn, sorghum, and soybeans on one load whenever practical, based on product availability.

2. We will accommodate dealers who elect to change orders on returnable products prior to shipment, but dealers must work through their sales representatives.

3. We will accommodate dealers' special handling instructions if notified at the time of ordering and to the extent practical based on the judgment of the customer service coordinator.

4. We will notify dealers of the date and approximate time of delivery of their orders. When truckers are delayed more than three hours, dealers will be notified of the delay.

5. We will accommodate dealers on plant pickup if scheduled in advance with customer service coordinators. Dealers will be given pickup allowance based on normal cost per unit if product had been delivered to customer. Product not picked up within a reasonable time will be delivered by us in a routine manner.

6. We will deliver to dealers' customers in truckload quantities without additional charge if the delivery point is not farther than the dealer's delivery point. Freight charges will be made for delivery to a more distant point. Prior arrangements must be made, and the dealer must be present at the time of delivery. Drop shipments of a minimum of 200 units may be arranged if the delivering branch can accommodate. A drop charge will be made to the dealer for this service.

7. Final disposition of refused product (returnable items only) delivered to a dealer will be handled on an exceptions basis by customer service coordinators.

8. We will back order five or more units per order for a dealer due to miscounts or damaged merchandise. Quantities involving less than five units must be reordered.

9. We will accommodate late rush orders after April 1 on a 48-hour turnaround when practical in the judgment of the customer service coordinator.

10. At the time estimated returns are counted, the sales representative will notify the dealer to gather together all product from his customers on a one-time pickup as arranged by the customer service coordinator. All subsequent pickups will be at the dealer's expense.

11. We will accommodate palletized shipments if notified at the time of ordering and to the extent practical based on the judgment of the customer service coordinator. The dealer will be charged $10.00 per pallet at the time of delivery. Credits will be issued when pallets are returned.

The manual that contains the headings listed on page 41 was written for internal use, as illustrated by the following excerpts from the texts under some of the headings:

Order Cycle Times

In order to maintain credibility with customers regarding delivery times, specific order cycle times must be stated as part of the customer service policy. Goals must be established; otherwise service cannot be measured. The order cycle times for the measured product groups are shown below. Standard times are from receipt of order.

Custom Manufactured Products Group	Standard Cycle Time	Stock Items Product Group	Standard Cycle Time
Class C-1	5 weeks	Class S-1	5 days
Class C-2	2 weeks	Class S-2	5 days
Class C-3	5 weeks	Class S-3	4 days
Class C-4	3 weeks	Class S-4	3 days
Class C-5	8 weeks	Class S-5	5 days
Class C-6	4 weeks	Class S-6	3 days
Class C-7	3 weeks		
All others	Negotiated		

Complaints and Adjustments

It is the sales representative's responsibility to report customer complaints to the customer service representative. However, if a customer brings a complaint directly to customer service, the customer service representative will proceed immediately with its resolution and will keep the sales representative informed of its status.

In order to maintain credibility and customer goodwill, as well as to ensure repeat business, credits or deductions up to $200 may be allowed without requiring proof of shortage, damage, or quality problems. Complaints involving greater amounts will be reviewed and resolved as follows:

Complaints up to $500	Customer service representative
Complaints from $501 to $2,000	Customer service manager
Complaints from $2,001 to $5,000	Administrative manager
Complaints over $5,000	Division manager

Order Status Reporting

It is the responsibility of customer service to maintain automatic delivery follow-up to keep sales representatives and customers informed of any delays or other problems. On supplier direct orders, the sales representative will be notified by customer service if the entered shipping date cannot be met. If the sales representative is not available and the information is critical, customer service will notify the customer directly. If a customer has previously called customer service on an order, then customer service should call the customer direct if there are any changes from the most recent information given the customer. The sales representative should be notified of all such communications.

For practical reasons, it is generally preferable to develop policies and procedures *after* your mission statement is complete and as a separate project. Of course, if you already have policies and procedures in place, but not a mission statement, you need to develop a mission statement and then revise or adjust policies and procedures to be sure they're consistent.

Policies and procedures should be organized into a manual arranged in a logical format and indexed for easy reference by your reps and yourself. A suggested format appears in Appendix A. As explained in this chapter, many of your policies and procedures can be incorporated into decision rules employed in your computer system.

Policies Must Be Specific

It's permissible to wax philosophical in a mission statement, but policy statements must be factual, specific, and understandable to anyone who works with them.

Policies should not be confused with advertising slogans such as OUR POLICY IS THAT THE CUSTOMER IS ALWAYS RIGHT! An easy way to test such a policy is to make a $5 purchase from the company and employ this syllogism: "You owe me $5,000. Your policy is that the customer is always right. I am your customer. Therefore, I am always right, and you owe me $5,000. Pay up!" You will almost certainly get a response to the effect of, "Oh, our policy doesn't mean right in *that* way!"

Home improvement companies advertising FREE ESTIMATES — NO JOB TOO LARGE OR TOO SMALL sometimes find themselves in trouble with consumer agencies when they decline to make estimates on jobs that are in fact too small. Suggestion: Arrange with your advertising department to provide you with copies of advertising and sales promotion materials *before* they're released, enabling you to check for slogan-type statements that affect your service obligations to customers and, in some cases, for extremely burdensome or impossible-to-perform obligations.

The subject of advertising is dealt with in detail in Chapter 12, and as you'll discover, lack of awareness of ad content on your part and your reps can create a number of embarrassing situations!

It is extremely important that policies be highly specific and that they also be practical and doable in terms of the resources available to you in the customer service department. Although wording of policies is often similar to the "terms and conditions of the sale" that many companies print on order forms or acknowledgments, terms and conditions of sale are generally binding on both yourself as seller and the customer as buyer, and policies are not necessarily binding on customers. In general they are binding on your organization only to the extent that you publish them and customers rely on them in dealing with your company.

Typical policy statements that companies might apply in customer service operations include:

"It is our policy to resolve all claims under twenty-five dollars in favor of the customer."

"It is our policy not to accept third-party checks."

"It is our policy to add a ten-dollar surcharge to all orders under $50."

"It is our policy to refuse service to persons who appear to be intoxicated."

"It is our policy to absorb freight charges on all orders over $500."

"It is our policy to issue rain checks for sale items that are not in stock at the time of your visit."

"It is our policy to refund shipping charges as well as the cost of merchandise on all returns."

"It is our policy to deduct seventy-two dollars from your invoice if we do not deliver within three working days — seventy-two hours."

"It is our policy not to deny boarding to senior citizens, families with small children, or children traveling alone."

"It is our policy to investigate all claims before payment."

"It is our policy to give priority to service calls from customers in disaster areas."

A satisfaction guaranteed policy is not actually a policy; it is a guarantee that the seller will do something to make up for the customer's lack of satisfaction with the transaction. In other words, sellers can only guarantee what *they* will do, not how the customer will respond. A policy need not be stated in legal language. The statement "If you are dissatisfied with your purchase in any way, you may return it for a full refund or exchange, as you prefer" is a guarantee, not of satisfaction per se, but to give customers their money back or a substitute product if they are *not* satisfied.

It's also proper, if the company wishes, to adopt a policy of "Always give the customer the benefit of the doubt." Even though this sounds vague and more like a philosophy, it has a specific foundation: that there is a doubt to begin with. In other words, the policy is only applied when there is a doubt.

In customer service a policy is essentially a rule indicating how a company will handle specific situations or classes of situation. Unfortunately, many companies seem to have more policies stating what they will *not* do for the customer than what they *will* do.

Standards as Policy

A policy of providing excellent customer service is not a policy because the term *excellent* is not defined in terms of specific service levels. "Our policy is to respond to all service calls within 4 hours" is a specific statement of a policy backed up a measurable standard. Is 4 hours "excellent" service? It could be in one situation and not in another. If management wants to use the word *excellent* in its policy statements, that's perfectly acceptable, as long as *excellent* is defined in measurable terms. For example, which of the following is preferable: (1) "It is our policy to provide excellent response to 911 calls;" or (2) "It is our responsibility to respond to 911 calls by taking no longer than 7 minutes to arrive at the calling site." Is seven minutes "excellent" in this context? To a coronary patient it's certainly preferable to wondering precisely what "excellent" means!

The examples of policies cited above do not necessarily contain numbers, but they are measurable in binary terms—"yes" or "no." They set forth in broad terms what the company will do and will not do.

Procedures Reflect Company Policies

Ideally, procedures are step-by-step instructions designed to ensure uniformity of customer service performance within the framework of company policies. On a large scale, they detail how the functions assigned to the customer service department are performed in relation to other departments, with particular emphasis on the information flow and authorizations.

Within the department, one of the most common procedures is the set of instructions concerned with entering an order for products or services. These probably include instructions on what to do when the product or service isn't available, if the customer's credit isn't acceptable, and so forth. The process is essentially the same whether the customer is ordering an airline ticket from Washington to Los Angeles or forty thousand pounds of plastic pellets.

Many procedures are now built into computer programs so that a central function in order entry is to use a terminal to enter the appropriate data into the system in response to various prompts. The computer uses a number of databases and decision rules to translate the original input into the fulfillment process.

In the case of the airline ticket, the computer searches the inventory of seats available for the particular flight segment and date, posts the charge to the designated credit card, adds the passenger's name to the manifest, prints out the ticket and boarding pass, deducts the seat from the available inventory, and more.

In manufacturing, the order entry program searches inventory, prints out order assembly pick lists, shipping documents, acknowledgements, invoices and the like. The database may be queried to check inventory levels, order status, prices, and in some cases offers a range of substitution possibilities for items not currently in stock.

More advanced programming enables customers to query the database directly (within limits, that is, excluding proprietary data) and place orders without dealing with vendor personnel. This ordering is usually done computer-to-computer using special protocols, but a number of applications simply use a touchtone telephone as the basic input device.

Procedures in the service industries are also increasingly computerized. Some sophisticated programs used by insurance companies evaluate claims input directly from terminals in clinics and hospitals by comparing them to a series of databases and then issue checks in the proper amount, along with a letter explaining the settlement.

Another growing computer application of customer service in the service industries is remote diagnostics of software problems, user-serviceable equipment failures, and similar applications, including "sick" computers that automatically transmit their symptoms to other computers, which can "cure" them from a distance. Applications such as these have been accelerated because of the difficulty of recruiting and maintaining field engineering staffs who are readily available virtually anywhere in the world on almost a moment's notice.

The net result of this type of procedural computerization is that conventional written departmental procedures as instructions are more likely to deal with exceptions than with routine activities, which are largely automated. Examples include how the airline might handle overbooking, flight cancellations, and similar events resulting in complaints; how the manufacturer might deal with stockouts, returns, exchanges, and the like. Procedures may also cover such contingencies as product recalls, hazardous spills, freight loss and damage, undocumented insurance claims, customer errors, and more.

The increasing tendency to regard customer service as a total process is causing major changes in procedure design. Some of the issues you should be thinking about as you develop these "new look" procedures are discussed next.

Policies on Returns, Exchanges, and Adjustments

Administering product returns, exchanges, and other types of adjustments is usually a function of the customer service department. Your task is likely to be complicated by the fact that the actual policies governing returns, exchanges, and adjustments are usually drawn up elsewhere in the company. A 1987 survey conducted by the Schering-Plough consumer operations/customer service department of 47 companies of different types showed these discrepancies between the responsibility for setting policies on product returns and the responsibility for ensuring adherence to those policies (see page 48).

These statistics illustrate that policies on returns and exchanges often reflect the bias of the departments responsible and not necessarily what's best for the relationship with customers. For example, if the sales and marketing department develops the policies, there's a tendency to discourage returns because they reduce commissions, points, or other incentives for high sales performance. Similarly, if the finance department develops the policies, accepting returns or issuing credits to customers is likely to be seen as "giving away the store," and often meets high-level resistance.

What's ironic about both of these viewpoints is that the cost of administering restrictive policies on returns and exchanges is often greater than any

Setting Policy		Adherence to Policy	
Sales	18.8%	Customer Service	63.7%
Sales/Finance	14.6%	Sales	10.6%
Sales/Customer Service	14.6%	Traffic/Distribution	8.5%
Marketing	10.2%	Claims/Adjustments	4.3%
Sales/Marketing	8.3%	Sales/Logistics	4.3%
Finance	8.3%	Finance	4.3%
Customer Service	6.3%	Other	4.3%
Corporate Management	6.3%		
Distribution	4.2%		
Other	8.4%		

amounts saved by imposing them. The only difference is that the cost shows up under another heading. For example, in a New England company all returns and exchanges must be personally authorized by the treasurer, who runs a very tight ship. He undoubtedly saves his company money by doing so, but the time he spends dealing with relatively trivial amounts is far more expensive than any savings he generates, and he has little time left over for the financial planning that his company so sorely needs.

The companies involved in the Schering-Plough studies were mainly manufacturers selling business-to-business. In consumer marketing, there is a better understanding that liberal return and exchange policies are a marketing tool designed to create confidence in the organization and to encourage customers to make purchases with the assurance that if products aren't satisfactory they can be returned.

Most major retailers readily accept returned goods, and some do not even require proof of purchase. Sears Roebuck, for example, accepts merchandise back without a sales slip. To avoid abuse of the policy it posts notices that refunds for such returns will be made by check mailed to the customer's home. Direct marketing companies vary from the extremely liberal guarantees of L. L. Bean to more restrictive practices of other companies imposing time limits and other conditions such as resaleability.

Relatively few of these companies compensate customers for return shipping or postage charges, and only a few retailers issue extra credits or give small gift certificates to customers to compensate them for their time and trouble in returning unsatisfactory goods. Ironically, a major retail chain instituted a gift certificate program in order to lure dissatisfied customers back into the store, only to see the program shot down by the store managers. Instead of setting up a separate budget for such certificates, management decided that their cost would be subtracted from each manager's bottom line, thus reducing the manager's annual bonus based on sales. It's easy to understand why the program went over like a proverbial lead balloon!

Since services are generally consumed at the time they are provided, they can't be returned in the same way products are returned. Adjustments for services can also be complicated by high and sometimes unrealistic expectations on the part of customers. Air transportation provides an example of this. Passengers whose flights have been delayed or canceled often blame the airlines when in fact the actual cause is weather, the air traffic control system, or safety considerations and requirements—all of which are far more in the passenger's interest than simply leaving and arriving on time. The fact that some airlines provide compensation or adjustment to passengers who have been inconvenienced is simply a matter of good business: When a meal, hotel, or travel voucher is issued to a passenger who has been inconvenienced, that passenger will be less likely to blame the carrier for the problem.

The medical and legal professions, and health care generally, are also areas where expectations often cloud the issue of whether service is adequate and appropriate. The profusion of malpractice and liability suits in these areas illustrates the point. But perhaps the most common of all examples of unmet expectations is the home repair business, which traditionally generates more complaints to better business bureaus and consumer agencies than any other kind of consumer-oriented business.

The difficulty of establishing what constitutes good service is exemplified in education and entertainment, where the service is consumed as it is provided and where refunds or other adjustments are seldom offered.

Needed: A Practical Policy on Adjustments

The previously cited examples illustrate some of the practical difficulties of developing a hassle-free method of managing adjustments in the best interests of the company. Yet if your company has a genuine objective of being the best in its field—a truly excellent company—as customer service manager you are going to have to wrestle mightily with the complex problem of developing policies and procedures for adjustments that satisfy customers as well as different elements in your own organization. And, yes, there will almost certainly be some interdepartmental disagreement along the way.

Here are some factors to consider in developing your policies and procedures on adjustments of all types in both product and service environments:

Legal Requirements

Most products or services sold in normal commerce are covered by a so-called implied warranty of suitablity or fitness. Regardless of whether a product or service is covered by specific, limited warranties, a customer can still sue if the product or service doesn't meet the suitability or fitness test. A canoe that leaks, a balloon that won't hold air, or a wheel that isn't round—all these are clearly unfit for the intended use and the only way a seller can avoid responsibility for such unfitness is to sell them on an as-is basis. Although inadequacy of service is often more difficult to prove, the same rule applies: services that don't meet acceptable standards are judged to be unsuitable and subject to refund or other adjustment.

The legal issues involved regarding suitability can take several forms: (1) *the basic suitability issue*, where the customer seeks simple reimbursement, refund, or cancellation of a contract based on suitability; (2) *out-and-out liability for direct damages*, e.g., a defective or improperly repaired heater that causes a fire, and (3) *consequential damages*, such as loss of a contract because a bid was not delivered in time by the messenger service.

As customer service manager, you will want to teach your personnel how to identify any of these issues and where to refer them: to your legal department, quality control, design engineering, or elsewhere. They probably won't arise very often, but they are always present as a less desirable alternative to policies that are considered sufficiently fair that customers don't feel compelled to take legal action to get the service they feel they're entitled to under a conventional sales contract.

You should also be sensitive to the legal requirement that all customers in a given class be given equal treatment in the matter of actual service as well as adjustments. This clearly doesn't mean that you have to be as generous in making adjustments for a $1,000-a-year-customer as for a $1 million-a-year-customer. What it does mean is that if you are more generous with the $1,000 customer than with another, your generosity may be construed as an illegal rebate. Since it is perfectly legal under most circumstances to be more liberal with your larger customer, there is every reason to base your adjustment policy on account size and revenues.

There are also numerous legal requirements governing handling of returns and adjustments involving controlled or hazardous substances or services that must be provided by licensed individuals. These vary significantly from one industry to another and obviously need to be incorporated into your underlying policies and procedures.

Avoidable Causes

The basic reasons for returning merchandise or requesting adjustments include one or more of the following:

- Returnable goods under policy
- Quality problems
- Billing errors
- Goods not as represented
- Discount not given
- Duplicate order already received
- Warranty claims for adjustment
- Goods damaged or delayed
- Incorrect product(s) shipped
- Customer error in ordering
- Service not as represented
- Advertising and other allowances
- Failure to make delivery appointment
- Inability to unload

Some of these problems can be prevented altogether, whereas others can be reduced significantly in number as well as in frequency and cost. For example, customer errors in ordering may be a result of inadequate product knowledge, lack of technical expertise, or insufficient training in economic order quantity (EOC) buying. For example, the FMC Fire Engine Division found that a significant number of its warranty claims resulted from improper use of equipment by fire department personnel. It developed a training program in equipment use that it provided free to two people from each fire department (usually the smaller volunteer departments). Additional people could attend at a nominal charge. The immediate result was a 15 percent drop in warranty administration costs, which more than often offset the slight cost of the training course. Similarly, a major manufacturer of building materials found a significant payoff in reduced customer errors when it provided customers free self-training courses in economic lot ordering. In 1989 it was reported that L. L. Bean's generous return policies were causing considerable added expense when customers would order three sizes of a garment, try them all on, keep the size that fit best, and return the other two. It was able to restrict this practice by providing improved instructions to customers on ordering, particularly on orders placed by phone.

Claims or requests for return or adjustment that result from problems in your own operation—inaccurate data entry, for example—can often be reduced significantly simply by improving those operations. Statistical process control techniques that are already widely used in manufacturing are rapidly being adopted in customer service as well, with a major objective of correcting errors at the source rather than after the fact. This is why it is important to maintain good statistical records of errors and where they originate. Of course some very basic procedures should be looked at, such as clerical accuracy, suitability of the management information system (MIS), order picking procedures, accuracy of catalog descriptions, and clarity of invoices and other documentation.

In addition to training customers, it may also be desirable to train sales personnel in proper procedure, since a good percentage of errors—particularly the error of overcommitment—are the direct result of actions taken by salespeople. Although some managers favor imposing sanctions on salespeople who overpromise, oversell, or otherwise create unrealistic expectations, others feel that sanctions would be a strong demotivator that could also affect relationships between salespeople and their customers.

Customer Friendliness

As discussed in Chapter 3, adjustment policies that seem perfectly reasonable from the seller's viewpoint can annoy and frustrate customers. It's reasonable to want to protect the interests of the seller as well as the buyer, but many policies seem to be based on a distrust of customers rather than an attempt to treat them equitably. This perception is usually created by time-consuming procedures, forms to fill out, and multiple signoffs, which add little more than delay. Many companies require advance approval and the use of special forms and labels when returning goods, which creates additional delays and heightens the perception of mistrust.

Although some companies have strict standards requiring prompt issuance of credits, the majority give very low priority to this function. Customers often perceive this slowness as a device used by vendors to gain interest-free use of cash that should rightfully be working for its proper owners—the customers—rather than their vendors. Delays in issuing credits or approvals for returns simply generate additional calls and pressure from customers, all of which bring considerable added cost in time and stress for your already overworked customer service representatives.

Product returns typically fall into three main categories:

1. *Returns for full credit.* Medicines, books, periodicals, and similar time-sensitive materials may usually be returned for full credit after a certain amount of time has passed. Often these items cannot be resold. Other products that can be resold are often accepted for full credit provided they are in resaleable condition. A few companies such as L. L. Bean will accept goods back without a time limit and often without any stipulation of credit. Some of these companies will also pay all shipping charges. Returns of goods that are shipped in error or fail to meet quality standards receive full credit for both goods and shipping charges.

Goods that are damaged may or may not be allowed full credit, depending on whether they were shipped FOB origin or FOB destination. For goods shipped FOB origin, title would pass to the buyer at the time of shipment, and the buyer would normally have to recover the cost of any loss or damage from the transportation or delivery company. Goods shipped FOB destination and damaged in transit would still belong to the seller; thus it would be the seller's responsibility to replace the goods for the buyer.

In certain industries—furniture is one example—the seller may offer the buyer substantial discounts for keeping a product that is damaged in transit as opposed to returning it for credit. This situation is often the case when the seller drop-ships from several destination points, and returning goods would place a burden on the customer as well as on the vendor. There are also cases where the seller issues full credit upon guarantee that the buyer will destroy the product. This is characteristic of certain products that are either too costly to return or can't be returned because of the Food and Drug Administration (FDA) regulations.

2. *Returns for partial credit.* Generally, resaleable items that are taken back by the vendor subject to a restocking charge fall into this category. This charge purports to compensate the seller for the costs incurred in placing goods back in storage, updating inventory records, and so forth, but in reality it's frequently intended as a deterrent to returning goods or, conversely, an incentive to keep them. The amount of the restocking charge may increase in proportion to the length of time that the goods have been kept, on the premise that the seller's opportunity to resell diminishes with the passage of time.

3. *Returns for no credit.* As an accommodation to customers a seller may accept returns of toxic or hazardous materials or goods that are difficult to dispose of without issuance of credits but with assurance that the materials will be disposed of safely and legally. Some sellers charge for this service, particularly in the case of custom formulated products that have no resale potential.

Although most business-to-business returns policies require the customer to obtain written authorization from the seller before returning goods, a few companies have adopted honor system policies whereby customers can return merchandise on their own authority, even to the extent of deciding which of the three categories of returns theirs will be accepted under.

In a truly user-friendly policy, one commercial company encloses preauthorization forms and labels with every order it ships. Although some fears were expressed that the practice would result in a precipitous and costly increase in returns, no such increase resulted. What did happen was that the company was able to save some $60,000 annually in administrative costs by eliminating much of the red tape and streamlining the receiving and accounting through precoded labels and return forms. The company recognizes that making it difficult or time-consuming for customers to return merchandise simply delays future orders and discourages account growth. They know, as many direct marketers have learned, that quick resolution of credits and adjustments is one of the best ways to create customer confidence and build future business.

Economics of Restrictive Returns Policies

Although many companies feel that it's necessary to limit returns for economic reasons, in actuality restrictive policies often cost more than they save in two main areas: the actual administrative costs involved in authorizing and validating returns and the impact on future sales.

As an example of the latter, manufacturers and retailers often order extra stock so that they won't run out and be unable to fill their own orders. If goods or materials are left over, they are returned for credit. However, if returns policies are restrictive, these customer groups are likely to underorder and end up buying less from their vendors because they are manufacturing and/or selling less themselves. Overly restrictive policies may also open the door to competition: one company serving the construction industry with industrial fasteners fills the gap caused by underordering by delivering directly to jobsites using radio-dispatched vans carrying full inventories. By providing this service, it protects its own accounts that have underordered and gains access to accounts that are currently buying from other sources—but may not be for long.

Some companies feel that returns policies that are too liberal encourage careless buying and added cost. Other companies find it's more effective to help customers forecast their needs more accurately and order in economic lot quantities with sufficient lead times, reducing the likelihood that liberal returns policies will be abused, at the same time ensuring that they are in place when a legitimate need arises.

Pros and Cons of "Satisfaction Guaranteed" Policies

Although many companies advertise "Satisfaction Guaranteed,"* the phrase is actually a contradiction in terms. Satisfaction is a state of mind. A seller cannot guarantee that a buyer will have a specific state of mind any more than a lover can guarantee that his or her lover will return the sentiment. When a company advertises SATISFACTION GUARANTEED OR YOUR MONEY BACK, that is clearly *not* a guaran-

---

*A more detailed discussion of guarantees and warranties is included in Chapter 8.

tee of satisfaction: it's a guarantee that money will be refunded if the customer isn't satisfied. Even this phrase is vague, because it doesn't define satisfaction.

If you are thinking of adopting a policy of satisfaction guaranteed or money back, consider this example. A builder offering such a guarantee builds a house to the exact specifications of the owners. Upon the final inspection of the property, the owners say they are dissatisfied with the size of the closets and want their money back. Are they entitled to have their money back? You may say that the owners have no right to recovery since the house was built to their exact specifications. But the guarantee was a guarantee of satisfaction, not a guarantee of workmanship. It turns out that the owners have a pretty good case!

Of course there's nothing wrong with a money-back guarantee if you state it in precise terms and are prepared to meet those terms without question or delay. YOUR MONEY BACK IF NOT COMPLETELY SATISFIED is a form of guarantee often used as an inducement to buy. IF IT DOESN'T FIT, BRING IT BACK AND WE'LL REFUND YOUR MONEY is another commonly used inducement to purchase. Even so there are usually stipulations about the condition of the returned item, the need for a sales slip, and a time limit. And there are many items for which such guarantees would generally be impractical, such as goods that are personalized or designed and built to customer specifications or services that have been rendered exactly as requested by customers.

Although there are some proponents of unlimited guarantees of satisfaction as incentives to companies and their employees to provide high quality goods and services, open-end guarantees of this kind inevitably require higher prices as a form of self-insurance against excessive refund claims, particularly in the case of high-priced and customized services and products. It also enables competitors to offer comparable services and products at lower prices enabled by specific warranties rather than open-end or unlimited guarantees.

Warranties: A Better Solution?

While written warranties don't have the appeal of unlimited guarantees as an advertising slogan or incentive to buy, they are widely accepted as a practical and reasonable alternative. Most written warranties are called "limited" warranties because they spell out the conditions under which the seller or manufacturer will repair or replace the product or refund the customer's money. Such a warranty is very much like a contract in which both parties are aware of the specific terms and conditions. Like a guarantee, it's a form of insurance in which the costs are passed along to customers. But in the case of warranties, these costs are considerably less because there are practical limits on adjustments.

Automobiles, for example, are warranted for a specific period of time or number of miles, and to qualify for warranty repairs or adjustments the owner is usually required to perform certain maintenance services at specific intervals. Many consumer goods are warranted for periods ranging from ninety days to a year and are supported after warranties expire by so-called service contracts that are essentially the same as the original warranty and run from year to year. Extended warranties are very much the same.

Warranty administration is often handled in the customer service department and in general is handled much like conventional adjustments. It's particularly important that warranties be administered uniformly to all customers. If any given customer is given service or an adjustment in excess of that specified by the written warranty, the action could be interpreted as an extension of the warranty that must now be applied to all customers covered by the same warranty. An automobile dealer made an adjustment over and above the terms of the warranty and the end result was a class action suit requiring the automobile manufacturer to offer the same service free of charge to some 80,000 other owners with the same model and warranty coverage.

This is an excellent reason for making policies on adjustments fair and reasonable in the first place. You'll find very little argument from your customers!

6

Positioning and Organizing the Customer Service Department

As a customer service manager aspiring to head a department that renders as near perfect a degree of service as possible, you must be well-informed on the broad issue of positioning the customer service department and hands-on *capable* of organizing and staffing it. This chapter tells you how to meet both needs fully, with fresh information on both subjects.

This dichotomy between positioning the department and organizing it occurs because separate management levels are usually involved:

▪ *Positioning* the customer service function — deciding where it reports and whether it is centralized or decentralized — is usually resolved at a senior management level. But you can and should have a voice in the decision because of its impact on the quality of service the organization provides.

The more you know about the pros and cons of the different positioning possibilities, the more positively you will be able to influence the final decision. And unless your management is reading this book over your shoulder, you will be significantly better informed than they, simply because what follows on reporting patterns and the centralization/decentralization issue isn't available elsewhere.

▪ *Organizing and staffing* the department is your direct responsibility, and you will be judged on how well you handle it. Even though you may have to operate initially under constraints of headcount and grade levels, with experience you should be able to overcome those constraints through rewriting job descriptions and through cost-justification of increased staffing as described in chapters 14 and 15.

Customer service departments have changed dramatically within the last several years, and the information on organization in this chapter reflects the four main forms that evolution has taken. You won't find this information else-where. Use it well!

Positioning the Department

Pros and Cons of Five Reporting Options

Clearly no single organizational reporting pattern for customer service fits all types of businesses. The effectiveness of different reporting relationships varies by industry or type of business, as well as by the way management has defined the customer service department's mission. Here are the pros and cons of the principal reporting patterns:

Pros of Reporting to Top Management. For service companies such as banks and insurance companies seeking to break away from the traditional view of customer service as a backroom operation, reporting at the top sends a message throughout the organization that management is genuinely committed to cus-tomer service, It's also likely to be the best way to break away from the embed-ded rituals and procedures that have hindered customer service in the past.

In many newer and high-tech companies outside the service industries, a top-level reporting relationship is taken for granted and has proved to be a valuable competitive tool. In businesses predicated on customer service— direct marketing is one example—it's not unusual for top management to be directly involved in setting customer service policies and monitoring customer service performance on a day-to-day basis. And it's becoming relatively com-mon for top management in the manufacturing industries to participate in weekly meetings to review overall customer service performance.

Cons of Reporting to Top Management. There are no significant negatives for having customer service report at the top, provided of course that the cus-tomer service manager has line authority on a level with that of other depart-ment heads. If the manager repeatedly has to turn to top management for approvals and signoffs on routine matters, the reporting relationship may be ineffective because top management isn't always that accessible.

Pros of Reporting to Sales and Marketing. Without getting into the fine dis-tinctions that some companies draw between a sales department and a market-ing department, there is excellent logic for incorporating customer service into the department. As a sales-support function, customer service can make a multi-thousand dollar contribution to increased field sales productivity by per-forming a number of administrative tasks and giving field salespeople more face-to-face selling time with their customers.

Where there is a close relationship with the sales department, a properly staffed and trained customer service department can take over sales to marginal accounts and make them profitable. It's also easier to institute order enhance-ment programs and handle lead qualification in the customer service depart-ment when it reports in this way. And if the company is planning to follow the trend to use customer service as a marketing strategy, then this particular reporting relationship is almost mandatory.

Cons of Reporting to Sales and Marketing. Although reporting to sales and marketing is the most common relationship, several negatives have to be overcome. The first is the tendency of sales personnel to view customer service people as clerks and personal assistants rather than as part of the sales team. Also, field sales personnel tend to have short-term goals—for example, making the next sale, showing good results for the month or the quarter—while the customer-keeping function of customer service is basically a long-term strategy. If the sales and marketing departments are short-term minded, they may resist investment in customer service improvements with a long-term payout. Finally, there may also be resistance on the part of field salespeople to such customer service innovations as automatic adjustments and liberal return, exchange, and refund policies, all of which can adversely affect salespeople's commissions.

Pros of Reporting to Operations. This reporting pattern is fairly widespread, since the term "operations" can include logistics, distribution, materials management or the traditional backroom operations in banks, stock brokerage firms, and similar organizations. In manufacturing industries, particularly grocery products, chemicals, health and beauty aids, paper, and building materials, the relationship is common and has proved to be an effective marketing tool because of the importance of maintaining strategic inventories in the marketplace.

Also, the management science applications used in developing cost-effective distribution are quite often useful in developing cost-effective customer service logistics by coordinating product flow with information flow and vice versa.

Cons of Reporting to Operations. The heavy cost orientation of most operations functions, even when operations exists as a department in its own right, can be a serious detriment to effective customer service. The long tradition of many companies to look at customer service as an out-of-pocket, reducible expense is likely to be reflected in resistance to attempts to upgrade customer service to marketing strategy status in terms of personnel, policies, systems, and budgets. In a large operations activity, lack of career pathing and opportunities for promotion may result in high turnover and uneven service levels.

Pros of Reporting to Finance. A heavily systems-oriented finance department can offer excellent support to customer service in computer and communications systems, electronic data interchange (EDI) and electronic funds transfer (EFT), and similar areas. Also, since breaking out customer service costs by customer is going to be a virtual "must" in the demographics-oriented company of the future, the ready availability of financial personnel to extrapolate such data gives the customer service manger a powerful tool for cost-justifying proposals for customer service enhancements of all types—staffing, systems, policies, and procedures.

Cons of Reporting to Finance. In spite of these advantages in the reporting relationship, the tradition of regarding customer service as "cost adding" can be very difficult to overcome. Where the financial and comptroller's department see themselves as guardians of the company's finances, customer service goals are certain to be overshadowed by accounts receivable and credit collections, a bias that will most likely be reflected in the attitude of customer service representatives toward their customers.

Pros of Reporting to Manufacturing. This reporting relationship is often preferred for custom manufacturing operations, where customer service personnel have a technical or engineering background and in some cases are involved in every phase of product manufacture from design and development through to the delivery and installation or application of the finished product.

The printing industry is one example, where the vast amount of technical detail involved in the process makes an interface between manufacturing and customer service at the plant level highly desirable. From a marketing viewpoint, the relationship may be a good one because it frees salespeople for selling and builds a stable relationship between customers and inside personnel that is likely to remain even when salespeople are lured away by competitors.

Cons of Reporting to Manufacturing. If manufacturing management is not fully sensitized to this customer-keeping function of customer service, this particular reporting pattern cam be extremely harmful to a company's relationships with its customers. Remember that manufacturing managers are usually rated on unit costs and capacity utilization, that is, the highest levels of productivity based on present plant equipment. The incentive to meet specific needs of customers is frequently overshadowed by the incentive to meet the needs of machines, that is to schedule manufacturing equipment in the most cost-effective manner with little if any regard for what customers need here and now. This attitude can be particularly damaging in cases of supply shortage or customer emergency. In this environment, customer service is often viewed as an annoyance that interferes with manufacturing efficiency and customer service should certainly be reporting in more friendly surroundings.

Centralized Customer Service Operations

A centralized customer service activity can take on one of several forms:

- A single department at a single location responsible for all customer service activities for a company or division of a corporation.
- Two or more regional customer service departments that are, in effect, a single department split among several regions for operational convenience and reporting to one manager or director.
- Divisional customer service departments of a corporation at one or different locations. Each of these is still considered centralized in terms of the division it serves.
- A corporate customer service department serving all divisions. This form is relatively rare.

- A centrally dispatched field service organization. Although the field engineers themselves may be located all across the country, they form a single department reporting to a manager at a central location.
- A customer service group composed of individuals working at home but with phone connections to a central switchboard or ACD system and terminals accessing a central mainframe computer. This kind of arrangement is increasing.

Note that centralized departments aren't necessarily located at corporate or divisional headquarters. Joanna, a multiplant division of CHF Industries, Chicago, consolidated six regional customer service centers into a single centralized operation at Tempe, Arizona. Similarly, General Electric Lighting Division closed 22 regional customer service departments and opened its national customer service center in Richmond, Virginia. Union Carbide Specialty Chemicals Division, headquartered in Danbury, Connecticut, closed five regional customer service centers and centralized customer service operations at South Charleston, West Virginia. Notable about the Union Carbide move was that three other customer-oriented functions—shipment scheduling, accounting, and inventory planning and control—were also moved to the new location on the premise that the interaction would increase productivity. And it did. Reps' productivity increased 75 percent, from eight orders a day to more than fourteen.

Rorer Pharmaceutical Corporation in Fort Washington, Pennsylvania, took a slightly different course by establishing a customer support center, which is essentially a corporate, rather than divisional, customer service department handling all customer service matters for Rorer's five divisions.

Decentralized Customer Service

Decentralized customer service is typical of multilocation companies where customer service people are stationed at individual locations and report to a manager at that location rather than at the headquarters location. Here are some typical examples:

- *Multiplant companies.* Decentralized or locally reporting customer service organizations are generally the rule at custom manufacturing or make-to-order plants.
- *Manufacturers' and wholesalers' distribution centers or sales offices.* These are usually quite small and are accountable only to local management.
- *Manufacturers' field service organizations.* Some of these organizations report centrally, but in the case of home appliances, office equipment, and similar products, the customer service function typically reports locally.
- *Retail chains.* The function almost always reports locally, quite often at the store level.
- *Consumer-oriented national or regional businesses or organizations that are local in nature.* These range from hospitals to restaurant chains, franchise operations, public utilities, and similar organizations.

Printing and converting companies such as Meredith-Burda and James River Corporation tend to have their customer service departments at the plant level because the nature of the business requires close interaction between customer service and production personnel. Within recent years, Copperweld Corporation set up new customer service centers at producing plants in Shelby, Ohio, and Chicago, Illinois. Overall, relatively few national companies have gone from a centralized to a decentralized customer service operation.

Figure 6-1 lists the principal advantages and drawbacks of each type of organization.

For typical customer service operations, logic indicates that a centralized customer service department will assure a consistently higher level of customer service, will be more cost effective, and will provide economies of scale seldom possible in a decentralized organization.

With today's telecommunications capabilities, distance from customers or from the home office is seldom a factor, and large decentralized customer service operations can be found in locations as diverse as South Dakota, New Jersey, Indiana, Oklahoma, Florida, Arizona, Virginia, Maine, and New York. Although the specific time zone differences may require an adjustment of working hours in order to offer national coverage, this adjustment is readily achieved through flextime or staggering working hours. A number of the larger departments—mail order and credit card companies are good examples—now operate 24 hours a day.

The organizational pointers that follow are predicated on this concept of a centralized department where you are responsible for developing the most efficient organization for your company's needs.

Organizing the Department

The four basic ways of organizing customer service usually reflect the way customer service personnel are assigned to handle calls from customers. And that derives mainly from the nature of your business, the size of your customer base, and the level of skill needed to serve it. The following four types of staffing arrangements can be applied to either in-person or remote operations. Chapter 10 deals with them in terms of call center applications:

1. *Next available rep.* This method of staffing is the most common in high-volume customer service operations. Whether customers are serviced in person or by the phone, the principle is basically the same. Customers are handled in order of their arrival or call by the next rep who becomes available. The in-person version is common at airline ticket counters, in banks, government offices, and similar operations. The call center version can be found in airline, car rental, and hotel reservation operations and in phone ordering and inquiry applications of all types.

From a staffing viewpoint, the next-available-rep arrangement is highly productive and cost-effective in customer service operations where there's a

Figure 6-1. Advantages and disadvantages of centralized and decentralized customer service operations

Centralized Customer Service Operations

Advantages	*Disadvantages*
Economies of scale permit high levels of productivity	Emphasis on productivity, downsizing may undermine productivity
Practical for state-of-the-art communications, computerization	Vulnerable to natural disasters
Can be adapted quickly to some competitive situations	Less sensitive and responsive to unique local or regional needs
Easy to measure performance and ensure adherence to standards	Uniform standards may not be suitable for all locations and markets
Allows specialization within the department	Less hands-on, front-line practical field experience
Ensures standardized application of policies, procedures	Highly structured approach may discourage individual initiative
Enables faster access to top decision-makers	Limited opportunity for one-on-one contacts with key plant personnel
Opportunities for career paths help attract quality people	Difficult to maintain sense of team in large organization
Highly suited for high-volume consumer goods manufacturing	Unsuited for custom manufacturing, many types of service organizations

Decentralized Customer Service Operations

Advantages	*Disadvantages*
Close to customers	Remote from central support functions
Sensitive to local conditions and problems	Difficult to administer procedures, policies uniformly at all locations
Fosters good relationships with local customers	Difficult to measure service quality and maintain consistent standards
Close to line managers in field	Limited access to top decision makers
Smaller, more flexible group	Higher costs, few economies of scale

Good sense of team	Limited opportunities for career pathing, advancement
Few layers of management	Customer service personnel often diverted to other tasks
Well suited to custom manufacturing operations	Difficult to coordinate when customers deal with several locations
Required for local-type businesses and institutions	Smaller staffs difficult, expensive to train in customer service

fairly narrow range of services and a high volume of customers seeking those services.*

Reps are generally at the same level of expertise, and their principal function is to access the database to perform the transaction—enter an order, update a record, or provide information—requested by the visitor or caller. A ration mainly depends on three factors: (1) the accessibility of a rep when a customer visits or calls; (2) the degree of sophistication built into the computer program; and (3) the skill of the customer service rep in working with the computer in applying that sophistication in fulfilling customers' requests.

Most visits or calls in this kind of system are relatively short. As long as there are enough service givers, no customer waiting in line is seriously inconvenienced if one of those reps takes extra time with a customer. Great emphasis is placed on productivity, and the rep normally makes very few actual decisions. Decision rules generally reside in the program itself and can't be overridden by the rep. If she can't deal with a particular situation, the matter is usually forwarded to a superior for exceptions handling.

The principal drawback of the next-available-rep staffing arrangement is that it can be both boring and stressful and may result in excessive turnover. Ways to deal with this problem are discussed in detail in Chapter 17.

2. *Assignment by account, region, or industry group.* This type of staffing is highly desirable in mid-volume business-to-business situations. It provides both the personalization and the degree of specialization needed to provide a level of service that's customized to the individual account's needs. It also provides an excellent morale factor for the individual reps.

When reps are assigned by account, territory, or industry, the stress, burnout, and turnover factors are likely to be considerably reduced by the "pride of

---

*Bear in mind that if you provide free parking at an in-person customer service site, the longer it takes you to service customers, the more you will have to budget for parking, either in space or in fees to third-party parking operators. Next time you go to your supermarket, you'll see that if lines are long and slow at checkout stands, the parking lot will probably be full and congested.

ownership" that characterizes such situations. The downside is that staffing the system is much more complicated than in the next-available-rep configuration because of workload balancing issues.

3. *Assignment by specialty.* The most common example of this staffing method is assigning one or two reps to handle export-import customer service or designating individuals to handle claims, promotional payments, credit adjustments, bilingual transactions, or whatever. This method is good from a morale viewpoint, but generally is cost-effective only in larger departments. However, the development of specialties of this type is one of the best arguments for a centralized customer service department where it's much more practical to staff in depth than in a decentralized organization.

4. *Assignment by tiered level of expertise.* This method of staffing and call distribution is becoming more common, particularly in telephone operations at high-tech and software companies and in field service and engineering applications involving remote diagnosis.

In a typical system, as many as four tiers may be involved: The first tier consists of one to four reps, depending on the call volume, who screen incoming calls and decide which level to assign them to based on the type of problem. Some calls can be handled at this level, but the majority are handled at the second level where the largest number of reps is assigned. Matters requiring a higher (or different) level of expertise are directed to the third or fourth tier. These are normally higher-level engineers or scientists who do not normally handle phones but are available to handle complex problems and may also be called into service to help level the workload during peak periods.

A similar type of staffing may also be found in field engineering staffs, where engineers are dispatched to customer sites based on the level of skill required at each location.

Division of Labor

Depending on the size of the department, there is likely to be a further division of labor in actual tasks performed. For example, Readers Digest Association has two major divisions in its customer service department: (1) reps who handle telephone calls and (2) reps who respond to letters. In direct marketing or mail order companies such as L. L. Bean and New England Business Service, the division is customarily between reps who take orders from customers and enter them into the order processing system and those who handle inquiries, returns, exchanges, credits, and complaints. In most instances both groups report to the same manager, but in some companies order entry and customer service are two distinct departments reporting to different managers.

In manufacturers that sell to other businesses, it is much more usual for customer service reps to handle orders as well as account service on returns, credits, expediting, and the like, particularly where reps are assigned by account or specialty. In many ways, reps act as consultants to customers in determining the most suitable products or product configurations, applications, delivery methods, and other details.

By contrast with direct marketing companies where one rep may enter several hundred orders in a day, a customer service rep at a manufacturer may enter as few as three or four in a day but representing far greater dollar volume, with some individual orders in excess of $100,000. In some instances a rep may be responsible for a single major customer account. In one large company, one rep handles an account that bills $1 billion a year. There are similar situations in the service industries: banking, insurance, financial services, training, information services, consulting, engineering, and others. The requirements for these customer service jobs, which are essentially account management, are considerably more stringent than in the next-available-rep departments.

Software companies are essentially service organizations where order entry is a relatively minor part of the customer service job. Most of the customer service reps' time is devoted to supporting the software installed at customer sites, in effect talking users through the problems they encounter. A typical customer service organization may be divided into two groups, the "fixers," who find a temporary solution for software problems, and the "changers," whose job is to eliminate the underlying causes of software problems.

In conventional customer service departments, depending on department size, there are usually support personnel who don't normally deal with customers but may perform data entry, call screening, and clerical functions. Personnel may also be assigned to a specific function such as credits, displays, exchanges, traffic, or promotional payments. Larger departments may have an industrial engineer, a programmer, or a trainer as part of the permanent staff. There is usually a departmental secretary and quite often a secretary to the manager as well.

Departmental Hierarchy

Most customer service departments follow a conventional format, with a manager, several working supervisors, then several senior reps or team leaders (depending on departmental size), and the support staff if any. Some very large operations may have two departments — customer service and customer support — each headed by a manager and reporting to a director or vice-president. In a major credit card operation such as American Express there are likely to be several customer service sections based on account size. Several sections handle corporate accounts, one of which handles only the very largest corporate accounts.

At the other extreme, there are a great many departments with as few as six reps reporting to a supervisor where there is little if any structure. And many companies do not have a formal customer service department but divide the functions among sales, credit, shipping, purchasing, and production.

There has been significant increase in the number of formally organized customer service departments in recent years, and there's every reason to believe the trend will continue in customer service in much the same way that distribution departments have evolved in the last thirty years.

Some Typical Customer Service Jobs

Although titles such as "customer service manager" and "customer service representatives" are found in almost every type of organization, there's almost infinite variation in actual job content. In some organizations, almost anybody who has contact with the public is called a customer service representative. In others, the title is applied only to customer service department personnel who perform certain specified tasks related to the delivery of a service or product to customers.

Companies vary considerably from one to another and from one type of business to another, and the list of responsibilities shown in Figure 6-2 is very general. The list was originally developed by Customer Service Institute and later adopted by the International Customer Service Association for use in its periodic customer service salary surveys.

Laying Out the Department

Customer service people work under considerable pressure, and the physical environment in which they work affects their productivity as well as their motivation. While most larger departments are planned by professional designers, in smaller operations the manager may be more directly involved. In either case, you should make sure that certain basic conditions are met:

- *Privacy but not isolation.* CSRs like to have their own space, but they also enjoy a sense of community. Most customer service departments are divided into individual cubicles with relatively low dividers. The dividers provide sound absorption and a sense of privacy yet other members of the team are close by.

- *Personalization.* Some companies have very rigid rules about the appearance of cubicles, whereas other companies allow considerable latitude in how reps may decorate their cubicles. In some departments, aisles between rows of cubicles are adorned with "street signs" bearing the names of different members of the department. In the face of the continued stress that's characteristic of the job, some concessions to individuality seem in order.

- *Team grouping.* If the department is organized into teams, you may want to look into the cluster arrangement. The centralized customer service department at Union Carbide Specialty Chemicals Division is arranged in a series of five "pods," each of which has workspaces for about seven customer service reps and interfacing disciplines: three sales accountants, a shipment specialist, an inventory planning and control specialist, and two distribution coordinators. Carbide officials describe this consolidated arrangement as "highly successful."

- *Ergonomics.* There has been considerable concern about the physical stress associated with data entry jobs and the relative immobility of customer service work generally. Some managers have introduced stand-up terminals

Figure 6-2. List of responsibilities assigned to customer service personnel

Customer Service Director
Has overall responsibility for directing the operational and administrative functions of the customer service department(s). Engages in long-range planning and is responsible for seeing that the corporate/division strategy and mission is carried out by assigning goals and objectives to the customer service manager(s), and provides direction and implements policies. Responsible for planning budgets, hiring, and setting standards.

Customer Service Manager
Responsible for meeting specific departmental objectives/goals. Responsible for training person-nel, monitoring performance, introducing more efficient procedures, writing and/or updating customer service manuals and maintenance of customer files. Recommends changes where appropriate and has functional responsibility for receipt of order processing, billing, returns, adjustments, product and order status inquiries.

Assistant Manager of Customer Service or Customer Service Supervisor
Has functional responsibility, under the customer service manager, for one or more areas of customer service, for example, order processing claims and returns above a certain dollar

limit, and warranty administration. On behalf of the customer service manger, performs actual liaison with sales, credit, inventory control, warehousing, shipping, traffic, data processing, and the customer. Serves as operating head of the department in the absence of the customer service manager. Occasionally delegated to perform special functions; customer research, preparation of the customer service manual, customer visits, etc.

Order Processing Manager/Supervisor
(Rank equivalent to assistant manager of customer service or customer service supervisor.) Responsible for receipt of orders, order editing and review, credit check, order entry, manual or computerized systems, mainten-ance of records associated with order processing system: order status, inventory levels, back orders, order fulfillment ratio, etc. Responsible for training, motivat-ing, and supervising order entry clerks and support personnel. Controls access to customer records and computer data-banks, and maintains security as necessary. Supervises entry of new data, changes, product descriptions, weights, price information, etc. Responsible for order processing, supplies, maintenance of equipment, service contracts, etc.

Source: International Customer Service Association   *(continues)*

Figure 6-2. (continued)

Senior Customer Service Representative or Assistant Customer Service Supervisor
Often functions as a team leader, account executive or working supervisor. Primary contact for customer, responsible for taking orders, handling routine inquiries and complaints, claims, credits, and refunds below a certain dollar limit. Is expected to have extensive knowledge of account requirements and special situations, ability to cut red tape and get results for customers. Handles exceptions, substitutions, allocations and other special problems. Often possesses specialized technical knowledge about company's products and their applications.

Customer Service Representative
Receives and processes all incoming orders and prepares appropriate forms for pick lists, invoice generation, etc. Gives customers product availability and delivery information, initiates credit checks when necessary, advises supervision of unusual situations. The primary contact for customers for inquiries, complaints, product information, and returns.

Order Entry Clerk
Responsible for auditing and batching order entry documentation for computer output or, with on-line systems, enters orders on CRT terminal, and maintains entry reports.

Customer Service Clerk
Performs routine filing, clerical, typing, and similar functions.

reps can use when they're tired of sitting, and a few have workstations that permit working in either position. These are said to be popular with reps.

▪ *Information storage.* Information storage is a major element in customer service. The more information that can be accessed in the computer, the less you have to be concerned with the location of hard copy files. It's preferable to have frequently used hard copy files or references in individual or group areas.

▪ *Facsimile.* The increasing use of facsimile has already led some companies to put individual machines in group areas, and it seems quite likely that some companies will soon be placing them at individual workstations handling a significant amount of hard copy communications.

▪ *Noise abatement.* Carpeting, sound-absorbing dividers, acoustical tile in ceilings—all these are absolutely essential in any customer service department. Some firms are using white sound, a form of electronic sound masking that overcomes the dead atmosphere created by too much sound-absorbent material in the workplace.

- *Lighting.* Like noise abatement, proper lighting is essential in the customer service environment. Particular attention should also be given to the illumination on terminal screens.

- *Workflow.* If any appreciable volume of paper or other materials actually moves through the department, you may want to call in one of your company's industrial engineers or a space designer to help with logistics.

- *Don'ts.* Don't neglect to observe how often customer service personnel get up to use the files or the copier. Don't overlook the possibility that you may need to redesign jobs as well as the workflow. Don't forget to link up new workflow patterns with other departments. Don't expect the process of relayout to be accomplished when you were told it would be. Above all, don't forget to consult your personnel and listen to their ideas *before* you talk to anyone else!

7

Setting Quality Standards

Standards play a central role in customer service management. As manager, you will find them to be among your most useful tools in running an efficient department and providing consistent levels of quality service to your customers. Standards are a yardstick for measuring performance, quality, duration, length, height, weight, purity, and so forth. They are particularly useful as a measure of uniformity and consistency in the performance of customer service and in the quality of the service itself.

Standards have different uses and applications. You will be concerned equally with work standards that measure the performance of customer service personnel in your department and in related functions such as warehousing and shipping and with customer service standards that measure the quality of the service you give customers.

Work or Performance Standards

Work or performance standards refer to the amount and quality of work or output workers are expected to produce within a given time frame. They are usually stated in numbers: keystrokes per minute, telephone calls per hour, orders per day, tons per man-hour, error rate not to exceed one-half of one percent. They are often referred to as "measures of productivity" and used as a means of cost control as well as incentives for improved performance.

The numbers represented in work standards are generally a high average of output for a typical cross-section of jobs performed by a typical cross-section of workers in a typical work environment. They are developed through time-and-motion studies and thousands of precise observations by industrial engineers. An operation such as filling out a return authorization form is usually divided into a series of discrete elements, with the time required to perform each element stated in time measurement units (TMUs), each TMU representing one one hundred-thousandth of an hour. Look at Figure 7-1 to see how a series of elements might be stated as the components of one specific operation.

Standards such as these are carefully engineered to allow for rest, fatigue, and the varying complexity of tasks. Some standards also allow for different

Figure 7-1. Components of a document processing operation

Element	*TMUs*
Obtain document or form	42
Scan sheet for reference points	60
Verify stock number	152
Verify item description	51
Verify unit of description	67
Enter individual's name (14 letters)	343
Enter date (4 digits)	104
CSR's signature (14 letters)	172
Total normal time	991 (35.68 seconds)

skill or expertise levels. In Figure 7-1, variations in the length of the document, or the detail to be entered, would tend to average out quickly.

Standards for medium- to high-volume telephone operations take several forms. The actual standards could vary considerably from one type of company to another, but a typical ACD report enables measurement of performance against a number of different work standards by printing out these data by individual employee:

Name of worker
Number of calls inbound
Number of calls outbound
Number of internal calls
Number of calls transferred
Type of calls
Length of calls
Total time on-line
Total time off-line

Some managers make this information available to workers every day so that they know on a continuing basis how well they are doing as individuals and how well the group is doing as a team. Other managers prefer to use them only when there appears to be a serious problem with an individual's performance. But even then, they point out, the performance report should not be used for punitive reasons. Of course if performance continues to be unacceptable, the ACD reports will ultimately justify your terminating individual employees, provided that all individuals in the same job category are measured in the same way.

For a company where calls are likely to be longer and more complex, it may be desirable to set standards for individual segments of the call in terms of both time required and quality of response, with time measured in seconds and quality rated on a 10-point scale. Figure 7-2 shows how a service-type call can be broken down into its individual components, which are then measured by actual live observation and subsequently compared to standards for the specific type of call.

Figure 7-2. Components of a service-type call

Call Element	Time	Quality	Comments
1. Greeting	___	___	___
2. Caller response	___	___	___
3. Probing	___	___	___
4. Process:	___	___	___
Name	___	___	___
Address and zip	___	___	___
Phone number	___	___	___
Equipment	___	___	___
Rented/owned	___	___	___
Model number	___	___	___
Serial number	___	___	___
Repair/service code	___	___	___
Special request (exchange, pickup)	___	___	___
5. Marketing questions/ upselling	___	___	___
6. Additional customer comments	___	___	___
7. Close/wrap-up	___	___	___

As the figure shows, work standards do not have to be concerned exclusively with output that's measured in units of work per unit of time. Output measures must be validated against the actual quality of work performed, and most companies employ some form of monitoring to ensure that the quality meets certain predetermined standards. Since quality is often a subjective judgment, its important that all supervisors involved in rating the quality of telephone performance employ the same rating system, as shown in Figure 7-3, which is used to supplement ACD reports in a large consumer call center.

The actual standard in this case would probably be a requirement that the individual score an average of 7 or better in order to project the image desired by the company. If scores fall below that point consistently, it may be a sign that productivity standards for the number of phone calls to be handled within a given time frame are set too high, and reps are sacrificing quality in order to meet

Figure 7-3. Sample rating form for telephone performance

Name _____ *Date* _____

| | *Customer Interaction* | *Quality Points** *(From 0–10)* |

1. Identified oneself properly   _____
2. Listened actively   _____
3. Used friendly, pleasant, patient tone _____
4. Used empathetic phrases,
   customer satisfaction skills   _____
5. Maintained customer's self-esteem   _____
6. Communicated clearly, used good
   grammar, no in-house jargon   _____
7. Enunciated clearly   _____
8. Directed and controlled flow
   of conversation   _____
9. Did not place blame on
   another department or person   _____

Identification/Resolution

1. Asked appropriate questions,
   got customer to respond   _____
2. Assessed and diagnosed problem
   correctly   _____
3. Applied appropriate procedure to
   solve problem or otherwise deal
   with the situation   _____
4. Reached agreement with customer
   on specific action to be taken
   or what to expect next   _____

*Where   0 = Lowest,   5 = Average,   10 = Exceptional

standards. The format also enables the manager to spot areas where individuals, as well as the entire group, may need additional training and skill-sharpening.

Although work standards are often considered as exploitative of workers, if they are properly engineered they are eminently fair. Obviously, workers need to be told before taking a job what standards they'll be expected to meet and what the consequences will be if they don't meet them. If they feel that the standards are too demanding for the salary offered, they don't have to take the job. In this respect output is no different from any other measure of qualification for a job: typing, language skills, experience, education, and so forth.

Standards also ensure that all workers are measured in the same way, allowing for differences in skill levels and complexity or difficulty of tasks.

Rather than exploit workers, work standards are designed to ensure that every worker does his or her fair share and that workers who do their fair share aren't exploited by those who don't.

In a large publishing organization, for example, some customer service representatives who had worked without standards for a number of years were told by management that, starting the following month, they would be subject to various standards, depending on their specific job assignments. The announcement brought a strong negative reaction from the group, even though the standards were based on the group's own performance, as measured over a significant period of time. The reps saw the standards as a "speedup," although in fact their intent was to maintain productivity at levels within the group's proven abilities. What management had failed to explain to the group was the delicate balance between productivity in the customer service department and laid-down costs of the firm's books and publications in the marketplace.

Belatedly, management pointed out that reductions in productivity would necessarily result in increased subscription rates for the publisher's magazines, and although this would bring in some additional revenue it would also cause a drop in circulation. With advertising rates pegged to circulation, it would actually have to *reduce* advertising rates and suffer big revenue losses as the final result of any drop in productivity.

Additionally, this management had been experiencing, along with many other companies, significant deterioration in the quality of the available workforce. It shared its concern about this deterioration with existing staff and was able to show them how the standards being imposed would actually protect present workers by screening out future job applicants whose work would otherwise undermine the performance of the entire department.

The lesson to be learned from this company's experience is that, if you don't already have work standards and you're planning to start using them, make sure that workers understand their intent and allow plenty of time to sell the concept within the department. Figure 7-4 shows a poster developed to address employee concerns about work standards. You may also want to consider having your reps develop the standards themselves. Companies that have done so find that the standards are fair, reasonable, and workable and allow for different skill levels plus training new personnel. Best of all, reps buy into them from the outset, which makes your selling job a great deal easier.

Work Standards Pluses and Minuses

Work standards are most effective in customer service departments where the following conditions apply:

1. *The volume of work is fairly steady.* The volume of work given to individual workers should approximate the conditions under which the standards were established. In high-volume telephone operations, fluctuations in the volume of incoming calls are offset to some extent by adding or subtracting staff. A number of companies also employ different standards during extremely

Figure 7-4. Poster telling employees how standards help them

WHY STANDARDS?

1. **Standards are good.** They tell us exactly what's expected of us.
2. **Standards are positive.** They show us how well we're meeting those expectations.
3. **Standards are constructive.** They show us how and where we can improve our performance.
4. **Standards are fair.** They measure us and our co-workers by identical criteria and without personal bias.
5. **Standards are relevant.** They are based on the needs of the marketplace and the economics of competition.
6. **Standards are proactive.** They enable us to correct subpar performance before it impacts customer relations—and profits.
7. **Standards are challenging.** They give us goals and the drive to reach and exceed them.
8. **Standards are rewarding.** They give us a sense of accomplishment that cannot be disputed or diminished.
9. **Standards are supportive.** They build team spirit based on common goals and mutual support.
10. **Standards are THE DIFFERENCE.** They are what sets one organization—ours—apart from all the others. Standards reflect the quality of our service and the excellence of our people—the "best of the best" in our field.

Source: Customer Service Newsletter

high-volume call periods. But if the workflow is intermittent, standards are likely to give false readings and an inaccurate picture of productivity.

2. *The work is uniform and distributed uniformly.* If the work varies in complexity or difficulty, standards will create perceptions by workers that "it only counts if it's counted" and the difficult tasks are likely to be performed superficially or ignored altogether in favor of the easier ones. A conventional ACD system ensures that the workload of incoming calls is distributed evenly, but it can't guarantee that the calls will all be similar. If there's too much variation in the types of incoming calls, measuring performance against standards may be less important than seeing that calls are routed to individuals according to their skill or experience levels.

3. *Workflow and work must be readily measurable, preferably as a byproduct of the actual work.* Measurements such as keystrokes, phone calls, and tons or transactions per man-hour are usually generated by the task itself. Measures such as checks or credits per day can be based on the worker's actual output. However, if measures have to be recorded manually, either by workers or by

somebody else, it automatically adds time to the operation as well as the potential for inaccuracy.

Work standards are generally most useful in large, standardized operations such as hotel and airline reservation systems, car rental call centers, catalog order departments, banks, and public utility customer service departments. But as the organization moves from the standardized to the specialized, the use of standards becomes less and less practical. Many smaller operations simply don't lend themselves to the use of work standards because of frequent interruptions, changeovers from one task to another, and differences in work assignments within the department.

Using work standards may be counterproductive, even when there are cash and other incentives for high performance. Rewarding quantity rather than quality is likely to discourage creativity and innovation. When a customer service rep is handling a problem for a major account, what counts is the quality of the solution, not the length of the call.

A well-known chemical company sometimes shows visitors a videotape of one of their reps taking an order from a customer. The transaction takes about 10 minutes, with numerous social exchanges, conversations about children, grandchildren, forthcoming weddings and so forth. At first glance, it seems like an efficiency expert's nightmare. Then the customer service manager points out the value of the order the CSR has just entered during those ten minutes: $60,000. At an average rate of seven orders a day, she handles about $2 million a week or about $1 billion a year in bookings. It's one of a number of instances where conventional standards are irrelevant in measuring performance.

Should you use weak standards in your department? Industrial engineers who are also customer service managers report that in the typical business-to-business customer service department, only about one third of customer service activities lend themselves to measurement by standards, and even then record keeping can be a thankless chore. As long as you understand their limitations, standards can be applied to certain operations such as routine phone transactions in order to provide a fair picture of how your representatives are performing relative to one another. But you will still want to test those standards on the job to ensure that when your reps actually meet or exceed those standards the quality of their work remains consistent with your customer service goals.

In other words, when you develop work standards, your goal is not to decide how many calls your reps *can* handle within a given time frame but rather how many calls they *should* handle once you have decided what the format, content, and length of those calls should be. And for that you will want to look at an entirely different kind of standard: customer service standards.

Customer Service Standards

Customer service standards reflect the levels of service that a company has decided it needs to provide to meet marketing goals and profit and market share objectives. Customer service standards fall into two main categories:

1. *Visible or external standards,* which reflect the kind of service the customer actually experiences in dealing with the company. Many of these standards relate to *response*: speed of response to telephone calls; accuracy and speed of response to orders for service or products; response to claims, adjustments, and complaints; response in emergency or problem situations; response to requests for information; and more.

2. *Invisible or internal standards,* which generally refer to the support activities within the company required to meet the external or visible standards. For example, a telephone company with a government contract is required to observe a standard that all complaints be resolved within 5 working days. That's the external or visible standard. But in order to meet that standard, it's necessary for the customer service manager to get information and action from other departments: quality control, accounting, field engineering, and others. Thus the company has set an invisible standard or internal standard requiring that when such a situation arises the department(s) contacted by customer service respond or take responsive action within 3 working days. This in turn gives the customer service manager sufficient time to develop and/or negotiate the resolution with the customer within the time frame indicated by the external standards.

Three Requirements for a Customer Service Standard

1. *A customer service standard must be specific and whenever possible stated in numbers that can be measured against.* Thus:

- "Excellence" is not a customer service standard because excellence is not defined in measurable terms.
- "On-time" shipment/delivery is not a standard because on-time is not defined: Is it the time specified by the customer or the time promised by us? Is it the time shown in a timetable?
- "Eighty percent of orders under $500 shipped complete the same day as received" is a valid customer service standard because every element can be measured.
- "No caller kept on hold more than 30 seconds" is a valid customer service standard.
- "All credits posted within 48 hours (2 working days) of receipt" is a valid customer service standard.
- "All calls from a customer with a 'system down' condition to be returned within 15 minutes" is a valid customer service standard.
- "As soon as possible" is *not* a valid customer service standard.

Specific standards can and should be developed for every aspect of customers' dealings with the firm and vice versa, with first emphasis being given to those most discernable by the customer:

- Standards of response
- Standards of courtesy

- Standards of availability—
  person, product, or service
- Standards of accuracy
- Standards of completion
  or followthrough

2. *A customer service standard must be fully supported by an appropriate commitment of resources.* These resources will typically be inventory, personnel, skills or specialties, communications or information systems, and whatever else is needed to enable the company to perform its mission. Although it has become popular to talk about customer service in terms of "team spirit," "empowerment," "exceeding expectations," and other buzzwords, in reality, most good customer service reflects a willingness to set high customer service standards and commit the resources necessary to meet them. Most poor customer service reflects either a reluctance to commit those resources or, just as often, an absence of them.

As important as it is, the training and motivation of personnel is only one step—and usually the final one—in developing an effective customer service system. For example, if the company set the standard cited above for shipping 80 percent of orders under $500 complete the same day as received but then failed to allocate sufficient inventory, all the CSR training in the world would not enable the company to meet its standard. Commitment of resources to inventory and to improved forecasting and production planning capability would be the direct route to averting customer service failure and far more cost effective than spending money to train personnel in all the different ways to pacify customers and say "I'm sorry."

As customer service manager, you are going to have to overcome those well-entrenched and well-meant but completely fallacious notions that motivating and inspiring your troops is the key to customer service excellence. The key is to set the right standards and commit the resources necessary to meet them.

3. *A customer service standard must be supported by an appropriate discipline throughout the organization.* In the example of the telephone company cited earlier, the 5-day standard for complaint resolution was supported by an internal discipline requiring that all departments contacted by the customer service department respond within 3 days. In the company offering same-day shipment of orders under $500, that discipline would extend to the warehouse manager, shipping department, credit personnel, and others involved in the total process. In many situations, the discipline would include the accountability of the purchasing department for supplying packaging and labeling materials and outsourced parts and supplies of various kinds.

As customer service manager in a typical organization, you are quite likely to be held accountable for customer service failures beyond your control because of a lack of accountability elsewhere in the organization. You don't like to point the finger of blame at someone else in the organization, and your customers won't appreciate it, either. To avoid this type of situation altogether, make sure that the standards you establish meet all three requirements.

Examples of Customer Service Standards

Customer service excellence—what differentiates your company from its competitors—ultimately boils down to a multitude of standards covering a multitude of corporate activities and an effective system for measuring performance against those standards. The typical standard is discrete, that is, relatively narrow in scope and confined to measurable service features. Some examples of such standards include:

- Process and post credit memos within 7 days of receipt.
- Post all adjustments within 7 days: All adjustments must be current at month's end.
- Keep busy signals below 5 percent of all incoming calls.
- Maintain hold or wait time at less than 2 minutes.
- Maintain 99.5 percent accuracy on order entry and assembly.
- Ship 98 percent of orders to A customers within 24 hours.
- Respond to computer user hardware problems within 15 minutes.
- Distribute standard user reports at 10 A. M. daily.
- Central processing unit uptime to be within 98 percent of available hours.
- Process special reports within 24 hours of request.
- Review all credit holds a minimum of once weekly.
- Process credit applications within 15 days of receipt.
- Reception: Escort visitors to proper location within 10 minutes of arrival.
- Salespeople: Write 98 percent clean and complete orders.
- Salespeople: Contact customer service once daily.
- Switchboard: Answer 95 percent of calls by third ring.
- Switchboard: Connect callers correctly on 98 percent of calls.
- Inquiries: Respond to 90 percent of routine inquiries on-line, in real time.
- Inquiries: Where research and consultation is necessary, complete all call-backs within 72 hours.
- Inquiries: Interdepartmental information requests from customer service to be serviced within 48 hours in order to meet published customer response standard.
- Voicemail: Return all internal and external calls within 8 working hours.
- Limit "no answer" on internal and external calls to 1 percent or less.
- Human resources: Fill 90 percent of nonexempt jobs in customer service within two weeks of vacancy.
- Human resources: Set staffing as necessary to meet engineered productivity standards; add/subtract personnel as the workload varies.
- Complaints involving $100 or less are to be resolved immediately up to twice per quarter per customer.
- Complaints over $100 and under $500 are to be resolved within 2 weeks or less.
- Invoice deductions up to $25 are allowed up to twice quarterly per account.
- Retail: When more than five people are in queue at any checkstand, another is to be opened immediately—operated by supervisory or management personnel if necessary.

- Order turnaround: 93 percent of orders filled complete within 72 hours.
- Order line fill: No less than 98 percent line fill at all times.
- Field service requests: system partially operable, onsite service within 8 hours.
- Field service requests: system completely down, onsite service within 4 hours or less.
- Field service: critical parts availability, 99 percent immediately shippable.
- Maintenance: MTBF (mean time between failures) no less than 2,000 hours.
- Travel: involuntarily denied boarding not to exceed one-half of 1 percent.
- Banking: data transmission 99.8 percent on time and accurate.
- Banking: customer check order cycle ten days or less; corrections, 5 days, premium delivery costs absorbed.

As you review this list of standards, you may wonder why so many standards appear to be less than 100 percent. The reason is a practical one: cost. To develop a completely fail-safe system in customer service, as opposed to one that operates in the mid- and high-90th percentile, would increase operating costs and push prices to unacceptable levels.

In customer service as elsewhere in business, the cost of doing business is sharply impacted by *capacity utilization,* which is simply the extent to which the company makes use of its assets, including personnel, inventories, machines, space, and systems. The objective is to utilize these assets as fully as possible, so that there is a minimum of idle time or unused capacity. In the manufacturing business, machinery is scheduled for as much running time as possible and as little down time as possible. The same is true in scheduling aircraft, trucks, and trains in the transportation industries. Your dentist has three assistants and four chairs so that he can maximize the use of his skills and not have to dilute valuable earning power waiting around while you are prepped for or deprepped from his ministrations.

The classic example of the capacity utilization problem is the cost of inventory that would be incurred in attempting to support a standard of 100 percent product availability in retailing. Although you can usually get what you're looking for in the size and package you want, it's not always there. And there's a reason. In a typical supermarket, to make absolutely certain that the specific product you're looking for on any given day will be 100 percent available in the exact quantity you want would require doubling safety stock inventories on many of the 20,000 line items typically stocked in such a market, requiring a significant increase in the shelf price—a price that you and other consumers would be unwilling to pay. Any increase in sales due to increased product availability would be marginal at best and more than offset by decreased sales because of consumer price resistance.

A similar scenario would hold true for any attempt to make personnel 100 percent available for immediate servicing of customers' needs and eliminating queues altogether in retail stores, at airline ticket counters, sporting events, and so forth. To have technicians immediately available to repair computers, telephones, printing presses, even washing machines, would require costly backup staffs who, like the Maytag Man, would be paid mainly for sitting around waiting for calls that rarely come.

Certain businesses, health care, for example, do have 100 percent standards where the cost of providing the service is passed along to the consumer in one way or another. It's estimated that over $500 of the cost of a new car represents the cost of the health care benefits of the manufacturer's work force. A different kind of passalong occurs in the federal government. The Government Printing Office in Washington, D.C., which is required by law to publish the *Congressional Record* daily when Congress is in session, has 24-hour service contracts for virtually instant repair of its critical printing equipment. The added cost of ensuring that the daily rhetoric of Capitol Hill is available in hard copy form each morning is passed along to the taxpayers.

Given the cost constraints imposed by capacity utilization economics, most companies have to realistically set standards, not in terms of "excellent" or "ideal" customer service but in terms of what customers are willing to pay. The coach sections of commercial aircraft are considerably larger than the first-class cabins for practical reasons. In business the process of setting standards is a matter of striking the delicate balance between what people need and what people want, on the one hand, and what they are willing to pay for it, on the other.

As the above list of standards suggests, customer service standards are a company's best answer to a very basic question: Given our corporate objectives, what kind of customer service should we be providing our customers?

This question is complex. The popular notion that a company should automatically offer "excellent" service reflects fuzzy thinking because *excellent* means many things to many people and is always tempered by customers' willingness or ability to pay for the cost of the service. Customer service standards must be defined within specific boundaries, such as the following:

- What types and levels of service do customers need in order to continue buying from us?
- Assuming this level requires improving present service, will we be able to absorb the cost, or will we have to pass it along to customers?
- If we pass the added cost along to customers, will they be willing to pay it?
- What types and levels of service are our competitors offering?
- What are they offering that we're not?
- What are we offering that they're not?
- How do our customers rate our service, feature by feature, versus the competition's? Which features are most important? Least important?

These practical questions all require specific answers. It isn't enough to know whether customers will be satisfied with a given level of service. We need to know whether service improvements will pay for themselves, what effect they will have on our customers' future dealings with us, and whether we should set different customer standards for different kinds of customers.

How to Set Customer Service Standards

Preparing the Ground

Who should set customer service standards? Logically, the customer service manager and his or her staff should prepare detailed standards like those listed earlier. But once standards have been developed, it is critical that they be approved and supported at the highest management levels. For without the commitment of resources plus the establishment of a customer service discipline in all sectors of the company, standards of any kind are going to be difficult, if not impossible, to meet.

Start your discussion of standard-setting as close to the top as possible and certainly in those quarters where you're likely to get the most support. To the extent that customer service standards are recognized as a strategic marketing tool, marketing is normally a logical starting point. Marketing can determine the principal standards most suitable to overall marketing strategy: the standards that will generate the highest profits and/or market share for the customer service dollars invested.

Marketing should be able to provide important support in setting appropriate standards in three main ways:

1. Recognizing and countering competitive service offerings
2. Making it known elsewhere in the company that being Number 1 in customer service may not always generate the highest profits
3. Using customer research, simulation, and other management science techniques to answer "what if" questions about potential changes or improvements in customer service

Interfacing departments should also be involved in developing standards because they may be required to change or modify existing practices. In some companies, management has appointed a cross-departmental committee for developing and implementing practical internal as well as external customer service standards. This approach is excellent because (1) it ensures that standards adopted are workable, and (2) it ensures that each department represented has a stake in making the standards work. When management appoints such a committee it is essential to include a sufficient complement of front-line, hands-on workers to ensure practicality, and it must give a fair estimate of what kinds of resources it's willing to commit to implement standards recommended by the committee.

The customer service manager will naturally be involved in the development of standards developed by such a means or otherwise. He or she has the best first-hand knowledge in the company of customers and their needs plus any practical hurdles to overcome to make standards work. The added involvement of customer service reps provides incomparable real-world guidance and serves as an excellent morale factor for the entire department as well.

You may be thinking that you are perfectly capable of setting standards without participation by others. That is probably true in theory, but going it alone presents three serious problems that normally don't exist when others are involved:

1. Just as other departments are likely to support standards they've had a hand in setting, so are they likely to oppose and even undermine those imposed on them without their involvement.

2. Management is more likely to accept proposals that have joint sponsorship than those that are unilateral and may be perceived as empire-building.

3. Customer service managers who set their own standards without support and involvement of others may unconsciously attempt to circumvent these problems by setting standards that are immediately acceptable to everyone. In so doing, they may fall into a common trap of setting standards reflecting what the company *can* do with its present makeup rather than what it *should* do even if it means making some basic changes in policies and procedures.

So, as a practical matter, you will want to undertake standard setting as a joint venture with others. If it's a major exercise in standard setting, the entire project may take a year. But in the meantime, you can adopt new standards as they're approved and debug and modify as you go along.

If you're in a hurry to get standards in place, don't overlook the opportunity presented by unexpected customer service failures to get immediate management support for instant standards and decision rules that will minimize the possibility of further failures of the same kind.

Brainstorming the Candidates

Start by listing all candidate customer service activities that impact the customer directly. You may want to list them under whichever of the following categories apply to your situation, bearing in mind that in brainstorming you *do not prejudge* practicality, feasibility, or acceptance by others. Just write 'em down!

1. *Response time.* The most universal standard, it applies to almost every facet of customer service, in every type of business.
2. *Accuracy.* Another universal standard, ranging from accuracy of diagnosing equipment problems to accuracy of interpreting customer needs, accuracy in fulling orders, documentation, etc.
3. *Availability.* Relates to products and services as well as to availability of personnel to provide service, availability of computer time, hotel rooms, airline seats, etc.
4. *Length of queue.* Derives from item 1 and reflects an estimate of how long customers are willing to wait for service. The process of queuing is explained in detail in Chapter 11.
5. *Reliability.* A customer service feature that is often more important to customers than response time. Measured by percentage of deviations from standards in performing services or tasks and also in elements such as mean time between failures (MTBF).
6. *Quality, measured.* Relates to standards of quality as measured objectively for products or services: product integrity at time of receipt, on-time delivery, conformance with purchase order terms. Can also refer to measured performance of individuals against quality standards for telephone performance and other activities.
7. *Quality, perceived.* Recognizing that in many instances "Perception is reality," these may be standards of dress, appearance, courtesy, and pro-

cedure that are not central to the quality of service but that normally enhance the customer's perception of it.

8. *Training and performance.* Closely related to both aspects of the quality standard, this standard sets forth the skill and training levels required for specific tasks, as well as the way performance will be measured. It also recognizes that the perception by customers that employees are well trained can have a major, favorable impact and thus may emphasize highly visible features of training such as those displayed at Disneyland and some airlines and first-class hotels.

9. *Complaint resolution.* The time required to resolve a complaint has great effect on customers' perception of the firm and often overshadows the actual quality of resolution. Thus standards for complaint resolution should emphasize speed and recognize that for complaints under a certain dollar amount, no-fault adjustments may be the only means for meeting an appropriate, time-based standard.

10. *Recovery.* This increasingly important standard in customer service specifies actions to be taken in the case of customer service failures, problems at customer sites, unique customer needs, or natural disasters.

11. *Special services or features—differentiators.* These are not necessarily standards in themselves but are often characterized by standards — for example, a customer hotline that must be accessible by customers within x minutes and provide a 95 percent on-line question-answering capability.

These are the main categories of external or visible customer service standards and those that are most likely to affect customers' perceptions of your company and to influence their future dealings with it. Bearing in mind that customer service standards are being set for strategic reasons, you will want to set tentative standards for each activity commensurate with its strategic importance, with a key stipulation to guide you: *There is seldom any value, strategic or otherwise, in providing customer service that is better than needed, assuming that you have properly assessed customer needs in the first place.*

As you set tentative customer service standards, you should consult three sources to help you set priorities and the actual service levels you think are most suitable to your strategies:

1. *Customer research,* to help you decide what's most important to your customers in terms of service and service levels. Different classes of customers may have markedly different needs.

2. *Competitive offerings,* to assure you that your service offerings are both competitive and relevant. Actually being better than the competition doesn't ensure that you're *perceived* as being better, and your research should take this into account.

3. *Marketing intuition,* to calculate the value of enhancement as well as pricing issues and price elasticity or inelasticity in your markets that may affect the standards you decide on.

If you have properly brainstormed your candidates for customer service standards of this type, selected those that fit your strategy, and set tentative service levels, your next step is to assess their practicality in terms of cost as well as operational feasibility.

Determining Feasibility

Assessing the feasibility of a standard has two phases: (1) Can the desired level of service be provided? Is it within the state of the art or technology to provide it? and (2) What will it cost or, alternatively, will it pay for itself? Three brief case histories illustrate this stage of setting standards:

Example 1: A standard calling for responding to and resolving 95 percent of requests for information while the customer is still on the phone, with no more than a 30-second hold. The objective here is to distinguish the company from its competitors by the quality of its service, with an important secondary objective of avoiding the high cost of off-line research and callbacks to customers, which now characterizes the company's response to some 40 percent of all inquiries. The feasibility of this standard depends on the availability, levels of performance, and cost of these supporting components:

- Trained personnel: sources, cost
- On-line, real-time information system
- Database capacity and scope
- Ease of system access by inquiry handlers
- Speed of system, search-and-find features
- Ease of update by other departments
- Practicality of real-time updates
- Number of additional data entry people needed
- Design year factors, that is, allowance for growth, expansion, or enhancement
- System for measuring performance against standards
- Payback, or potential savings over present system

Since a system of this type represents a major investment, it must be carefully costed out. Apart from the known benefits of improved customer service overall, the system offers significant savings over the present system with its 60 percent response level. For example, the present system requires off-line research and callback on 40 percent of present inquiries. The callbacks involve an added, and particularly hidden, cost: the fact that it is often necessary to make several callbacks to reach a particular individual. The research itself involves two kinds of costs: the actual labor costs and the opportunity costs for the personnel involved.

Since systems of this type are already in place at General Electric, Eastman Kodak Co., and Abbott Laboratories, it's clear that they are feasible and can be cost-justified in cost-conscious environments.

Example 2. A maximum 2-hour response on field service calls that involve machine-down situations. The objective of this standard is to build confidence in new equipment, sign up more customers for service contracts, and set the company apart from its competitors who are currently offering 4- to 6-hour response in similar situations.

Determining the feasibility of the standard requires determining the availability and cost of these resources:

- Addition of trained personnel
- Improved inventory of critical parts
- Improved tools and test equipment to shorten repair time
- Improved remote diagnosis to free up field personnel
- Improved remote or walk-through servicing to free field service engineers from user-serviceable assignments
- Vans for engineers to ensure adequate parts inventory (possible alternative: requiring customers to maintain on-site inventories of critical parts)
- Computerized dispatch system
- Car phones for field engineers
- Additional training (free?) for customer personnel
- Redesign of equipment for user friendliness, improved mean time between failures (MTBF)

All the items listed are within the state of the art, and there are significant opportunities for improving service while actually reducing costs overall. The investment in free customer training is often more than offset by a reduction in warranty administration costs, whereas remote diagnosis and self-repair on user-serviceable components are often preferred by customers to waiting for an engineer to arrive on-site for minor repairs. A two-bin parts inventory in vans facilitates inventory management and at the same time reduces the possibility that engineers will arrive on-site without the right part. Advanced diagnosis and computerized dispatch aid in this as well.

Example 3: Improve order response and order fill to 97 percent line fill and 92.5 percent complete order fill. The objective is to be designated a sole source supplier in an extremely competitive market. As in the previous examples, a number of service features and components need to be researched and costed out:

- Improved forecasting capability.
- Improved production planning, greater flexibility.
- Increased investment in inventory.
- Provision for cross hauls where necessary.
- Strategic use of air freight to minimize need for maintaining local inventories of high-value products. Feasibility of negotiating contract or volume rates?
- Direct order entry and inquiry by customers using electronic data interchange (EDI) or remote (captive) terminals.
- Just-in-time arrangements (see section on "JIT standards" later in this chapter).
- On-line, real-time capability for stock status and commitment.

- Improved tracing and expediting.
- System of rolling warehouses—railcars or trucks—with full capacity for diversion and reconsignment to customers with immediate need (variation: local combined peddler and delivery vans that can be field dispatched to customer locations).
- Decision rules for unforecast large or unusual orders, for example, place order directly with plant rather than at local distribution center. Offer customer lower price for longer lead time.
- Computerized substitutability system for items not in stock. Offer concessions to customers, for example, higher priced item for same price as item originally ordered.
- Decision rules for allocating stock during shortages.
- Partnershipping arrangements with carriers and public warehouses to assure preferential treatment.

All of the items described above have been employed by companies with the objective of developing sole-source relationships with their customers and, in some cases, simply protecting an existing relationship from competitive threats. In dealing with large-scale distribution of the type envisioned in this example, there are almost always very large cost tradeoffs. For example, the use of air freight for shipping high-value merchandise, such as fashions, pharmaceuticals, and software and circuit boards, enables substantial reductions in localized inventory safety stocks. With vaccines valued at several hundred dollars or more per pound, and some circuit boards costing as much as $25,000, it doesn't take long to offset the added cost of shipping by air! It's also been demonstrated that investments of say $100,000 in improved forecasting systems can actually reduce inventory investments in the millions.

The Discipline: Setting Internal or Interdepartmental Standards

This aspect of setting practical and meaningful customer service standards is understandably one of the most difficult yet critical. Management, department heads, and line workers must recognize that customer service is everybody's job, and to prove it the company has specifically defined those standards and the levels of accountability associated with them.

The three previous examples can be used to illustrate how internal standards and/or interdepartmental accountability are determined.

Example 1. 95 percent on-line response to information requests. Internal support of the information system and timely response to internal inquiries are both critical to the standard. Since the system envisioned requires real-time input for almost every major department in the organization, strict accountability of each department concerned must be written into the standards, with a provision that failure to meet those standards within the designated time frame will be automatically reported to the next level of management for appropriate action.

Nine typical internal or interdepartmental performance standards, with the actual times to be determined by the individual companies, include:

1. Response time on inquiries beyond the scope of the system or front-line personnel: applications inquiries, technical inquiries, software or systems support inquiries
2. Response time on order or production status inquiries
3. Response time on shipment status inquiries
4. Response time on credits, refunds, and other adjustments
5. Response time on approvals, releases, and other sign-offs
6. Standards on data completeness
7. Standards on data accuracy
8. Standards for immediate notification of customer service department of relevant changes in policies, procedures, personnel assignments, product design, pricing, deals
9. Standards for timeliness of system updates

Many of these standards refer to operating features not normally visible to customers but nonetheless critical to overall service levels. It's not going to be easy to persuade other department heads of the value of increased accountability of the type mentioned here, but it is well worth the effort!

Example 2. Two-hour response on critical field service calls. Many firms seeking to establish a standard of this nature have to make substantial improvements in their internal support of the field engineering or technical services department and associated support services. Strict accountability for each department must be written into the standards, with automatic escalation to the next level of management when those standards are not met.

Eight of the main interdepartmental performance standards essential to meeting a 2-hour or similar field engineering customer service standard include:

1. Maintain adequate inventories of critical parts; no "stealing" of parts by production department for assembly or any other reason.
2. Reorder parts from third-party vendor within 24 hours of reaching a designated reorder point.
3. Fill parts orders promptly.
4. Report practicality of correcting design defects and software problems versus continuing to service in the field.
5. Notify field immediately of engineering and design changes.
6. Respond promptly to requests for high-level technical support when problems reach a designated level of complexity.
7. Respond promptly to additional staffing needs when service calls reach a specified point and designated customer service standard cannot be met with existing staff.
8. Respond promptly to requests for manual pages and documentation required by field service engineers and customers.

Field service engineering is currently undergoing many changes. If it is part of your customer service responsibility, you are already aware of the difficulty of getting competent and motivated people for what is frequently a difficult, stressful job that requires a great deal of travel and separation from family, and is almost 100 percent occupied with negative situations, that is, machinery breakdowns that cost the customer money and may cost even more before the problem is resolved. These circumstances give an extra urgency to the kinds of interdepartmental support listed above.

Example 3. 97 percent line fill and 92.5 percent complete order fill standards. In the manufacturing or distribution environment where these standards are not uncommon, the internal support of manufacturing, warehousing, and shipping or distribution is essential. In direct marketing or retailing where there is no manufacturing operation as such, the purchasing/materials management/ procurement function is a critical element in meeting order fill standards. Some typical internal or interdepartmental standards essential to meeting the external customer service standards for line fill and complete order fill include:

1. Production and inventory level standards to be met by manufacturing and/or purchasing
2. Order entry standards including data entry staffing
3. Credit approval or clearance standards
4. Packaging materials or inventory standards
5. Warehouse order assembly standards
6. Carrier selection, routing, and documentation standards
7. Response standards on requests for premium transportation
8. Customer pickup standards
9. Consolidation or "area shipping" incentives and standards
10. Shipping standards, including staging, pickup, transit, and delivery
11. Standards for handling change orders within acceptable time frame
12. Approval standards for fill-ins, orders below minimums, and other exceptions

In this category of standards, you will see many similarities to the just-in-time, or JIT, standards discussed next. Because of the complex system of internal support required to meet such standards, they present an exceptional opportunity for you to introduce statistical process control techniques for the kind of service quality control that will make your company a true leader in customer service.

JIT Standards

Just-in-time (JIT) standards are widely used in the manufacturing industries and refer to a complex system of delivering raw materials, parts, and components within very narrow time windows so that they will appear just in time to be entered into processing or manufacturing operations. JIT standards differ from conventional customer service standards in that they are actually set by the individual customers. JIT standards are usually unique to each customer and are likely to go into such detail as requiring suppliers to have EDI hookups using software compatible with theirs, generating invoices and packing slips in a specified format, and generating specified reports.

Although JIT standards are generally imposed by major manufacturers who are generally in a position to dictate their own terms, there are examples of JIT standards in wholesaling, retailing, agribusiness, and construction industries as well.

The primary objective of JIT standards, from the customer's viewpoint, is to reduce inventory and warehousing or storage costs, and at the same time obtain maximum return on capital used in the business. In the construction industry, particularly in metropolitan areas, JIT, or timed jobsite deliveries, may be required by the extremely limited storage space at the site. In retailing, JIT deliveries are generally coordinated with seasonal merchandising programs and advertising campaigns, with the immediate objective of maximizing inventory turns and return on the advertising investment.

From the vendor's viewpoint, JIT has the advantage of an assured market for its products. But the arrangement is likely to be one-sided in favor of the customer and unreasonable as well. For example, some manufacturers do not pay for parts and components delivered to them until they are actually assembled into finished products on the assembly line. It's not unusual for retailers to specify that orders be delivered to their warehouse at specific times and then to refuse to accept delivery at those times. Major discounters and "warehouse stores" usually require special packaging or bundling as well as prepricing and other accommodations.

However, the volume of JIT business available is so attractive that many suppliers are willing to put up with its frequently exacting standards. If you are in a company that has JIT customers, your main concern will not be in setting standards, but rather in ensuring that the standards set by your JIT customers are in fact met at a cost that is consistent with your own company's profit goals.

Work Standards vs. Customer Service Standards

Work standards are essentially measures of productivity rather than customer service quality, but they play an important role in ensuring that quality standards are met. In each of the three examples cited, it's necessary to perform designated tasks within a certain time frame and at a designated level of service quality: accuracy in providing information, skill and speed in diagnosing and repairing equipment, accuracy and fast turnaround in filling orders. One of your most important jobs is to ensure that the work standards adopted for these critical functions allow these tasks to be performed at the desired level of quality and that your staffing levels in customer service be increased as necessary to maintain that level of quality.

As you start this complex job of setting meaningful, strategic customer service standards for your company, you have a great advantage over almost every other company in business today. Relatively few companies have standards that are genuinely tied to company strategy, a surprising number have no standards at all, and an equally surprising number don't know the difference between work standards and customer service standards. You're in an enviable position!

Summary of Rules for Setting Customer Service Standards

- *Set customer service standards for strategic reasons:*
  1. Set standards that achieve a marketing goal: profits, increased market share, sole-source destination, etc.
  2. Do not confuse customer service standards with work or productivity standards, which simply measure output per unit of time.
- *Set customer service standards on a realistic economic basis:*
  1. Set standards high enough so that they meet customer needs and achieve a fair economic return or competitive gain but not so high that they exceed customers' needs or willingness to pay.
  2. Use actual numbers to describe desired service levels. Avoid use of terms such as *excellent,* or *quality,* which cannot be measured in a uniform way.
  3. Do not confuse customer service standards with goals or targets established to motivate your personnel. They are two entirely different kind of standards. As customer service manager you are responsible for meeting customer service standards; your personnel are responsible for meeting, or trying to meet, whatever goals you set for them.
- *Set customer service standards for service features most important to customers:*
  1. Research helps determine the relative importance to customers of different service features and thus the levels at which standards for those features should be set.
  2. Research also helps uncover service features that customers may no longer want or need, and which therefore can be eliminated, freeing resources for features that need strengthening.
  3. Research identifies service features that customers would like to have but are not currently receiving.
  4. Research also helps determine whether there are significant differences in the service needs of different types of customers.
  5. Research uncovers competitive offerings that may have to be met or competitive weaknesses that can be taken advantage of.
- *Set standards that are workable and measurable:*
  1. Involve all department heads who influence the meeting or nonmeeting of standards.
  2. Secure management commitment on the standards, the resources, and the required accountability of all parties.

8

Managing Complaints and Adjustments for Profit

Although *complaint* is widely used in connection with customer service, the connotation of irate and unreasonable customers that it evokes is generally inaccurate. An analysis by telemarketing consultant Lee Van Vechten showed that fewer than five customer calls per hundred to a typical customer service department were classed as "irate" and fewer than one per thousand as actually rude. In a total of 846 calls none were classified as abusive.

This doesn't mean that customers don't complain. Instead, it means that the majority of complaint calls—calls that customers make to express dissatisfaction or request an adjustment—are considered routine by both parties and are generally handled by them in a courteous, businesslike way that strengthens the bond between the company and its customers.

Indeed, the majority of complaints aren't actually complaints but are likely to be tallied as errors, exceptions, credits, adjustments, returns, exchanges, and so forth. In a typical business operation, there may be from thirty-five to fifty such categories under the complaint heading, depending on the type of business. The following list includes some representative categories; other categories may be peculiar to your industry or circumstances:

- *Pricing.* Too high, incorrect discount, freight allowance, etc. (A high proportion of complaints in this category may suggest that there are equally as many undercharges that are *not* reported.)
- *Communications and instructions.* Customer could not understand printed materials from company or attempted to follow instructions and failed to get appropriate results.
- *Insufficient support.* Not enough trained personnel to answer questions about technical applications, software problems.
- *Misbilling, performance.* Product billed but not shipped or service charged for but not performed.
- *Misbilling, account.* Service or product has been billed to the wrong account, division, or department.

▪ *Misdirection.* Product shipped to wrong location, service performed at wrong site. (An extreme example of this occurred several years ago when a building demolition company knocked down the wrong building.)

▪ *Quality.* Product or service doesn't meet specifications.

▪ *Features.* Product or service not as represented.

▪ *Application.* Product or service fails to perform.

▪ *Availability.* Customer is unable to procure product or service.

▪ *Delays, access.* Customer was delayed unreasonably in accessing department or placing order for product or service.

▪ *Delays, commitment.* Failure to meet commitment on time.

▪ *Inaction.* Failure to respond and failure to meet action commitments of various types.

▪ *Damage, physical.* Product arrived in damaged condition.

▪ *Damage, financial.* Vendor's misperformance caused financial damage to customer.

▪ *Damage, other.* Vendor's misperformance caused embarrassment or emotional suffering to customer.

▪ *Allowances.* Vendor failed to provide co-op advertising and/or promotional allowances.

▪ *Other errors and omissions.* About thirty to forty categories, depending on the type of business. Usually, a high proportion of these complaints relate to billing matters: incorrect posting, failure to credit, checks that cross collection notices in the mail, double billing, etc. Another large segment concerns correctness of orders, primarily errors of count or errors of substitution or wrong product.

▪ *Returns.* Product is returned or service discontinued for unspecified reasons under vendor's guarantee.

▪ *Personnel.* Customer received poor service or was offended by perceived poor attitude of service givers.

▪ *Policies, specific.* Customer felt policies applied in his or her case were unfair, harsh, or discriminatory. (Note that in many cases complaints about personnel are actually complaints about the policies their companies require them to administer.)

▪ *Incorrect information.* Customer received incorrect information about policies or procedures. (Also likely to be registered as a complaint against personnel rather than the information itself.)

▪ *Policies, general corporate.* Customer disagrees with corporation's policies on the environment, overseas investments, hiring, etc. Complaints in this category are often handled by a separate entity responsible for consumer affairs or public relations.

▪ *Wrong party.* A certain number of complaints are misdirected: complaints intended for one company are sent to another company with a similar name or sometimes with a completely dissimilar name. Some companies use these misdirected complaints as sales leads and have decision rules and scripts offering discounts, free trials, or trade-in allowances or credits on competitive products or services.

■ *Miscellaneous and oddball complaints.* These may range from criticisms of advertising tastes to an off-the-wall paranoiac complaint that your logotype contains the evil eye, which is fixed on unsuspecting consumers throughout the supermarket aisles of the civilized world.

■ *Contamination and personal injury.* Although these enter the system as complaints, they are usually referred immediately to the legal department and are handled outside the complaint management system under the direction of the legal department. Front-line personnel should be trained in the correct procedure in the first-stage handling of this category of complaints.

■ *Threats.* Threats of legal action or harm to persons or property come under the umbrella of complaints but are almost always referred immediately to the legal department. Companies that receive a higher-than-average number of threats because of the nature of their business (hazardous chemicals, cigarettes, etc.) usually provide front-line personnel with specific scripts for handling threats and identifying the caller before routing the call to a designated member of the legal department.

Many of the complaints in this list are predictable exceptions that in many instances can be resolved on the spot via a computer entry or posting of a credit. Informal surveys of managers suggest that in virtually every type of business about 90 percent of complaints are resolved in favor of the customer and with very little ill will or emotion in the process.

There are exceptions, of course, and every complaint management system must allow for the emotion that sometimes erupts when a customer has been seriously inconvenienced, embarrassed, or financially damaged; or when he or she feels that customer service personnel have been unacceptably rude, insulting, or obstructive.

Irate Customers Are Made, Not Born

Much of the emotion associated with complaints arises *after* the complaint has been registered. In a typical situation, the so-called irate customer wasn't irate when he or she called to register the complaint but rather was *made* irate by the way the complaint was handled or mishandled. Suppose a consumer reads a product label or a catalog notice giving a toll-free number to call in case of service or product dissatisfaction. The individual then calls and either hears a busy signal or is placed on a lengthy hold. What started out as simply concern, or perhaps a motive to provide constructive criticism, ends up as impatience, irritation, and sometimes anger. When the customer's call is finally answered, the slightest hint of impatience, insensitivity, or defensiveness on the service-giver's part is likely to exacerbate the customer's initial concern into the prototypical unreasonable near-fury associated with irate customers in general.

In one reported instance, an insured calling her insurance carrier about a routine matter, an apparently misbilled premium notice, was transferred five times, ending up finally with a supervisor who provided incorrect information and failed to follow through on a commitment to correct the misbilling. The net result was an *extremely* irate customer who filed a lengthy complaint with the insurance commission in her state and threatened the insurance company with punitive legal action as well. When the insurance company finally made the adjustment representing some $260, the insured promptly canceled all three of her policies with the company and secured coverage elsewhere. Based on one of the standard rules of thumb associated with complaints, she then told at least twelve friends or associates about the experience. If she was angry enough, she probably also wrote the Office of Consumer Affairs in her city or state, the local Better Business Bureau, and her congressperson.

While this type of case is often used by consumer advocates to illustrate the insensitivity and sometimes deliberate malfeasance of business, usually it is simply a reflection of lack of a proper system for handling exceptions, Whereas the irate customer's anger is likely to be directed at the people with whom he or she has to deal, the underlying problem is that personnel either haven't been instructed in how to deal with complaints or the instructions they've been given simply don't work.

What's unfortunate about this case is not just the business the company lost—everybody involved was probably glad to get rid of the irate customer—but also the excessive internal costs generated in the process of alienating the customer, and which presumably would continue to be generated in dealing with similar exceptions in the future.

Although this sort of thing is likely to happen in companies where senior management takes a highly defensive posture against customers (which might be expected in an insurance company sensitized to fraudulent claims), it is just as likely to happen in companies that place too much emphasis on *preventing* problems but not enough on *correcting* problems that occur nonetheless. In short, an efficient customer service system is designed to minimize problems to the extent that it's economic, but at the point that prevention becomes *un*economic it becomes absolutely essential to have a complementary system or subsystem in place to deal with the problems that do occur in spite of everybody's best efforts to avoid them.

An excellent example is the airlines' baggage handling system. The system handles some 700 million pieces of luggage a year under all kinds of conditions, and loses, damages, or misroutes fewer than one percent of these. Yet it's backed up by a sophisticated baggage recovery system and an effective compensation system that minimize the impact of failures that do occur. Many airlines supplement this system further by providing free toilet and travel kits to passengers to tide them over until lost items have been recovered or can be replaced. Many hotels, recognizing that they are part of the travel system, too, offer toothbrushes, shaving kits, and the like to guests who are stranded without these necessities.

This is only one example of the complementary interaction between a customer service system—baggage checking—and a complaint management system for recovering or compensating for lost baggage. Indeed, airline management recognized that it is more likely to be judged on the way it handles the one percent of lost or damaged baggage than on the way it handles the 99 percent of checked baggage that arrive on time at the right destination!

Developing a Complaint Management System

This chapter discusses developing systems to correct problems after they occur, which includes a panorama of complaints and adjustments and other negative events that are basically handled within a body of policies, decision rules, and procedures known as the *complaint management system.* The system is called by many names—or sometimes by none at all—but it is always present in one form or another.

Although you have probably been exposed to many anecdotes about complaints—positive as well as negative—they are used in this chapter only to illustrate significant principles, not to glorify or demean individuals or companies. Here's one such anecdote that a colleague wrote down for inclusion in this chapter:

> I bought a trivet with a tile insert at Montgomery Ward's at Wheaton Plaza [he writes] and when I took it out of the box at home, it was cracked. I didn't feel like driving back but my daughter volunteered to drive me there.
>
> As she dropped me at Ward's main entrance, she asked me what time I would like her to pick me up.
>
> "Give me half an hour at least," I told her. "You know, I'll have to fill out all those forms—name, rank, serial number, mother's maiden name, date of birth, nearest next-of-kin not living with you, and so forth."
>
> "I know," she broke in, "and they'll ask you what you did to damage the tile, and that'll make you mad and you'll demand to see the manager. O.K., I'll pick you up here in 45 minutes."
>
> So I went into the gift section where I'd bought the tile. A pleasant young man approached me.
>
> "Can I help you?" he asked.
>
> I took the tile out of the box and showed it to him, explaining that I'd bought it there earlier and hadn't noticed the crack until I got home and took the tile and trivet out of the box they were packed in.
>
> "Gosh," he said, "I'm sorry you had to go to all that trouble, coming back out here and everything. Would you like another?"
>
> I said I would and he took one down from the display, examined it microscopically, and asked me to do the same. He explained that some tiles got damaged in transit, and although they always tried to screen them out, once in a while one would get through.
>
> He put the replacement tile set in its box and then in a bag, which he handed me.
>
> "What about the forms?" I asked.
>
> "Forms?"
>
> "Yes, you know, the forms. The forms I have to sign giving my

name, rank, serial number, mother's maiden name, plus the reason for the return and all that."

"You don't have to do any of that," he said. "I'm just sorry you had to go to the trouble. Thanks for letting us know!"

I was stunned by the lightninglike speed of the transaction and the complete absence of defensiveness, or accusing me of breaking the tile, and so forth. As I looked at my watch I realized that the whole process had taken less than 5 minutes. I still had 40 minutes to kill before my daughter was to pick me up.

So, I looked around. The first thing to catch my eye was a SALE! sign. And there was a huge display of brass desk lamps, marked down from $97 to $79. I'd always wanted one for an old-fashioned desk we have at the house, so I bought one.

By the time my daughter picked me up, I had three shopping bags full of goodies, and I'd spend a total of over $200. All because of a trivet set that cost me something under seven-and-a-half dollars.

Wouldn't I have bought all that stuff anyway? Heck, no! First, I wouldn't have had the time. Second, I wouldn't have had the inclination.

Fact is, if they'd given me a hard time about exchanging that tile, I would have stood in the middle of the parking lot in an Arctic blizzard for those 40 minutes rather than spend a nickel in their blankety-blank store!

This story-with-a-happy-ending is not a paid advertisement for Montgomery Ward but rather an encapsulated illustration of almost every major principle of effective complaint management in business. Even though it's a retail situation involving only a small amount of money, these rules can be applied to any kind of business, manufacturing, business-to-business, and service industries in both consumer and industrial markets. The same rules apply to virtually all the routine complaints that are made and at least 80 percent of the nonroutine or one-of-a-kind, oddball complaints that come your way:

• *Effective complaint management is a marketing strategy.* It is not a cost-cutting procedure designed to minimize the company's payout, nor is it a defense mechanism designed to protect the company. Where marketing strategies are often thought of as designed to attract customers, complaint management is designed to keep customers whom the company already has spent money to get on board. To keep them and keep them spending. As the anecdote illustrates, the customer was not only "kept," but was back spending money in a matter of minutes!

• *Effective complaint management uses a no-fault approach whenever possible and/or practical. No-fault* means simply that the issue of liability or responsibility is never raised if it can be avoided and it usually does not affect the way the complaint is resolved. In the tile example, note that the sales clerk never asked how the damage occurred, knowing that it probably would have angered the customer by projecting a defensive attitude.

In fact, just to make sure that he wasn't even suggesting the customer might be at fault, the sales clerk acknowledged that the tiles sometimes cracked in transit and the damage wasn't always caught, even though it was standard practice to check the tiles before displaying them. Note that there's a strong secondary message here that says: "It's not our policy to sell damaged merchandise, but we recognize that it can happen."

▪ *Effective complaint management is based on sound economics.* Complaint management typically involves several different sets of economics:

The cost of adjudicating a complaint and then resolving it on its merits, for example, paying or not paying on the basis of who was actually at fault. Warranties usually fall under this economic heading, since they typically define the situation under which payouts will or will not be made. Thus claims or complaints in warranty situations must be investigated before a payout can be made. This complex issue is discussed later in this chapter. At this writing, most companies accept that the cost of making a formal investigation of a complaint, that is, creating a file, getting the facts, and then deciding responsibility, is between $50 and $100.

The cost of a no-fault approach, that is, not investigating but automatically paying out up to a certain limit. The cost of investigating the cracked tile brought in by the customer clearly would have far exceeded the cost of simply giving the customer a replacement.

Some managers will argue that the investigation should be made just the same, for quality control purposes, but this is a separate issue. In the example, it was the store's option to turn the tile over to its quality control department, but since it already had a no-fault policy and would have replaced the tile anyway, there was no reason to make the customer await the outcome of the quality investigation before doing so.

The cost of a lost customer. Not every complaint results in a lost customer, but a customer whose complaint is badly handled is much more susceptible to competitive offerings and may even go looking for them. In many instances, it's easy to calculate the cost of lost customers or the decrease in business that usually results from a poorly handled complaint.

Another way to compute the cost of a lost customer is to calculate what it would cost to replace that customer. All you need to know is the cost of a sales call and the average number of sales calls it takes to make a sale or sales equivalent in value to the account you're about to lose.

The value of a retained customer. This cost is essentially the reciprocal of a lost customer cost, except that in this case you are asking yourself: How much are we willing to invest in keeping this customer? In the example, keeping the customer was considered well worth the $7.50 adjustment involved, particularly since the store probably didn't actually lose any money on the transaction anyway.

Obviously, these economics must be balanced out. An adjustment on a $3,000 sofa would have taken longer and might not have had the same outcome, that is, it would be adjudicated on the merits of the case. Yet a supplier of aluminum extrusions to the airframe industry might allow $5,000 or $10,000 as a goodwill or no-fault adjustment without requiring anything more than the customer service manager's signature.

▪ *Effective complaint management requires a clear statement of corporate policy that is periodically restated and reinforced.* In the example, the sales clerk knows the store's policy and is applying it the way it is intended to be applied — quickly and on a no-fault basis. The store is under no obligation to adopt a no-fault policy, but it happens to have chosen that option. Had it adopted a policy requiring filling out forms and justifying the exchange, it would be just as important to spell that policy out to employees and ensure they apply it properly.

Unfortunately, it doesn't always happen that way, in industrial complaint handling as well as in retail situations. For example, although service givers may be familiar with a company's no-fault policy, they are also influenced by the perceived attitude of the customer, as well as by a sense of loyalty to their own employer. A rude or abusive customer, or one whom the service giver perceives as dishonest, may not always get the full benefit of a no-fault policy unless service givers are fully instructed to apply it across the board, in all kinds of situations. Otherwise, you are very likely to hear responses such as "Oh, I didn't think it applied to situations like *that!*"

Not surprisingly, something similar is likely to happen in the application of more restrictive complaint policies. Service givers will be inclined to bend the rules for customers for whom they have empathy but to stand firm against complainers who rub them the wrong way. In extreme cases, this could trigger a class action suit by disfavored customers or possibly prosecution by the Federal Trade Commission on the grounds of favoring some customers over others. This problem is discussed in greater detail under Warranties and Guarantees.

▪ *Effective complaint management requires appropriate scripts.* The Montgomery Ward story doesn't suggest that the sales clerk was "reciting" a script verbatim or by rote, but clearly he had been coached (or had coached himself) in these four main steps in complaint response:

1. *Tone of response.* Projecting empathy, concern, and helpfulness; patience; suppressing defensiveness and responses in kind to angry and emotional or unreasonable customers.
2. *Format of response.* The typical complaint response should follow a standard sequence, starting with acknowledging the complaint, then moving through the interrogatory or fact-finding stage to resolving the complaint.
3. *Content of response.* Content of response refers to the specific information that is given to and obtained from customers in order to resolve the complaint. In some cases, CSRs may follow a script verbatim for legal reasons, for example, interpretation of clauses in an insurance policy in explaining to an insured why a claim was denied.
4. *Offer to resolve.* This is scripted to be a no-fault resolution that benefits the customer and is fair to both sides. The basic purpose of scripting is to ensure standard responses to typical complaint situations as well as equal application of complaint policies. Although actually reading a script may not seem desirable, there may be cases where it's the lesser of two evils: For example, when you don't have time to train your personnel in complaint response, you can always program responses that they can call up on their terminal screens and then read or paraphrase to the customer on the other end of the line.

Figure 8-1. Example of a simple yes-no decision rule

1. Is it our product/service?

Yes	*No*
Ask Question 2.	Refer to correct source, if known.

2. Is it an approved customer?

Yes	*No*
Ask Question 3.	Refer to regional sales rep.

3. Is the adjustment requested
   $50 or less?

Yes	*No*
Issue credit or check in amount requested in accordance with Procedure III.B.1.	Refer to procedures manual "Claims over $50."

■ *Effective complaint management requires decision rules.* Because they ensure a standard procedure and consistent resolution of complaints, decision rules are a critical component of delegating authority or empowering front-line personnel. One of the best investments you can make is to work with your reps to develop decision rules for the most common complaint situations that arise. Once decision rules are in place and reps are comfortable with them—as they will be when they're involved in developing them—you'll find them coming to you less and less for help on the majority of complaints.

By the same token decision rules are an excellent way for front-line personnel to spot serious complaints that you should be handling personally, such as product recalls or hazardous spills, major customers placed on credit hold, and so forth. Decision rules fall into two main categories:

First, *yes-no decision rules.* A simple rule of this type of illustrated in Figure 8-1. The process is virtually identical to troubleshooting an automobile that won't start. (Does the motor turn over? If no, check the battery: if yes, check the gas tank. Is the battery charged? If yes, check the terminal connections; if no, charge it. Is there gas in the gas tank? If yes, check the ignition; if no, fill the tank.)

Second, *index or matrix decision rules.* These usually consist of an index of symptoms keyed to pages in a manual as shown in Figure 8-2.

Figure 8-3 is a more complex version of a matrix decision rule that introduces a second variable, namely the size or importance of the account. In complaint handling it is practical and often desirable to have different decision rules for different classes of customers. As one manager put it, "If we have a million dollar customer who destroys $500 worth of tooling, we'll replace it free of

Figure 8-2. Sample index decision rule

Out-of-warranty repairs	pg. 21
Proof of delivery requests	pg. 10
Retrofit malfunctions on out-of-warranty equipment	pg. 47
Returned items, no record of purchase	pg. 16
Returned items, not our product	pg. 15
Returned items, overstocked	pg. 16

Figure 8-3. Sample matrix decision rule

Event or Complaint	*Customer Group*			
	A	*B*	*C*	*D*
Possible loss of account	1	10	19	28
Equipment/line down	2	11	20	29
Environmental/OSHA	3	12	21	30
Special promotion	4	13	22	31
Lost sale	5	14	23	32
Stockout	6	15	24	33
Billing error	7	16	25	34
Quality complaint	8	17	26	35
Other complaints	9	18	27	36

Note: Numbers refer to specific instructions in procedures manual.
Source: Customer Service Newsletter

charge on a goodwill basis. If it's a thousand dollar customer, we won't, and we're not expected to." The differentiation may be on grounds other than account size, such as the criticalness of the need: A health care manufacturer may give precedence to its hospital customers over its wholesalers/distributors on the premise that the hospital's need is more immediate and likely to be critical, whereas that wholesaler/distributor is buying for inventory.

▪ *Effective complaint management requires standards and ongoing performance measurements against those standards.* These standards typically relate to three specific areas:

First, *speed of acknowledgment and/or resolution of written or messaged complaints.* This area refers primarily to complaints other than those received directly in person or by telephone. Included would be complaint letters sent by mail, fax letters, messages left on an interactive system, voicemail, or conventional recorders, and complaints registered through a third party such as a salesman, broker, or agent.

In some instances, a distinction is made between acknowledgment and resolution, and in others they are considered the same. For example, if a customer writes a detailed letter about failure of a service or product and demands a substantial refund or compensation for consequential damages, the complaint should be acknowledged immediately but the actual resolution comes at a later date after the facts have been ascertained and the complaint adjudicated. If the amount of money involved is under the amount designated under a no-fault policy, acknowledgment of the complaint also includes a check to resolve it.

Many complaints do not require a resolution per se, and the complainer does not expect one. For example, a customer writes about how long she had to wait in a checkout line at the supermarket. An excellent way to handle this complaint would be to immediately acknowledge the complaint with a letter covering these points:

"We are sorry you had the problem and appreciate your calling it to our attention."

"We are working on the problem by opening new express lines and testing a new scanning method."

"If your schedule permits, you might want to do your shopping at [specified hours] when the store is less crowded and the lines move faster."

"As a token of our appreciation, we've enclosed a book of coupons [or a gift certificate] to use the next time you visit the store."

There's no need for a separate acknowledgment and resolution in this instance, provided that the complaint is responded to promptly. The suggested points do contain a form of resolution in suggesting that the customer may want to avail herself of alternative shopping times. It also "compensates" the customer by including coupons or a gift certificate.

Complaints to the manufacturers of many consumer products are usually acknowledged and resolved in a similar fashion. For example, if a consumer complains that he did not get good results with a cake mix, the manufacturer will acknowledge the complaint, send a refund check, and include a certificate good for purchasing—not another box of the cake mix, but a package of the firm's frozen pies or desserts. Obviously, if the company is flooded with letters from consumers who had a similar problem, it will want to do a quality check on the product and also verify that the mixing and baking instructions are accurate and understandable. But that should not be a reason for delaying the combined acknowledgment and response.

The actual standards that should be applied in this area of complaints are at the discretion of the company, of course, and should take into account that many of these complaints, particularly those sent by mail or via field sales personnel, may have been "in the pipeline" for as long as a week to ten days, and some customers may actually be expecting a response before the company has received the complaint itself!

In short, timeliness of acknowledgment is very important from the customer viewpoint. If you can't resolve a complaint becasue of its complexity or for other reasons, then you should acknowledge its receipt by card, letter, or phone, and let the customer know the timetable for resolution. If you need further information from the customer, request it at the time of acknowledgment. And be sure you ask for *all* the information you need at one time. Otherwise you will be perceived as stalling on resolving the complaint.

▪ Second, *speed of resolution of complaints made by phone and in person.* Since these complaints are acknowledged at the time they are registered, the standards concentrate on what happens after that. Some telephone complaints can be handled similarly to the written complaints described above. For example, a customer complaining about the long checkout lines would find the complaint acknowledged in essentially the same way and then would be told to expect the coupons or gift certificate within a given period of time. The sooner she receives the coupons or gift certificate (which will of course be accompanied by a personalized letter), the more effective the complaint strategy is in bringing that customer back in the store. In no case should the interval be longer than 2 weeks, and ideally it would be 2 or 3 business days.

Time standards for other types of complaints are normally based on the dollar amount and the amount of research and other internal action that needs to be undertaken. If a company has a good information system and/or a practical no-fault policy on complaints, many can be handled at the time of the call. For example, here is a typical conversation between a corporate credit card holder and a CSR in the credit card company's customer service department:

Cardholder:	My card number is 123456789.
CSR:	Is this Mr. Donovan?
Cardholder:	Yes, it is—and you've posted what should have been a forty-dollar credit as a forty-dollar debit.
CSR:	I see that we have, Mr. Donovan, and I'm terribly sorry for the error on our part. Here's what I'm doing: I'm posting a credit of eighty dollars, which will wipe out the forty-dollar debit and give you the forty-dollar credit you were supposed to receive. Is that satisfactory?
Cardholder:	Sure is. Thank you very much.
CSR:	Thank you, Mr. Donovan.

This narrative represents the entire transaction, which at the most took 2 minutes. On the surface, it appears that such a speedy resolution was possible because the CSR could instantly access and correct the database. But the speed of resolution could also represent something entirely different: Perhaps the credit card company has a policy governing its corporate credit cards that all adjustments under $50 requested by cardholders will be automatically allowed. So although a good information system allows fast resolution of complaints based on the actual facts, it's clearly not essential in the case of no-fault or goodwill adjustments. What's more important is that the lack of a good information system is not a valid excuse for delaying complaint resolution.

▪ Third, the *quality of the way the complaint is handled.* Quality standards for complaint handling derive largely from the policies, format, content, and scripting described earlier. A regular part of the quality control process should be to monitor correspondence and phone calls related to complaints as described in Chapter 9 and to reinforce or retrain as indicated.

The best performance in the world by your reps cannot overcome policies that are perceived as harsh or unfair by customers. Many managers send follow-up questionnaires to customers who have complained to determine their satisfaction with the way the complaint was resolved as well as with the actual handling of it by the CSR.

In all three areas described above it's essential that performance be measured on a continuing basis and that action be taken to rectify substandard performance.

Although you can handle most of the performance quality issues inside the department as part of the training process, improving performance against time standards often depends on elements outside the department and beyond your immediate control. Thus in developing those time standards it's important to build in accountability by including a statement to this effect: "All complaints not resolved within this time period to be referred automatically to the next level of management for action."

Fact and Fiction About Complaints

In the light of the preceding discussion of requirements for an effective complaint management system, perhaps you're inclined to start improving your present system or developing a new one from scratch. Before you do, however, you will find it helpful to run through the following true-or-false statements to make sure your program is on target:

1. *Complaints are largely random and unpredictable.*   □ True   □ False
False. If an effective quality control program is in place, it is usually possible to forecast complaints by number and type based on deviations from standards. At a major publishing company, for example, the quality control manager samples packaging and shipping operations, and, based on incidences of errors discovered in checking, calculates the percentage *not* caught. From this, she forecasts the number of complaints that customers will call in to the customer service department. And she's remarkably close! The customer service manager staffs so that there will be enough personnel on duty and, if necessary, prepares scripts for them so that complaints will be handled uniformly and in accordance with company policy. The net result is that when those calls start coming in, there's sufficient staff to minimize busy signals and holds, and complaints are handled quickly and effectively. With advance notice, there's sufficient time to determine whether to give the customer a credit or otherwise neutralize the problem. And the entire process illustrates the value of setting standards and monitoring performance against those standards!

2. *The objective of a quality program should be to eliminate complaints altogether.*
□ True   □ False
False. Although a 100 percent error-free service level is in theory an excellent goal to shoot for, in the practical business environment it's usually unaffordable. You've heard it said that quality is free? It is—up to a point.

As Chapter 6 demonstrates, poor quality service incurs high rework costs and high customer turnover costs. A reasonable investment in training and monitoring reduces those costs and produces savings that can be passed along to customers in the form of price cuts. But the underlying problems haven't been eliminated altogether. To do so would bring the law of diminishing returns into force; the cost of eliminating errors, rework, and customer turnover altogether would far exceed the savings realized by doing so, and the added cost would have to be passed along to customers.

In this case, quality would be free, up to a point. Beyond that point, it would be mighty expensive!

If you'll recall the airlines' baggage handling system discussion, you'll see an excellent case in point. The system isn't perfect, but to make it more nearly so would incur costs that would have to be passed along to passengers already complaining about high costs and would probably require doubling or tripling advance check-in requirements. Again, the improvement in quality would cost far more than would it worth. The investment in a sophisticated recovery system is an effective balance between cost and service.

In developing your complaint management system you need to accept the premise of an allowable level of complaints or, if you prefer, an economic level of complaints. This concept is sometimes very difficult to sell to senior management, which has been used to a diet of "excellence," "zero defects" and the like, and it is even harder to sell to senior management with an engineering background. Yet the fact is that relatively few of your customers expect perfection, and none of them would be willing to pay the price you would have to charge if you could achieve it.

3. *All complaints need to be passed through a quality control investigation and responsibility established before being resolved.*   □ True   □ False

False. In the majority of complaints, responsibility for causing complaints and the manner in which they're resolved are two separate issues. When a company adopts a no-fault policy, it doesn't foreclose itself from investigating the causes of complaints. It simply divorces resolution from investigation for all complaints below a specified dollar amount. Complaints above that amount are investigated before resolution. The extent of the investigation is proportionate to the cost or seriousness of the complaint. Even then, reasonable time standards must be applied to the interval between notification of the complaint and its final resolution. Hence, the requirement that when resolution standards aren't met within the prescribed period, the complaint be escalated to the next level of management for resolution.

4. *In order to deal with complaints, front-line personnel should have high levels of training in transactional analysis and similar interpersonal skills needed to deal with angry customers.*   □ True   □ False

False. With sound policies and procedures in place, the large majority of complaints are quickly resolved without confrontation. Training personnel in how to implement policies and follow those procedures should take precedence over teaching them esoteric skills, which they'll seldom use. The proportion of irate customers in a typical mix of customer service calls is extremely low. If there are truly high-pressure emotional situations in connection with complaints, it may be more cost-effective to train a senior rep or supervisor in handling them than to invest in across-the-board training.

5. *If you delegate too much authority to resolve complaints to lower-level per-sonnel, they will end up giving away the store.*   □ True   □ False

False. This misperception on the part of senior management is one of the most common and is probably the biggest single contributor to the problem of irate customers. The historic levels of approval that are frequently required for even the smallest adjustments in some companies create red tape and delays far beyond the few occasions of over-generosity that front-line personnel might display in making those same adjustments without having to go through approval channels.

Most managers find that front-line personnel err most frequently on the side of under- rather than over generosity in making adjustments and often have to be prodded to apply automatic adjustment and no-fault or goodwill policies equally to all customers. They also find that if customer service reps are instructed to give customers the benefit of the doubt, they will usually check with their supervisors if in fact there is any doubt. Indeed, in most companies CSRs are much less likely to give away the store than are the firm's sales personnel.

6. *Reviewing a cross-section of our complaints is a good way to measure over-all customer satisfaction.*   □ True   □ False

False. It's axiomatic that the complaints you hear usually represent a mix of (a) your most costly problems and (b) your most articulate customers, but not necessarily your most *critical* problems or your most *important* customers. Problems that involve out-of-pocket costs for customers usually result in complaints, regardless of who the customer is; and some customers complain about a wide variety of problems in addition to those involving money. But your record will not tell you about nonmoney problems that were not complained about, whether by large or small customers, nor will it tell you whether major cus-tomers you haven't heard from are satisfied with the service they're receiving.

You should also be aware of these basic "complaint economics":

- Smaller customers are likely to complain more because they have more problems resulting from hand-to-mouth buying, poor planning and fore-casting, more emergencies, and more credit problems.
- Smaller customers may get attention on their complaints out of proportion to their value as customers, when in reality they often don't have any alternative vendors to turn to because of credit ties to their present vendor.
- Larger customers may be dissuaded from complaining if they feel that it won't get results.
- Larger customers typically have a number of alternative sources to turn to, and in fact may already be negotiating with one or more of such sources at the very moment that you're deciding they must be satisfied because they're not complaining!
- The number and mix of complaints that you record is strongly influ-enced by how easy or difficult you make it for customers to complain, and by extension how much you are willing to invest in the kind of com-munications required to facilitate that kind of feedback.

7. *Complaint handling costs should be charged as a marketing expense, not an operating or a manufacturing expense.*   □ True   □ False

True. An effective complaint management system is designed primarily to strengthen the relationship with the customer and make it more profitable. When complaints are handled well, customers' confidence is increased and they are more likely to concentrate their purchases with a vendor who has proved ready, willing, and able to settle complaints promptly and fairly.

The vice-president of sales of a New England yacht building company reported that his yard was so busy with orders from existing customers trading up to more expensive yachts that it couldn't take on any new business and that the majority of the trade-up business was from customers who had complained in the past. The reason for this phenomenon? The customer's complaints had been handled so well that even though competitive builders offered price inducements, these customers didn't want to give their business (usually in the hundreds of thousands of dollars) to builders with whom they had had no experience in after-sales service generally, and complaint handling in particular.

Customers who have experienced good service in complaint resolution are also more willing to try new products or services from a vendor they're already dealing with than from a company they've had no experience with. Here again, the cost of the complaint management system that makes this possible is a legitimate marketing expense and should not be charged as an operating cost.

8. *It costs five times as much to GET a customer as it does to keep that customer.*

           □ True   □ False

True. You've heard this one before, and, as you probably know, the cost differential is caused largely by these principal differences:

Customer acquisition — selling — is labor-intensive and incurs substantial support costs in advertising, direct mail market research, and travel expense. A commercial or industrial field sales rep can seldom make more than four or five calls per day and often spends as much time traveling and waiting as in actual face-to-face selling. Buyers do not always keep their appointments, flights are delayed, and other events intervene to reduce efficiency. Because of the combination of these variables and the relative remoteness of field selling, it's also relatively difficult to control. Finally, the "hit rate" in field sales aimed at new business is extremely low. A major account may require as many as 10 years of sales calls before the salesperson lands it and she may never land it.

Customer retention — customer service — is by contrast highly equipment intensive and relatively efficient. Customer service reps make anywhere from a few dozen customer contacts a day to one hundred or more. Because customer service is an "inside" activity, it is relatively easy to structure to meet specific situations such as seasonal surges and increases in the complaint level. And a well-managed customer service operation typically has a much higher "hit rate" in customer retention than field sales does in acquisition, primarily because its statistical process control system helps identify endangered customers very early in the process in plenty of time to rectify the problem and re-entrench the customer before the competition is even aware there's a problem.

What does this have to do with complaint management systems? It demonstrates not only that it costs much less to keep customers than it does to get them, but also that it costs much less to save existing customers who are in danger of leaving than it does to capture new customers to take their place if they do leave. In short, *an effective complaint management system is a high-yield investment in customer retention.* And it's one more argument to use to persuade your management to commit the necessary resources to upgrade your complaint management system.

9. *It isn't always how WELL you resolve complaints that counts, but how FAST you resolve them.*   □ True   □ False

True. The late Professor Dik Twedt of the University of Missouri conducted research on complaints that led to the conclusion that the speed of complaint resolution played a much more significant role in customer satisfaction than the details of the eventual settlement. Although Professor Twedt didn't offer a theory for this phenomenon, the most likely reason is the deeply embedded conviction in the American public that bureaucratic delay in responding to complaints is equivalent to stonewalling and connotes an intention to wear the complainer down rather than resolve the complaint. An equally uncharitable view is that delay simply means that the company is doing everything possible to cover its behind, as the saying goes.

If delay is perceived as bad, then promptness is perceived as good, and in the case of complaints, a fast response is interpreted as a desire to correct the problem, willingness to negotiate, and an underlying desire to satisfy the customer and maintain the relationship.

That may seem a great deal of weight to attach to fast response on complaints, but remember one of the basic laws of customer service: perception is reality. One of your first considerations in designing your complaint management system should be to set time standards for complaint resolution that reflect what customers think is appropriate rather than what you or your management feel is reasonable.

10. *If you involve customers in the complaint resolution process, they will quite often accept less than you would have been willing to offer.* □ True   □ False

True. Often one of the most effective approaches to complaint resolution is just to ask the customer, "What would you like us to do?" or "What do you think would be fair?" If you haven't already done so, you'll find to your surprise that the customer's response will be quite reasonable, and in many instances significantly less than you would have been willing to offer in a negotiated resolution. People are much more likely to support a decision they've had a hand in than to accept the same decision when it's forced on them unilaterally. In fact, some companies are adopting the practice of allowing some customers to write and authorize their own deductions. Some companies give phone approval to adjustments requested by customers, thereby eliminating 90 percent of the paperwork and 95 percent of the delay. In the direct marketing business, it has become common practice to preauthorize returns, often without requiring customers to state a reason. The policy works very well, mainly because it's a combination of cost-sharing, letting customers do more of the work, and empowerment, or giving them a piece of the action.

Computerized Claim Resolution

Bearing in mind that the word *complaint* embraces a variety of adjustments, the current state-of-the-art practice in claims payment in the health care insurance industry has widespread application in other industries and is largely compatible with current electronic data interchange (EDI) and electronic funds transfer (EFT) practices. Here's how it works for one of several Blue Cross-Blue Shield units currently using computerized claims resolution for as many as 80 percent of claims:

1. Hospital, clinic, or doctor's office enters claim information on remote terminal and transmits to central Blue Cross computer.
2. Blue Cross computer edits data transmission for errors or omissions, conformity to required format.
3. Computer verifies customer status, coverage, and eligibility.
4. Computer compares input data with a series of relevant databases and adjudicates the claim accordingly.
5. Computer calculates the amount to be paid.
6. Computer generates letter of explanation and barcoded check in the indicated amount.
7. Bar coding initiates automatic collation and insertion of checks and letters, plus sortation by zip-plus-four and metering of appropriate postage.
8. Computer enters the transaction into the appropriate database.

The manager of one such installation says that duplicating the output enabled by this particular application would require hiring an additional 900-plus people and equipping them with terminals in order to access a massive mainframe that doesn't exist. Would the result be better with human operators? Possibly in some details, but the probability is minuscule that 900 reps making individual judgments would get overall results superior to those programmed into the system—and they would take a lot longer and cost a lot more, all of which would eventually revert to insureds in the form of increased premiums.

What these companies are doing is not very different from the sequence of events that follows a customer's return of merchandise to a vendor, except that the customer fills out a form manually and sends it back with the shipment, where it is entered into the database and run through a series of decision rules to determine what kind of credit or refund the customer qualifies for. At this point, the appropriate documentation is generated, including checks, correspondence, and the like. With the trend toward preauthorized returns and deductions mentioned earlier, two steps have been eliminated: the customer's request for return authorization and the vendor's preparing and mailing the authorization form or label.

The increasing use of optical character recognition (OCR) and bar code scanning broadens the possibilities for computer applications by enabling data entry without keyboarding, an important factor in handling returned goods, for example. If a customer claims product failure, the claim can be adjudicated on a no-fault basis in a matter of minutes, and the database comparisons determine the payout, as in the Blue Cross example. Or a quality inspection may be dictated by the dollar amount of the claim, in which case the computer calculates the amount of time required for the investigation and adjudication and prints out a letter to the customer accordingly.

What's the application to nonproduct complaints? You may not know it, but when you write a complaint letter and get a very nice response within two or three weeks, there is every likelihood that, like the Blue Cross claims payments, that letter went out to you untouched by human hands.

About 80 percent or more of the letters received in a consumer response unit fall into a relatively small number of categories and many can be answered with generic letters using roughly the same sentences and paragraphs. Thanks to word processing, the CSR can evaluate a complaint letter and indicate a response, whether to substitute Paragraph 3c for Paragraph 2b, and so forth. The letter then goes to a word processing unit where the appropriate paragraphs are plugged in—with internal personalizations, of course—and you get a letter that makes you feel pretty good. After all, it responded to the problems you mentioned in your letter, spelled your name correctly, and used it several times in the text and in the P.S.

Of course if you read the letter closely, you'll see that it didn't refer specifically to the incident you wrote about but rather to the class of incidents to which it belongs. For example:

You wrote: I am writing to you about a serious breach of sanitation at your hotel, where I observed a waiter removing dirty glasses from a table by sticking his fingers inside them, and then a moment later bringing clean glasses to the table in the same fashion, with his fingers stuck inside them.

You got this response: Thank you for your letter. I was sorry to learn that you had been inconvenienced during your stay and assure you that the matter has been taken up with the individual's supervisor in order to prevent a recurrence.

The letter was signed by somebody with the title Consumer Response Specialist.

Was this about the waiter's germy fingers, or was it about the bellman who didn't bring your suit back from the valet service?

You realize it could have been either, and now you're annoyed. You took the time and trouble to write the manager of the hotel about something that concerned you—and should have concerned her—and you got a lousy form letter back, not even signed by the manager but by somebody called a Consumer Response Specialist—a professional letter-writer. What a waste of everybody's time, and certainly deficient in the major ingredient that complaint management is supposed to be all about: giving you an inducement to return and continue being a customer of the hotel.

This illustrates the shortfall of today's semicomputerized complaint response letters. In some respects they're a step up from the traditional check-the-box form letters; in others they're a step down. The original check-the-box form letter was designed to communicate information quickly and clearly, whereas the computerized letter attempts to project the "we care" attitude that's so highly valued, and often fails miserably.

Computerized letter response often leaves much to be desired because it usually lacks many of the refinements of the computerized claims payment system. Incoming complaint mail is sorted by type and turned over to "interpreters," whose job it is to analyze each letter and specify the appropriate programmed response. The material then goes to the word processing section where it's typed, signed (with an Autopen) and mailed.

Like the word processing operator, the interpreter is an hourly employee who is required to scan and interpret a specific number of letters per hour. It's a fairly high number, and every once in a while he gets stuck with a twenty-four page letter devoted mostly to birds of the Everglades or astrological portents for the present administration. Subsequent letters have to be read, scanned, and interpreted twice as fast. Well, you know the rest—you just got one of that interpreter's letters!

Now let's take some of that Blue Cross sophistication and apply it to this now-infamous hotel you stayed at. Before grinding out a response, the hotel computer takes a look at its database and recognizes your name and sees that you have an account history. So it massages that computerized form letter with a few embellishments:

Dear Mr. Aardvark:

Thank you for notifying me so promptly and in such detail about the problem you had in the dining room on your recent visit. The information you gave me will be very helpful in preventing a recurrence of this type of incident, and we have discussed your letter with the personnel involved.

Mr. Aardvark, I know you've been a customer of ours for a number of years, and we value your business highly. Please use the enclosed free dinner certificate next time you are with us, and by all means call me while you are here if I can be of assistance.

Sincerely,

Jack Spratt

Jack Spratt, Manager

What's different about version 2 is that when your name was entered into the database, the computer discovered that you were a 10-year customer and incorporated this information into the letter, using it as a decision rule to send you version 2 along with a dinner certificate. This letter goes into no more detail about your letter than the first letter, except that it personalizes with information about you, not just repetition of your name. Topped off with the dinner certificate, the letters leaves you with a feeling that the hotel does value your opinion as well as your business. And the certificate will get you back there!

By the way, the second letter didn't take any longer to generate than the first, and it produced the dinner certificate as a byproduct, just as the Blue Cross computer produced checks in settlement of claims. It's easy to visualize a version for first-time guests, families with children, convention attendees, senior citizens, and more. First-timers, for example, could be offered room upgrades, families with children or senior citizens, special discount rates, conventioneers extended checkout times. None of this targeted complaint resolution would require any additional labor output from the scanner/interpreter.

This type of application isn't limited to hotels, and in fact is being applied with great success by American Airlines in its AAdvantage Gold program for high-mileage business travelers. Credit card companies, banks, and department stores also follow similar practices. The segmentation by account value described in Chapter 14 is particularly applicable to complaint management of this type, where you have limited resources for complaint management and want to invest them in the way that will generate the optimum profit or return on investment (ROI).

In industrial relationships, the size of the account rather than the length of the relationship generally sets the complaint management priorities. In consumer relationships, years of business, charge versus cash, average purchases, credit and the like may all be criteria. Your sense of altruism may make you want to respond to all complaints equally, but your sense of profit should be telling you that if you don't provide service to your top accounts in complaint response as elsewhere, somebody else will show you how to do it—after they take the account away.

Pareto's Law and Complaint Management

Although Vilfredo Pareto is considered somewhat of a scoundrel for having provided inspiration for the infamous fascist Benito Mussolini; his 80–20 rule—or, if your prefer, his 20–80 rule—is one of the most useful tools we have in customer service management, particularly in designing complaint management systems. The best known application of Pareto's Law in customer service management is simply stated in the following paragraph.

Twenty percent of your customers give you 80 percent of your business. This axiom naturally has a reciprocal: *Eighty percent of your customers give you 20 percent of your business.* Now, translate this into the complaint management arena. *Twenty percent of your complaints involve 80 percent of the dollars.* And, finally, the important one: *Eighty percent of your complaints involve only 20 percent of your dollars.*

Now, assume that complaints are handled, as they are in many companies, in linear fashion, one after the other as they are registered. So the situation evolves into this further extension of Pareto's Law: *You are spending 80 percent of your time and effort processing 80 percent of your complaints representing only 20 percent of your dollars.* And finally, *you are spending only 20 percent of your time and effort on 20 percent of your complaints representing 80 percent of the dollars.*

If you are thinking that it seems illogical to concentrate 80 percent of your time and effort on 20 percent of your dollars, you are quite right, but it's still done that way in a lot of companies. You can save money in administering your complaint management program and, more importantly, save the customers who will make you money for years to come.

Figure 8-4. How to use Pareto's Law to maximize efficiency

The chart shows a curve with the y-axis labeled "Percentage of Dollar Value of Complaints or Claims" (from 0% to 100%) and the x-axis labeled "Percentage of Number of Complaints or Claims" (from 0% to 100%).

Setting Automatic Adjustment Levels:

Step 1: Determine the dollar amount of complaints or claims below which 80% of all complaints or claims fall, and above which 20% fall, i.e., the dollar amount represented by the intersection of the two dotted lines below.

Step 2: Determine the total dollars of complaints and claims *above* this point, and then the total dollars *below* this point.

Step 3: Determine the relative percentages of total dollars, e.g., 20%–80%,30%–70%, etc. Normally, the top 20% of complaints and claims will account for about 80% of the total dollars, but there will be some exceptions.

Step 4: If the 80%–20% rule holds true, set this dollar level as the automatic adjustment cutoff, i.e., investigate claims *above* this point but not below.

Step 5: If the 80%–20% rule does *not* hold true, test other combinations until you arrive at the cutoff point for 80% of the dollars, and automatically adjust all claims below this point and investigate all claims above it.

Source: Customer Service Center

Figure 8-4 illustrates how you can measure the Pareto distribution of your claims by dollars as well as numbers. Note that the illustration comes out perfectly on the 80-20 nose because it was intended to. In the real world, your distribution may come out 70-30, or 85-15, but the same principle applies: you need to concentrate your time and effort where there's the most dollar potential.

Figure 8-4 suggests that if you determine the break-point between the bottom 80 percent of your complaints and the top 20 percent you will come up with a dollar figure defined this way:

Eighty percent of the complaints are below this dollar figure.
Twenty percent of the complaints are above this dollar figure.

Whether the dollar figure is $300, $500, or $150, doesn't matter. Whatever the dollar figure, *if you provide automatic, no-fault adjustment to all complaints BELOW that amount, you will almost always come out ahead!*

The reason is very basic: Most of those smaller complaints in the 80 percent sector eventually are paid or resolved in favor of the customer anyway. Yet every minute they're in the administrative pipeline they're costing you money and alienating customers. They're keeping your personnel from concentrating on the larger complaints, where the real money is and where the expense of investigating and negotiating a settlement is worth its relatively high cost.

There's a very simple rule of thumb: Whatever it costs you to investigate a complaint in the conventional way (and the going rate at this writing is between $50 and $100), multiply that number by ten and you will have your breakeven point for goodwill adjustments. If it costs you $75 to open a file and investigate a complaint, you can afford to pay out $750 on a no-fault basis without investigating.

After querying several hundred customer service managers at random, I've concluded that there's a 90 percent chance you would have paid that complaint anyway, so it would have cost you $825, the $75 cost of investigating, plus the $750 payout. After you've paid out nine complaints costing you a total of $825 each ($75 investigating, $750 payout), you've spent $7,425 to pay out $6,750 worth of complaints. You decide not to pay out the tenth $750 complaint, so you spend only the $75 investigative cost.

That adds up to a $7,500 total you've spent to pay out $6,750 worth of complaints. Wouldn't it have been better to have paid out all ten complaints of $750 each on a no-fault basis and saved all that time and trouble at the beginning? It wouldn't have cost you a penny more. And if that's not enough, remember the opportunity cost—your people could have been working on something much more valuable, like larger dollar amounts—and the fact that a fast, fair adjustment almost always keeps the customer, while slow resolution is almost certain to strain and sometimes break relations.

Of course, no-fault systems need policing just like every other customer service system. On the relatively rare occasions when a customer takes advantage of a liberal complaint policy, you can detect it almost immediately with your conventional measures. At that point, it's simply a matter of letting the customer know, diplomatically, that you'll have to start investigating each complaint again on its merits. That usually ends any policy abuses without offending anybody.

Unvoiced Complaints: What You Don't Hear Can Hurt You

If you keep a record of complaints, it is usually broken down by type, cost, and matter of resolution. The one category that's seldom represented is the unvoiced complaint. It's not on your list because you didn't hear it. Apart from the fact that some customers are more articulate than others, customers have a variety of reasons for not complaining, even when there's something to complain about:

> "It wasn't a major problem anyway."
> "Thought you knew about the problem."
> "My assistant was supposed to have called you."
> "It wouldn't have done any good to complain."
> "I forgot."
> "You make it too difficult to complain, too much red tape."
> "Didn't want to get anybody in trouble."

"Decided to use it for leverage later on."
"I wasn't aware there was a problem."

Here is a typical example of an unvoiced complaint:

Customer:	I'm calling about my order. It's supposed to be here this afternoon.
Vendor CSR:	There's been a slight delay. It'll be there tomorrow morning. Is that OK?
Customer:	Sure, as long as it's here tomorrow morning, that'll be fine. Thank you.

Doesn't sound like a complaint, does it? And chances are it isn't recorded as one, either. But what if it happens 2 or 3 weeks running and at some point does inconvenience the customer? The cumulative psychological effect of these minor incidents can concentrate themselves into one very tense situation.

But it doesn't always happen that way. Sometimes there are customers who never complain but one day just leave. Too late, you ask them why. They tell you a litany of problems and you say: "But you never complained before." They reply: "It wouldn't have done any good anyway." If you dig deeper, you may find that a competitor has wooed them away by promising better and more reliable service. And all the while you thought they were perfectly satisfied!

Taken singly, unvoiced complaints don't represent many dollars, and not a whole lot in the way of problems or hard feelings, either. But appearances are deceiving. Some experts claim that in a typical business-to-business setting there are as many as ten unvoiced complaints per one hundred orders—substantially more than the one-half of one percent error rate everybody brags about. And the cumulative effect of those unvoiced complaints can be damaging.

Fortunately, by the time you finish reading this book you will have access to some of the finest preventive medicine available:

- A system of standards based on customer needs and wants that will let you know exactly what kind of service you should be providing
- A system of measurements that will immediately tell you when you're *not* meeting those standards, most of the time before customers themselves know there's a problem
- The know-how to survey customers day by day as a double check of your own performance as well as to identify any changes in their service needs—and any competitive service offerings you may need to take into consideration

Warranties and Guarantees

Almost every kind of service or product that is sold, leased, or otherwise furnished comes with some type of warranty or guarantee. Besides the policy issues discussed in Chapter 5, there are four main varieties that you should be familiar with because they underlie much of the complaint and adjustment activity in the customer service department.

Implied Warranty

An implied warranty is the legal requirement (in common law as well as in statutory law) that a product or service must be suitable for the purpose for which it was sold. If you buy a chair from a furniture store and it collapses the first time you lower your 90-pound frame onto it, you don't need a written warranty to know that the store will have to give you your money back on the implied warranty that a chair must be suitable for sitting in, the same way that a boat must float, a pen must write, or a plane must fly. (Of course, you may also want to sue the store about the lower back injury you suffered when the chair collapsed, and if you win you may not need to read the rest of this book!)

The problem with implied warranties is that they don't define *how* suitable that chair should be for sitting, how floatable that boat has to be, how suitable the pen is for writing, or how flyable the plane. A purchaser may have specific expectations as to suitability, but vendors may have their own ideas as to what constitutes suitability. This is why buyers develop precise specifications and why industries develop industry standards. It helps avoid a lot of arguments and court cases. In manufacturing industries, for example, it's generally accepted as a trade convention that in custom runs, fabrications, or compoundings, there will be overages and underages within certain limits and customers will be charged accordingly.

Many complaints and adjustments fall into this gray area of implied warranties simply because it's impossible to write policies and procedures for every possible situation where services or products aren't perceived by customers as being suitable for what they thought they would be suitable for. Many companies' no-fault and goodwill adjustment policies are based on the premise that it's usually more convenient and cost-effective to write broad policies that purposely favor the customer.

Manufacturers and processors of food items, sellers of health and beauty aids, and manufacturers of a variety of consumer goods usually refund the customer's money on any expression of dissatisfaction by the customer.

The Montgomery Ward story is a case in point. There's a very good chance that the goodwill exchange would have been made in the same way if the customer had acknowledged scratching the tile. If you think otherwise, consider this hypothetical conversation:

Customer: I want to exchange this tile. I broke it on the way home.

Clerk: How did you break it?

Customer: I dropped it on the sidewalk when I got out of the car.

Clerk: Sir, I'm sorry, but we can't be responsible for damage that you caused yourself.

Customer: If you'd had halfway decent packaging instead of that lousy cheap cardboard, the tile never would have broken.
Clerk: Oh, all right...

Without realizing it, the customer is falling back on the implied warranty of fitness of the packaging to protect the tiles, and he's opened a whole new line of argument. If the clerk had persisted in resisting, sooner or later the manager would have entered the picture and conceded to the customer. The customer, having wasted 45 minutes arguing, would have taken the replacement tile and walked out of the store with a bad taste in his mouth and no additional purchases.

Confrontations such as this gain you nothing but ill will, whereas the original (and true) conversation won the store a good deal of business along with a substantial amount of goodwill.

Where larger amounts of money are involved, however, you may want to move into an area where buyers' and sellers' rights and obligations are specifically spelled out.

Limited Warranty

A limited warranty is similar to an insurance policy. It's a printed document telling what coverage you have if the product fails to perform—what the manufacturer will do to repair or replace the product and what is excluded or not covered. For example, most warranties on consumer appliances, automobiles, and the like exclude coverage if they are used for commercial purposes. Dry cleaners typically exclude plastic buttons or ornaments and limit their liability for loss or damage to specific dollar amounts or multiples of dry cleaning charges.

Limited warranties may also require certain actions by the customer, for example, changing the oil and lubricating the automobile at specified intervals. Be aware that the exclusions you print in limited warranties do not necessarily have legal force, that is, they don't necessarily limit your obligations to customers. Some states have laws giving customers broader rights than your limited warranty may allow. A warranty is not a contract in the usual sense. It binds you but doesn't necessarily bind the customer or prevent her from seeking legal remedies beyond what you offer.

Warranty interpretation is unique to each company and is usually spelled out by the legal department. Always remember that warranties, terms and conditions of sales, contracts, and other documents are generally perceived as relative rather than absolute—rules of the game that maintain orderly behavior but aren't always enforced. They're seldom rigidly enforced because companies realize that by the time they're in court, they've already lost the customer and they could lose the court case as well.

This doesn't mean that warranties are to be taken lightly. It's a reminder that they're far from an absolute remedy from bridging the gap between what customers expect and what your company can actually deliver. Although your primary concern as customer service manager is with the adjustments and payouts made under your company's warranty programs, be aware that warranties are as much a marketing device—an inducement to customers to buy—as they are a document to protect the company.

Guarantees

Without getting into fine legal distinctions, the kind of guarantees encountered in customer service are used widely in advertising and sales promotion to increase sales. Some typical examples include:

"Guaranteed satisfaction or your money back"
"Guaranteed lifetime service"
"Guaranteed to remove stains or your money back"
"9.9 percent APR guaranteed for one full year"

From your viewpoint as customer service manager, adjustments and complaints covered by your company's guarantees are relatively easy to administer. Since guarantees are widely used in advertising, they're usually very clear and unambiguous about what's actually guaranteed and what customers need to do to collect under the guarantee. This assumes, of course, that the guarantee is made in good faith and that there's not some fine print somewhere limiting it to senior citizens accompanied by both sets of grandparents. For example, the cover of a recent Christmas catalog trumpeted in 36-point type:

GUARANTEED SAME DAY SHIPMENT OF YOUR ORDERS!

Underneath this banner headline, but in 10-point type, was the subhead:

ON ALL IN-STOCK ITEMS.

That's not a real guarantee, of course, because it's like saying "We guarantee to deliver your pizza order to your door in 27 minutes—if all our drivers show up for work." It also fails because the customer isn't offered any compensation if the guarantee isn't met. Not that the compensation element must always be present in guarantees, but it certainly makes them more credible when it is. Companies that use guarantees as an inducement to buy and then renege on those guarantees become sitting targets for the Federal Trade Commission, better business bureaus, consumer advocates, and legislators and quickly find that there's not much percentage in showing bad faith in the matter of guarantees.

Yes, you will get some oddball claims. The customer who bought a pair of "guaranteed for life" shoes 30 years ago and now wants them replaced free of charge because they wore out. What will you do? You'll compile as many case histories of that type as possible, and then ask management to help you work out decision rules for each situation that truly reflect corporate policy. Then collect them all in binders and give them to your CSRs to guide them when *they* make the adjustments!

Make sure that guarantees are used only in good faith and that any requirements or limitations are clearly spelled out. Resolve complaints and requests for adjustments under guarantees immediately. After all, customers made purchases in good faith and full confidence in a prompt refund if not satisfied, and you have no reason to delay honoring that guarantee. The minute you start shading it, you wash away a lot of the advertising dollars that went into it and along with those dollars a lot of good will.

If you honor guarantees quickly and enthusiastically you'll get an incredible amount of free publicity, some solid referral business as a result, and that priceless repeat business you regenerate when you create customer confidence that your organization really cares.

At the risk of seeming redundant, let's say it again: In customer service as elsewhere, actions speak louder than words. Some experts claim that only 30 percent of customer satisfaction is attributable to the "words"—that is, the courteous manner of the CSR—while the remaining 70 percent is due to the actual results of the transaction.

Expectations

An expectation is not a warranty or a guarantee per se—or is it? Many complaints are charged to the fact that somebody created expectations on the part of the customer, and the company failed to meet those expectations. It's customary to blame field sales personnel for "selling products that haven't been invented yet," or making commitments beyond the normal capability of the customer service department to meet. In fact, in a few companies, every commitment by a field salesperson has to be approved by a committee that includes the customer service manager. Some commitments are rescinded because they can't be met.

Salespeople could often benefit from a little more restraint than they normally show, but they also have to make sales. Sometimes the only way to make a sale and land an account is to accommodate certain needs of that account or offer a higher level of service than the account's present vendor. In short, salespeople create expectations that may be difficult and sometimes impossible to meet.

But expectations are also created by advertising and sales promotion and by other departments in the company making commitments they don't keep. Some of these are created by the customer service department making promises to do something "as soon as possible" (which may mean next week in the department but is likely to be interpreted by the customer as this afternoon). The warranties and guarantees discussed above naturally create expectations —they're supposed to, but they don't necessarily created the expectations they were intended to create. It may depend on how closely the customer reads the fine print. Word-of-mouth and testimonials or referrals also create expectations. Customers who are looking for solutions to specific problems often jump to conclusions that certain services or products will solve those problems and they create their own unassisted expectations. So it isn't just the sales department that's out there creating expectations.

Whether intentionally or by default, *one of the most important missions of the customer service department is to bridge the gap between what customers expect and what the company can practically give them.* Only human beings are capable of bridging this gap, and as long as it exists your job as customer service manager will be secure. You might mention this point to your CSRs next time they complain about complaints and problems. The day the phone stops ringing is the day the customer service department goes into the Smithsonian Museum with other relics of the past.

Efficiency — From Whose Point of View?

Some warranties require considerable training and expertise because of the amounts of money involved and the complexities of consequential damages: Did the gasket manufactured by Company X cause the manifold manufactured by Company Y to blow resulting in the fragmentation of the piston rings manufactured by Company Z, causing scoring in the cylinder wall of the block manufactured by Company A? Or could it have happened the other way around? The resolution could be the difference between replacing a $17 gasket and a $7,000 industrial gasoline engine.

When warranty administration involves difficult issues, you're naturally inclined to develop specialists within the department rather than try to train everybody. That's efficient, and it makes sense. But it must also be efficient from the customer's viewpoint. If warranty administration (quality inspections fall into this same category) creates a bottleneck because you have too much work and too few people, you're right back into one of those queueing situations where you're operating at very high efficiency and customers are becoming angrier and more frustrated as they wait longer and longer for their turn.

This issue goes well beyond routine customer service management, but it returns you to the central focus of your job as a function of strategic marketing, not just "operations" or "after sales service."

How Much Should You Invest in Customer Retention?

Few managements have openly asked or answered this question, although it's implicit in most customer service situations, particularly in complaint management. As an example, assume that a subscriber to a weekly magazine calls to complain that she hasn't received the last three issues. Some publishers will extend her subscription by several months and hand-deliver the current issue to her home. This may seem like a great expense to keep a subscriber who probably bought a cut-rate subscription in connection with a million-dollar sweepstakes to begin with. But the publisher is buying her renewal because renewal rates have an important bearing on advertising revenues, and it's often far less expensive to maintain the loyalty of an existing subscriber than it is to alienate that subscriber and then go to the considerably greater expense of acquiring a new subscriber to maintain circulation levels and the ad rates that are pegged to them.

Another good example of this type of approach is the *Beaver County Times*, a daily newspaper in Beaver, Pennsylvania which employes 1,000 youth carriers to deliver newspapers to 47,000 subscribers. To begin with, all subscribers receive a "Subscriber's Owner's Manual," subheaded "How to get the most out of your newspaper." The booklet introduces the editorial content of the newspaper and takes readers through the appropriate steps to correct specific types of problems. The booklet also lists editorial personnel along with their phone numbers and gives tips on "how to get into print," covering the territory ranging from fairs to fundraisers to funerals.

The *Times*'s complaint response is worth noting. When customers complain about nondelivery, the redelivery is made in the conventional fashion. Then, a customer service rep hand-delivers a small gift along with an "Oops! We slipped!" card with a Mightygrip jar lid gripper attached to it—to prevent slipping, of course. The card repeats instructions for reporting problems and lists phone numbers to call. After that, the subscriber receives a double post-card questionnaire asking her to rate the way the complaint was handled. The card also does some carrier recruiting and, in line with its community image, asks subscribers to suggest topics for editorial coverage.

When a small newspaper sends personnel to hand-deliver token gifts along with apologies, it represents a good deal more than a token investment or a token gesture. Management clearly recognizes that the investment pays off in retained customers whose loyal readership drives advertising rates and profits. Even so, long experience shows that senior management often responds to proposals for adopting similar procedures by saying, "But *we're* different!" So it may be up to you to develop questions such as those in Figure 8-5 that relate to your specific industry and company.

One argument against this approach is that you don't necessarily risk losing an account every time a complaint is registered. That's true, but the degree of risk tends to be proportionate to how well or how poorly you handle the complaint. More importantly, you risk loss of account confidence, potential account growth, sole source designation, referral business, and more, and you increase your vulnerability to the competition.

Invest in Making It Easy for Customers to Complain

Part of the investment should go into opening channels of communication so that your customers know how and where to complain. Here are a couple of excellent examples:

 • *Royal Bank of Canada, Montreal.* A folder called "Straight Talk About Making A Complaint at the Royal Bank" tells depositors the principal steps to take in making a complaint:

1. Make the initial complaint to the individual's local branch or credit card center, by letter, phone, or personal visit, providing specified information.

Figure 8-5. Sample questions for determining the costs of acquiring, keeping, or losing an account

---

Step 1

How much does it cost us to acquire an A customer?	$ _____
How much does it cost us to acquire a B customer?	$ _____
How much does it cost us to acquire a C customer?	$ _____
How much does it cost us to acquire a D customer?	$ _____

Step 2

On the average, how much revenue will we lose when we lose an account in one of these categories? (The revenue loss occurs over the period until that account has been replaced by one of similar value.)

Average revenue loss from loss of an A account	$ _____
Average revenue loss from loss of a B account	$ _____
Average revenue loss from loss of a C account	$ _____
Average revenue loss from loss of a D account	$ _____

Step 3

Add the acquisition costs from step 1 to the revenue loss figures from step 2:

Average acquisition cost + revenue loss, A accounts	$ _____
Average acquisition cost + revenue loss, B accounts	$ _____
Average acquisition cost + revenue loss, C accounts	$ _____
Average acquisition cost + revenue loss, D accounts	$ _____

These numbers represent the potential dollar loss every time an account receives poor service, registers a complaint, or receives an attractive offer from a competitor!

Step 4

Now, how much are we spending to maintain those accounts?

Average cost to maintain an A account	$ _____
Average cost to maintain a B account	$ _____
Average cost to maintain a C account	$ _____
Average cost to maintain a D account	$ _____

Step 5

Knowing how much we have at risk in these different categories, how much more are we willing to invest

1. To avoid endangering the accounts through poor service?
2. To keep the accounts when endangerment has already occurred?

	Maintaining Accounts	Keeping After Endangerment
A Accounts	$ _____	$ _____
B Accounts	$ _____	$ _____
C Accounts	$ _____	$ _____
D Accounts	$ _____	$ _____

2. If the initial contact doesn't resolve the matter to the depositor's satisfaction, the depositor is urged to contact the bank's senior vice-president in that province.
3. If step 2 doesn't produce satisfactory results, the depositor is asked to write the president at the bank's head office.
4. If the depositor is still dissatisfied, the folder gives the address of the Superintendent of Financial Institutions, the government agency that regulates banking practices, whom the depositor may contact.

The folder ensures depositors that all complaints will be acknowledged within 5 working days and that in many cases the complaint will be resolved at that time as well. But it adds, "Since some situations may be complex, you can expect that these will take longer to resolve."

The value of the folder is not only that is has high credibility, thanks to the inclusion of the government agency but also that it projects the image of a bank that respects customers' right to complain and makes it easy for them to do so, and, particularly, that it provides valuable feedback and minimizes the likelihood of festering unvoiced complaints.

▪ *Intergroup of Arizona.* For anybody who has ever dealt with the hassle of doctors' bills being sent to their homes instead of to their insurance companies and all the subsequent complications that arise, this health maintenance organization has developed an effective "instant de-hassler." It's an oversize, postage-paid business reply envelope with a cartoon-illustrated foldout flap headed "Save this envelope."

The left-hand side of the flap illustrates "the way it should work," with the doctor's bill going directly to the insurance company. The right-hand side illustrates "The way it shouldn't work—but might, and how to fix it," and shows the bill routed to the individual rather than to Intergroup. The panel urges the patient not to throw away the bill on the assumption that Intergroup has a copy but instead to forward it in the attached envelope. "And you relax, because Intergroup takes care of it."

This envelope is an excellent investment in heading off complaints before they occur. Like the Royal bank folder, it also does an excellent job of personalizing the company and bringing it closer to its customers in an industry not always noted for its personal touch and concern for customer service.

Writing a Complaint Procedure

The general format of complaint procedures is outlined in Figures 8-6 and 8-7. You can adapt material from either or both of these for your own procedures, but it's essential that you observe the system requirements outlined in the early part of this chapter, particularly those relating to policy.

Involve your reps in writing the procedure, particularly because it will help them identify with complaints as a customer-keeping strategy rather than the unpleasant chore it's generally considered. And, the procedure will work, because they will make it work. Training CSRs in complaint management then becomes mainly a matter of training them in procedure. If you have good policies and procedures, the essential interpersonal ingredient of complaint management—empathy—is already there. CSRs recognize the legitimacy and importance of customer complaints and their own responsibility for resolving complaints consistently with your customer-keeping policies and strategies.

There will always be some tense situations and some excessively difficult customers. Whenever possible these situations should be handled according to a set, three-part rule:

1. If you are not going to yield any further to the customer's demands, it's up to you as manager to take the bad guy role and say "no" to the customer. This action protects your rep's relationship with the customer by redirecting any ill will toward yourself. That's part of the job of being a manager.

2. You are going to meet the customer's demands, then reroute that information back to the customer through your CSR so that he can continue to be the good guy in the relationship, the person who goes to bat for the customer. If you don't reroute good news through CSRs, they will lose face and credibility with customers, and their morale will suffer as well. Soon all customers with complaints will be coming directly to you instead of to your reps. Is that what you want? It's one way to keep busy.

3. After customers have heard you say "no," they naturally have the option of going over your head to the next management level. If you sense or know that this is going to happen, you should immediately notify the individual at that level who will be receiving the complaint and let him or her know your recommendations. If the complaint has been escalated because you don't have the authority to change the policy, that's different from a situation where you have the authority but don't elect to exercise it. Either way, your arrangement with your supervisor should be that good news should be relayed to your rep through you, and the rep should inform the customer, whereas if the answer is still going to be "no," it's the responsibility of your immediate supervisor to put on his black hat and be the bad guy who says "no."

The Disaster Recovery Approach:
Use Negative Events to Create a Positive Image

This approach is based on the well-known (to customer service managers) theory that day-to-day excellence in customer service often goes unnoticed,

Figure 8-6. Example of basic complaint procedure

1. *Definition and accountability.* Since individuals as well as companies differ in their interpretation of what constitutes a complaint, it's essential that a definition be established that everybody understands along with a clear statement of accountability at all levels.

2. *No-fault process.* It should be made clear that the complaint procedure is essentially a no-fault process for resolving complaints and, where indicated, for correcting problems in the best interests of the company. It must not be seen as an attempt to pin blame, or it will fail. It must be made clear that accountability refers specifically to accountability for following the designated complaint resolution procedures according to the standards that have been established.

3. *Standards.* These should be established by complaint category, usually within specific time frames: "All complaints under $25 to be resolved on the first call"; "all complaints involving hazard or an 'A' account to be reported immediately to the designated individual or backup"; "all complaints not resolved within ____ days to be referred up to the next level of management"; etc.

4. *Notification.* Since virtually any employee is a potential recipient of complaints concerning the firm's services or products, it is absolutely essential that all employees be informed of: (1) what constitutes a complaint (see above); (2) where and how it should be referred or routed; and (3) the applicable standards. Periodic reminders should be issued as well.

5. *Receipt and logging.* Complaints received by phone should be entered on a standard form with a serial number and include the account name, contact, address, etc., plus details of the complaint. Where credits are allowed as deductions from outstanding invoices, the form may also be used as a credit authorization to accounts receivable. Complaints received by mail or fax may simply be stapled to the form. All complaints should be logged in regardless of their nature.

6. *Identification by type and severity.* It is vital that all complaints be classified as quickly as possible by a trained and knowledgeable person. This is particularly important where the company's services or products may relate to life-threatening or environmental situations. It is also important in kanban or just-in-time arrangements, or where there are particularly sensitive or "flagged" accounts.

7. *Action/routing.* In some cases, the individual receiving the complaint may be authorized to handle it on the spot; in others, it will be referred elsewhere. Some of the options include:

   - Immediate resolution under an automatic adjustment policy.
   - Immediate or timely resolution within the department.
   - Immediate referral (by phone or in person) of high-severity complaint to predesignated individual elsewhere in the company.

(continues)

Figure 8-6. (continued)

- Routine referral elsewhere in the company. Examples: quality complaints, credit matters, and complaints about advertising.
- Further research by individual receiving the complaint.

8. *Decision rules.* Although each person handling complaints is expected (and allowed) to exercise judgment in investigating and resolving complaints, the use of decision rules assures uniform treatment of routine and repetitive complaints and, by pushing the decision further down in the chain of command (and closer to the customer), enables faster and generally more satisfactory resolution of the complaint. In addition to automatic refunds, decision rules can cover such matters as warranties, removing late or penalty charges, extension of credit, exchanges, deduction, etc.

9. *Monitoring and follow-up.* The customer service department will normally be responsible for monitoring progress on the complaint when it is referred to other departments as well as when it is being handled within the department. This is where time standards and accountability prove their value, because lack of a timely response from another department enables the problem to be escalated to a higher level of management, e.g., from a quality control technician to his/her supervisor or manager, or from a manager to a director, etc. The responsible individual in customer service is expected to follow up personally to make sure all promised actions are actually taken.

10. *Resolution.* Complaints will normally be resolved by the designated individual using decision rules or interpreting company policy. The actual resolution may take one of several forms:

- Automatic adjustment (see above)
- Resolution accepted by customer (this may include a determination that the complaint is not valid, as well as a full settlement, a partial settlement, an alternative or a substitution, etc.)
- Decision appealed by customer and escalated or referred elsewhere

11. *Reporting—Observance of communications and action standards.* The substance of all complaints as well as the action taken will be reported to designated individuals/departments with an interest in the matter. Where applicable, time standards will be observed, both in communicating such information and in acting on it. For example, release of orders in excess of credit limits when decision has been made to raise limits, issuance of refund checks, authorization of replacements, etc.

12. *Tabulation—Statistical process control.* The substance of all complaints by classification, cost, and other features will be reported in a designated format and tabulated for statistical quality control purposes.

Figure 8-6 (continued)

> 13. *Review and recommendation.* Statistical and descriptive data will be reviewed and analyzed at designated intervals, including frequency and cost as well as effect on the company's relationships with customers and others (e.g., regulatory officials, the local community, etc.). This data will be forwarded to management and others with recommendation for changes in procedures and policies where indicated. It is particularly important that the no-fault atmosphere be maintained, but equally important that all recommendations be fully supportable by the record.

whereas your real recognition comes from how well you respond in emergencies. In practice, this theory is only partially correct.

In the business-to-business environment, many of your customers measure and rate your service on your day-to-day performance. If the president of your company intervenes in a problem situation and makes one of those spectacular "saves" you read about in the media, you can bet that it doesn't carry nearly as much weight with the customer as does the question of whether your president is going to do something to improve the condition that created the crisis—a condition that's due mainly to his or her inaction in the first place. Most customers know instinctively that when the president makes one of those spectacular saves, he or she just robs Peter to pay Paul and doesn't really correct the underlying problem.

On the other hand, if it's a genuine crisis and not a red tape foul-up, and the customer service department can spring into action and solve it, then you win a lot of brownie points for the company and the department. Just keep your sights set on these twin targets:

Target 1. Solve a problem for the customer.
Target 2. Create high visibility for your customer service excellence.

Emphasis on Recovery

Do it fast, do it differently, do it innovatively, do it memorably, and your service will become highly visible and likely talked about in a very positive way. Consider these incidents:

• *The sub-zero seminar.* The heating unit serving one of the meeting rooms at the Holiday Inn O'Hare/Kennedy in Rosemont, Illinois, ceased functioning on the coldest day of the year, and great gusts of arctic air swept through the vents—frozen open, naturally. A seminar on customer service management was in progress and the seminar leader was mindful that only a short while before at a well-known hotel in another city, it had taken some 45 minutes to

Figure 8-7. Example of procedure for handling nondurable consumer goods complaint

1. *Provide warranty, hotline, and similar information on package or label.* Give telephone number, complete mail address, and other data that will ensure that the complaint moves directly to the right person. Using a separate post office box number will help avoid mail room delays, misrouting.

2. *Respond quickly, regardless of the seriousness or apparent triviality of the complaint.* "Grudges" against companies are more often related to delays in replying than to the seriousness of the complaint.

3. *Apologize.* Monitor performance to make sure reps don't get defensive or hardened to hearing customers sound off. "I'm certainly sorry to hear that. Let's see what we can do to straighten things out" is a good start.

4. *Replace a product the customer says is defective.* If the customer says the product is defective, this suggests that he/she wants to continue doing business with you—that the complaint isn't directed toward your line generally, but to the single purchase or package. This loyalty should be rewarded and reinforced before the customer has a chance to waver. If the problem was caused by wrong use of product, replace anyway and diplomatically instruct customer in proper use.

5. *Make prompt refunds to customers who ask for them.* It costs more to delay and investigate than to automatically issue refunds in nominal amounts. And delay antagonizes the 90-plus percent of customers who make their request in good faith.

6. *Send "dissatisfied" customers a different product.* If the customer does not claim product defects per se, but just doesn't like the product itself or feels it doesn't meet expectations, there's still a chance to retain that person as a customer by sending him/her a refund and another product from your line along with a letter thanking the customer for his/her comments.

7. *Send a coupon of equal or greater value.* If it's impractical to send the product, a coupon for other items in the line will keep customers in-house.

8. *Require proof of purchase only where it's reasonable to do so.* Don't expect customers to save sales slips for relatively inexpensive items.

9. *Require return of product only when there's a useful purpose—and reimburse the customer.* Show the customer how to pack the product if necessary. Quibbling about who pays the freight costs more than paying it.

10. *Tell customers what you're going to do in advance of the event.* Tell them the longest time interval—"No later than..." and surprise them pleasantly by beating it.

11. *Determine satisfaction level by follow-up mail or phone survey.* This tells you how well your complaint strategy is working and also gives you an opportunity to ask customers if they've bought your products since.

> 12. *Track subsequent purchases where practical.* They'll usually increase as the result of effective complaint handling. Tracking enables you to justify the cost, time, and effort of your organized approach!

procure a screwdriver, with union electrician attached, to tighten a screw on an overhead projector. He did not expect much different in the present crisis.

So, it was with considerable surprise that he learned from the head houseman that, while the arctic air had been wafting through the vents, workers had been busily setting up another meeting room—unasked—and it was now ready, and would he please bring his seminarians to the new site to continue the seminar. Somebody at the Holiday Inn knows three things:

1. Good hotel service is normally transparent or invisible. When there's a chance to make it visible, just do it!
2. People who use hotels for business meetings and seminars tend to work under considerable pressure, and they tend to return to sites where they get the most support and the least hassle.
3. There's a lot of competition from newer and more luxurious hotels in Rosemont.

As a footnote, Holiday Inn has had this particular business—four to six meetings a year—for about 14 years.

▪ *Wonderful Westinghouse.* A customer placed an order with a Westinghouse division by phone. The customer service rep who took the call felt that the order did not sound just right and queried the customer as to its accuracy. The customer insisted that the order was correct, but even after hanging up the rep felt that something didn't sound right about the order. So he called the customer back. This time the customer showed some annoyance and again insisted that the order was correct, and by the way, let's get it into the works. The CSR was still not satisfied and called back a third time, at which time the customer realized his specs were in error and corrected them. Net saving: $100,000 and the business of an important customer.

▪ *No flies on Orvis.* A direct marketing firm widely known for its fly fishing schools and fishing gear generally, Orvis by mistake posted a $15 charge to a customer's credit card order for merchandise that was back ordered—a no-no under Federal Trade Commission rules. Before the customer became aware of the error, Orvis sent him a letter of apology indicating that the charge had been reversed and enclosing a $25 gift certificate and a catalog (don't forget that detail), which inspired the customer to place an order for some $150 worth of additional merchandise. Orvis recovered the cost of its gift certificate as well as the customer.

In each of these minicrises the recovery was fast, noteworthy, or innovative and exceeded the customer's expectations. They all resulted in excellent word-of-mouth advertising for the organizations involved and some kudos in print as well. Note that none of them required intervention by the company president; policies and philosophies were already in place, and front-line empowerment took care of the rest.

Rules for Implementing a Disaster Recovery Approach

You can use this approach for the entire spectrum of negative events that fall into the category of complaints and problems the customer service department must deal with. You are using negative events to create a positive, customer-oriented image as part of your overall customer-keeping strategy.

Negative events occur at three probability levels:

1. *High probability:* stockouts, shortages, work overload, errors, delays, service and product quality problems
2. *Medium probability:* work stoppages, hazardous spills, computer down, phone system down, skilled personnel shortages
3. *Low probability:* natural disaster at own and/or customer sites, illness in vital jobs, major product recall

Note the inclusion of contingencies at customer sites in item 3. If you have just-in-time (JIT) arrangements with some customers, you have probably already experienced potential line-down situations and how important it is to have standby supply plans, even when the problem was caused by the customer and not yourself. It's a great way to shine when distributors and other customers are hit with a natural disaster and you provide help.

Low probability events tend to be the most costly to deal with because, in general, events are usually costly in inverse proportion to the degree of anticipation that is allowed them. If you know your plant is going to be struck in six months, it's a little easier to accommodate and a lot less costly than the wildcat strike that's going to erupt tomorrow morning but you don't know about it yet.

Three Basic Rules of Disaster Recovery

1. *Have decision rules in place for all negative events where there is little or no forewarning.* You cannot afford to be ill prepared when a serious crisis erupts: blizzard, fire, hurricane, earthquake, phone lines down, product recall. Start writing contingency plans now for all the worst-case scenarios you can think of. You don't need anybody's permission to develop plans where none currently exist, and you'll get a lot of credit for working them out.

Hardly any businesses in the area were equipped to deal with the week-long phone outages that followed the Hinsdale, Illinois switching station fire on Mother's Day, 1988. Elkay Manufacturing in Oak Brook, one of the few companies that had a contingency plan in place, was up and running at an alternate site within four hours. Congratulations to Stan Bandur, CCSE (Certified Customer Service Executive), manager at Elkay. At the time of the crisis Mr. Bandur was manager of sales service and production planning and he and his cohorts at Elkay provided excellent, topflight customer service management. Other companies that were not so well prepared gave a number of customer service managers a chance to show their resourcefulness and dedication in getting back on-line in a matter of days, but some companies had no service for as long as two weeks and suffered seriously because of it. Since that time, "hot site" and contingency planning have achieved a higher priority in many companies, and with good reason. With no anticipation and no advance preparation, disasters can be very expensive for the customer service department!

2. *Develop an early warning system for serious events of higher probability.* This category includes such events as strikes, shortages, and production overload. Use a milestone, critical path method (CPM), or production evaluation and review technique (PERT) approach. If you're not familiar with these planning techniques, your friendly industrial engineers can show you how to apply them to contingency planning. The basic premise is that you set up "milestones" or "trigger" dates on which you take anticipatory action in a predetermined sequence of events.

For example, in the case of a possible strike, your first milestone might be three months before contract negotiations begin when you notify customers of the possibility of a strike, suggest they may want to start stockpiling, and offer them extended terms to make the suggestion more attractive. Other milestones would call for preparing for shipment from alternative sites, confronting issues such as crossing picket lines, and so forth. You should use a similar approach whenever a possibility becomes a probability, no matter how slight. The planning process will add to your managerial skills and gain you a lot of valuable exposure throughout your company.

3. *Delegate high-volume, relatively low-cost complaints to the lowest level of authority, front-line personnel, for immediate disposition using standard procedures and decision rules.* Don't overlook the possibility of carrying empowerment one step further by letting customers resolve some of their own adjustment issues, thus freeing up your own personnel to work at the top of their skills where they will bring a much greater return to the organization.

9

▪▪▪
▪▪▪
▪▪▪

Auditing Customer Service Performance and Quality

One of the most valuable contributions you as customer service manager can make to your company is to set up a sound method for auditing customer service performance and quality. This will help you gain recognition for customer service as a legitimate management discipline with measurable results, not just a clerical job. It will also ensure that your customer service program stays on target and makes a provable contribution to the bottom line.

As its name implies, an audit is a composite of measurements and cross-checks that enable you to assess the entire customer service operation, not just isolated parts of it, and at the same time to pinpoint specific problem areas that could compromise your objectives. Your customer service audit will have six major phases: (1) *internal measures of work output and productivity*, (2) *internal measures of customer service quality*, (3) *external measures of customer service quality*, (4) *measures of customer service offerings by competitors*, (5) *benchmarking*, and (6) *measures of corporate customer service culture*. Some of these measures can be applied continually, since they're typically generated as a byproduct of routine telephone transactions, whereas others are generally applied periodically on a project-type basis.

Measures of Output and Productivity

Output is a measure of the volume of work performed without reference to its rate of efficiency. Output may also be referred to as production, as in, "Our total output [production] last week was 4,000 shipments." Measuring output is a necessary first step in measuring efficiency. Output measures are also used in so-called activity reports, which are essentially a tally or profile of the work performed by the department during a specific time period, classified by type of work: so many orders, so many inquiries, and so forth.

One customer service call center reported its weekly activity in phone calls as follows:

Type of Call	Number of Calls	Percentage of Total
Price inquiries	4,279	22%
Stock availability	4,092	21
Orders	3,243	17
Part numbers	3,118	16
Applications	1,944	10
Expedites	1,132	6
Adjustments	452	2
Other	961	5
Misdirected	211	1
Total 19,432	100%	

Such activity reports can be extremely useful in analyzing the workflow of the customer service department. For example, this breakdown would suggest to the manager that there appear to be unusually high percentages of calls relating to pricing, stock availability, and parts numbers and a relatively low percentage of orders.

You would want to determine whether the large number of price inquiries is the result of price volatility in your market, confusing price lists, or an intense competitive situation. You would want to know the reason behind the large number of calls relating to part numbers. Is there a cataloging or numbering problem that can be corrected? The discrepancy between calls about stock availability and actual orders suggests a significant stockout problem, but you would want to check orders received by fax and electronic data interchange (EDI), since the proportion of phone orders is dropping in most companies.

Output or activity reports also indicate how much business the company is doing and what kind of business, but such reports don't tell how many people it took to do the work, or how long it took them, or the relative productivity of the department.

In short, output or activity reports are well suited to measuring how much work was done and what types of work were performed, but they are definitely not measures of the quality or efficiency of individual or departmental performance. Although activity reports are frequently used in charting trends or making historical year-to-date comparisons, they don't allow for variables such as total man-hours or the difficulty of the work itself or the skill levels of the worker, all of which are key elements in the performance measures to be described shortly.

For examples of some telephone activity reports, see Figures 9-1 and 9-2. Both figures compare fiscal years 1990, 1989, and 1988 for the company in question. Figure 9-1 measures units of work produced for these three fiscal years (note that the chart in the lower right-hand corner denotes fiscal years 1990 and 1989 only). Figure 9-2 measures the rise or decline in service quality in four areas.

Productivity measures the actual rate of output in units of work, often per man-hour, and enables accurate historical comparisons as well as comparisons between individuals performing similar work. While the term *productivity* itself

(text continues on page 136)

Figure 9-1. Telephone activity reports measuring units of work produced

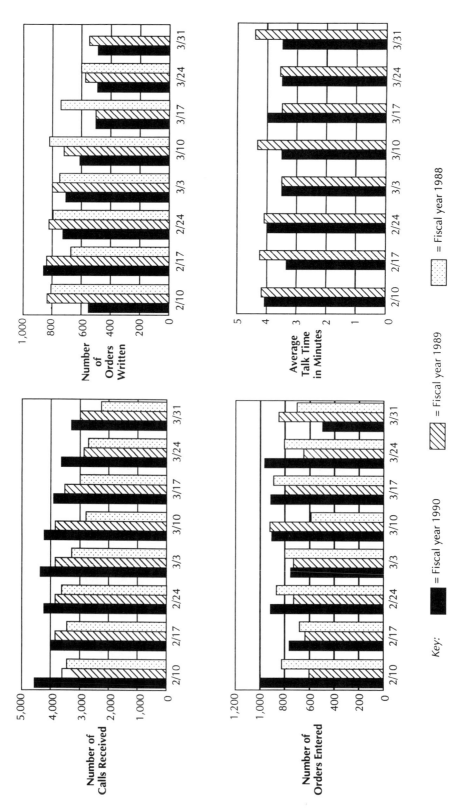

Source: Ball Seed Company

Figure 9-2. Telephone activity reports measuring quality of service

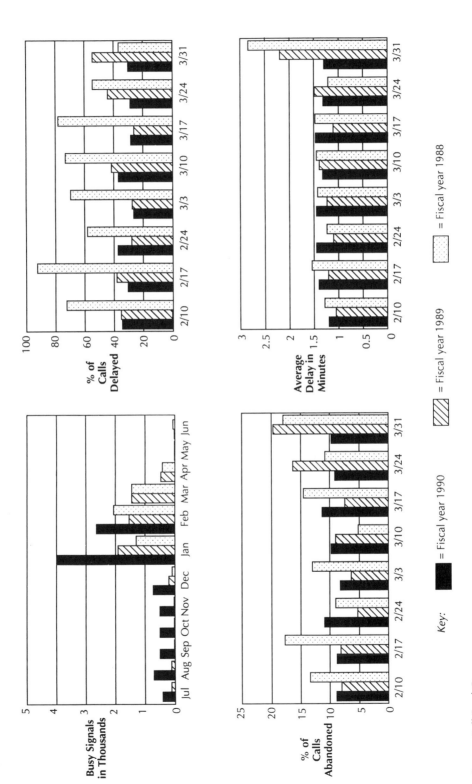

Source: Ball Seed Company

does not necessarily connote efficiency, "high productivity" implies a high degree of efficiency and "low productivity" the opposite. Productivity is sometimes used to mean *relative* productivity—relative either to a standard of productivity, or as a percentage of the output that's theoretically possible for a given time frame.

But there are some loopholes in productivity measures, too. For example, an insurance company rated its claims personnel on the number of claims they resolved during an 8-hour day. What the company did not factor in was that some workers were pulling out all the "easy" claims, most of which could be resolved in less than half the time it took to analyze and resolve the more complex ones. As a result, the agents with the easier claims appeared to be more productive than their co-workers when in fact they were less so in terms of actual work performed.

Measures of productivity are most useful where the workers you are measuring are performing roughly the same work, for example, where calls are distributed via an ACD system. In the case of the insurance company, balancing the workload in terms of difficulty or complexity of the claims would enable a valid reading of the relative productivity of the workers. But this isn't always possible. Where a department is organized by territory, specialty, account, or industry group, measures of productivity are much less reliable in making comparisons between workers than when everybody handles an equal mix of work.

Overall productivity, that is, productivity stated in percentages, is relatively low in typical customer service department operations, mostly because of the frequent interruptions and changeovers from one task to another that are characteristic of a typical customer service operation. Customer service managers surveyed informally at seminars over the last several years generally rate the efficiency of their department—what they actually produce versus what they could potentially produce—in the range of 60 percent to 70 percent, and some as low as 50 percent. In large, high-volume call centers handling reservations or small orders, the percentage is likely to be over 80 percent.

The most common measures of performance in customer service pertain to two types of work:

1. Discrete units of physical work, as in words per minute in typing or keystrokes per hour in data entry.
2. Discrete transactions, as in orders per day or orders by type; or discrete elements, as in lines per order. Some typical measures in this category would include:

   - Calls per hour (or day)
   - Orders per hour (or day)
   - Inquiries answered on-line
   - Outbound/inbound calls
   - Leads qualified per day
   - Average minutes per call
   - Average lines per order
   - Average cost per call
   - Keystrokes per hour
   - Claims resolved per hour (or day)
   - Credits issued per hour (or day)
   - Inquiries researched for call-back
   - Internal calls
   - Documents filed/retrieved per hour

- Calls by type
- Average dollars per order
- Average cost per order
- Orders shipped per day

These measures may be compared historically on a day-to-day, week-to-week, or month-to-month basis to reflect business activity and/or work output at different periods. Bear in mind the distinctions between measures of production and measures of actual productivity. You must ensure consistent quality of output for productivity comparisons to have any significance. For example, let's say that your twenty customer service reps now handle 1,000 calls a day, an average of fifty calls per day per rep. You've heard other managers talking about seventy or eighty or even one hundred or more calls a day being the norm. So you decide to institute an incentive program to raise that average to at least 1,200 calls per day, or sixty calls per rep. The results look good: At the end of a month, you're averaging 1,200 calls a day with that same staff—a 20 percent increase. It almost seems to be too good to be true. And it is. Because you didn't keep score on three other critical measures:

1. *Accuracy.* A comparison of error rates before and after the incentive program would quite likely show a sharp increase in error rates coinciding with the beginning of the program.
2. *Call length.* Calls are considerably shorter since the program started. Isn't this a good sign? Not necessarily. Your reps may be omitting vital information, leading to costly misunderstandings or errors by customers. Or they may be skipping the simple courtesies that distinguish your company from its competitors.
3. *Callbacks.* A certain percentage of the additional calls being handled are likely to be callbacks from customers who didn't get enough information on the first call. Your incentive program discouraged your reps from their former practice of volunteering helpful information, even when customers didn't specifically ask for it.

If you measure these other elements and find them unchanged, it's pretty safe to assume that you've racked up significant gain in productivity. But be aware that when you compare output on a historical basis, you're simply measuring *relative* rather than *actual* productivity.

And there's an important difference: Relative productivity is a measure of your output now versus then; actual productivity is the measure of the output against what you know it should be, that is, the work standards you've developed, as described in Chapter 7, to reflect a high average of what output should be in your department, under your conditions. (Note that work output in another company's customer service department is not a reliable measure of your own department's productivity.) As an example, if you use work standards, you might realize that the 20 percent output increase caused by your incentive program reflected an increase in productivity actually exceeding the standards you'd set for the department. Or, it might reflect improvement from bad to mediocre, which in turn may suggest that your incentive program by itself may not be nearly enough and will probably run out of steam in the very near future.

For when productivity is low measured against actual work standards that have been developed specifically for your department, there's a better-than-average likelihood that you have some deep-seated morale and motivational problems in the department and quite possibly some systems and procedures problems as well. There's one other possibility: that the work standards themselves are unrealistically high for your department.

Finally, remember and emphasize to everyone in your organization that measures of output and productivity are not necessarily measures of customer service quality. A supermarket cashier who handles an average of twenty checkouts per hour is highly productive, but if there's a constant queue of ten people at her checkstand, each customer has to wait in line an average of half an hour—hardly what you'd call good service. Similarly, a CSR handling 150 calls a day might be seen as highly productive, but that level of productivity implies that there is always at least one call already waiting, and quite possibly more. How long have they been waiting, and how long will it take for a caller to progress from the end of the queue to the front, and how well will they be serviced by the CSR who knows that there's another wave of customers waiting behind them?

Don't overlook the opportunity of using output data to support requests for additional personnel and/or equipment or as the basis of continuing incentive programs with built-in quality controls. In a number of companies, managers have developed work standards for call handling; when call levels exceed the capacity of the department to handle them at those standards, then the manager is automatically empowered to hire additional staff. Of course, he is also required to reduce staff if call volume drops below a specified level. As discussed in Chapter 7, the actual call standards should be based on a level of call content and detail (or scripting, if it's used) that reflects the actual customer service quality you want those calls to exemplify.

Internal Measures of Customer Service Quality

These measures are mainly those that you have established to reflect the levels of customer service you are currently providing—the actual quality of customer service—versus the goals you set for the company when you established customer service standards as described in Chapter 7. Many of these measures are expressed in percentages such as:

- Percentage of orders entered versus received
- Percentage of orders processed/filled within 72 hours
- Percentage of lines filled versus ordered
- Percentage of orders filled complete
- Percentage of orders shipped on time (company's standard)
- Percentage of orders delivered on time (customer's request)
- Percentage of dollars filled/shipped versus ordered
- Percentage of calls answered by the third ring (about 12 seconds)
- Percentage of inquiries resolved on-line, on the first call
- Percentage of credits issued within 5 working days
- Percentage of claims resolved within 10 working days
- Percentage of field service repairs completed on first visit

Many of these measures can also be applied to service environments, including equipment and software support, institutional service, and the like. For example, a fast-food chain may have a standard that 90 percent of customers must be served within 5 minutes of queueing up at the counter. This is simply a variation on a standard that 90 percent of calls should be answered on or before the third ring, or that 95 percent of orders should be shipped complete within 72 hours.

Or, a bank may set a standard in its cash management activities that 98 percent of deposits be reported on time and accurately; an airline that 98 percent of flights be at 100 percent capacity or less (that is, no more than 2 percent of flights overbooked); a computer support group that 95 percent of machine-down situations be responded to within 30 minutes or less, and so forth. The standards were set to reflect the levels of service the organization felt were necessary to maintain for strategic marketing purposes or simply to hold on to its customers.

Remember that, in all of the examples cited here, the objective is to meet the standard but not necessarily to exceed it. Thus, if you find that you are shipping 98 percent of orders complete within 72 hours and your standard is to ship 95 percent, it could be a sign that you are spending too much money for one of two reasons:

1. A high proportion of shipments are being sent out by costly premium or expedited service just to meet the standard.
2. Inventory levels are too high and are incurring excessive investment, ownership, and storage costs.

Even if these costs aren't being incurred, it's possible that you are giving customers better service than they need or want, and you shouldn't assume that it's all right to continue doing so. First of all, if you provide service beyond what customers want or expect, they will very soon be taking it for granted and you'll find it very difficult to cut service back to a reasonable level. Or, if service is better than it needs to be, some customers may resent what they perceive as being made to pay for services they don't use.

If you find that your service does in fact exceed your standards, two strategic opportunities are suggested:

1. Reallocate your service resources so that you can provide something extra to your top customers to reward and protect them: Reward them for being good customers and protect them from being lured away by competitors.
2. Reduce service to the targeted level and split the savings with customers in the form of price cuts that will make you more competitive.

In the more likely event that your service is not on target, measuring performance against standards has the advantage of pinpointing specific problem areas early so that you can correct them before there's any serious harm to your overall customer service effort.

Exceptions reports are mainly reports of specific types of customer service failures that are also stated as percentages:

- Percentage of calls in queue more than one minute
- Percentage of calls blocked
- Percentage of calls abandoned
- Percentage of complaints to orders
- Percentage of complaints unresolved after x days
- Percentage of errors to orders
- Percentage of backorders, overbookings

Although most managements don't like to acknowledge that there's such a thing as an allowable error rate or an acceptable complaint ratio, in reality exceptions reports such as these are simply the reciprocals of conventional standards. For example, a standard calling for 98 percent line fill will have a reciprocal of 2 percent lines back ordered, while a standard of 95 percent of orders shipped complete will have a reciprocal of 5 percent of orders shipped incomplete.

The value of exceptions reports is that in a typical customer service operation, there are far fewer failures than there are successes, far fewer deviations from standard than there are on-standard performances. Managing by exception just means that you are working with manageable numbers that enable you to quickly apply statistical process control (SPC) techniques to nip problems in the bud and avoid the costly rework that's often incurred when problems are discovered after the fact.

As necessary as performance reports of this type are to maintaining quality customer service operations, any reports that show a dramatic increase in performance should be scrutinized very carefully. For example, a sudden drop in the number of back orders suggests that your inventory position has improved significantly. Yet it hasn't. What really happened is that your out-of-stock condition has lasted so long that customers are no longer entering orders for those items, so the percentage of back orders to orders plummets. Instead of doing better, you're doing worse.

In another report, you find that you have an exceptionally high score in the "on-time delivery" category. Investigation reveals that you met your *promise* dates, but a relatively small proportion of these reflected your customers actual *want* dates. So your measure doesn't reflect service quality at all but rather your ability to plan and to make and keep a commitment. Of course, you can correct this by requiring that reports show the customer's request date, your commitment date, and the actual delivery date. Or, you can set standards specifying order cycle time from receipt to actual delivery.

External Measures of Customer Service Quality

"Quality is what the customer says it is." "Customer service is what the customer says it is." No matter how carefully you research your customer's service needs and wants, no matter how precisely you measure and adjust your service levels to meet your standards, your customers ultimately assess the quality of your customer service program. And the most critical part of your measurement program, the phase that should certainly take precedence over all others, is researching the quality of your customer service performance from your customers' viewpoint, which may be surprisingly different from your own.

An example of this was recently furnished by an award-winning Midwestern service company, beyond question the leader in its field. By every measure—and it applied entire batteries of measures—it was rendering near-perfect customer service. Yet research conducted among its customers revealed that they regarded the company as no better than average in its customer service offerings and certainly not distinguishable from its competitors.

What the research really revealed was not that the company's service was average and undistinguished, but rather that customers *perceived* it to be average and undistinguished. It turned out that most of the company's customers had never dealt with its competitors and thus had no standard of comparison. Based on the survey, the company wisely decided that its best course was not to change its customer service profile but rather to educate its customers to the benefits and advantages of the present service.

In another situation, a Canadian cosmetics company surveyed customers and found to its surprise that the customers who were getting the best service were the most dissatisfied, whereas those who were experiencing the most service problems were the most satisfied.

In both instances, customer research revealed significant differences between perception and reality that were undermining the companies' best efforts to provide high levels of customer service. Had they not conducted their research, both companies would have risked losing a strategic service advantage and quite possibly their best customers as well.

Who Should Do the Research?

Customer research can be conducted in several different ways: You can perform the research yourself, using departmental personnel; you can turn it over to your company's marketing research department; or you can have it done by an outside organization. The principal factors are cost, convenience, and credibility.

Self-conducted research is extremely low in cost and can often be conveniently programmed into other customer service activities, such as enclosing questionnaires with orders or asking customers about service issues when they phone in. Turnaround time to obtain and tabulate information can be as short as a single day. If your findings run contrary to popular beliefs in the company, however, you may find that credibility becomes an issue. That's not all bad, however, because you can then propose further research, either by your own marketing research department or by an outside agency. And their findings will lend further credibility to your own.

Marketing research department research is more costly, of course, but your company billing practices determine whether it's actually charged back to your department or performed by the other department as a staff or support activity. Research that's designed and conducted by professional researchers obviously has a great deal to recommend it in terms of sampling, accuracy, reliability, and credibility. Its main drawbacks are time and, occasionally, complexity. Where it may be enough to get a few "quick-and-dirty" statistics, market research people may insist on developing a highly structured sample, testing questions beforehand, inserting cross-checks in the survey to measure validity of responses, developing confidence level percentages, and otherwise defeating your purpose of simply testing the waters in an informal way. It's their job to conduct research properly, and if you need the high level of credibility that they bring to customer research, you'll have to do it their way, which often means delays as well as survey procedures and formats that you don't entirely agree with. However, if you're concerned with major issues in customer service with proposed major policy changes, professional research of this order is a virtual "must."

Third-party research is similar in many respects to research conducted by your company's marketing research staff, but it has the added advantage of objectivity or neutrality. An independent research agency has no stake in the outcome of a survey other than accuracy and reliability of results. It can also ensure unbiased responses from your customers by not revealing your company's name as the research sponsor, which can be quite valuable when you are assessing customers' perceptions of your service versus the competition. Third-party researchers are also better equipped to conduct field research, that is, interviewing customers at their companies or at trade shows, store locations, or elsewhere. And most are equipped to conduct focus group research in which groups of customers are videotaped or recorded as they discuss customer service offerings of one or more companies in a particular field.

Third-party research can be expensive and, more often than not, is likely to be initiated by senior management, often without even involving you in the decision. It may be one phase of a consulting contract where management consultants have been engaged to assess your company's overall customer service practices. If you are conscientious enough to be reading this book and applying its principles where appropriate, the chances are that outside consultants will improve rather than undermine your position. They often need a good deal of educating by you, and your best bet is to give freely of your time and expertise in providing that education. You will find that ideas you have proposed often gain great credibility and a much higher degree of acceptance when they're supported by somebody charging your company $2,000 or $3,000 a day for their expertise.

You will get a great deal for your money when you use outside consultants to conduct customer research, but you won't get it very fast and it won't be in simple form, so if all you need is basic data in the yes-no or "twenty questions" category, conduct your own research!

Customer Research Methodology

Regardless of who actually performs the research, the methodology will be basically the same. There are three principal methods available that enable you to determine how customers assess your customer service performance: personal interviews, telephone surveys, and mail questionnaires. I've described the procedures as if you and your staff are doing the research yourselves.

Personal Interviews. You can conduct these yourself simply by visiting customers on-site or by inviting them to visit your company in groups. You can also send your reps out on customer visitations as an incentive and motivator, as discussed in greater detail in Chapter 17. Either way, face-to-face interviews with customers are a valuable means of gaining a great deal of information about different customers, both as to how they do business and as to how they rate your customer service performance. They will also be flattered by the attention. Visitations by reps can have a very positive effect on both reps and customers in terms of their future relationships.

Although you should generally ask all the customers you visit the same basic questions, your primary goal should be to conduct qualitative or individualized research rather than to develop statistics.

It's certainly all right to ask customers to rate different features of your customer service performance on a 10-point scale or compare it to the competition, but don't, under any circumstances, pass up the opportunity to find out *why* they feel the way they do about your service: what you're doing wrong that they feel needs to be corrected, what you're doing right that they'd like to see more of, and what you're not doing at all that they feel you should be doing.

One common pitfall of face-to-face interviews with customers is that they may tell you what they think you want to hear rather than what they really feel. This will be particularly evident if you ask them about specific individuals in your department; customers don't want to get them in trouble with you or to jeopardize an existing relationship for the future. If you need to ask about a specific person, ask in positive terms: "Where do you think Bill could stand strengthening?" You can also assure customers that specific information of this type will be held in confidence, although you will certainly want to pass along any and all compliments.

If you plan to conduct personal interviews on a continuing basis (and it's a good idea to do so), here's a five-step approach that has been used with considerable success by a large Midwestern pharmaceutical manufacturer.

Step 1. Decide which customers you want to interview. Normally, these will be your larger customers or key accounts intermixed with a few smaller accounts that you feel have real growth potential. You may also want to include some start-up accounts where there's new technology or business practices suggesting trends that you need to know about for the near future.

Step 2. Call and ask permission to visit and interview these individuals and make appointments at your mutual convenience. Tell them you'd be glad to meet with others in their companies. Allow two hours per interview whenever possible, and if any of your customers offer you a plant tour along with the opportunity to make the acquaintance of some of their inside personnel, by all means accept. Write a brief letter confirming their acceptance, being sure to include the date and time and approximate duration of your visit.

Step 3. About two weeks before the appointment, write a letter that includes the main questions you'll be asking or the topics you hope to cover, giving your customer time to collect data for your interview and also to line up others for you to talk to during your visit. It's also a good exercise for you, and it will make the interview more productive for yourself as well as the customer.

Step 4. Conduct the interview using a tape recorder if it's acceptable to the customer. Otherwise take notes, but don't get so bogged down in note-taking that you miss the nuances of the interview. With a little experience, you'll find it fairly easy to reconstruct the interview later as long as you don't let too much time elapse.

Be sure to start by asking open-ended questions such as: "Tell me about some of the kinds of problems you run into in your business" or simply "Tell me more about your business" or even "Tell me a little bit about your job and the kinds of problems you run into." Avoid starting with closed-ended questions that can be answered with one or two words, for example, "How are we doing?" or "How would you rate us on a ten-point scale?" Opening with such questions inhibits the discussion and suggests that you're only fishing for compliments. Save your closed-ended questions for later, when the discussion is more relaxed!

As you start getting answers to your open-ended questions, your customer is likely to touch on subjects you want to know more about. At this point you narrow the focus of the interview by asking probing questions such as "Can you tell me a little more about the problem you had with the documentation?" And, as you get further into the interview and want to redirect the flow of the conversation, simply ask a closed-ended question such as "What day was that?" or "Who handled the transaction?" or even "Were you satisfied with the way the problem was handled?" In most cases, the customer will answer with one or two words and then stop briefly. This hiatus will provide you with an opportunity to introduce a new subject or to ask other closed-ended questions including numerical ratings of your service versus the competition.

Be sure to ask for copies of any specific reports the customer has compiled on your service, including any comparative data involving competitors. If the customer is highly critical of your company's performance, remember that you're there mainly to get information, not to defend the company. Whatever the case, always thank the customer for the information, and use the same type of questioning approach to bring out as much negative information as the customer may have stored up. Naturally, if there are any outstanding or unresolved problems, the visit to the customer is an excellent opportunity to show how quickly you can resolve them!

Step 5. Write a report covering the main points of your interview as soon after returning as you can (or dictate one while you're traveling). Add any statistical data or numerical ratings to the data you already have from other interviews and circulate the report to interested persons. Make a brief presentation to your own personnel, being sure to emphasize all the positives before you get into any negatives, which are best described as "areas where customers feel we could improve our service." Write a follow-up letter of thanks to the customer and any others who may have participated, then tool up for your next interview. Use each interview to improve the next one and also to suggest further subjects for discussion. By the time you've conducted three interviews you'll be an old hand, developing priceless firsthand information and enjoying every minute of it!

Telephone Surveys. Some of the features of a personal interview can be incorporated into a telephone interview. However, interviewee fatigue is likely to set in quickly and you should plan to spend no more than 30 minutes on any one interview, unless the customer expresses willingness to talk longer. As with the personal interview, you should conduct the interview by appointment and furnish the customer with a list of questions in advance of the actual interview.

Because of the physical limitations of telephone interviews of this type, you may want to focus on a narrower range of subjects on individual calls. The flexibility of the telephone enables you to call many more customers overall than you could interview in person, and you'll end up with roughly the same amount of data at considerably less cost.

A very effective form of telephone survey that costs very little and accumulates data rapidly is opportunistic in nature. When a customer calls in to place an order or make a routine inquiry, your customer service rep handles the call in the usual fashion and, before signing off, asks: "While I have you on the phone, could I ask you a few questions for a survey we're conducting?" Most customers will agree and, by parceling out different questions among your reps, you can quickly assemble a great deal of information. If you have the appropriate software, your reps can enter responses directly into the system and give you a running total of survey findings.

You can also use the telephone for conventional questionnaire-type surveys that in the past were conducted primarily by mail. The advantage of the telephone over the mails is that it's faster and more flexible, and at the present time only slightly more costly than a mail survey. You're also likely to get a higher response rate simply because it's easier for customers to respond verbally than to fill out a form and mail it back. Other than the difference in response methods, you can use basically the same types of surveys and questions as described under Mail Surveys.

Mail Surveys. Mail surveys are usually the easiest and least costly surveys to conduct and the least demanding on departmental time. A formal mail survey has these steps:

Step 1. Prepare a balanced list or sample of your customers as the basis for your survey. Weight the list in terms of customer importance, or plan to key your questionnaires to the different account categories.

Step 2. Develop a quality survey package, including a personalized letter on good quality stationery (not an obvious computer letter), hand or autopen signed; the questionnaire itself, preferably on one side of a single sheet; and a postage-paid reply envelope or card. Include your fax number for respondents who may prefer that mode of reply—another reason for printing your questionnaire on one side of a single sheet. Ask respondents to sign their questionnaires, and allow plenty of room for them to write their comments. Signed questionnaires containing handwritten comments give your findings a great deal of credibility when you show them to others.

Step 3. Test the survey to make sure the questions are understood by recipients and that there aren't any ambiguities that might invalidate your findings.

Step 4. Mail the survey, allowing two to three weeks for responses. Follow up by phone on nonrespondents. If you get questionnaires back with specific complaints on them, follow up immediately by telephone; it's excellent public relations. Aim for a 30 percent or better return to ensure validity of your findings.

Step 5. Present the results in multimedia form: an executive summary, tables of data, graphs, and actual copies of significant signed survey forms with handwritten comments. These always get top attention!

Bounceback Surveys and Other Formats. These are typically brief surveys sent to a customer in connection with a specific event: a purchase, a service call by a technician, auto repairs, claims submitted to an insurance company for resolution, or other interactions with the company. The customer is asked to rate the quality of the service performed in the specific instance and to indicate the degree of her satisfaction. The format may also include specific questions about availability of parts, availability of information, skills and courtesy of customer service reps, and more. The surveys are usually but not always self-mailers; one common version is the familiar questionnaire found in hotel rooms and some restaurants. Bounceback cards may also be included with shipments, invoices or refund checks, or claims payments.

As a variation on the bounceback card, many organizations provide hotlines enabling customers to relay a complaint or report a specific problem and get an immediate response. Although hotlines are intended mainly to allow a fast response to individual complaints, they can also be a source of valuable statistical data and should be reported accordingly.

Another variation on the bounceback card, which has been tested by American Airlines, is a video booth set up in the baggage claim area of a major airport, where deplaning passengers can record their comments about service on the trip they have just experienced. This approach has several excellent values including its immediacy and relevance to a specific experience. The videotape can also be a useful training tool for the flight crews on the particular route segments rated. Some firms use voicemail or recorders to capture feedback from customers, but neither audio nor video taping should be considered a substitute for a live contact when customers are looking for an immediate response.

Measures of Customer Service Offerings by Competitors

This extremely important phase of the audit has three main subsets: (1) the specific nature of competitive offerings, including policies on exchanges, refunds, and other adjustments; warranties or service guarantees; special customer support services; (2) actual customer service performance on key indicators: response rates, error rates, fill rates, mean time between failures (MTBF), and similar quantitative measures; and (3) customers' perceptions of your service versus the competition, and vice versa.

Competitive Practices and Policies

There are a number of sources of information about your competitors' customer service practices and policies. Some of the most common include:

▪ *Catalogs, advertising, and similar materials*. Much of this literature is readily available from your distributors, who will be glad to provide it. They're very much in favor of competition between their vendors.

▪ *Feedback from your own CSRs*. Alert your people to the importance of competitive information of any kind, not just pricing. Customers are generally very open with CSRs, and if you provide reps with a means for documenting the tidbits they pick up in casual conversation with customers, you'll end up with valuable information for improving you own service. Research has shown that feedback from field sales reps is relatively unreliable, so whatever your source of information, always satisfy yourself that your information is accurate before acting on it.

▪ *Trade and professional association meetings and conventions*. One or more of your competitors are likely to be represented on the program in either panels or formal presentations. You'll learn a lot just by listening! If the organization publishes proceedings, so much the better. Don't pass up the informal or social sessions, either. You can pick up useful tidbits even during coffee breaks. Just don't talk about costs or pricing practices!

▪ *Newspaper and magazine articles*. These are helpful, but bear in mind that writeups in tradepapers are often one-sided—they omit all the negatives—because the company that's written up is an advertiser or potential advertiser. In this respect industry newsletters that don't carry advertising are likely to be more unbiased, although much of the information they carry is already in the public domain.

Competitive Customer Service Performance

There are two good sources of this type of information:

1. *Independent surveys of your industry*. Such surveys may be conducted by your trade association or by a third party. They often go into considerable detail on customer service performance, but they rarely cite performance data for individual companies. Some surveys will identify the participants but not their responses. One consulting firm maintains a continuing database of customer service performance in major industry groups. Companies that participate are given detailed statistics on how they rate against others in the same industry group, although the actual participants are never identified. In applying industry standards or averages to your own company's performance, bear

in mind that they are not absolute measures of how well or how poorly you measure up against your direct competitors or vice versa. However, such statistics are often quite useful in making a case with your management: if you're below the norm, a case for added funding for your operation; if you're above it, proof of how well you're doing. Either way, you come out ahead!

2. *Customer records.* Some of your customers likely keep records of vendor performance (including yourself and your competitors) on response, delivery, order fill, adjustments, MTBF, errors, and the like, depending on your type of business. They will usually share this information with you freely, and in fact may try to use it as leverage for getting better service from you. Which is why their data may be suspect. Always check their data on your performance against your own, and if there are discrepancies, find out why. They may be charging you with poor performance resulting from their own actions, for example, failing to pick up at the appointed time or charging you with concealed damage or shortages occurring on their own premises.

If you have just-in-time (JIT) arrangements with customers, this type of problem is less likely to occur because you've usually agreed beforehand what the measures of performance will be and how they'll be applied. It is usually your larger customers who keep competitive records, and the likelihood is that they are already getting better-than-average service because they demand it. Thus their records may not reflect the quality of service second-level customers are getting from you and your competitors. This is why it's critical to survey your customer base.

Customers' Perceptions of Competitive Performance

Since relatively few of your customers actually measure your performance precisely, your best assessment of your own performance versus the competition is likely to be obtained through a conventional rating survey conducted in one of the ways described earlier in this chapter.

When you ask customers to rate your performance against the competition you're likely to be measuring perception as much as you're measuring actual performance, but that's all right: the familiar saying that "perception is reality" is one of the givens in customer service management.

The survey is often done in a matrix format listing principal service features applicable to your industry and asking three basic questions about each service feature:

1. How do you rate our performance on [*named service feature*]?
2. How do you rate [*named competitor's*] performance on it?
3. How important is this service feature to you?

It's important that you use this format and not omit question 3 (or your industry's version of it); otherwise you can get false readings about your own company as well as its competitors.

Benchmarking

The term *benchmarking* has various definitions. The most relevant, in terms of customer service, is "the structured search for industry best practices, not confined to one's own industry." Benchmarking is not a direct measure of your own company's performance but rather a reflection of "the best of the best" against which you can measure your performance and that of your competitors.

In its purest form, benchmarking is a strict discipline involving formal procedures whereby study teams visit outstanding companies of different types and apply a battery of measures to their performance. An absolute essential is that the study cover companies outside one's own industry group as well as inside. For example, a benchmarking study group from the metalworking industry might study practices in the apparel industry or even in the hotel industry.

The practice of benchmarking was perfected by the Japanese who came to the United States in large numbers in the 1970s and 1980s and studied practices in virtually every type of industry. Their study teams made detailed and meticulous notes and debated and discussed and refined their findings. Much of the competitive advantage they gained was from the realization that methods in one industry might be usable in another, unrelated industry.

The nature of American business tends to place emphasis on short-term results within the confines of a given industry. This tendency has clearly hurt the United States in world markets as well as at home. As customer service manager you need to look well beyond your own industry for ideas and techniques that can be adapted to improve your service and assure your company's continuing growth and profitability.

You may not have the opportunity to participate in a formal benchmarking project conducted by your company (although you should jump at the opportunity if it presents itself), but there are dozens of opportunities for informal benchmarking. These include seminars, workshops, and conferences of managers from businesses of different types—the more mixed the audience, the better. Concentrate on the ideas and principles that do apply rather than on the details that don't. Professional organizations that cut across industry are excellent arenas for benchmarking: the International Customer Service Association, Council of Logistics Management, American Management Association, American Marketing Association, American Production and Inventory Control Society, Association of Field Service Managers, and National Association of Service Managers are all examples of organizations where you will find a healthy cross-section of practices you can compare to your own and vice versa.

Be sure also to read the so-called horizontal business publications that cover all industries as well as "vertical" magazines that cover only your own. Publications such as *Plant Engineering, Sales & Marketing Management, Inbound-Outbound, Voice Processing, Transportation & Distribution,* and *Direct Marketing* are examples of horizontal publications that typically contain a great deal of case history material that can be used for informal benchmarking. These publications don't always report the downside or negatives of some of the new systems and applications they report. Sometimes there's a tendency to emphasize the "gee-whiz" aspects of new technology over the practical applications. And don't put too much stock in the superficial writeups that deal in "management by anecdote," using isolated examples of dramatic customer service "saves" rather than practical descriptions of effective customer service systems. With these reservations, the trade press can give you a lot of good ideas, and the case histories contain the names of other managers you can network with for your mutual benefit.

Of course whenever your local chapter of whatever organization you belong to offers a plant tour, sign up right away, even if you're in the hyperballistics engineering business and the plant tour is at a sand and gravel company!

Measures of Corporate Customer Service Culture

The term *customer service culture* is widely used to describe companies where concern for customers pervades the entire work force. This is an exaggeration. In reality, a corporate customer service culture is just a reflection of sound business practice. Management recognizes customer service as a legitimate business strategy and supports that strategy.

That support is evident in the company's policies and procedures and, above all, in its system of accountability. Because of the way the company is organized and managed, employees understand that it is genuinely customer-oriented. Even if they don't understand this, the system of accountability ensures that they adhere to the standards of customer service that management has set for them.

The key factor in a customer service culture is that it represents the way management has chosen to run its business and achieve profit and market share objectives. This doesn't rule out concern for customers. In fact it suggests that management recognizes that customers are its most valuable asset and makes sure that they are treated accordingly.

In a number of companies, management *talks* a great deal about customers and customer service, but beyond the words there's very little tangible evidence of a genuine management commitment. For there's nothing vague about a customer service culture. Its presence—or absence—can be identified by any number of tangible indicators, the most common of which are reflected in the Corporate Culture Scorecard found in Appendix B.

You may want to supplement this with a roundtable discussion with others in the company addressing such questions as:

- How does the company view the marketplace?
- What obligations does it feel toward its customers?
- To what extent does it respect its customers?
- Do policies accurately reflect company philosophy?
- Are they carried out at all levels?
- Is there accountability at all levels?
- To what extent is customer service viewed as marketing strategy and given equal consideration with other marketing elements in the commitment of resources?
- How effectively do logistics and operations support marketing strategies?

- How effectively do systems support logistics?
- *To what extent is there a genuine corporate culture of customer service reflected in attitudes as well as performance throughout the organization?*

It's suggested that you print these questions on the pages of a flipchart, one per page, and then run through them one by one, writing comments or observations on the respective pages. As you finish each question, tear off the sheet of paper and put it up on the wall with masking tape. When you finish, you'll have a reasonable profile of your company's corporate culture. Of course, you don't have to do it in a meeting format: You already know the answers to many of the questions. The meeting is a good format, however, because it will nudge other department heads to buy into such a culture, simply through their participation in the deliberative process.

There are no "right" answers to these questions, but it will be very easy to discern the gaps between philosophical acceptance of a customer service culture and the policies and operating realities that are necessary to make it work. Closing those gaps is one of your most important missions. Good luck!

Section III

Customer Service Operations and Logistics

10

■ ■ ■
■ ■ ■
■ ■ ■

Proactive Management of Inbound Communications

The most visible part of customer service is the way a company handles its contacts with customers. If those contacts are handled well, they become a powerful marketing tool for winning and keeping customers. If they are handled poorly, the company suffers loss of reputation, customers, and market share—all to the benefit of its competitors.

One of the first things you learn as a customer service manager is that almost everything that happens in a customer service department is triggered by inbound communications from customers—communications that may flood in by the thousands daily, each one setting off its own chain of responses and reactions. Much of your attention is centered on systematizing those communications and making them efficient, cost-effective, and at the same time so highly acceptable to customers that your competitors don't stand a chance of getting a foot in the door. This chapter helps you in that complex and challenging task.

Inbound communications in customer service cover just about every form of information exchange except perhaps carrier pigeons and smoke signals. The three major categories you are most likely to be involved with are hard copy, electronic data interchange (EDI), and voice processing. The mix of these is influenced by your type of operation, the volume of communications you handle, and the needs and wants of your customers.

One of your major goals should be to set standards of communications and information handling quality that meet your customers' needs and staffing and productivity goals that won't force you to compromise those standards. To do so, you must be familiar with the basic technologies and how they can be best applied to your operations.

Hard Copy Technology

The words *hard copy* are used to describe a document or record that exists in physical form, as opposed to verbal or digitized data. The term usually connotes authenticity, but the hard copy doesn't have to be an original document.

It can be a photocopy, computer printout, microfiche, or more. Hard copy communications include the following media:

Postal Service

The postal service is widely used where cost is critical and time or tracing capability are not and original documents are required for legal or other reasons. Primary advantages of mail are that it requires no special equipment, it is highly flexible, and in domestic first-class service it is delivered everywhere at a uniform rate. Customers use mail mainly for order confirmations, checks, and non-time-sensitive communications. There is a widespread perception that mail is slow and unreliable, and few customers use it for sending in orders or other communications requiring a reasonably fast response.

Yet there are several applications for mail that as manager you don't want to overlook. Mail surveys and bounceback cards to follow up on service contacts are excellent, low-cost means for measuring performance as viewed by customers. Hard copies of questionnaires signed by important customers will convince management of customer likes and dislikes in a way that none of your words could accomplish. And the originals of complimentary letters written and signed by customers are powerful morale builders within the department as well as the company. Whistler, a Massachusetts consumer electronics firm, displays all such letters on a "wall of fame" adjacent to the customer service department.

Surprisingly, there's a personal quality to a letter that doesn't exist in phone calls and other media. Writing letters to customers to thank them for their business or for being cooperative in a difficult situation is one of the most impressive things you can do, because hardly anybody else bothers to do it.

Courier or Document Delivery Services

Courier or document delivery services include premium mail service and next-day or second-morning service offered by Federal Express, United Parcel Service, and others. These services are widely used when it's desirable to send originals and when urgency and tracing capability outweigh cost.

These services are also generally used for emergency shipments of small parts or critical supplies to customers. Their relatively high cost is usually justified by the much higher costs that would be incurred if the parts or supplies weren't received quickly and by the value of keeping a customer who might otherwise be lost to the competition.

Facsimile (Fax) Transmission

Widely used as a substitute for mail and for certain types of telephone calls, facsimile has the advantage of speed, accuracy, and reasonable cost. It's also preferred by many customer service people because the fax machine doesn't have to be answered the way a telephone does. When information, inquiries, and orders are received in hard copy format, they can be evaluated, prioritized, queued, accumulated, postponed, or expedited in whatever way is most convenient at the moment.

Having this capability helps level the workload and improve departmental productivity. It's hard to do this with telephone calls because they must be answered which they're received, and often there's no way of knowing how important a call is until it's answered. With a hard copy, you can decide right away whether the matter needs immediate attention or whether it can be handled later during a slow period.

Here is an example of strategic applications in managing inbound communications that shows significant benefits for both the vendor and its customers and demonstrates how to get an edge on the competition at relatively low cost. In 1989, Brown Shoe Company launched a program to link some 1,600 accounts via facsimile to its St. Louis operations. Brown offered its dealers high-grade fax machines at a low group rate and in return provided them with an 800 number to recover the cost in reduced telephone charges plus faster inventory turns, better reorder capability, and increased sales. Gene Spilker, director of customer service, said, "All we want to do is to provide better, quicker, and less costly service to our customers." Yet the move was sound marketing strategy—making it easier for customers to deal with Brown than with competitors. And it is operationally sound, too. The arrangement keeps costs down for Brown as well, and it minimizes calls asking for confirmation (as would be the case with regular mail) since the fax machine automatically acknowledges receipt of orders.

Since some facsimile transmissions may fade over time, if you want to retain a facsimile to meet legal requirements, write the date and your signature in black ink on the margin and make a copy on your photocopy machine. Staple the facsimile to your copy and file. Your signature and the date won't fade even though the original transmission does. With the date and signature appearing in the same location on both copies you can always validate that your photocopy is a true copy of the original transmission.

Facsimile transmission has been approved by some lower courts for transmission of depositions, and it seems likely that its use for orders and order acknowledgment will have comparable legal status.

Telex and Remote Terminal Messaging

In this application, messages are typed into a terminal at a customer location and printed out on a printer at the vendor location. They may also be used between the customer service department and the warehouse or shipping department to transmit shipping documents, releases, pick lists, or other material.

Some companies place captive terminals free of charge at customer locations and absorb the line charges generated. The purpose is to give the vendor a competitive edge by making it easy for that customer to place orders and otherwise communicate with the vendor. As with other hard copy media, this arrangement also contributes to efficient workload planning and leveling.

Videotape Communications

You will certainly want to use videotape—and perhaps videodiscs—to inform and educate customers and train them in repairs, retrofits, or other procedures. Where expensive telephone time is currently being taken up talking customers through different procedures, videotapes may be a more cost-effective way of conveying that information to the customer, especially where it can be used to train numbers of people. For some time, Ralston Purina has been providing customers with videotapes to train their workers in the proper handling of bagged goods, thus reducing problems of returned and damaged goods adjustments. Don't be surprised if some of your customers start sending you videotapes showing you how to improve your service to them!

Electronic Data Interchange

Computer-to-computer technologies have taken over much of the traditional mechanical activity of customer service reps who receive inquiries or orders from customers via phone, input the data into a computer terminal and, in many cases, read back the computer output displayed on the screen. EDI enables customers to access vendors' computers directly through their own terminals and computers rather than going through a human interface. This EDI use speeds processes and reduces the possibility of error. It also frees the customer service rep to do other, more important work where human interface is essential.

With 10,000 active users of EDI in 1990 and an annual growth rate of 45 percent, EDI has already supplanted reps and telephones in order processing applications of this type in a great many cases where companies are doing a high volume of business with one another, including suppliers to retailers and vendors to original equipment manufacturers. The Big 3 automakers, K Mart, Wal-Mart, Bergen Brunswig and Pacific Telephone are among major users of EDI, many of whom require their vendors to develop EDI interfaces compatible with their own.

EDI is particularly suited to situations where input created by customers for their own computers can also be used as input for the vendor or host computer, as in the case of purchase orders, bills of materials, and the like. It can also be used for inquiry and data retrieval by authorized parties. For example, a firm's salespeople and designated customers may access the computer for data on inventory availability, order status, pricing information, delivery, and more. In some inquiry applications the computer can be accessed by either touchtone telephone or computer terminal and generate verbal responses.

In terms of customer service operations, EDI is essentially a means of delivering or exchanging information that doesn't materially change procedures after the output has been generated. From your point of view as manager, the technology is not nearly as significant as the twin benefits EDI provides: improved operational efficiency and closer linkage with your customers. Of the two, linkage with your customers should certainly take precedence:

the system needs to be user-friendly to make it easy to order from you, and it should have tangible benefits for customers.

As an example, Herman Miller, the Zeeland, Michigan, manufacturer of upscale contemporary furniture, offers its dealers a hardware-software package costing them in the neighborhood of $6,000 but offering them ease of communicating orders and obtaining order status information and regular daily updates directly from the host computer at Miller's headquarters. In addition, orders entered via the computer automatically get priority over orders received by other means.

Is EDI acceptable to customers as a replacement for the former method of phoning the order in to a live rep? Apparently the speed and convenience outweigh the loss of the personal touch for most companies, but there are some exceptions. Firestone Tire and Rubber in Akron, Ohio, reported that in dealer sales its middle-range customers had readily adopted its EDI package, but its very largest and very smallest customers still preferred to deal with a live CSR.

EDI is already being used by the federal government on a pilot basis in its procurement activities through the Government Services Administration. If your organization does any government contracting, or plans to, you should be preparing for this EDI use, which is expected eventually to cover most of the GSA's bid, procurement, and contracting activities. The Veterans Administration and other agencies are following suit.

Voice Processing Technology

Although the conventional voice telephone—a customer talking with a company representative—has been the underlying medium of business communication for almost a quarter of a century, many of its traditional functions in customer service have been taken over by facsimile and EDI, mainly because they are faster, cheaper, and better suited to the particular task. And the technology of the telephone itself has undergone important changes, which have a number of customer service applications.

There is a strong feeling that the telephone personalizes transactions between customers and the company, and it's certainly true, particularly in business-to-business transactions, that many customers form their opinions about their suppliers mainly on the basis of the way they're treated on the telephone.

But the high volume of calls, high labor costs, and personnel shortages have made it increasingly difficult to handle calls to the satisfaction of large numbers of customers. Busy signals, lengthy holds, multiple transfers, and inadequate responses from company personnel tend to dilute much of the value of the person-to-person contact the telephone affords. Instead of creating a positive image of the company, these contacts often leave a very poor impression of the company, as well as customers who are annoyed and irritated rather than pleased with the personal contact.

As customer service manager, you are quite likely to find yourself under pressure to improve the quality of your department's telephone communications and at the same time reduce the cost of handling the ever-increasing volume of calls.

Depending on your organization, you may also run into resistance to the idea of using one or more of the many forms of automation that are coming into use in customer service operations. You may even have to overcome some of your own biases against depersonalizing the relationship with customers.

Yet if you do a little sampling among your customers, you will find that their main interest in their day-to-day contacts with your firm is fast and accurate service at reasonable prices and the ability to reach qualified personnel by phone when problems occur that need special, nonroutine handling. As for the image of your company that's projected, it's one of the basic axioms of customer service management that customers tend to judge a firm by how it reacts when things go wrong, not by its routine, day-to-day operations.

When you examine your department's telephone traffic, the statistics will almost certainly show that many of those exceptions or nonroutine events aren't getting the attention they deserve because your people are spending too much time on the phone handling routine matters that could be handled by facsimile, EDI, or some of the newer voice processing technologies which do not require a human attendant on your end of the line.

If you sell through dealers, distributors, or retailers, you should be aware that conventional telephone responses at that level are often handled very poorly and could be seriously hampering your own sales through those channels. For example, *Marketing News* (1986–1987) reported that a series of calls made to about 5,000 Yellow Pages advertisers by a research organization resulted in over one-third being handled unacceptably, even by the most relaxed standards, and 10 percent handled so poorly that no sale could possibly result.

If your company depends on these channels to generate business, and particularly if you give co-op allowances for Yellow Pages advertising, your concern with customer service telephone contacts goes well beyond the confines of your own company.

You have plenty of reasons to consider all the available voice processing alternatives, regardless of how off-the-wall they may seem right now. Your first step is to profile your call system as it now exists, then test the different technologies that are available to achieve the levels of quality and efficiency you need for your customer service operations.

First of all, look at the basic methods whereby incoming calls are typically received and distributed within different kinds of customer service departments. This function is often handled by an ACD system. There are hundreds of ACD configurations, from very basic single-function systems at one location to highly sophisticated multifunction configurations tying together a number of locations. To decide which kind you need or whether you need one at all, start by tracking the methods used to handle information flow between customers and your department. In short, who answers the phone when the customer calls?

▪ *Next available rep.* This method of call distribution is most common for high-volume call centers used for reservations, mail order, public utilities, banking, and similar operations. It is highly productive and cost-effective in such situations, with calls routed automatically to the rep who has been off the phone the longest and a variety of real-time computer readouts enabling supervisors to manage the operation efficiently.

If you're working with this kind of high-volume system you know that staffing is a major concern in two respects: (1) having the right number of phones and the right number of people on the phones to handle the daily (and sometimes hourly) fluctuations in the volume of incoming calls; and (2) attracting and retaining qualified people by finding ways to minimize the burnout that is inherent in what is basically both a boring and a stressful job.

Of these two concerns, the "how many" issue is the easiest to deal with. Most ACD systems forecast your numerical staffing requirements on a real-time basis, some for segments as small as 15 minutes. The problem of keeping people and avoiding stress and burnout is much more complex and is one of the reasons you should look very closely at some of the voice processing formats available to handle routine transactions.

▪ *Assignment by account, region, or industry group.* Where CSRs (or sometimes small teams of CSRs) are assigned to specific groups or categories of accounts, inbound calls can be routed in several different ways. In some organizations, a switchboard or a secretary in the department routes the call to the appropriate rep. The secretary simply asks the caller for the account number, location, or zip code or area code and from this knows where to assign the call.

Where there's a continuing relationship between a designated rep and a particular group of customers, you may give the rep a direct number so that incoming calls don't have to be screened. Then, customers can either dial direct or go through the secretary or switchboard. A variation on this method is self-directed switching, where the caller can direct the call by touchtone telephone once it's been received into the system.

Most ACD systems can be tailored to meet the needs of specialized call distribution within the department. Two applications are illustrative:

1. Calls routed by origin area code. This system is common where reps are assigned by territory. When a call enters the system, the origin area code is automatically "read" and the call switched to the rep or reps handling that territory.
2. Calls routed by automatic number identification (ANI). The system reads the originating phone number, identifies the account, and routes it to the appropriate individual's terminal where it calls up the customer's file and displays it on the screen so that the rep knows who (or at least what account) is calling before actually connecting with the caller. ANI can also be used in a number of next-available-rep configurations to enable personalizing the response. One financial services firm uses this system for its major accounts; although they're handled on a next-available-rep basis, the rep who answers can see who the account is and will respond to the effect of: "This is the [account name] desk. How can I serve you?"

Although the account management form of staffing illustrated here is preferred both for the morale factors and for the higher service levels it usually enables, take special pains to be sure that whatever combination of technology and staffing you use, it assures high levels of accessibility of assigned personnel to customers.

▪ *Assignment by specialty.* From a call management point of view, you'll use mainly the same technology and staffing principles as for assignment by account. Calls made to a specific number can be switched by an operator or by the caller. One organization publishes one number for English-speaking callers, another for Spanish-speaking, another for Japanese-speaking callers and so forth, so that the incoming call goes to the CSR speaking that particular language. Other specialties can be handled in the same way.

▪ *Tiered staffing.* This method screens inbound calls and assigns them to a tier of support personnel according to the level of expertise required. Although the screening is generally done by live operators, it can also be handled as a caller-routed, menu-driven application. Systems in use input the customer's information into the database, avoiding the necessity of the customer having to repeat the information if the call is transferred. In other instances where all personnel are busy and callbacks are required, CSRs can access the database and research and often solve the problem before calling back.

Alternatives to Live Call Handling

Since call distribution systems with multiple stations can be expensive to design and install, one of the first steps you need to take in evaluating your staffing alternatives is to determine whether all the calls that are coming in have to be handled live by a customer service rep or whether an alternative technology may be more suitable. You also need to determine whether they all have to be handled at the particular times they're being handled, and in some cases whether they have to be handled at all: the "Is this call necessary?" kind of call.

Regardless of how you staff your department and route calls, your inbound phone traffic is likely to contain numerous inefficiencies that you need to identify and remove whenever possible.

When you measure inbound calls by number and type (the first step in rationalizing any phone system), you are very likely to find that many are repetitive questions on similar subjects that can be answered with relative ease by accessing the computer. If you can arrange for customers to access the computer directly, as many banks do, this may enable less sophistication (and less cost) in the live response system.

If you analyze individual calls, you will discover that as much as 50 percent of a typical call is taken up in making the contact and identifying the caller, account number, and the inquiry or subject of the call, all before the customer service representative has entered the inquiry into the computer for a response. This suggests an excellent opportunity for ANI, which enables more calls to be handled by fewer reps and a smaller capacity ACD system. ANI also reduces line charges as well as labor costs and at the same time enables greater accessibility and better service to customers calling in.

Many customers are opting for facsimile and EDI on their own, and these media are well-suited to a considerable range of transactions. They are considerably less costly because they don't require a human being in attendance.

If you find your phone system overburdened with routine calls or lengthy orders that could be faxed, for example, you might want to follow the example of Jerome Sherwin, sales service manager of Alkco, Franklin Park, Illinois, who discontinued his firm's 800 numbers for voice calls and connected them instead to fax machines. With toll charges now assessed on regular calls, customers had an excellent incentive to use the free calls to the facsimile system for many of their communications that previously had been telephoned. Many other companies have installed multiple fax machines connected to ACD systems in various configurations.

Or you may want to consider a simple recorder. Lift Parts Manufacturing Co. in Des Plaines, Illinois, found that an extremely high volume of stock orders were being phoned in, tying up phones and reps to the extent that customers calling in with emergencies, needing a single critical part for an out-of-service machine, for example, couldn't get through. To remedy this costly situation, the firm installed a hotline serviced only by a conventional answering machine. As an incentive to use the hotline, which was restricted to emergency orders, customers were assured that all orders received by a certain time would be guaranteed shipment that evening by premium transportation. By using the hotline, customers could also order a special-of-the-month item, available at a reduced price only to hotline users.

An Indiana automotive parts manufacturer found a similar situation where a customer needing a critical part to get a passenger bus back into operation could not get through (sometimes calling on a pay phone from a remote rural location) because other customers were calling in regular stock orders consisting of 300 lines or more. And a very different type of call was compounding the problem, that is, frequent calls from hand-to-mouth buyers placing very small orders. To offset this situation, the firm created an incentive program to motivate customers to place larger orders and to communicate them in hard copy format. In this case the incentive was a free accessory or kit available only to customers placing orders for $500 or more in hard copy form with the required lead time. The program was promoted through distribution of a calendar showing each month's special and serving as a reminder of the program each month. As a bonus, the program also gave the hand-to-mouth buyers reason to plan their purchases more systematically to consolidate their orders so they could take advantage of the free offering.

Balancing Inbound Calls

Leveling the call center workload is one of the most difficult problems you're likely to encounter in managing the customer service department. But the task becomes a lot easier when you realize that calls don't *have to* come in when they come in. Even though you can't actually dictate when your customers must call, you can influence them to call at the times that are most convenient to you.

This idea may surprise you, coming at a time when most companies are working to improve their accessibility to customers via extended hours, 7-day/24-hour availability, and other services. These arrangements presuppose that customers automatically call when it's most convenient for them to do so, when in fact the opposite is often true.

For example, how many people call their doctor's office and say: "I want an appointment at 2:45 P.M., Tuesday, October 23"? They are more likely to say: "I'd like an appointment the week of the twenty-second. Do you have anything available?" And the doctor's office is likely to respond: "We can give you an appointment at 10:30 A.M. on Thursday, the twenty-fifth. Is that all right?"

Now, let's write another scenario. An individual has a heart attack and dials 911 for emergency help. He obviously expects immediate response, not an appointment at the rescue squad's convenience. There is a clear parallel in the way customers prioritize their business calls:

1. They would *prefer* making routine calls at their convenience.
2. They are willing to make their routine calls at an alternate time that is reasonably close, that is, within the same general time frame.
3. They feel that they *must* be able to get through when they call on matters of high priority.

Not all customers feel this way of course, and different customers define priorities in different ways. But at this juncture you're not concerned with *all* customers, you're only concerned with whether you can motivate *enough* customers to change their calling patterns to help you level your workload, or at least improve it sufficiently to make the effort worthwhile.

And you can. Many companies simply tell their customers the most convenient time to call. Many credit card companies, for example, suggest to customers that they call on Wednesday, Thursday, or Friday rather than Monday and Tuesday, which are high-traffic days. IBM found that when it told customers the best time of day to call its parts department in Greencastle, Indiana, enough customers changed their calling patterns to save IBM the cost of adding more telephone lines and personnel to man them. When L. L. Bean, a 365-day, 24-hour operation, found its lines clogged with daytime calls, it added a message to its catalog and order form suggesting that "For better service, call after 9 P.M. and before 10 A.M." The result: Enough telephone traffic moved to the nighttime hours to save Bean the expense of adding equipment and personnel to improve response to daytime callers. The Holden Group sent its customers mailers suggesting that calling during off-peak times would provide faster access (see Figure 10-1). This helped level Holden's call-handling workload and solved staffing problems for the company. Because of the time difference between its West Coast location and the East Coast, where many of its major customers are located, Everest & Jennings, the California wheelchair manufacturer, found that morning calls from its California customers were blocking afternoon calls from its East Coast customers and vice versa. It alleviated the situation simply by requesting its California customers to call after 2:00 P.M. Pacific time whenever possible. By this time, most of the firm's East Coast cus-

Figure 10-1. Mailer developed to advise customers on how to avoid delays in getting through to customer service

LESS MUSIC, MORE TALK.

If you've ever called our Customer Service Department, you've found that you can rely on:

- Fast, accurate answers to your questions
- Illustrations tailored to your income needs
- Assistance in changing addresses, beneficiaries and general account updating
- Latest interest rate information
- Courteous resolution of problems.

Customer Service is available every Monday through Friday, from 7:00 a.m. to 5:00 p.m., Pacific Time. But sometimes, getting through to us can mean delays if you're calling during our peak times.

Although our selection of music is fine, to avoid waiting on hold we suggest you call us before noon or after 2:00 p.m. PT, Tuesday through Friday. Then you can get less music, more talk.

(800) 225-8899
CA: (800) 241-4455
CA: (213) 312-6100

Source: The Holden Group

tomers had closed for the day. The arrangement made it easier for customers on both coasts to access the customer service department.

Another approach to balancing the call workload is to provide customers with an incentive to place their orders on certain days of the week. Howmedica, Inc., the New Jersey manufacturer of knee, hip, and other implants, set up a free shipping program whereby customers in designated zones would receive free shipping if they placed their orders on specified days of the week. The savings achieved in workload leveling throughout the customer service, warehouse, and shipping departments more than offset the relatively slight cost of the shipments, which went out in the form of low-cost freight consolidations to the designated areas.

A final method of balancing call traffic is to move some calls from the inbound to the outbound category. This move is useful where customers place orders at more or less regular intervals. A Firestone unit found, as an example, that a number of its customers were willing to be called at a regular time each week, an arrangement that enabled CSRs to schedule the calls at times of relatively low inbound activity. It also reduced routine interim calls by customers, who simply saved up these matters for the weekly call-by-appointment. Meanwhile, the CSR had time to review inventories in anticipation of the customer's order and to develop lists of items that could be substituted for items currently back ordered.

Eliminating Unnecessary Calls

"Is this call necessary?" Your reps ask themselves this question a number of times every day. And with good reason, because by some estimates as many as 25 percent of the inbound calls you receive each day are unnecessary. Here are some typical examples of such calls, along with suggestions on how they can be reduced or eliminated:

▪ *Hasn't read instructions or documentation.* This type of call is quite common in the software industry, but it occurs in other areas as well. A Midwestern software company tallied calls for assistance by customer site and found that a small number of customers were making an excessive number of calls, which in turn were overburdening the customer service department and creating added costs. By imposing a surcharge on calls beyond a certain number and length, they were able to reduce the total number of assistance calls significantly.

▪ *Can't understand instructions or documentation.* In this situation the instructions are unclear or confusing, resulting in an excessive number of calls for clarification. An Ohio-based manufacturer of specialized paint additives found itself in such a situation, receiving a flood of calls from end users who couldn't understand the instructions on the products' labels. Inspiration! The job of rewriting the labels was turned over to the reps who had been handling the calls and were naturally aware of what was confusing buyers. Result: a significant drop in inbound calls and, therefore, a better image for the product and an increase in the number of satisfied customers.

A Midwestern manufacturer of hospital lab equipment places customer service reps on its new product review committees to ensure that when new products are introduced to the marketplace, their controls and operation are user-friendly. The reason: the company realizes that its customer service reps get more direct feedback and know more about the likes and dislikes of lab technicians who actually use the equipment than anyone else in the company.

▪ *Errors.* Errors of any kind naturally generate inbound calls. An organization with some 400,000 members mailed out a bulletin containing an incorrect date for a future meeting. For the next week, the switchboard was jammed with phone calls from members concerned that they had made a mistake in planning their own schedules. There was no remedy in this case, since the damage was already done, but one alternative would be to divert calls through an announcement-only call answering system, where persons calling on other matters could default to a customer service rep. In any event, the example illustrates the value of careful proofreading.

The experience of the customer service manager of a West Virginia chemical company bears this out. He found that some 60 percent of paperwork that came into his department from other departments contained errors. His department was able to correct those errors and ship out 99 percent error-free orders. This naturally reduced the number of inbound calls from customers that would have resulted from the high percentage of billing and shipping errors that would have otherwise gotten through. As an added bonus, it speeded up payment on invoices because customers didn't have to call to correct errors in pricing, discounts, and terms of sale.

▪ *Changes in invoice format.* A firm that wanted to increase the confidentiality of its discounts to customers changed its programming so that the computer calculated the discount on each invoice but did not print it out. The net price included the discount, but the percentage and dollar amount of that discount did not appear on the form. Some customers realized that the discount had been allowed, but many more did not and, on each of the many calls they made to the firm's customer service department, customer service reps had to walk them through a lengthy explanation of why the invoices were correct. The process was not only time-consuming and costly, but also significantly delayed payment of those same invoices.

By contrast, when McCormick & Co., the Baltimore, Maryland, spice and grocery products firm, changed the format of its invoices to make them easier to understand, it prepared an eight-page booklet diagramming the new invoice format and explaining it line by line. Before using the new invoice, it furnished all customers with a copy of the booklet. The result: no confusion on the part of customers and an immediate and substantial improvement in cash flow.

▪ *No-confidence calls.* These check-up calls are calls made by customers to the effect of "I'm just calling to make sure my order will be going out on time" or "The service man is supposed to be here at 11 A.M.; it's 10:30 now. Is he going to be here on time?" Some of these calls come from perennial worriers among your customers, but the majority come from customers who have had a bad experience with your company in the past and want to avoid a recurrence. A New Jersey electrical manufacturer faced with this kind of situation developed an early warning system to notify customers when orders were likely to be delayed. After the system had been in place and customer confidence restored, total inbound calls to the customer service department dropped by 25 percent.

▪ *Clarification calls.* These callbacks are mainly from customers who didn't get complete information on a previous call. A typical introduction: "I forgot to ask you..." These calls are usually made because the customer service rep responded to specific questions asked by the customer but did not volunteer any related information. An example would be a customer calling to ask where the airport limousine service leaves from, being given the information, and then calling back a minute later to ask what time it leaves.

New England Business Service in Groton, Massachusetts, discovered that by training its reps to volunteer information of certain types even when customers didn't ask for it, the total number of inbound calls could be reduced significantly, along with total talk time. One manufacturer of pallet racks related cases where customers might call back as many as five times after placing an order, each time asking for one more piece of information; shipping date on one call, carrier name on the next, pro number the third time, transit time on the following call, and shipping costs on the fifth and final call. Developing a standard script delivering that information to the customer when ordering eliminated the majority of added calls.

The Issue of Holds

Holds are distasteful to customers and expensive to the company. Current technology enables announcements telling callers how long they will have to wait and offering them a better time to call or the option to leave a message. Useful information or even advertisements or new product or service announcements are preferable to music, which many callers find annoying. Furthermore, companies that rebroadcast radio music on their answering systems may be required to pay substantial royalties to ASCAP, which has become increasingly vigilant in monitoring this use of licensed music.

The hold time can also be used to prepare the caller for the transaction, saving valuable talk time and avoiding the necessity of a callback: "Please have your catalog and credit card handy so we may serve you better," "Please be sure you have the model number and part number so we can expedite your order."

When customers are told how long the hold will be, it does not seem as long as if they're not told, because by staying on the line they have in effect "bought in" to the announced delay. For the same reason, whenever reps place customers on hold, they should ask their permission and offer the option of a callback. In some cases, it may be preferable *not* to offer the option either way. If there are very few calls in queue, it may be preferable to put the customer on hold briefly. This assumes the rep will be able to connect back in less than 30 seconds or so. In other cases, it may be that the wait will be so long that callers should be told they will be called back and asked what times they would prefer. This function can be handled by diverting overflow calls to a basic answering machine programmed for that purpose.

Holds are particularly expensive on toll-free numbers because you are paying for dead time on the telephone, at the same time blocking additional calls. Ironically, holds are frequently the result of understaffing and headcount policies designed to cut costs, when in fact the cost of staffing adequately would be less than the company is currently spending for that dead telephone time.

If you suspect this problem in your company, calculate the cost of hold time over a year's period. You can derive most of this data from your ACD reports. Then calculate the cost of hiring enough personnel to avoid these holds. The hold cost is likely to be two or three times the personnel cost. Don't forget to toss in the fact that when customers have to hold too long, they waste a valuable minute or two of connect time taking out their irritation on the rep who has finally picked up. So, reducing hold time adds two bonuses: happier customers and reduced talk time!

Interactive and Automated Response Systems

Voice messaging systems are the next step up from the conventional telephone attended on both ends, and they range from the basic recorder, which simply takes messages "at the sound of the beep," to sophisticated voicemail systems where callers can route their own calls using a touchtone telephone.

The basic recorder or answering machine lends itself well to captive situations, for example, where field sales personnel can call in their orders after hours without tying up lines during the day. It can also be used in announcement-only situations where the volume of calls is too great to handle, for example, calls to the electric company during power outages. The announce-only mode can also be used for retrieving standardized information obtainable by calling a specific telephone number: weather reports, flight schedules, drive instructions from the airport to a specific hotel, and so forth.

Another application that the basic answering machine shares with voicemail is leaving a message that does not require a response or acknowledgment: "Just calling to let you know the shipment arrived safely."

Voicemail, a step up from conventional recorders, includes a routing capability that enables the caller to route a message to a specific individual and, if she isn't there, either leave a message or divert the call by default to a secretary or other individual. Voicemail and recorders are often preferable to leaving messages with live call-takers because they ensure that the message is received in the caller's exact words and not distorted in being transmitted through a third-party. However, voicemail should not be misused to the extent of making callers feel that they're being given the runaround.

Interactive Voice Response Units (IVRUs)

IVRUs are a step up from voicemail or voice messaging because they enable callers not only to route their calls by touchtone telephone but also to interact and perform transactions with the underlying system. The distinguishing feature of IVRUs is that customers who call the system get specific voice responses to their inquiries as well as acknowledgments of their transactions.

Banking and financial applications for IVRUs are becoming quite common. A Dallas bank's system is currently handling 11,000 calls a day—mainly inquiries about balances, deposits credited, or checks cleared—while thirty-five reps are handling a total of 3,500–4,000 calls a day. A Boston investment firm is handling 45,000 calls live daily and another 48,000 with an IVRU. The manager says he would have to hire another 200–250 people to equal the call-handling capacity of the IVRU system.

When interactive systems are used for entering orders for services or products, the system can be programmed to offer alternatives. Some can be relatively sophisticated, using a voice response to this effect: "We don't have that available in twelve-packs; would ten twenty-fours be acceptable in place of twenty twelves?" or "The noon flight is fully booked; do you want a seat on the 2:00 P.M. flight?" Interactive systems are also being increasingly used in registering for college courses, public seminars, and similar events. These uses are a variation on simple order entry.

In virtually every type of interactive application, the effectiveness of the system is highly dependent on the decision rules underlying the prompts. By proper framing of questions or "branching" it's possible to reduce over a million possibilities down to one, using fewer than twenty questions to do so. This principle makes it practical to develop IVRUs for a wide variety of applications. Similar logic is employed in what some interactive systems describe as "thought recognition."

An advanced IVRU application is for remote diagnosis and repair of equipment. Systems exist that will walk the caller through the entire process of troubleshooting, based on yes-no responses and the appropriate branching, then on to adjustment, repair, and parts replacement. These systems have the advantage of presenting information in standardized form and logical sequence. This method is often preferable to having the information relayed by a field engineer, who may be good at making the repairs but less expert at conveying the information to the user over the telephone. In addition, such systems are usually far more cost-effective, both in warranty and service contract situations, than sending an engineer to the customer site to perform the repairs.

Voice Recognition Systems

Voice recognition systems have been around for some time, but only recently have they been debugged to the extent that they show promise for general customer service applications. When they become practical for customer service use, their application will be just about the same as for current IVRUs except that input will be by voice rather than touchtone telephone. This will broaden the appeal and ease of interactive systems considerably, at the same time enabling diversion of even more routine calls to an automated mode. As customer service manager, you will want to keep a close watch on developments in this area.

Thought Recognition in Communications

Thought recognition is only a matter of time and not as far-out as it seems. It's not so much a matter of technology as it is of understanding human thought processes and logic. Most interactive systems are based on thought recognition and simply offer the customer the options he or she is most likely to choose under a given set of circumstances.

When a customer uses a bank's automatic teller machine (ATM), he or she selects from a limited number of functions: deposit, withdraw, check a balance, and so forth. Thought recognition is the process of determining those options most likely to be suitable for a given customer base. Basic customer service applications like the ATM are relatively simple because so many customer transactions fall within a narrow range that is readily machinable.

More sophisticated versions used in equipment diagnostics or insurance policy interpretation may link together as many as 1,000 or more screens following logical thought processes, and it's almost certain that even more advanced versions will be in use within the next few years.

In telephone transactions, the thought recognition process has been refined to the extent that a customer can call a company and carry on a conversation with a machine, asking and answering questions without realizing that he is talking to a machine, not a live human being. With a voice-activated recorder/announcer on the receiving end, it's possible for a customer to call and order a cab, a pizza, or merchandise from a catalog; to register for a course; or any of dozens of similar applications, all without realizing that the prompts are all mechanical and induced by the caller.

The same process can be used in reverse, that is, in automatically dialing customers to get specific information: order numbers, delivery confirmation, payment requests, and more.

Both the inbound and outbound applications are practical business uses that often benefit the customer as well as the vendor by speeding up processes that would otherwise take much longer. The use of the outbound version for telemarketing is a relatively recent practice. It hasn't been fully accepted yet, but probably will be in the changing selling environment where face-to-face selling is becoming increasingly expensive and underproductive.

Much of the automation discussed here is already being used in larger customer service operations characterized by high-volume communications and well-defined customer bases. As the general public becomes more sophisticated, interactive systems will be taken for granted in virtually every kind of business-customer contact.

They won't replace the human contact, of course, but handling routine and repetitive transactions quickly and cheaply will make the human contacts that do occur much more productive and cost-effective than they could ever be without the automation. To use these systems in customer service you don't need a degree in engineering but rather an understanding of which applications will work best in your environment.

How to Select the Communications Technology Best Suited to Your Business

1. Measure the volume of calls by type and complexity. If you have a high volume of calls asking for relatively simple data such as account or order status, a basic interactive system will be practical. Then, the calls that must be handled by trained reps can be the basis for your staffing projections.

2. If calls are diverse, it may be necessary to determine the real reasons people call. In some cases, callers can't understand instructions or aren't using the documentation you provide them. Rather than try to figure out how to handle large numbers of such calls, it's usually practical to reduce their overall volume by rewriting manuals and instructions into more user-friendly format, assessing charges for certain types of calls to discourage customers from calling needlessly, or educating customers in how to use their documentation.

3. Tally calls that can be handled more effectively by other means such as fax. Orders and similar documents that are essentially one-way in nature can be handled more efficiently in hard copy form. They can be batched, queued, and prioritized in the most efficient fashion, whereas phone calls must be handled in sequence as they come in, a relatively inefficient process for transmitting information.

4. Decide on the level of automation appropriate for your customer base and mix of calls. Don't be too conservative because acceptance is increasing all the time, and too little automation will leave you behind the competition.

5. Develop requirements for your live calls in terms of volume, length of calls, and acceptable hold, busy signal, and abandonment rates (the number of people who hang up rather than being kept on hold), as discussed in Chapter 10. Consult your telecommunications engineers at this point to work out the technical configuration of your system, allowing for expansion to meet a growing volume of calls. Over time your voice calls will probably increase at a slower rate than your automated calls, and you may want to design the capacity for each accordingly.

6. Before you make any decisions, brainstorm with your reps on desirable features and functions of the system and incorporate these features to the extent that's practical. It is important that your reps see automation as a tool to help them work at the top of their skills, not a means to reduce headcount.

7. If you are involved in the selection of equipment vendors, get them to give you references from other customer service managers and inspect their operations personally if possible. And talk to their reps as well.

8. Don't delay. Automation takes a long time, and the longer you postpone it, the more likely it is that you'll have to settle for a lesser degree of automation than your situation really requires.

11

Queueing: Key Element in Excellent Customer Service

The customer service department is the front line of your company, and the ease or difficulty customers experience in getting through to or accessing your department, even before you start servicing their needs, can be a major determinant in the way they regard you and the degree to which they do business with you, if they do it at all.

Is your company perceived as easy to reach and easy to do business with? As a customer service manager, you should be familiar with the function known as queueing, which is almost always involved in the delivery or performance of customer service. Queues can be visible or invisible. They can involve people or objects, tasks or functions. They can involve actual physical queueing or electronic sequencing. They can be fixed or flexible. They can be single or multiple, single-purpose or multipurpose. Examples include:

■ *People in queue.* This kind of queue is the most common. People stand in line to buy airline tickets, to check out their purchases at the supermarket, to receive services in a clinic, to exit a parking lot, and so forth. In a well-engineered queue, people stand in a single line and are directed to the next available service giver. This practice is followed by many banks and airlines, but it's seldom found in supermarket checkout, where it would normally be less efficient in existing store layouts. The Kroger Co. has been experimenting with a variation, however, that separates the scanning/bagging functions from the cashier function. And many markets have express checkout lines of different kinds.

These are all examples of *physical* queues. In most of them, people actually form a queue, although in some instances they sign in and are called by name in order of signing in, or in others they take a numbered check in order to be called in turn.

■ *Objects in queue.* A common example is sequencing orders in the warehouse so that all orders for the same items, or with a common destination, or using a

173

particular delivery service, are queued separately from other orders. A variation on this is to queue orders by pick zone, or to queue small orders separately from large orders, or to queue heavy shipments for truckloading ahead of light shipments in order to maximize cube-density factors in the truck and also to avoid crushing the lighter weight freight. Another example is queueing of trucks to make deliveries to a warehouse or receiving dock with a limited number of doors. A similar situation exists with shipments. At one company, all shipments are made through a single dock door for security reasons, and a queue of trucks is maintained in a nearby holding area so that loading can be carried on continuously throughout the day. This particular company also queues shipments in reverse order of delivery, that is, last order first, to speed up and facilitate delivery and unloading.

▪ *Tasks or functions in queue.* This queue usually involves dispatching field service personnel, pickup and delivery trucks, or taxicabs. Dispatch is sometimes based on a first come, first served rule, but for practical reasons it's more likely to be based on zones, distance, and general economics. For example, if Caller 3, Caller 7, and Caller 11 are located closer together than Caller 1 and Caller 2, they're likely to get their shipments picked up before Caller 1 and Caller 2. Similarly, each member of a company's field service group may have their assignments for the day queued up in the most economic sequence from a mileage or proximity viewpoint.

▪ *Electronic queues.* Call sequencers and ACD systems are the most familiar forms of electronic sequencing, and as discussed in Chapter 10 there are numerous variations.

Some electronic queues have a key account override, which automatically places calls from designated accounts at the head of the queue, regardless of how many other calls are already in that queue. Electronic queues are also involved in accessing a mainframe or database. Although in some instances the queue may not be discernible to the user, in some customer service applications the cumulative delay for all terminals may be significant.

Electronic queues are basically invisible, although it's possible to use an announce-only feature to inform callers how long they'll have to wait and to give them the option of leaving word for a callback.

▪ *Interdepartmental queueing.* A common problem facing customer service departments occurs when their requests for information or action are delayed by being held in queue at credit, engineering, production planning, traffic, and other departments. This delay is usually the result of a lack of accountability in the form of interdepartmental standards setting time limits on how long inquiries and requests for action can be held up in other departments. These problems, along with suggestions for overcoming the "forever in queue" syndrome that so many customer service managers and their staffs have to cope with, were discussed in Chapter 7.

Postponement and the Economics of Queueing

Queueing exists out of simple economic necessity and represents a practical way of dealing with an uneven workload and fluctuations in demand for the services of your personnel. Although it's desirable to provide a fast response to incoming calls, for example, in a typical customer service operation, it's virtually impossible to respond immediately during peak calling periods as illustrated by the following case history:

The management of a large direct marketing company with some 250 customer service reps handling phone calls asked its telecommunications engineers to calculate the cost, including hardware, software, and staffing, of a system where it would be possible to answer every inbound call, whenever it might occur, on the second ring. With the existing system, reps were handling 95 percent of the calls by the second ring, but management was anxious to improve the service level to 100 percent.

After studying historic call patterns over a typical period, the engineers came to the conclusion that, while it would be theoretically possible to install and staff a system enabling the desired levels of response, it would be prohibitively expensive—more than twice as costly as the present system. Management realized that if it attempted such a system, those additional costs would have to be passed along to customers. They knew that customers would not accept higher prices just for the sake of marginal improvements in response, which roughly 95 percent of customers wouldn't be aware of in any event, and would not normally object to brief holds in queue during peak calling times.

In effect, this company determined that it was more economical to actually *postpone* responding to calls than to attempt to handle all calls as they came in. In this kind of situation, postponement takes two main forms:

1. *Let the phone ring longer.* When personnel aren't available when the phone rings, letting it ring four times (or more) before responding either live or mechanically postpones placing the call in queue and in some instances may even avoid it altogether.
2. *Place the call in queue.* At the designated number of rings, if there's no live response, the call is automatically answered mechanically and placed in queue.

The principle involved is simply that peaks of phone activity will be followed by valleys, and postponing live response for an acceptable period of time is an effective way of evening out the workload without adding the cost of increased staffing.

A third form of postponement, which in some situations may be preferable to lengthy or slow-moving queues, is busy signals. While callers will not tolerate continuous busy signals over an extended period, a significant number prefer a busy signal to either being put on hold or leaving a callback message.

Many ACD systems forecast staffing requirements in increments as small as 15 minutes, but few companies can afford to have people on standby unless they are performing other, lower priority tasks that can themselves be postponed. Thus the cushion afforded by a queue is usually the most economical way to deal with short-term workload fluctuations.

This principle holds in banks, supermarkets, and similar businesses where there are practical limits on the number of service givers and workstations or checkout stands. At peak periods, the lines get longer, and patrons can elect to either wait in line a little longer or leave and return at a less busy time.

You are probably thinking, as you read this, of the tendency of store managers to close checkout stands during off-peak periods, so that queues are just as long, and sometimes even slower, as during peak periods. This practice reflects poor planning on the manager's part; by reducing incentives to shop during off-peak periods, the practice also encourages customers to make their smaller or fill-in purchases at convenience stores where such delays are seldom encountered. It's also a reminder that in your own operations you can never afford to let short-term savings overshadow or compromise your easy-to-buy from mission. Note, too, that slow-moving queues in retail stores require larger parking lots to accommodate all those patrons in queue.

Queueing and Unit Costs

Let's assume that it's your department and you want those phones to be answered on the second ring at all times, without queueing. This increase is approximately 5 percent over current service levels, and we already know from the previous example that your costs will at least double.

If yours is a typical customer service operation, your unit cost—the fully distributed cost, including personnel, equipment, line charges, overhead, supplies, and miscellaneous costs—is about $5 per call handled live. If you bring your response rate to the 100 percent level, your unit cost per call will be $10. At this point, you will probably decide that your 95 percent level is just fine. In fact, you might even decide to lengthen the queue slightly and cut that cost per call to $4!

But bear in mind the *optimum queue*, which represents the amount of time most callers will wait before becoming irritated and hanging up. This optimum varies from situation to situation, as well as with the expectations or needs of the individuals. Callers who would become irritated after a 2-minute hold on a call to a supplier would be delighted to call their local department of motor vehicles and only have to wait five times as long!

Engineering Aspects of Customer Service Queues

In business engineering, the term *queueing* refers to the way activities are sequenced in order to maintain the highest levels of productivity of personnel and equipment consistent with service levels. *Queueing theory* is simply the application of mathematical formulas to answer questions such as these:

▪ How many phone lines and how many staffers do we need in order to provide an acceptable level of telephone response, given the number of calls we expect to be receiving next year at this time?

▪ How many active checkstands do we need to ensure that no line has more than five people in it and no person in line has to wait more than 10 minutes before being served?

■ How many service positions and food placements do we need in our cafeteria, and how many cashiers, to ensure that nobody spends more than 10 minutes in line, and (this one is more complicated!) how many tables do we need in the cafeteria to ensure that no one will ever have to wait more than one minute for a table and also so that at meal times there will never be more than five empty tables at one time?

The answers to these and similar questions can be found through the use of the *queueing tables* used by industrial engineers in planning workflow and processes of various kinds in manufacturing plants, warehouses, stores, offices, schools, research labs — any environment where people perform activities that require sequencing. Much of this sequencing can now be done by computer, but as manager you need to be conversant with the overall approach, although you shouldn't have to get involved in the actual engineering process. Give your industrial engineers the data they need, and let them massage the numbers and come up with the answers that reflect the combination of service level and cost that best meets your needs. But remember: as customer service manager, it's up to you to spell out your requirements in very specific detail.

Defining Queue Requirements

Here are some details to consider when you approach the queueing issue in customer service, not only in telephone call sequencing but in workload planning generally:

■ *Workload.* Workload is the number of events that occur and require service within a stated period of time. It includes telephone calls, letters and fax messages, inquiries, credits, deductions, complaints, and other transactions for which handling time standards have been established. If you don't have time standards, your engineers can help you develop them.
The workload must be defined not only in the number of occurrences but also in terms of the time required to service each occurrence (that's where time standards come in) and the average frequency per time unit.

■ *Available capacity.* Available capacity usually refers to the number of staff members who are on hand to service the workload and the equipment they have available to work with. If you are still estimating staffing requirements, you need to define the acceptable level of service in terms of time: the maximum amount of time a person or occurrence is allowed to wait in queue before servicing.

■ *Sequence in the queue.* It's necessary to determine which of the following three sequencing methods will be applied to persons or occurrences in the queue:

1. *FIFO.* First in, first out is generally the most acceptable form of queueing where people actually stand in line or wait for the kind of service provided in a restaurant, store, or similar situation. FIFO may also be applied to storage situations where flow racks are charged from the back and picked from the front.

2. *LIFO.* Last in, first out is used mainly in storage situations, loading of transportation equipment, and the like. LIFO can also be applied to handling non-time-sensitive documents or tasks.
3. *FILO.* First in, last out is the reciprocal of LIFO and it is typified by the truck trailer that is loaded in reverse sequence of stops to deliver orders.

▪ *Exceptions.* Normally, customers in a queue will be served on a FIFO basis. Will you vary this and provide for exceptions? Some examples: airline passengers scheduled on a soon-to-depart flight are allowed to move to the head of the line at the ticket counter; calls from key customers are automatically jumped to the head of the queue, or transferred to a customer service representative assigned to that account. Be sure to consider all the different types of situations that you might want to handle on an exceptions basis. But remember, too, that the more exceptions you have to handle, the more costly your operations overall.

▪ *Division of labor and distribution of workload.* "Division of labor" refers to assigning different tasks to different workers, for example, some individuals handling orders only, others handling inquiries only, others handling deductions only, and so forth. This system can be efficient in a high-volume operation, but it may require a customer to get into several queues, which can be a time-consuming and frustrating experience. Division of labor also presents somewhat more complex staffing problems than the typical next-available-rep configuration.

"Distribution of workload" refers to the system of assigning work so that all personnel have the same amount of work to do. On a standard ACD system, the system does this automatically by routing any given call to the rep who has been off the phone the longest. But, as specialties develop it becomes necessary to staff functions in greater or lesser depth, according to the rate at which the specialized transactions are presented and the speed at which they can be completed.

For example, if transaction type A takes 12 minutes to complete and occurs at the rate of ten per hour, it would normally require twice as much staffing as transaction type B, which takes 6 minutes to complete and occurs at the same rate, ten per hour. Or, if transaction type C takes 12 minutes to complete but only occurs at the rate of five per hour, it would usually require the same staffing as transaction type B occurring at twice the rate but only requiring half the time to complete. These are relatively simple principles, but they are often difficult to apply in actual practice because of workload fluctuations and other variables.

▪ *The most efficient queues.* These are queues where the range of transactions is very narrow and virtually everyone in the queue is calling or presenting himself for the same purpose: making a hotel or airline reservation, checking a balance or paying a bill, placing catalog orders or inquiring about order status over the telephone. Most of the capability for performing the actual transactions resides in the computer, and training personnel to initiate those transactions is relatively easy. Fluctuations in workload can often be adjusted for by a combination of flextime, overtime, and part-time staff. Fair and accurate measures of productivity and quality can be applied against uniform standards, and high levels of productivity are usually experienced. The company can establish and maintain any desired level of service that it's willing to pay for.

▪ *The least efficient queues.* These typically involve mixed transactions, for example handling routine orders along with inquiries or complaints requiring extensive research. A familiar example is a sales clerk who is expected to answer the telephone while waiting on customers at a sales counter, or a hotel front desk clerk who must answer the phone and solve guest problems while checking in new arrivals. Another example is the multistage queue where customers have to go to different workstations or departments to perform different transactions. While these may be efficient from a manpower utilization viewpoint, they are usually anything but in terms of customer convenience.

▪ *Benchmarking pros and cons.* Standards for a company's queueing practices should reflect the firm's best estimate, preferably supported by research, of the levels of service it must give customers in order to maintain and/or increase market share and profitability. Basing standards on benchmarking, that is, on standards used by other companies in the same industry, is only valid when all conditions are identical among the companies—and they almost never are. While benchmarking seems like an easy way to set standards for queues and other customer service activities, in actual fact it can be risky and expensive.

Optimizing the Queue: Basic Marketing Strategy

The ideal queue doesn't exist or, it's the absence of any queue at all. The *optimum* queue, on the other hand, is economic from the company's point of view and acceptable from the customer's, at least to the extent that it is not perceived as a significant inconvenience or impediment to doing business with the company. Indeed, some queues may be so well designed that customers don't even realize they are in queue. The use of properly worded "announcements on hold" telling customers what information will be needed to service their calls, or providing technical or applications information, may be perceived as an information service rather than as a queueing device.

Intentionally or otherwise, your queueing methods can have a big impact on your company's marketing results because of the way queueing influences customers' perceptions of your company and the attitudes they develop toward it: fast service and brief holds or short, fast-moving queues are equated with concern for customers and an action orientation. If reps are supported by good management information systems with ready access to databases, they can handle most transactions without delays or callbacks. This not only enhances the image of your company, but also makes it easier to deal with than the competition is—and easier to give more business to, or designate as a sole source supplier.

By contrast, customers perceive slow response and lengthy holds as indifference to their needs and lack of appreciation for their business. Indeed, customers usually cite lengthy holds as the most irritating aspect of their vendor contacts. And music played during holds usually increases their irritation.

Beyond that, holds are very costly to companies using toll-free numbers because they are paying for hours of dead time on their systems and in many instances are blocking calls from customers wishing to place orders. And customers who are already having trouble reaching your company are hardly inclined to increase the volume of their business and have to deal with you—or attempt to deal with you—that much more frequently!

It's difficult but not impossible to calculate the potential loss of business caused by excessive holds. If the product or service is generic, excessive holds will lead the caller to abandon the call and contact another vendor. One company found that 43 percent of callers who phoned to place orders and found their calls blocked did not call back but actually took their business elsewhere. Since the company knew the size of the average order, it readily calculated that it was losing $43 for every $100 of business that would have been placed. The total amount involved was staggering, and the company quickly made major improvements in its system and way of handling calls. The new system cost well into the hundreds of thousands of dollars but paid for itself (in business captured rather than lost) in barely 6 months.

The most suitable queue balances economics with marketing considerations, that is, it balances reasonable cost with the level of service that makes it easier for customers to deal and continue to deal with your company than to turn to a competitor. Even though your company may have a virtual monopoly on a particular service or product, ignoring the importance of creating an easy-to-do-business-with climate can have very costly consequences.

A New York State manufacturer widely known for the quality of its products had such a monopoly for its top-of-the-line products. It paid little attention to customer service niceties, knowing that customers had no place else to go for these particular items. What it overlooked was that its other products had plenty of competition. Competitors offering better service ultimately skimmed most of this profitable secondary business away form the manufacturer by offering competitive pricing and better service. The manufacturer was forced to cut its work force by more than one-half and was left with empty buildings and only its top-of-the-line business, which was barely enough to pay the rent and the remaining work force.

The easy-to-do-business-with theme should be present throughout your company's marketing effort. And the queueing issue is an excellent place to start. The three main steps in queue optimization that you should be considering for incorporation into your marketing strategy are discussed next.

Optimization Step 1: The Exceptions Approach

Optimization doesn't necessarily mean making the queue as short as possible but rather as acceptable to as many customers as possible and then handling customers to whom it's unacceptable on an exceptions basis. This is another example of what's known as working with the percentages, or designing customer service strategies on the premise that if a sufficient proportion of customers conform to a policy or other requirement, the nonconformists can be handled the way they want to be handled.

For example, a St. Louis company offers customers in queue the option of leaving their orders on a recorder when all other lines are in use. Not all customers exercise that option, but those who do help shorten the waiting time of those who prefer to wait in queue to give their orders to a human being rather than to a machine. A Dallas bank gives depositors an incentive to make routine inquiries to an automated answering system. Not all depositors use this alternative for their routine calls about balances, checks cleared, and so forth, but enough do so that those who prefer live calling can get through with little if any delay.

Another way to handle exceptions is through separate queues for different kinds of transactions. For example, a large supermarket dedicates two of its checkout lanes to customers with orders of fifteen or fewer items, another to customers with orders of nine or fewer items paying in cash only. Similarly, industries have special lines for orders for only one or two line items or for critical parts requiring same-day shipment. A Midwestern direct marketer of office supplies has installed an interactive system that directs callers ordering two items or less to "punch 2," which connects them to a third-party fulfillment organization and frees their own personnel to respond more quickly to larger, more complex, and more profitable orders in the queue.

Some of the exceptions you should consider when planning queueing in customer service operations include:

• *Major accounts.* Increasingly, companies are moving toward special numbers and sometimes even dedicated phone lines enabling top accounts to bypass any calls in queue and go directly to an account manager or representative. American Airlines has special phone numbers for its Admirals' Club and AAdvantage Gold members, as do some other airlines, car rental companies, and hotels. Companies using automatic number identification (ANI) can program their call handling system so that calls from key customers are automatically "jumped" to the head of the queue. Using ANI for this purpose is also discussed in Chapter 10.

• *Emergencies.* Most electric utilities have emergency numbers for reporting lines down and life-and-death situations or service problems involving persons on life-support systems. Similarly it may be desirable to have hotlines for reporting hazardous spills or for ordering emergency supplies in the wake of natural disasters. A company selling to health care providers may provide one number for wholesale and retail drug companies placing stock orders and another for hospitals calling in emergency orders.

• *Product lines and/or applications.* In a diversified company with a variety of products or applications, it is often desirable to furnish different numbers for the different lines or uses. A company such as Clairol, for example, furnishes a toll-free number for consumers seeking advice on product use and a different number for wholesalers and retail chains ordering the product for resale. A railroad that serves the automotive industry, textile manufacturers, and chemical producers provides separate numbers for each to use. Of course it does not provide separate numbers for every type of business it serves; lower-volume customers are probably handled through a general or regional queue.

• *Specialization and service giver skill levels.* In some industries—software is a notable example—the customer service department may involve as many as five or six different skill levels, and it's very important that calls be routed to the appropriate skill level and no higher or lower. Many companies separate order entry or its equivalent in service companies from other customer service functions. In the American Airlines AAdvantage Gold program, there are two levels of service givers: those who handle routine inquiries about programs or mileage and make reservations for members and those who are empowered to make adjustments.

Normally, this type of organization will be staffed in pyramidal fashion: the largest number of staff will be at the bottom of the pyramid handling routine calls and transactions, with successively smaller groups as calls become more complex and time consuming. The actual staffing numbers are determined by the volume of calls per skill level, an arrangement that minimizes the amount of time any one caller has to wait in queue before having her particular need taken care of.

   ▪ *Special situations or conditions.* A common example of this exception is the issue of jobsite or timed deliveries. A typical jobsite delivery usually involves heavy equipment or machinery and often requires that the customer have special crews of riggers, electricians, or other tradespeople on hand to receive and install the equipment—at very high pay rates. It is critical that the vendor's customer service people be immediately accessible so that any problems or delays that arise can be taken care of immediately. Note that in this example, it's also critical that customers be immediately accessible so that they can be notified of delivery delays in time to reschedule work crews without incurring excessive standby costs.

   ▪ *Special customer groups and different customer skill/sophistication levels.* A Dallas bank makes special provision for handling calls from senior citizens who don't like talking to machines and who often have substantial sums on deposit. Similarly, many public utilities and government agencies have special numbers for Spanish-language callers. Some companies have multi-lingual interactive systems where the caller can select which language to be informed in. For instance, the Los Angeles International Airport information system has four languages available at this juncture—English, Spanish, Japanese, and Korean—and plans for six more to be added shortly. The automated telecommunications system (IVR) for each language has its own number, which is promoted to that particular public, and uses a menu-selection approach to provide information on traffic, parking, ground transportation, and the like. Although the menu-selection process takes longer than a live attendant, the cost of any added lines that may be incurred is more than offset by direct labor savings.

   A New Jersey company allows sales reps and designated customers to access its mainframe computer for entering orders, querying product availability, or determining status on orders already entered. Since skill levels vary significantly among the individuals actually calling the computer (via touchtone telephone), callers are offered a choice between a "short form" and a "long form" access mode, enabling the more experienced and sophisticated users to get on and off the line faster, which in turn frees up more access time for those who take longer.

   Many database services, such as Compuserve, which are available on a subscription basis, offer their subscribers similar options so that frequent users can bypass menus and instructions and go directly to specific databases, which in some cases produce higher revenue per minute than regular connect charges. The option may also enable the service to handle more customers overall, thus increasing revenues without having to add lines to shorten queues to an acceptable length.

The underlying principle in all these examples is that if 80 to 90 percent of customers will accept the constraints of a given queueing system, the other 10 to 20 percent can be handled on an exceptions basis. This system is far more economical than attempting to devise a system that will be acceptable to everybody.

It is rarely practical or necessary to offer equal service to all customers under all circumstances, but two conditions must be met when making exceptions to your queueing practices:

1. *Rules for making exceptions should be clear and reasonable.* The usual way of making exceptions is on the basis of account size combined with the severity of the incident or the potential consequences if action on an exceptions basis is *not* taken. Most front-line service givers and their managers are highly motivated to provide equal service to all customers, but in many situations such an approach can be extremely counterproductive.

It's often necessary for managers to reeducate themselves and their personnel in this respect, and the best way to do so is through a system of decision rules that classifies customers by account value or criticality and instructs the service giver when to make exceptions and handle the customer ahead of others in the queue.

The airline that gives precedence to passengers in queue whose flight is due to leave shortly can apply a simple rule: If there are lines at ticket counters within *x* minutes of scheduled departure time, the agent simply announces that anybody standing in line for that flight should move to front of the line. Yet the airline can't overdo it; in one instance a passenger who was waiting in line to purchase a ticket for a flight later in the week was jumped three times in this fashion. Most airlines now alleviate the situation by providing gate check-in for passengers who have carry-on baggage only.

Clear decision rules are also a far more practical way of handling exceptions than the conventional squeaky wheel measure whereby the customer who makes the most noise gets the most attention. Front-line personnel and managers should recognize that the function of decision rules is to ensure that accounts are handled commensurately with their value to the company. It's not a question of "discriminating against the little guy" but rather one of keeping the company in business by providing adequate levels of service to customers the company can't afford to lose.

Of course, it is clearly illegal to discriminate against customers on racial, ethnic, or religious grounds, and it is particularly important that service givers who deal directly with consumers understand the potential consequences of doing so. Here again, clear decision rules are essential. In all instances, service givers must understand that appearance, language, manners, and educational level or perceived status can't be permitted to influence judgments about when to and when not to make exceptions in either business or consumer environments.

2. *Allowing out-of-queue exceptions should not significantly impede service to customers remaining in queue.* In the ideal situation, persons already in queue are not aware that the queue has been bypassed. As long as the delay is not

significant and the caller is not aware of being bypassed, this method of handling exceptions is practical and economic. Of course it's only practical with electronic queueing where the queue itself is not visible to the customer. If bypassing happens often enough to significantly lengthen hold or wait time, serious consequences are almost certain to arise:

- Customers annoyed at waiting so long will waste precious talk time complaining about the long wait, which requires some type of response by the service giver. The time consumed in this ritual will further delay responses to callers behind them in the queue, and the situation will repeat and compound itself with each successive customer in the queue.
- If upgrading service to a few customers results in significant (and visible) downgrading of service to customers remaining in queue, more dissatisfaction will result, more and more exceptions will have to be made, and very soon exceptions themselves will have to be queued.

Optimization Step 2: The Redesign Approach

The redesign starts with identifying the bad queues in the customer service system and then taking steps to improve them. This process is likely to involve procedural changes, which are not always easy to sell within the organization, even to the people who will benefit the most from them.

An everyday example of a bad queue occurs in a department store where cashiers are required to handle time-consuming returns and exchanges along with conventional purchase transactions. The problem can be alleviated by streamlining the returns procedure so that it doesn't take any longer than a regular purchase transaction, which many organizations are reluctant to do, or by setting up a separate queue for returns and exchanges, which may not be cost-effective, or if it is cost-effective is usually understaffed and an annoyance to customers. Some department stores compound the problem by requiring service givers to handle phone calls as well as customers present in person and, typically, the phone call gets precedence.

Another solution to the mixed-queue problem practiced by some department stores is to have enough cashiers available so that no customer has to wait more than x minutes or that no line have more than y customers in it, regardless of the transaction.

By contrast, a do-it-yourself hardware chain on the West Coast was observed to have about ten checkout lines for regular purchases but only one for returns and adjustments, and that particular line had about twenty individuals in queue compared to about five at each of the ten regular checkstands. This chain's management appears not to recognize that, because the respective queues are highly visible to all customers, it is creating a perception that it discourages returns and exchanges. This perception is likely to divert some customers, particularly those in the adjustments queue, to other sources. A better solution, for this example, would be to dedicate a second checkout lane to returns and exchanges, reducing the returns queue by one-half and lengthening the regular checkout queues by no more than one person each.

Some divisions of labor can also cause bad queues. For example, a Florida citrus organization rotates the responsibility for handling complaints on a daily basis: Rep A on Monday, Rep B on Tuesday, and so forth. This practice creates several problems. The first is that complaint handling is branded as an undesirable chore, like KP in the army, and other reps are reluctant to pitch in and help Rep A when it is his day for handling complaints, regardless of how many may come in. The second problem grows out of the first. Customers who call with complaints feel that they're being downgraded when their calls are transferred to the "complaint-handler of the day," and in fact they may be placed in queue for relatively long periods of time, which further intensifies the perception of being downgraded.

A variation of this practice, which is likely to cause resentment, is to have a disproportionate number of lines available for entering orders and relatively few available for customer service calls inquiring about orders already placed. Some companies do this by having a toll-free number for orders but a separate, non-toll-free number for inquiries. Having a non-toll-free number will take care of the queueing problem on inquiries by discouraging calls, but it is also likely to discourage future business. However, it is probably preferable to a toll-free number where customers have great difficulty getting through at all. One practical solution to this problem is to offer both a toll-free and a non-toll-free number for customer service. Some customers prefer paying for the call to waiting in queue, which in turn reduces the number of callers in queue on toll-free lines. Yet another option is to make 900-numbers available for customers who truly don't want to wait and are willing to pay several dollars per minute of connect time. This is coming into use in customer service departments responsible for software support and has been well received by customers. Some companies have even had to add personnel to handle the added call load!

The following are some additional bad queue situations found in typical customer service operations, along with suggestions for remedying them:

- *Wrong queue.* A wrong queue occurs when customers are held in queue for a period of time, only to find that they have been connected to the wrong person or department. This error may require their entering a second queue and experiencing further delays in reaching the right person. Wrong-queue calls usually result from one of two causes: (1) the customer calls the wrong number to begin with, for example, calls the number for technical support instead of the number for technical applications, or the number for customer service instead of the number for placing orders; or (2) the switchboard connects the customer to the wrong number.

The wrong queue condition can often be corrected by giving printed who-to-call directories to customers, to other departments, and to switchboard operators. Many companies issue directories containing photographs and direct phone numbers of contact personnel, along with descriptions of their responsibilities.

Rodale Press in Pennsylvania issues a subject directory, so that if a customer calls and doesn't know which department she wants to talk to, the operator can look up the subject of the call alphabetically. Looking up "Aqua-culture," for example, indicates that the call should be given to the research department at the extension listed. Other subjects are similarly cross-referenced to the appropriate departments and extensions, and in some cases specific individuals. Rodale goes one step further and issues a departmental directory showing each department's responsibilities and, as a final touch, a list of items that each department does *not* handle. This latter feature minimizes the practice common in many companies of dumping "unknown" calls into the customer service department.

A Chicago company, which issues updated phone directories quarterly, includes a subject index with each directory. The directory lists which plants manufacture which products, who has pricing responsibility, changes in personnel, and so forth. Because the index, which is arranged by subject, is stapled into the phone directory so that it can't be overlooked, very few calls are misdirected. New and inexperienced personnel at the switchboard or elsewhere in the organization can use the subject index to locate the proper person or department in the directory.

▪ *Unacceptable delays that occur in answering customer inquiries.* In this bad-queue situation, the movement of the queue is slowed by the inadequacy or slowness of the information system, slow responses from other departments (when a customer is put on hold so that the rep can call another department), or simply the complexity of the question and the limited ability of the individual rep to answer it.

The question of interdepartmental response is discussed under Protocol delays. There are several ways of dealing with the overall problem of delayed response.

One way that is being used increasingly in software support is to store questions in the computer when all support personnel are engaged. When they are free they can review the problem and in many cases arrive at a solution before calling the customer back. This reduces hold time and at the same time speeds up the movement of the queue. This approach also enables questions to be answered by reps with the appropriate skills and avoids the problem of multiple transfers, which are expensive in both line charges and labor costs. It also saves the customer the annoyance of having to repeat the details of her inquiry to several different people.

Another solution coming into widespread use is automated response systems geared to the most frequently asked questions. The interactive systems used by banks and investment services often handle as many as 50 percent of all inquiries at about 10 percent of the cost of attended systems. Equally important, they give standard, accurate information and they free up lines with human attendants to handle the more complex questions sooner with faster movement of the queue. Here again, handling complex questions off-line and then calling back is often the preferable solution.

It's often necessary to prioritize and reprioritize as calls come in. For example, one computer company applies callback standards such as the following when calls come in from customers or from its own field engineers working at customer sites:

Situation	Call Back Within
When the system is completely down	30 minutes or less*
When the system is partially operable	1 hour
No problem; customer has a "how to" question	Same day
On-site field engineer needs help	30 minutes or less*

*Handle on-line whenever possible

The most practical solution to those queueing problems involving long and slow-moving queues is to adopt some form of customer participative interactive system, usually involving automation. Just as some retailers are testing customer-operated scanning stations for totaling their shopping bills to reduce visible queues, interactive telephone systems are being used to reduce lengthy phone queues.

Although the most widely used interactive systems are relatively simple and user-friendly and present no problems to teens and preteens who have grown up in a computer environment, an increasing number of much more advanced systems are being put into daily use. For example, Southern Pacific Company has an interactive voice response system for answering employee calls about work schedules. The system handles up to twenty simultaneous inquiries using concatenated speech, which splices together prerecorded words, numbers, and names in order to form sentences. The system contains recorded (and properly pronounced) names of some 9,000 Southern Pacific employees who call in to secure their assignments based on a complex system of seniority, work rules, job bidding, and more. What's notable in a system such as this is not so much the technology itself but rather the user-friendliness, the ability to handle many calls simultaneously with a single automated "agent," and the way it can speed up response to individual inquiries, speed up that particular queue, and at the same time allow more personnel to be assigned to lines requiring human response.

Some companies have similar systems for employees contacting their human resources departments for information about insurance, vacations, and other benefits. By handling routine calls the system shortens queues requiring personalized response and at the same time ensures that responses are accurate and consistent. A bank in Honolulu has a similar system that responds in English or Japanese, as the caller elects.

The more sophisticated automated response systems—including systems that "learn" correct responses through use—are found primarily in captive situations such as those described above or occasionally in more sophisticated customer groups, but there's no question that they will be widely used within a short time.

■ *Protocol delays.* Where response delays occur because inquiries must be referred to other departments, the best solution is to adopt internal or interdepartmental response standards as discussed in Chapter 7. This isn't always possible, however, and an alternative solution may be to seek expanded authority to access other departments' databases or on-line services.

For example, customer service reps at a New Jersey producer of bulk products frequently received calls from customers asking for location, arrival, and switching data on rail hopper cars of product en route to them. To secure this information, reps often had to place customers on hold and then attempt to reach their own traffic department, where they often had to wait for excessive periods because tracing and expediting personnel were already tied up or had other priorities.

Recognizing that he would have little success trying to impose a response standard on the department, the customer service manager did the next best thing: He secured approval to gain on-line access to the same car location reporting system used by the traffic department to obtain car passing reports, by car number, of the specific shipments being inquired about by customers. Thus it became possible to give customers fast answers on-line and, equally important, to quickly spot situations requiring expediting in order to avoid a customer's having to shut down a plant because of late product arrival.

A similar situation occurred in a California company manufacturing materials handling and packaging accessories. Many of its calls were from customers requesting pro numbers of shipments that had been made to them, numbers that were historically assigned by the carrier at the time of pickup. This information required calls to the traffic department with the customer on hold, and of course lengthened and delayed the queue when the information had to be searched out by traffic personnel.

Working with the traffic department, the customer service manager persuaded the carrier to furnish pro numbers in advance, as well as transit times between the manufacturer's location and principal customer sites, which not only eliminated the delay in handling inquiries but in many cases eliminated the calls altogether because the customer service rep could provide the pro number, shipping date, and transit time at the same time the customer called in the order.

▪ *Excessive holds.* Excessive holds may be caused by customers who: (1) prefer to be placed on hold rather than wait for a callback or (2) weren't given the option in the first place. This problem can be dealt with in several ways. The first way is obviously to offer the callback alternative via a voicemail-type interactive system. The second way is to make it the *only* alternative, that is, use a voice-activated interactive system to tell customers they will be called back, and ask them via prompts to leave specific information so that the research on their inquiry can be done off-line before the callback, thus minimizing actual time on-line.

A third way of dealing with the problem is for the customer service rep to make a judgment on how long the customer will be on hold and offer the hold-or-callback option to shorter-hold customers while telling longer-hold customers that they will be called back at a specified time. Whenever possible, of course, the customer should be given the option of being placed on hold or being called back, but when the volume of calls is high, the callback route may be the only alternative.

One other plus for callbacks: Where different lines are used for inbound versus outbound calls, transferring some of the workload to the outbound lines can reduce congestion on the inbound lines and at the same time provide better overall service. But it's essential that callbacks be made within a specified time that's acceptable to customers, and provision should be made for an alternative contact when the callback is made and the original caller isn't available.

Many companies call customers by appointment on a weekly basis to receive their orders and document any problems or inquiries. Their understanding with customers is that they call back immediately on high-priority issues and report back on others when they make their regular call the following week. Some customers are called several times a week.

Outbound as well as inbound calls may be automated. Although some of these, such as autodialed sales pitches, may be objectionable to a good many people, there are a number of legitimate applications: notifying customers when a delivery will be made, informing loan applicants that their loans have been approved (but use human beings for rejections!), and virtually any situation where a two-way dialogue is not necessary.

▪ *Uneven call mix.* In this typical situation, some calls are inherently much longer than others but all are lumped together in the same queue. Much of the problem can be eliminated by having different lines for different purposes, using alternative means such as facsimile, and arranging for callbacks on more complex matters.

Incentives for handling more calls in a given time period are usually *not* a solution. What happens is that reps often develop an "It only counts if it's counted" attitude and pay little attention to the quality of their treatment of calls. One company offered a cash incentive for calls above a certain number, and found that some reps were able to increase productivity by as much as 30 percent, but the quality and accuracy of those reps' transactions took a nosedive, and their curtness on the phone alienated more than a few customers. However, in some situations incentive points are awarded on the basis of the types of calls handled rather than the actual number, with more complex and sensitive calls receiving a higher number of points. These are an acceptable means of increasing productivity without compromising quality, but they are not easy to administer.

▪ *Uneven call patterns.* Normally, the length of the queue varies with the time of day as well as the day of the week and month. Some of this variation is the result of salespeople's incentives or compensation programs, some the result of sales promotions with cutoff dates. Calls have a tendency to peak at the end of the month, but they are also likely to be heavy on Mondays and during "seasons," which vary from industry to industry. If field salespeople phone on the same lines as customers even more congestion results.

Overall, there are likely to be high levels of customer dissatisfaction during such peak periods. The following five steps will help reduce that dissatisfaction considerably:

1. *Suggest to customers that they call at less busy times.* Enough callers will accept the suggestion to reduce the workload at the busiest times. One organization sends its members a folder with a clock face for each day of the week. The busiest hours are printed in red, the moderately busy hours in amber, and the least busy in green. It's easy to tell at a glance when it's best to call.

Customer Service, Sí... Message Center, No

The customer service department should be capable of handling customer calls quickly and conveniently, but it should not be allowed to become a "message center" for customers trying to reach field salespeople and vice versa. It's an inefficient, expensive practice that adds to telephone congestion, lengthens queues, and generally interferes with rather than improves customer service.

By now most salespeople should have their own voicemail along with the response standard. This enables callers to leave messages in detail, in the exact wording they want, and without tying up customer service lines. Appropriate controls on the voicemail will ensure that the caller receives a response within a specified time.

The goal isn't to discourage customers or salespeople from calling customer service, but rather to ensure that when customers and salespeople do call on customer service business, they don't have to go into lengthy queues.

---

2. *Use flextime to extend working hours* to accommodate customers in different time zones without necessarily adding staff.

3. *Set specific times for field salespeople to call.* Choose off-peak hours when there will be minimum interference with customer calls. This request will not be well received by all personnel, but enough individuals will comply to achieve your goals of distributing the call load more evenly.

4. *Ask that you be informed well in advance of special promotions or advertising campaigns and especially new product introductions.* This request may also meet with some resistance, but failure to staff up properly in advance of such events can result in hundreds of thousands of marketing dollars lost. In an increasing number of companies it's a standing rule that promotions aren't released until the customer service manager has prepared the staff to deal with them.

5. *Be prepared to add personnel, lines, and equipment when necessary.* Sometimes there is no alternative, and too much is at stake to compromise front-line contacts with customers over an extended period.

■ *Avoidable inbound calls.* These occur for various reasons. Customers who do not understand instructions, policies, forms, or invoices often call for clarification. Software firms receive many calls from users who simply can't understand their manuals. No-confidence calls from customers require assurance that commitments will be met. Errors in pricing or discounts, dates, quantities, and other information are also likely to generate avoidable calls. Although these and the other types of unnecessary calls can't be eliminated altogether, their number can be reduced significantly by correcting the conditions that cause them. See Eliminating Unnecessary Calls in Chapter 10.

▪ *Poor scripts or standards—or none at all.* In the absence of specific guidelines on how to handle different types of calls, personnel are likely to take too long on some calls and not long enough on others. Equally serious, they're likely to provide incomplete or inaccurate information that results in additional calls from customers or, worse, occasional costly service failures caused by those same customers relying on the inaccurate information provided in the first place. In addition to causing additional expense, service failures are also likely to compound existing call-handling problems by generating additional telephone traffic.

The clear remedy for this situation, which is not uncommon, is to develop appropriate scripts and standards.

▪ *Customer service reps performing mixed functions.* If reps perform several tasks, for example, handling customer calls and researching invoice deductions, productivity in both tasks is likely to suffer. If they must leave their workstations to pull material from files, queues of inbound calls will build.

One remedy for dealing with this bad queue situation is to allow reps to sign off the phone while completing specified tasks or to allocate time at the beginning or end of the day for reps to complete pending assignments without interruption from telephone calls.

Optimization Step 3: The Perception Approach

Assuming that all the applicable steps have been taken and you're left with the irreducible minimum queueing levels within your cost constraints, you're still wondering: how acceptable are our current queueing patterns to customers?

You might be surprised to find that, in spite of all the effort you've put into minimizing waits and facilitating access to your customer service personnel, in spite of all the user-friendliness and ease of doing business you've achieved, customers still consider you difficult to deal with.

And the reason for this is that you have overlooked one very critical factor in queueing: the role of *perception*. You have concentrated on the *mechanics* of queueing, as you should, but you've neglected to sell its benefits to your customers. For example, when a customer calls your department with an inquiry, your customer service representative says to the customer, "I'm going to put you on hold while I get that information." Perhaps that sounds adequate, but consider what your competitor's customer service rep has been trained to say: "Do you mind if I put you on hold while I get that information?" and then to wait until the customer assents. Your rep *told* the customer she was being put on hold, but your competitor's rep *asked* the customer's permission and received it.

In effect, your competitor was able to get the customer to "buy in" to the hold. The two situations were the same, but the customer's perceptions were quite different because of the way the hold was introduced. Even if your competitor's rep put the customer on hold twice as long as your rep, the customer would most likely have found it more acceptable. The reason? Perception. If a customer voluntarily enters a queue, it is more acceptable and doesn't seem as long.

Perceptions of queues can be enhanced by:

▪ *Citing a benefit.* The common recording, "Please stay on the line; your call will be handled by the next available agent," implies a benefit in waiting, a nonbenefit in hanging up. If the wait is going to be lengthy, it may be necessary to have intermediate messages with different wording. Continued repetition of the original message brands you as amateurish.

▪ *Stressing the fairness of the system.* An announcement that "all calls are handled in the order received" reassures callers that the system is fair and makes the wait more acceptable.

▪ *Indicating the probable length of the wait.* A wait of known duration doesn't seem as long and isn't as stressful as a wait of indefinite duration. With modern equipment, this information can be provided to callers automatically as the length of the queue varies. Such systems are well received by customers as well as by the companies where they're installed.

▪ *Offering an alternative or option.* The availability of an interactive option is perfectly acceptable to some customers and they appreciate the opportunity to avoid a lengthy wait. Other customers appreciate the callback option, still others are perfectly happy to call back at suggested times. Those who elect to remain in queue will get better service and will be aware of it.

▪ *Providing an instructive message.* This message can be designed to alert callers to information that will be required when the call goes live, or it can be used simply to inform callers about new products or services, applications, policies, new hours, holiday closings, changes in prices or specifications, or whatever. The fact that the hold time is occupied with relevant information (not advertising as such) makes the wait seem shorter — another facet of perception. In fact, the information provided often makes the succeeding live conversation shorter, and in a few cases eliminates it altogether. In some industries, the instructive messages introducing new products or services regularly generate sales. The savings and/or additional sales revenue will often more than pay for the cost of programming this type of response.

▪ *Explaining the delay.* If it's possible to tailor your message to a specific reason for a delay in response, callers will be more patient. "We apologize for the delay; our system is currently being worked on." In such cases it's often advisable to suggest that customers call back after a specific time. Otherwise you're likely to have a full queue with little movement and increasingly irritated customers.

▪ *Giving status to the customer's call.* The manner in which the call is handled when it goes live can have a major impact on the caller's perceptions of the company. Chances are the customer is already irritated by the delay. That irritation can quickly change to anger if the rep handling the call treats it impersonally or routinely, brusquely or hurriedly. Conversely, close attention by the rep, patience, expressions of interest and concern, and an absence of haste in the rep's manner works wonders to change a negative perception into a positive one.

▪ *Thanking the customer.* The statement "Thank you for bringing this to my attention" gives immediate status to a customer's complaint and helps blunt anger and negative perceptions. Statements such as "Thank you for your patience," "Thanks for documenting the information; it really helps," or "Thanks for understanding" remind your people as well as the customer that you *do* appreciate the fact that they're calling you and not competitors.

12

The Critical Communications Role of the Customer Service Department

The customer service department has been described as the "nerve center" of the company, but to customers it's the heart and soul of the company. And as manager, you have the primary accountability for most customer communications, and you have a vested interest in those that may be controlled by others.

Your company probably has a communications department responsible for preparing advertising and public relations literature that directly affects the kinds and numbers of customer communications you must deal with in the customer service department. It is very important that you develop a cooperative working relationship with this department, for your own benefit as well as theirs. Your company also has an MIS department and a telecommunications department. Their concern is primarily with the technology and media of communications rather than with the content and objectives of those communications, but you depend on them to keep your systems up. Historically these departments have not always given high priority to customer service systems problems, so you may need to be somewhat aggressive in making sure that your needs get the attention they deserve as part of that priceless nerve center of the company.

As you read this chapter, keep in mind that communication is such an integral part of customer service that aspects of it are actually mentioned throughout this book. This chapter in particular examines and assesses communications with customers via two critical measures:

1. *Quality.* Do all communications, in whatever media, reflect the quality image the organization wishes to convey? Is the organization perceived as it wants to be perceived?
2. *Efficiency/Effectiveness.* Given the nature of the company and its market, do all communications represent the most efficient way of giving, obtaining,

or exchanging information? Are these communications getting the desired result?

Inbound Customer Communications

Communications with customers typically represent 60 to 80 percent of a company's inbound communications in the form of orders, inquiries, and related communications. As noted earlier, these usually employ electronic media, and the telephone, which dominated such communications from 1975 to 1989, began by 1990 to be replaced in many applications by fax, remote terminals, electronic data interchange (EDI), and interactive systems of different types.

But electronic media of one kind or another continue to dominate inbound communications and far outnumber other types of contacts. Although there are occasional face-to-face contacts between CSRs and customers, either in the field or at company sites, the general ratio here is one face-to-face contact to about every 15,000-plus electronic contacts.

Similarly, written communications from customers are relatively rare except in a few specialized industries or in situations where original hard copies are required. The growth of facsimile has brought about somewhat of a resurgence in hard-copy communications from customers, but in reality a fax message is much closer to a phone call as a communications medium than it is to a traditional hard-copy letter.

Because inbound communications are so concentrated in electronic media, they are relatively easy to monitor and measure in the different ways discussed in earlier chapters. You will certainly want to take every advantage of the data that the system generates on call traffic and call-handling productivity, as well as supervisory observation of the quality of the call-handling process.

Outbound Customer Communications

Outbound customer communications are much more diverse and subtle than inbound and are likely to include a much higher proportion of hard copy than inbound communications, sometimes as much as 80 percent hard copy to 20 percent electronic communications. This hard copy includes invoices, correspondence, form letters, instruction books, catalogs, and product sheets as well as company literature in general, videotapes, and advertising or public relations materials.

In sheer quantity, outbound communications to customers are likely to outnumber inbound communications *from* customers on the order of hundreds of thousands to one, particularly in consumer markets. For example, one major consumer products company has a customer base of 40 million households that regularly receive its outbound hard-copy customer communications via the postal service, yet its staff for handling inbound communications from that customer base is fewer than 400 persons.

That's a ratio of one CSR to every 100,000 customers. Since reps rarely handle more than 150 calls a day, on any given day the company is receiving inbound communications from fewer than two-tenths of one percent of its entire base, while in some cases it is sending hard-copy communications several times a month to 100 percent.

In commercial or technical markets, the ratio of CSRs to customers is considerably smaller, of course, but there is still a disparity in quantity between inbound and outbound customer communications. WordPerfect Corp., the Orem, Utah, developer of the most popular word processing program, WordPerfect, has a ratio of one rep to every 6,000 customers. The company handles about 15,000 customer support calls a day with an on-line staff of about 675 people. This averages out at about twenty-two calls a day per rep, although there is likely to be considerable variation in the number of calls any one individual handles on any given day, on the basis of their length and complexity. Yet that 15,000 calls a day is less than one-half of one percent of the customer base of more than 4 million users, who have the company's outbound communication at hand, that is, the documentation telling how to use the software itself.

As you can imagine, outbound communications are much more difficult to control and measure than typical inbound communications, because they go out to customers in so many different ways, and a high proportion of hard-copy communications typically generates a relatively low proportion of feedback from those customers.

This chapter assumes that inbound communications *from* customers are person-to-person voice communications, with some exceptions in the form of EDI and interactive voice response (IVR) systems. Outbound communications *to* customers are generally assumed to be in hard copy form, with the exception of several items on the list in Figure 12-1.

Measuring the Quality of Customer Communications

The safest way to measure quality in handling calls from customers is to adopt the familiar saying, "Quality is what the customer says it is" and apply the three main criteria customers would be most likely to use:

1. *Ease of access.* How quickly and easily can the customer reach the person he needs to talk to?
2. *Suitability of response.* Did the customer get the information, action, or other results she wanted with minimum effort?
3. *Skills of service giver.* Was the customer's call handled by an individual who was empathetic, knowledgeable, and courteous, and who maintained the customer's self-esteem throughout the contact?

Some examples of the types of questions you need to ask about your organization in respect to these three criteria are shown in Figure 12-1. Some of the questions may strike you as elementary, yet they are frequently ignored by companies that ought to know better.

On personal contacts of these kinds, it's assumed that your CSRs have been properly trained, provided with appropriate scripts where necessary, and that

Figure 12-1. Questions to ask to determine the quality of call handling in your company

- Do customers know who we are and how we're listed in telephone directories and buying guides?
- Do our products and other materials all carry an address customers can write to or a phone number they can call?
- Is the address or phone number specific to a department or function so customers won't have to go through lengthy explanations of why they are calling and repeat this explanation several times?
- Are switchboard operators provided with subject indexes and up-to-the-minute information so they can route calls properly?
- In cases where customers may have to contact different people in the organization, do we provide customers with whom-to-call directories—and keep them up to date?
- Do we have toll-free numbers for orders and customer service?
- Can customers get through (without encountering busy signals) at least 95 percent of the time?
- Is the phone answered, either live or by machine, by the third ring?
- Do customers have the option of using voicemail or a voice response unit (VRU) if regular lines are busy?
- Is our voicemail or VRU system user-friendly, e.g., can callers default or escape to a live operator at any time?
- Do we have a system whereby top customers or special accounts can "jump the queue" and have their calls answered ahead of others?
- Do fewer than 20 percent of incoming calls get placed on hold?
- Are 90 percent of the holds for less than one minute and 98 percent less than two minutes?
- Do fewer than 5 percent of calls through our switchboard have to be redirected?
- Are incoming calls answered with the proper identification and with the interest and enthusiasm we wish to project?
- Do our CSRs probe effectively to find the purpose of the call and project a sense of knowledge and competence to deal with the issues raised by the customer?
- Are inquiries answered promptly and completely?
- When customers call to complain or discuss problems, do our CSRs use empathetic phrases and appropriate customer satisfaction skills?
- When customers enter orders by phone, are our order takers knowledgeable about the products or services being ordered?
- When customers phone, can CSRs quickly secure customer info from the database in order to personalize or tailor the call?
- Is the system programmed to enable CSRs to offer customers the benefit of the most economical order quantities?

Source: Adapted from "Checklist for an Easy-to-Buy-From Company," Customer Service Institute

- Will it suggest alternatives to products or services ordered that are not currently available?
- Will the system automatically flag orders that may be in error, i.e., don't conform to customers' past order history or profile?
- Are the other communications media (e.g., EDI, IVR, voicemail) offered to customers as options but not requirements?
- Are there clear incentives or benefits for customers when they use these alternative media?
- Do we survey our customers regularly to determine how well our inbound communications systems are meeting their needs?
- Do we return calls promptly?
- Do we make callbacks by the time we said we would, or sooner?
- Are there standards requiring our personnel to respond to voicemail messages within a specified period?
- Are these standards applied on internal calls—customer service querying production or credit, for example—so that timely response can be made to issues raised by customers?
- Do we call customers promptly when we learn of conditions or problems that may affect their current operations or future plans?

they are regularly monitored in order to maintain the quality of their contacts with customers.

You may want to consider a practice employed at New Hampton, Inc., the parent company for several direct marketing companies including Avon Fashions, James Creek Traders, and Brights Creek. All personnel in the parent company are required to call one customer a month and ask a predetermined series of questions about overall service quality. The findings are tabulated monthly and become the basis for management decisions on service improvement. Although the minisurvey covers aspects of service beyond communications, it's an excellent way of involving management and other departments in the quality process and a reminder to customer service reps that *their* communications are very much of interest to management!

Quality Considerations in Hard Copy Communications

Where a conversational problem in understanding can be corrected immediately, in hard copy communications the situation is far different. With thousands, millions, or more catalogs printed and distributed little can be done to correct a problem until the next catalog printing. Of course, the customer service department would be alerted to the problem so that scripts could be prepared to deal with it as necessary. In that case, there could be a substantial impact on departmental costs because of the added amount of talk time required to explain or clarify misunderstandings.

Because hard-copy communications have an almost indefinite life in mortal terms, it's not surprising that obsolete form letters, coupons, instruction books, and policy statements keep turning up to wreak havoc with the information flow. Or, customers keep writing to you at an address you moved from four years ago, and the problem is compounded by the postal service's limitation on how long it will forward first-class mail.

Hard copy can perpetuate errors in pricing and product specifications and even phone numbers. One company sent out a bulletin carrying its name and address correctly, but the wrong area code for its phone number, substituting the 202 Washington, D.C. area code for its own 212 New York City area code. For some time after that, an army master sergeant in a supersecret office deep in the Pentagon was receiving phone calls from pet shop owners seeking free samples of the newly-developed birdseed mix that had been advertised in the mailing.

Great care must be taken in the initial preparation of hard copy communications to ensure their quality, defined in this instance as clarity, accuracy, and relevance and the durability of their content. A major problem in some industries such as insurance and equipment manufacturing and software is that customers frequently neglect to insert in their manuals the corrected or updated pages that are sent out when errors are discovered in the originals or it's time for a revision. Problems can also occur because the updated pages reach the customer company but not the correct individual.

Although what hard-copy communications *say* clearly is more important than how they *look*, the communicability of hard-copy materials can never be completely divorced from their appearance, how well they are designed and produced, and the extent to which their language and contents project the desired company image. And this principle isn't confined to annual reports and fancy advertising pieces. Many companies overlook the importance of the layout and design logic of such "minor" items as package enclosures, labels, announcements of new policies or procedures, invoices, instructions, and form letters or cards. Poor design and a poor quality appearance can have a doubly negative effect: reduced communicability and lowered credibility.

Forms and form letters or responses that have been poorly duplicated on the office copying machine or that are blurred and blotched copies of copies send a message to customers that the company does not pay much attention to detail—a cardinal sin in customer service. The same message comes from forms that have become partially obsolete and have portions crossed out. On the other hand, standardized forms that are neat, well designed, and functional may be more effective than individual personalized and word-processed letters that look great but are poorly written and confusing to customers who receive them.

The U.S. Veterans Affairs Department discovered that one of its response letters was creating so much confusion among veterans and their families that it had to send out 56,400 new letters explaining the first letter. If the original letter had been more clearly written or perhaps printed with illustrations and boldfaced, step-by-step instructions, there might never have been a problem.

Many companies print folders and cards with photographs of their reps; it is an absolute must that you use professional quality photos as well as professional

Figure 12-2. Examples of photo business cards of customer service representatives

Source: Good Sam Club

quality printing for such materials. Don't forget that the competition may be doing the same, particularly if they're targeting your key accounts, and you don't want your department to look chintzy by comparison. See Figure 12-2 for some samples of well-designed photo business cards of reps. Such cards are an excellent way to introduce CSRs to customers, and they also serve as morale-builders for the reps themselves.

In preparing folders you can also use candid shots of personnel in the office environment, that is, you don't have to use studio portraits, but the photos should still be taken by a professional, properly lit and suited to halftone reproduction, with good contrast and detail.

Notify personnel in advance when photos are going to be taken so that they can dress and groom themselves accordingly. (You'll note that in the few real-life customer service departments that are depicted in national advertising, the individuals are tastefully attired and groomed. This may not reflect what they really look like, day-to-day, but the purpose is to project an image to customers, not to indulge in cinema verité.)

Naturally, the quality of the design and printing of such folders should be commensurate with the time, trouble, and money you spent in getting good photos. If you have a limited budget, remember that it's far less expensive to print a simple format in black ink on color stock than it is to print an elaborate two- or four-color folder on white or ivory, and in some cases the simple format achieves more. Black-and-white photos are much less expensive to print than color photos, and printed color photos don't always convert well to black-and-white.

For a small department, a group photo may be sufficient to introduce the department in a folder, but a printed piece with minibiographies and individual photos usually contributes a great deal more to departmental morale. If you have a large department, or if the department is broken up into teams, photos of the smaller groups make mailers more interesting than row after row of "mug shots." Remember, the basic purpose of such folders is to introduce your personnel as real-life people and at the same time project a friendly, caring image for the department and the company.

Departmental newsletters that you circulate to customers serve a very useful keep-in-touch function: introducing personnel, describing new procedures, explaining how to interpret invoices or packing slips, return or exchange goods and so forth. Surprisingly, a departmental newsletter represents one area where a homemade flavor is acceptable. It adds credibility when the newsletter appears to have been prepared in the department, and it's much more timely when you do it yourself than when it is produced elsewhere.

3PM/McKesson, a pharmacy software company in Livonia, Michigan, sends out a calendar that contains photos of personnel as well as customer service messages about the available services and products. Customers are positively reinforced about this company's customer services practices 365 days a year. See Figure 12-3.

Of course, whatever you distribute should not be sloppy, but computer-generated copy and illustrations are acceptable, as is ordinary typewritten copy and clip art. Some organizations preprint the masthead in color on a large quantity of sheets of letter-size paper then use the office copier to imprint them with typewritten newsletter copy.

If you can't quite swing a departmental newsletter, don't overlook opportunities for departmental coverage in your company's house organ. Whether these are circulated internally or externally, or both, house organs with pictures of people get high readership at all levels in the company (particularly by management, trying to find out what's going on!) as well as by customers.

Another intercompany form of hard-copy communications is shown in Figure 12-4. The customer service department at Abbott Laboratories, Ltd., in Montreal put out a pocket guide for the company's field sales reps. It contains detailed information on customer service policies and procedures and has proved to be an effective tool for avoiding miscommunications that arise when field salespeople are not fully aware of the details of customer service operations.

Measuring the Efficiency of Customer Communications

The typical customer service department is a unique mix of hardware, software, and people. As manager, you face a constant challenge to select the most efficient medium for a given purpose. And you will find a number of contradictions as you do.

For example, the efficiency of the telecommunications aspects of customer communications were discussed in detail in Chapter 10 on inbound communications. It was made evident there that the most common form of customer communications, a CSR talking to a customer on the telephone, is frequently the least efficient. On the other hand, Chapter 13 on telemarketing sets forth a number of ways this personal contact can be used to enhance orders as well as to build a lasting relationship with the customer. It might even be an argument for forgetting about automation and interactive systems altogether!

Yet if your lines are so cluttered with routine calls that customers are subjected to lengthy waits, your telemarketing efforts are likely to be largely wasted in any event. A West Coast company is currently faced with such a situation. Management has mandated an order upgrading program for the customer service department, yet the current information system is so slow that

Figure 12-3. A page from one company's calendar promoting customer services

June 1989

SUNDAY	MONDAY	TUESDAY	WEDNESDAY	THURSDAY	FRIDAY	SATURDAY
4	5	6	7	1	2	3
11	12	13	14 FLAG DAY	8	9	10
18 FATHER'S DAY	19	20	21 SUMMER SOLSTICE	15	16	17
25	26	27	28	22	23	24
				29	30	

Pharmacy System Services

Employing 18 people, the PSS department churns out more than two million prescription claims each month on magnetic tape. The claims flow from four separate sources including Stand Alone customers, On Line customers, and two "batch" processing systems, Economy-claim and 3PM's Data Entry.

Because the department meets the predetermined weekly deadlines of 105 different third party carriers, PSS is more commonly referred to as the Third Party Department.

3PM's Timely Reminder: Daily system backups are your most important computer maintenance function.

Fast Facts: 3PM's Systems Engineering Department provides software enhancements, research and development.

Source: 3PM/McKesson

Figure 12-4. Front page of a guide for field sales representatives of customer
service operations

Source: Abbott Laboratories, Ltd., Montreal

calls back up in queue and there is no time for telemarketing and no interest in being telemarketed on the part of customers, who have already been waiting impatiently for the system to grind out its data.

At this writing, the customer service manager has been unable to convince management that improving the information system will not only pay for itself in order upgrades but will also bring a handsome return in terms of increased productivity and improved moral.

As customer service manager, you are very likely to face issues of this type. And you should understand that, while improved speed and efficiency and reduced costs are usually the reasons for turning to automated telecommunications systems such as EDI and IVR, nothing prevents you from opting for a live voice system, if you can justify it in terms of cost and revenues.

Inbound telemarketing is one example of this. If a significant proportion of your inbound calls are inquiries that can be converted to sales, or sales that can be upgraded to bigger or more profitable sales, then there's no substitute for live voice communications in terms of efficiency. But if you find that only one call out of 100 can be upgraded, and then only for a modest amount, the cost of the attempts to upgrade probably exceeds the return and in the end shows up as increased customer service cost without any improvement in customer service.

If customers prefer voice contact and are willing to pay any difference it may make in their costs, then the relative efficiency or inefficiency of the medium aren't at issue. Your situation is analogous to the University National Bank in Palo Alto, California, which is reported to assess a $20 a month service charge on accounts that drop below $1,500 a month, the premise being that if smaller and less profitable accounts want the same level of service the bank's large depositors receive, they must be willing to pay the costs that such services incur.

Similarly, a number of banks with IVR systems for routine inquiries or transactions assess charges ranging up to $3 per call to depositors who have automatic teller machine (ATM) cards and elect to use the voice system for such routine inquiries and transactions. The premise is that if you have an ATM card, you know how to cope with automation; if you don't have an ATM card you are either a senior citizen or other individual not prepared to deal with this new-fangled gadgetry.

Another example of scaling service to the customer's willingness to foot the bill is the self-service versus full-service mix found in many gasoline service stations and the few that provide full service only, on the premise that there are enough customers in the area willing to pay the higher prices for the added services and/or the convenience of not having to pump their own gas.

(Note that in those few states that prohibit self-service gasoline stations different competitive marketing forces are likely to come into play. Note, too, that the higher cost of full service is not always reflected in good service, but rather in service performed by an employee of the station; the high cost of providing this service is attributable mainly to the extremely high costs for workers' compensation insurance for service station attendants. If customer service continues to be designated as one of the most stressful occupations, and compensation continues to be awarded for stress-based claims, you may find yourself in a situation similar to that of service station operators!)

How you resolve the human versus automation mix in your department depends on circumstances unique to your company and its communications traffic. Regardless of the extent to which you depend on voice communications, they can usually be made significantly more efficient by: (1) minimizing holds, (2) training personnel in how to control calls, (3) educating customers in how to make their calls, (4) having standby scripts and decision rules for routine inquiries or exceptions, (5) developing ad hoc scripts for unexpected events, (6) identifying avoidable situations that trigger phone calls, and (7) identifying individual customers who make excessive use of your phone support.

Improving Hard Copy Communications Efficiency

The permanence of hard copy communications makes it imperative that they be accurate, relevant, and timely. You have also seen the strain that inappropriate hard copy communications can put on the telecommunications system and on reps themselves. Even so, nothing should be permitted to overshadow the efficiency of the medium for certain kinds of customer communications.

Indeed the permanence and persistence of the printed word makes it far more efficient for certain types of customer communications than typical verbal communications. For the simple fact is that people forget. And they forget verbal (spoken) communications at an alarming rate. A popular theory among communications specialists is that:

> After one day, 28 percent of a verbal message is forgotten
> After one week, 48 percent
> After one month, 70 percent

Compounding the memory problem is the fact that people forget verbal messages in different ways:

- They forget the verbal message altogether. This is reflected in the statement, "It completely slipped my mind."
- They forget key parts of the verbal message, that is, they remember part but not all of the communication. This is exemplified by the customer who remembers to call by the specified date, but forgets to compile the data you need in order to make a quote.
- They remember incorrectly or wishfully. This may be the result of poor initial communications or terms subject to different interpretation such as "as soon as possible." It may also be the result of wishful thinking on the customer's part: remembering the commitment he wanted you to make rather than the one you actually made. Psychologists call this "secondary elaboration"; Mark Twain described it more aptly as "remembering big."

These limitations on the efficiency of verbal communications make hard-copy customer communications an absolutely essential part of the total communications mix, and you should constantly remind your CSRs of the importance of making hard copy confirmations of critical verbal communications. In certain industries it's a legal requirement that certain verbal transactions be taped, and in custom manufacturing it's the general practice to have customers sign off on specifications.

Special arrangements or services such as job site delivery that impose obligations on the customer should always be presented in hard-copy form. On routine matters, it's customary practice to periodically furnish customers with copies of the company's terms of sale. This should be done when those terms change, as well as in cases where companies no longer send out order acknowledgments that usually include those terms.

Communicating Complex Information

Hard copy communications can really excel in terms of efficiency in communicating complex information. The ability to combine step-by-step instructions along with keyed diagrams is one example. The use of color in highlighting portions of text or in making diagrams more understandable is another advantage. Hard copy instructions can be presented in cartoon or comic strip form to make them more understandable and interesting to people with limited literacy.

And then there is videotape. With the ready availability of VCRs and videotape projection equipment, industrial companies are turning to this medium to train customers in installation, use, applications, and maintenance of their products. Weil-McLain Co., of Michigan City, Indiana, has prepared a complete kit called H.E.A.T.—Hydronics Education And Training—combining videotapes and workbook plus a troubleshooting guide to train its customers' employees in the proper installation of its high-tech, gas-fired boiler systems. One of the advantages of this approach is that the workbook and troubleshooting guide employ diagrams and schematics to illustrate points of operation, and the videotape uses a real system with cutaways to show what the system actually looks like installed and in operation.

By contrast, it's a disappointment to many assemble-it-yourself consumers that so many companies publish instructions that are poorly written, poorly illustrated, and virtually incomprehensible to the audience for which they were intended. Stressed-out parents attempting to assemble doll houses, bicycles, or junior space ships on a holiday eve will testify to this!

Hard copy customer communications of any kind should be pretested *outside the company* and on an audience comparable to the specific customer audience for whom they're intended well before they're circulated to customers.

Remember that the measure being applied here is the actual efficiency of the medium rather than its esthetics. Clearly hard copy communications are far more efficient than verbal communications for certain applications, but if they're not properly executed they can incur substantial added costs on the verbal communications side when customers call for clarification or place orders based on incorrect information.

To illustrate: You would not mail a letter to the fire department to notify them your house was on fire; but in filing a claim with your insurance company you would most certainly want to use a standard claim form to make sure that all damage and losses were included and correctly costed out. Yet you would be very annoyed·at the insurance company if they asked you to fill out another form after receiving the first. You would feel, and with some justification, that the insurance company was simply using a delaying tactic in order to earn more interest on "your" money. If the insurance company wished to avoid this perception on your part, the agent could simply telephone you and ask for the additional information verbally, as some but by no means all insurers do.

Similarly, you would not want to use form letters or similar communications to notify customers of serious problems that require immediate attention. For example, you should not use form letters to notify dealers and distributors that they have been placed on credit hold when they have already made commitments to their own customers. Banks sometimes make enemies and lose accounts when they fail to phone key customers that they are overdrawn, and instead let them learn through insufficient funds notices sent via the postal service.

One longtime depositor at a local bank was understandably angered when her check for several hundred dollars for an insurance premium was returned by the bank because it exceeded her funds on deposit by 30 cents. It cost the bank far more to apologize to the customer after the fact than it would have to have telephoned in the first place. Of course, simply writing off the 30 cents altogether would have been the least costly response, but few bankers are *that* enlightened yet.

In spite of the unsuitability of the bank's response in this case, form letters and notices play an important role in responding to customer inquiries, and the almost universal availability of facsimile in business settings means that you don't have to depend on the postal service to deliver them in timely fashion. Consumer responses employing form letters by mail are generally quite acceptable when customers themselves write letters to the company. But total cycle time, that is, from the customer's postmark date to mailing the response should be less than 10 days.

Note that the controlling date is the customer's postmark date, not the date you received the letter. This is important, because you are dealing with the customer's perception and not your own internal measures of efficiency. If you take any longer, you are likely to be perceived as stonewalling or ignoring the customer.

Form letters or checkoffs come in handy in such situations because they permit fast turnaround. What's important to remember here is that, for routine matters, a printed response that goes out fast is almost always preferable to a personalized, word processed response that gets delayed because of a backup in the word processing department. Customers are more impressed by a fast response than by an elegant one. However, if urgent or serious matters or letters from key accounts are discovered in the process of scanning incoming mail, they should be singled out for a personalized response and quite possibly a phone call as well.

Remember, too, that although the postal service comes in for its share of criticism, it is still the only delivery service that is capable of delivering mail to every address in the country on every working day, and it does so at a fraction of the cost of competitive delivery services. For many communications, particularly where a standardized message needs to be delivered to large numbers of customers, it is unquestionably the most practical and efficient means of communicating.

High Potential for Shipment Enclosures and Stuffers

Don't overlook the potential of shipment enclosures, which can enjoy a free ride in the same packages as customer purchases and still reach the right people, particularly when shipping small parts directly to the individual who ordered them or to consumers who placed orders on their own behalf. It's also true of shipments to "mom 'n pop" customers.

In order to level its inbound call workload, an IBM parts unit printed up single letter-size sheets suggesting the best times for customers to call, basically during normally slack periods. Since the parts were shipped to the same individuals who actually placed the orders, the reaction was almost immediate. Enough customers changed their calling patterns that the desired call leveling was quickly achieved. The fact that the message actually arrived with the part gave the message more impact and relevance than if it had simply been sent through the mail. Similarly, St. Louis Music Supply Co. prepared a series of educational bulletins for customers—mainly smaller owner-managed music stores—which it simply enclosed with UPS shipments of musical instruments and supplies to the stores. The bulletins covered a variety of store management functions, such as advertising, credit and collections, as well as instructions on packing musical instruments for shipment, claims, returns, and similar items. Because store owners unpacked many of their shipments personally, the bulletins got immediate attention from the target audience, which in turn was quickly reflected in improved relations and operations between the St. Louis Music Supply and its storeowner customers.

You can also develop envelope stuffers for similar uses, and in fact can sometimes use the very same printed piece included with shipments. Some automated systems such as those used in mailing credit card statements automatically weigh each envelope and then compute how many more inserts the envelope can carry without requiring additional postage. It then automatically inserts that many enclosures—which probably answers your question about why there are so many single sheets in such mailings.

Direct marketers that sell to consumers almost universally include shipment enclosures instructing recipients how to make returns and preauthorizing them to do so, and some include labels to make the job even easier. The net effect appears to be that the cost of administering returns and exchanges is reduced without any increase in the number of such occurrences. It's obviously more efficient than having customers phone or write for instructions, particularly since the packing for return is right at hand.

Readership Problems

A final word on typical printed communications to customers: Don't count on them being read! Some managers find that it may take three or four repetitive mailings announcing a telephone number change before any appreciable number of customers start using the new numbers. In such cases, it may be more effective to send Rolodex cards or fluorescent-type stickers carrying the new number. Eye-catching formats are helpful, too. Figure 12-5 shows a well-designed mailer from Addison-Wesley Publishing Company. Its look attracts the attention of readers, who can then open it up to find a letter-size spread describing the company's new organization and order processing and shipment systems, developed to meet the customer's expressed needs.

It often helps to phone customers in advance of sending printed material, particularly in the case of customer surveys. Rockwood Research of St. Paul, Minnesota, found that phoning in advance of mailing a survey increased returns over enclosing a dollar bill as an incentive to respond by 7 percent, and 11 percent to 42 percent more than other traditional incentives. As proof that you can never take anything for granted in communications, a one-dollar bill outpulled a two-dollar bill by 4 percentage points!

Advertising and Customer Communications

Although preparing and placing advertising is usually outside the scope of the customer service department, the more you know how advertising works in general and how it interacts with customer service in particular, the more you, your department, and your company benefit. Since advertising by itself has been the subject of hundreds of books, it will be treated here only as it relates to customer service issues. Some basic definitions are in order:

Advertising. A broad term used to describe paid messages directed toward specific audiences with the goal of influencing their behavior. In business, advertising generally seeks to directly or indirectly influence purchasing. Outside business, advertising is used for political and social purposes, health and safety, fund-raising, recruitment, and more.

The most effective advertising is part of a total marketing strategy that very often includes an educational process as well as a selling one. Note that in business-to-business advertising, most ads don't ask for the order as such. Some ads are designed to make prospective buyers familiar with the features and benefits of products or services, in effect preselling the prospect so that salespeople can concentrate on actually closing the sale. Other ads are designed to create a positive image of the company in order to make the selling job easier or to gain acceptance for company policies and procedures.

Co-op advertising and promotional payments. Payments, allowances, or credits issued by your company to your distributors or retailers as a consideration for featuring your products in their local advertising and sales promotion activities. In some companies, this activity is handled by the customer service department; in others it is handled elsewhere. This area can be sensitive in your relationship with customers, because one of your responsibilities would be tracking their advertising and sales promotion to make sure they are actually spending the money as intended.

Figure 12-5. Company mailer that makes good use of design and contrast

Source: Addison-Wesley Publishing Company, Reading, Massachusetts

Media. The means by which advertising is actually delivered to the intended audience. The three principal media are: broadcast, which includes both radio and television; print, mainly newspapers and magazines; and direct mail, which is now generally referred to as direct marketing, which is largely made up of catalogs and brochures. Direct marketing users include credit card companies, seminar companies, membership organizations, and political candidates. Other media include outdoor advertising, point-of-purchase advertising, yellow pages and directory advertising, and theater advertising. The term *sales promotion* is often applied to secondary forms of advertising such as sweepstakes, premiums, package inserts, and the like, which reach audiences by different means.

Audience. Advertising is targeted to audience, or specific markets in terms of their buying power, need or use for the product or service, and their attentiveness or responsiveness to different types of media. Although advertising people are frequently criticized for the unsuitability of their advertising, the truth is that nobody in the advertising business knowingly targets noncustomers or nonprospects with their advertising. You have probably seen, heard, and used the term *junk mail* applied to direct mail. Actually, direct mail is much less wasteful in reaching its audience than advertising in magazines and newspapers—the two media it competes with most intensely and who are the principal promoters of the term *junk mail*.

Rates. Advertising rates are generally based on a per-thousand cost, so that media with the greatest circulation tend to charge the highest rates. This can be misleading, however, because so-called free publications with large circulations are often sent to large numbers of individuals who are only marginal prospects for your products or services.

Additionally, when people pay for publications they generally tend to read them more closely, including their ads, than publications that arrive free. Rates for renting mailing lists tend to vary with the quality and exclusivity of the list, but this should not be of great concern to you, because your own customer list is better than anything you could possibly rent from anybody else.

Measures of effectiveness. Advertising that is intended to persuade individuals to buy a service or product can be readily tracked by means of keys and coupons, business reply envelopes, and catalog order blanks. By contrast, advertising that is not designed to generate a direct response or purchase is more difficult to measure, and the usual practice is to test sample audiences to determine the extent to which they remember different ads or commercials. While it's a fact that companies with the largest market share also tend to be the heaviest advertisers, it's not conclusive whether advertising *got* them that share or is helping them *keep* it.

Customer Service Applications of Advertising

Your company's advertising reaches large numbers of your present customers. The bigger your company's market share, the more of those customers it reaches, which means that your company's advertising serves a number of useful purposes in communicating with those customers. The remainder of this chapter is devoted to examples, many of which you can adapt for your own use.

Overcoming Cognitive Dissonance

Cognitive dissonance refers to the feeling of uncertainty that individuals often feel after having made or authorized a major purchase. In many companies, specially-trained customer service reps are assigned to "mother hen" new accounts and see them through this period of uncertainty. Studies have shown that advertising that presents a strong image of the company can also play an important role in creating customer confidence and keeping customers at a time when they are particularly vulnerable to cognitive dissonance.

This type of advertising is particularly relevant where the ads feature the benefits of the company's services or products, thereby reinforcing the reasons the customer made the purchasing decision in the first place. Attractive ad photography of the product helps by addressing — or creating — pride of ownership on the customer's part.

Making a Public Announcement

When the company faces a major customer service problem, whether it's a strike, natural disaster, toxic spill problem, product recall, or whatever, it's critical that customers get the straight facts and get them fast, directly from the company. One of the best ways of doing so is to advertise via print (daily newspapers) and broadcast media. Although the ads will be seen and heard by the general public as well as by customers, the ads should be aimed directly at customers, not only to answer their questions and maintain their confidence and, when necessary overcome damaging rumors, but also to let them know what specific disruptions to service may occur and what you plan to do about them. Remember that it's your customers, not the general public that pays your bills!

Contingency planning for continuing customer service operations during a crisis is one of your responsibilities, and for that reason you should be ready to help prepare such ads when they're called for. The content of the ads should naturally reflect what your people are telling customers who call, and your people will need to be familiar with the ads so that their conversations with customers are consistent as well.

Mitigating Major Customer Service Failures

In January 1990, AT&T suffered a major disruption to its long distance service. Although the effect of the failure was lessened somewhat because the failure occurred on a federal holiday observed by many businesses — the birthday of Dr. Martin Luther King, Jr. — businesses remaining open as well as the general public experienced significant disruption to operations, particularly customer service.

To make matters worse, the service failure happened when AT&T was experiencing intense competition from a number of other long distance companies advertising better service and/or lower rates than AT&T. Compounding the risk of possible loss of market share, AT&T couldn't help but be aware of the potential damage to its public image and loss of confidence of investors. It was also well aware of how one regional phone company — Illinois Bell — had received criticism for what many customers considered mishandling of the customer relations aspects of a major service failure. A fire at Illinois Bells' Hinsdale, Illinois, switching station on Mother's Day, 1988, had caused outages in telephone service. (See Customer Service Institute, *Customer Service Newsletter*, Vol. 16, No. 7, July 1988.) And AT&T couldn't help but note the public criticism unleashed on Exxon Corp. for its management's failure to speak up publicly immediately following the disastrous Alaska oil spill in 1989.

So AT&T quickly went public. It prepared and ran full-page advertisements acknowledging and apologizing for its service failure, explaining how it happened and what steps were being taken to prevent a recurrence, and announcing the adjustments it was offering to subscribers to make amends for the service disruption.

One result was that competitors, perhaps realizing that it could happen to them, in general refrained from taking potshots at AT&T in their own advertising. Another was that AT&T was able to maintain its credibility, and by midyear the event was largely forgotten.

Influencing "Pull-Through" Behavior

From a marketing point of view, one of the most serious types of customer service failures occurs when the ultimate customer at either the retailer or distributor level specifies a product and it's not on the shelf or in stock. It may be the result of inadequate production and insufficient inventory to meet demands. But it may also be that retailers and distributors aren't ordering in large enough quantities or with sufficient lead times to meet the demand placed on them. In either case, there is high risk that the ultimate customer will buy a competitive brand simply because it's available and yours isn't. Of course, the real concern is that the ultimate consumer will permanently transfer his loyalty to that competitive brand once he has tried it.

Media advertising is quite often the most effective means of countering situations of this type. In one instance, Ralston Purina Company found that retail grocery chains were not maintaining sufficient stocks of a newly introduced dry dog food for large dogs. Because the dog food was for large dogs, it was in large bags, and grocers were reluctant to devote the necessary shelf space to the bags. As a result, consumers who had been exposed to the new product's advertising were often unable to find it in the stores and, as is often the case in supermarkets, simply bought another brand rather than voicing their concern to the store's management which, like the dog food, wasn't always available.

To counter this, Ralston ran space ads in local newspapers giving consumers a toll free number they could call to get the name and location of a grocery chain which *did* stock the product. When customers called, as many did, Ralston gave them the information and then asked them the name of their regular market. This use of an 800 number was relatively novel at the time (the mid-1970s), and it had several beneficial results for Ralston: (1) It stimulated sales and improved turnover at markets that had sufficient stocks, in effect rewarding those stores for ordering in sufficient volume; (2) because Ralston had obtained the names of callers' regular markets, its sales people could then go after these units to increase the size of their orders of the product; and (3) the ads served to maintain a presence in the marketplace, even when the product wasn't in all the familiar places.

When a shortage occurs simply because demand exceeds supply, some companies use local television advertising to maintain brand identity and customer loyalty during the interim. This advertising may also be critical to maintaining the loyalty of retailers who are understandably reluctant to devote shelf space to products that do not have high consumer recognition and loyalty.

As manager you should be aware that marketplace shortages caused by either inadequate ordering by customers or poor forecasting and production planning by your company can sometimes be averted by appropriate action on your part: either through the order enhancement strategies described in Chapter 13, or through providing "endangered customers" data to your management based on the feedback your department is getting directly from customers.

Supporting Your Customers With Their Customers

One of the earliest examples of this application may have been the famed toothpaste radio jingle of the 1930s: Brush your teeth twice a day; see your dentist twice a year. Twice-a-day brushing, not universally practiced at the time, would naturally increase demand for toothpaste and the toothpaste advertiser's market share accordingly. It would also increase business for dentists and dispose them kindly toward the advertiser in the matter of making recommendations or handing out free samples.

An excellent contemporary example is provided by the example of Genpak Corporation, Glens Falls, New York, a major supplier of polystyrene foam containers to the fast-food industry. At a time of widespread public concern with the proliferation of nonbiodegradable foodservice packaging, Genpak created a flier that its salespeople gave to buyers (smaller copies were also slipped into shipping cartons for a time). The purpose of the flier, headlined "What do you tell your customer?" is to help managers of fast-food restaurants respond to customers taking issue with them over their use of the nonbiodegradable containers. As you can see in Figure 12-6, the flier contains a credible array of facts about the environmental impact of disposable foam products and helps fast-food sellers justify (to themselves as well as to their customers) the use of foam

Figure 12-6. Flier providing customers with support and information for their clients

What do you tell your customer?

About the environmental impact of disposable foam foodservice products.

There are a lot of questions, information, and misinformation about disposable packaging these days, and it's easy to become confused. We'd like to give you a few simple facts so your decisions can be well-informed.

Disposable foam foodservice products are very popular today for many good reasons including sanitary benefits, convenience, and low cost. However, as you make choices on your foodservice carryout packaging, it is important to be aware of the environmental impact of the products you select.

Contrary to popular belief, polystyrene foam products have many environmental advantages. Here are a few:

Preservation of Natural Resources

Foam products are very efficient to manufacture, using fewer natural resources—including material *and* energy—than alternative disposable products. When producing foam foodservice products, virtually 100% of our internally generated scrap is recycled.

Is Biodegradable Better?

There is a general misconception that being biodegradable is synonymous with being beneficial to the environment. This is just not true.

When biodegradable products end up in landfills, they break down and form leachate and methane gas—two major environmental problems in current landfills.

Non-biodegradable materials—such as plastics —are far more desirable in landfills because they remain inert and harmless.

Space in Landfills

All foodservice polystyrene packaging comprises only 14/100 of 1% (.14%) of the total solid waste stream. In fact, in terms of solid wastes produced, foam disposables are very lightweight and compress in the landfill.

The Truth About Incineration

Proper incineration of polystyrene foam produces nothing but harmless carbon dioxide and water vapor. Combustion in an incinerator contributes no more to pollution than paper, wood, or even leaves.

And in a waste-to-energy incinerator, foam is an ideal fuel which burns clean, leaves virtually no ash, and produces four times the Btu's of average municipal garbage.

Recycling

Until recently, neither paper nor foam foodservice products were being recycled. However, because of their washability and high scrap value, used polystyrene foodware items from institutional cafeterias and fast-food outlets are now readily recyclable.

Our industry is aggressively pursuing programs to use recycled resin in such products as insulation and industrial packaging.

CFC's and the Ozone Layer

Since becoming aware of the scientific concern that CFC's were possibly depleting our ozone layer, our industry has continued to work extremely hard to find alternatives. Now, as a result, foam foodservice products have been CFC-free since 1988.

Even though our industry used only a very small portion of the CFC's in this country, we're proud to say that we are the first to aggressively seek and find a solution to this particular environmental concern.

What's Best for You?

As you weigh all the factors involved in your decision, consider if your community has a waste-to-energy plant; has a landfill problem; or is considering a recycling program. Disposable foam carryout containers should make sense in all these instances.

Do You Have More Questions?

We'd be happy to give you more information and answer your specific questions. Please call us toll-free at 1-800-458-7715. We're all working together for a better environment.

The disposable, carryout containers from Genpak are one example of combining the convenience and quality that are important for your foodservice operation with the ecological advantages that are important for our environment.

Genpak Corporation
an Innopac Company

P.O. BOX 727 GLENS FALLS, NEW YORK 12801
TEL. (518) 798-9511   FAX (518) 798-0834

Source: Genpak Corporation

plastic containers, which the public appears to prefer in any event. It also helps Genpak protect its own market share while distinguishing itself from others competing for it.

Advertising Customer Service and Commitment

This form of advertising appears to be very popular with top management and advertising agencies. It has advantages and disadvantages, and you'll have to decide for yourself which outweighs the other in your company's case. On the advantage side, if your company has reasonably good service, advertising will help your company establish a reputation for better-than-average service even though other firms may have comparable service. In other words, advertising can improve customers' *perception* of service.

As an example of commitment advertising, in the spring of 1990, Honeywell, Inc. ran a full-page advertisement in the *Wall Street Journal* featuring a photograph of Honeywell Chairman/CEO James J. Renier in the foreground of a typical group of Honeywell employees, with this headline "I'm in the *Wall Street Journal* to tell you what Honeywell people are saying about our customers." The text of the ad said, "Honeywell people worldwide have been reviewing our goals and priorities to make sure everything we do is aimed at putting our customers first." The result of this, said the ad, is a written goal "to serve customers to their full satisfaction, by careful identification of customer requirements, measuring our performance, and empowering employees to meet customer needs." The ad ended with a slogan-type statement: "Customers control our world."

The fact is that Honeywell has historically paid a great deal of attention to customer service, so this ad is certainly consistent with the experience of most of its customers, and may in fact make them more aware of the quality service they are receiving. Such ads can be an important factor in markets that are likely to be perceived by customers as generic, as many markets are. When the buying public in a particular market of this type is asked to rate service givers in that market, there is usually a strong correlation between their rankings and the amount of advertising and positive public relations individual companies in the market have underwritten.

There's nothing wrong with this, of course, because the purpose of advertising is to influence buying behavior and to reassure and retain existing customers. And good customer service is a legitimate reason for turning to a new supplier or staying with an existing one.

The risk in advertising of this type lies in a single word: credibility. The experience of customers has to be consistent with the claims made by the advertisement. Customers who might have experienced a service failure in dealings with Honeywell—or even with a local heating/air conditioning contractor servicing their Honeywell controls—would tend to be negatively reinforced in their perceptions of the company. And customers with no direct experience with Honeywell might find the absence of specifics in the ad reason enough to class it as another brag-and-boast ad offering golden promises but no proof of how they'd be kept.

It's true that in Honeywell's case the ad might have high credibility and warrant the high ad cost (about $100,000 at the one-time rate for a full-page ad in the *Wall Street Journal* national edition in the spring of 1990). But unless your company has an excellent and established track record in customer service, you would be well-advised to invest the $100,000 in customer service improvements and *then* advertise how great you are!

Advertising Customer Service in Terms of Standards

You are generally on safe ground when you advertise specific features of customer service where you've already established your competence. For example, in an advertising brochure directed to its dealers, Volvo Parts Operations in Rockleigh, New Jersey, published these standards:

Inventory Availability

Order lines shipped without back ordering	97
Stock back orders delivered in 4 weeks or less	99
Critical back orders delivered in 2 weeks or less	99

Order Processing Reliability

Critical orders received before 1 P.M. local time delivered within 2 working days	99
Stock orders delivered within 4 working days	98
Order lines shipped error-free	99.7

Order and Product Inquiry Turnaround

Order inquiries resolved within one hour	90
Order inquiries resolved within 2 hours	99
Product inquiries resolved during initial phone call	90
Urgent product inquiries resolved or status provided within 2 hours	99
Nonurgent product inquiries resolved or status provided within 4 hours	99

The organization also publishes its standards relating to credits and other areas of concern to customers. The brochure also contains a number of tips to Volvo's dealer-customers on how to obtain the best service: whom to contact, what information to have, documentation, timing, and other details. Worth adopting: Volvo's instructions to customers on what to do *before* they call and their gentle suggestion *not* to call about orders that are not late by Volvo's published standards.

Futura Home Products in Clearfield, Utah, goes a step further and guarantees that shipment of specified items will be made within 72 hours at a 90 percent or better fill rate. It tells its customers, who are mainly carpet installation companies, "If we haven't shipped your order for standard catalog carpet metal shapes 90 percent complete within 72 hours, we'll issue a $72 credit to you." Futura ships over 1,000 orders a month and sends out $72 checks on fewer than one percent. Customer Service Manager Wyn P. Holland reports an excellent response to the program on the part of customers.

Response and performance standards can be used equally well in service businesses, particularly if they are accompanied by guarantees. A number of fast-food restaurants offer the guarantee that if service isn't provided within a stated interval, the meal is free or discounted by a specified percentage. Some freight transportation companies offer free transportation for shipments where normal delivery standards aren't met.

Naturally, when you advertise specific standards of performance, your service offerings had better live up to those standards. Otherwise you will quickly lose credibility with customers, which they will reflect by shortening their lead times and calling you more frequently to verify delivery, turnaround on credits, and similar items, all of which add to your costs and make it more difficult to meet those standards.

Similarly, if you advertise a guarantee of some type associated with your service offering, you had better have procedures in place and personnel trained *before* the advertising is released. And you will be well advised to monitor performance of front-line personnel charged with administering such guarantees to make sure that they do in fact fulfill the expectations created by the advertising. There are cases on record where front-line personnel were so completely unaware of service guarantees that customers had to show them the guarantees in print before receiving their credit, refund, or other guarantee offering.

What's more, don't expect management to respond favorably to the notion of publishing service standards, either with or without guarantees. Even though you may have established an excellent track record and demonstrated your ability to perform well within the standards you elect to publish, there's something about incorporating those standards in advertising that strikes fear into the hearts of senior managers that somehow you won't be able to meet them and then the roof will cave in. In reality, the number of claims you deal with are usually quite small, as the Futura experience suggests, and sometimes infinitesimal. Over considerable opposition within the company, one freight carrier advertised free transportation for any shipment not delivered within its published standards and yet experienced only one claim within the succeeding year.

Advertising New Service Features

This straightforward use of advertising both reinforces ties with existing customers and attracts new customers. It's prevalent in service industries, which tend to be perceived as more or less generic: banking, transportation, public warehousing, credit cards, tax services, the lodging industry, even health care providers and law firms advertise service features designed to differentiate their service from the competition's.

Service offerings such as free parking, free delivery, or free consultation may be relatively commonplace, or they may be more complex, for example, free analysis of insurance portfolios, computerized calculation of optimum packaging dimensions for given pallet sizes and storage constraints, or providing customers with printouts tracking relative performance to standard on freight shipments.

Japan Airlines advertises more than a dozen different meal choices for passengers: kosher, Hindu, standard vegetarian, strict vegetarian, vegetarian with seafood, Moslem, low cholesterol, diabetic, salt-free and more. At this writing, Visa is advertising a wheel-type profit calculator for direct marketers, claiming that it will enable them to calculate the increased profit they will gain by switching their charge customers from American Express to Visa.

As manager, you should always be on the lookout for new service features that you can develop to help create such differentiation, and be sure that it's covered by your company's advertising. Even such unglamorous service features as extended hours and the availability of expedited or premium service need to be advertised. One-call processing, assignment by account, on-line response to inquiries about current values of investments—service features that you and your most active accounts may take for granted may not be known to less active accounts and noncustomers whom you'd like to bring into the fold.

Some of the best advertising is basically *news*: news about your company that will be of interest to customers because it helps them in some way. And that's an important point. Ads must provide or imply a benefit for the people they're aimed at. You've seen the ads headlined: GOOD NEWS FOR ARTHRITIS SUFFERERS! If you have arthritis or have a relative who has arthritis, you will most likely read the ad because it suggests you will benefit from doing so.

If you run ads directed at your market reading SAME-DAY SHIPMENT CUTS YOUR INVENTORY COSTS 20%! or CUT INSURANCE COSTS 7% WITHOUT SACRIFICING COVERAGE! you will get a lot more readership than if you run brag-and-boast ads telling how great and wonderful your company is and how committed it is to serving and loving its customers.

Advertising Endorsements and Testimonials

Although this type of advertising sometimes strains credulity, there's no question that it can be quite effective. Celebrities attract attention, and when they endorse a service or a product, the appeal of that product is enhanced considerably. Of course, a basketball star who advertises and wears a particular kind of shoe is going to carry more weight than a movie star endorsing a headache remedy that there's no proof she uses.

And the endorsers featured or quoted in ads don't necessarily have to be celebrities. Catalogs issued by the Vermont Country Store in Weston, Vermont, are laced with testimonials from customers all over the United States, almost all referring to the excellence of the company's customer service. In business-to-business advertising, the title and company affiliation of individuals providing testimonials are usually more important than their names. For example, if you're in charge of software support and you get a testimonial about the quality of that from the director of MIS of Ford Motor Company, McDonald's, or Procter & Gamble, your ad will achieve a great deal of readership and credibility across the board even though the subjects themselves may not be known by name outside their own circles.

The likelihood of getting such testimonials or endorsements from Fortune 500 companies is not too great, but don't overlook the possibility of implied endorsements from companies that issue certificates of service excellence or similar awards to suppliers who meet specific standards.

Awards given by trade or professional associations such as the International Customer Service Association are equally effective when used tastefully. The Malcolm Baldrige Award is considered the top award nationwide for quality in products as well as service. Both awards certainly have excellent advertising value as a form of endorsement, and they're equally effective in developing a quality service culture within your company.

"Meet-the-People" Advertising

Like testimonial or endorsement advertising, this type of media advertising is one of the most appealing mainly because it concerns people—and people are infinitely interesting to other people. In an environment where so much business is conducted over the telephone and customers rarely meet "inside" people face-to-face, ads, brochures and even videotapes featuring customer service reps get high attention.

By giving your service the personal touch, people-ads are often an excellent way of distinguishing your service from the competition. Naturally, such ads need to be credible. One way to assure that they are is exemplified in an excellent customer service department brochure published by Skinner Valve Division of Honeywell, where CSRs actually supplied their own quotes, making it an extremely believable presentation.

A number of companies are circulating brief videotapes showing their customer service people in their regular surroundings. An excellent 6½-minute video produced by Copperweld Corporation does a forceful selling job for the company and its products by linking product quality to service quality and interspersing dramatic plant shots with believable one-on-one dialogue with customer service department members.

One word of advice: When advertising the customer service department—and it's one of the best uses of advertising dollars you can make—keep your CSRs in the foreground, yourself in the background. Beyond the fact that you want customers to call your reps, not you, it's a great and highly appreciated compliment to your reps to see themselves featured center stage in your company's advertising. They will appreciate your letting them have their day in the sun!

What Customers *Don't* Know About Your Company

It can't be emphasized too much: Your customers are not nearly as familiar with your company and its policies and procedures as you sometimes assume they are. Whether your customers are consumers or other business people, specifiers, buyers, or only indirect buying influences, they typically deal with number of other vendors who may or may not have policies and procedures similar to yours.

From their point of view, they have enough on their minds without having to remember, for example, that you permit self-authorization of returns up to $1,000, while your competitor's ceiling is $1,500. Or that your competitor's invoice shows discount percentages while yours omits them in order to preserve confidentiality but applies them in calculating invoice totals. A central role of your customer communications is to ensure that customers are reminded and rereminded of deadlines, surcharges, penalty or late payment fees, cancellation clauses, and other procedures or requirements. And don't be such a stickler for procedure that your reps develop the attitude, as sometimes happens, that a customer who departs from procedure has committed a major crime.

You should be particularly wary of relying on contracts and terms and conditions of sale in your dealings with customers. Although such documents usually have legal force—your company's lawyers have seen to that—by the time you get your customer into court to "enforce" those papers, you have lost the account anyway. In other words, communications of this order are going to be called into play only as a last resort. It's far more profitable to educate your customers in gentler, kinder ways *before* the fact!

And while repeated publication of a policy allows a legal presumption that customers are well aware of that policy, there are some who will ignore it, just as there are others who refuse to use their instruction books or documentation and call your department instead. There's not always much you can do about it if you want to keep their business.

Actions Can Speak Louder Than Words Inside the Company

One of the most critical communications problems that some customer service managers have to deal with is their departments' lack of stature and authority in dealing with other departments. Sometimes, the problem results from long years of treating the department as the "order desk," and customer service reps as "order clerks." Sometimes, unfortunately, it's the result of lack of aggressiveness on the part of the department head.

For better or for worse, customer service management is one of those jobs where it's often necessary to communicate stature via highly visible actions rather than by words alone, in one or more of these ways:

▪ *Institute a dress code for the department.* It's not only a matter of maintaining self-esteem for individual reps but also one of projecting professionalism to others in the company.

▪ *Maintain parity with other departments in the work environment.* The physical surroundings should be on a par with other departments. If management doesn't think so, remind them that local labor departments and the federal government are already interested in such issues, and worker's compensation claims caused by a stressful environment are becoming more common.

▪ *Hold an open house in the department.* If standard invitations don't work, try an off-the-wall approach like Elvira Mazzoni's at Callaghan Co., Deerfield,

Illinois, where she is director of customer service. Mazzoni invited selected company personnel to a "cocktail party" in the customer service department during working hours. Curiosity prompted a large turnout, and when the promised cocktails turned out to be gourmet jellybeans in cocktail flavors, the visitors stayed around to meet department members and observe their work and in the process developed new respect for the department.

■ *Invite speakers from other departments.* In this case being a good listener will often gain more stature for you and your department than all the logic and reasons-why you can muster for winning their support. Hold meetings at lunch time and provide a buffet or free brown-bag lunches. At ICI Americas in Wilmington, Delaware, half the department attends every other month, while the other half handles calls. Volunteer speakers from other departments book themselves well in advance. It's an extremely popular event; seems that everyone wants to make friends with customer service!

■ *Learn how others are measured.* A major source of friction between customer service and other departments is often the simple fact that different departments are rated on different areas of performance and yours is probably the only one that's rated directly on measurable customer satisfaction. When you turn for help to production, engineering, quality control, underwriting, distribution, credit, or finance, very often you are asking that particular individual to do something that will adversely affect his or her rating.

For example, a CSR notifies the warehouse manager of a requested change order from a major customer. The warehouse manager agrees to handle the change order, but does so by requeueing it at the end of the current workload. Today being Friday, this means that the account's order won't go out until sometime late Monday. The warehouse manager refuses to handle the order today because to do so would require working overtime, and management has prohibited any overtime in the warehouse.

Had the CSR been aware of this conflict, so to speak, she might have identified other orders that could have been held over until Monday, allowing the critical change order to be worked and shipped according to its original schedule. In this case you don't want to have to quote policy on change orders (which is typically to requeue) to an important customer, but you can hardly ask the warehouse manager to risk being disciplined either.

Knowing in advance how performance is measured helps you work with rather than against other employees and achieve a result that is agreeable to you both. If yours is a service organization, you'll have no trouble recognizing parallel situations and developing strategies for dealing with them.

■ *Act as a shield for other departments and let them know when you do.* In spite of what you've heard, as customer service manager you're perfectly aware that the customer isn't always right, and in some situations customers demand services that are not only unreasonable but also unnecessary.

In many of these cases, you negotiate an alternative arrangement with customers without even presenting their original demands to the other departments that would be involved. In effect, you shield the other departments from as many unreasonable demands as possible and turn to them only when there's no practical alternative.

Of course, this requires that your people know their customers well and have guidelines on rule-bending and making exceptions, and be able to negotiate alternatives with customers as well as go to bat for them when it's warranted. What's important is that you let other department heads know just how you've shielded them from unreasonable demands. This not only sends them a message that you're on their side, but also lends credibility to the demands that you do have to place on them.

■ *Send a rep to represent you at an interdepartmental meeting.* Bring the CSR with you to a meeting as an observer first, and then the next time send her in your place. Obviously, you'll want to pick the right person and prep her, but it will give other department heads a chance to see at firsthand what your people are made of and it will send a powerful message to your own people.

■ *Gain recognition by giving it.* Always be sure that other departments are recognized for their role in customer service saves that win you compliments from management as well as customers. When an individual in another department has been particularly helpful, see that a letter of commendation goes to his manager. And consider undertaking a monthly customer service recognition program in which the only requirement is that the winner be somebody outside the customer service department.

■ *Meet with other department heads weekly to discuss Top Ten accounts.* If you're not already doing this, it's a most reasonable suggestion for you to make. After all, you're the customer service manager, and nobody is in a better position to report on account activity as well as on present or anticipated problems. The meeting doesn't have to be confined to ten accounts, of course, it can relate to different classes of accounts, distributors versus original equipment manufacturer (OEM) or direct accounts, for example, or A and B accounts versus C, D, and E accounts.

Such meetings are an excellent means for establishing your own credentials and at the same time they draw the attention of other department heads to what's needed from them to protect and retain key accounts.

■ *Keep messages to management brief and relevant.* Minimize activity reports that tell how much work your department does, and concentrate instead on reports that relate to new customer acquisition, account growth, profits and, particularly, "endangered" customers.

If you are asked to prepare reports that necessarily run to some length, write an executive summary of no more than two pages. This summary is what is most likely to be read by senior management, who will most likely pass it down to others for their analysis and recommendations. Be brief, be clear, and avoid any semblance of empire-building. Above all, don't try to bypass the chain of command in reaching top management unless you're prepared to put your job on the line. Going directly to the top sometimes works in bringing about change but not very often.

■ *Learn the art of "incremental encroachment."* This phrase was coined by the general traffic manager of the line materials division of McGraw-Edison to connote a managerial strategy of bringing about change by neutralizing the tendency of other managers to resist change when it threatens their turf. His strategy can be summarized thus:

> When you encroach on another person's territory, do it in very small increments so that he/she is not even aware of it at the time. Over a period of time, you'll get your foot in the door and open it all the way to change—and with minimum resistance.

Customer service managers have to work harder than most in bringing about change because there are so many "experts" on what customer service ought, or ought not, to be. Where top management would be very reluctant to tamper with traffic, industrial engineering, MIS or the tax departments, it—and a few dozen other managers as well—won't hesitate to veto the most logical plans for improving customer service that you might devise.

One of the best ways to overcome problems of this nature, and resistance to change generally, is to appeal to emotions when you realize that appeals to reason and logic aren't going to work. This doesn't imply anything underhanded. It simply means learning to word your proposals in terms of the benefits that appeal to the particular manager or managers with whom you are communicating.

If top management is totally finance-oriented, use good, solid bottom-line numbers that are very clearcut and not speculative. If its concern is with competition, few things will get a proposal approved as quickly as an observation that the competition has already started doing something similar. If management's concern is with corporate image and status, focus on the leadership role the company will be taking and the recognition it will get in the business community by implementing your proposal.

Above all, don't be intimidated by top management. Remember that senior managers are as human as you are and just as fallible. If you don't think so, think of all those "successful" companies you hear about that used to be in business but no longer are. It certainly wasn't their customer service managers that brought them down!

13

■■■
■■■
■■■

Telemarketing as an Element of Proactive Customer Service

Like the term *customer service, telemarketing* means different things to different people. The literal meaning, selling by telephone, is quite clear, but within that definition there are three separate disciplines:

1. *Outbound telemarketing* is what is most often meant by the term *telemarketing*. It's a form of marketing that in many ways parallels direct mail in the development of overall strategies, selection of prospect lists, preparation of the package or sales approach, and development of copy or scripts. Telemarketing permits a dialogue between seller and buyer and enables the telemarketer to try different appeals and strategies in making a sale.

Telemarketing has fairly strict economic boundaries, that is, telemarketers are usually expected to make a certain number of calls per hour and meet a specified hit rate or number of sales per every so many calls. In addition to strategic marketing considerations, some very complex logistics are included in staffing and managing a typical telemarketing operation.

Telemarketing is a legitimate form of selling that is sometimes abused, but that abuse gets bad press well out of proportion to its occurrence. If you have a service or a product that offers benefits for buyers, you should feel no compunctions about identifying those potential buyers and telephoning them to offer them that service or product, just as you would in person or through advertising. If your company sells to small accounts, the telephone may be the only economic way to make a sales presentation to your buyers.

The major concern of telemarketers right now is the pressure from consumer groups to impose restrictions on telemarketing in much the same way that door-to-door selling was virtually regulated out of existence some years ago. Much of the hue and cry against such marketing techniques as direct mail, billboards, and telemarketing comes from the daily press — newspapers whose advertising revenues are constantly threatened by the availability of these other media. Your own business very likely has legitimate telemarketing applications that could be compromised by the kind of regulation that's frequently proposed.

224

2. *Inbound telemarketing* refers mainly to calls originated by potential buyers as the result of advertising or media publicity. Many of the freebies offered in ads and press releases—free booklets, guides, cost calculators, and the like—are offered in order to generate telephone requests or inquiries that can be converted into sales. Inbound telemarketing may involve simply taking an order for an advertised product, although it is just as likely to involve attempts to enhance or increase the order or to actually convert an inquiry into a sale.

Discounted air fares and travel packages advertised on the radio are common examples when you "call for details," the inbound telemarketer will make a reasonable effort to convert your inquiry into a sale. That's why the ad was run in the first place!

There are abuses of inbound telemarketing, too, but here again the fault is not with the medium but with unscrupulous people who exploit it by using bait and switch and similar ruses. In fact, the majority of the abuses that occur in inbound telemarketing are unintentional—poorly trained personnel who don't know about the ad or how to answer the inquiry but try to make a sale anyway.

Try calling a yellow pages advertiser to find out about getting your venetian blinds retaped or some similar service, and you will see how much room for improvement there is in the field of inbound telemarketing—some of those yellow pages advertisers are *your* customers selling *your* products or services! (A good reason, if you sell through distributors, dealers, or retailers, to help train their personnel in the proper presentation of your product to inquirers.)

3. *Customer service* contains elements of both outbound and inbound telemarketing. Very often, CSRs are used in new product or service introductions to call mainly small customers and sign them up, if possible, for an order for the new product or service. In some cases, reps will call marginal or inactive accounts or customers with blanket purchase orders who haven't ordered lately. The only difference from outbound telemarketing as described in item 1 is that your reps are usually calling existing customers rather than prospects and they're people whom they already know from previous dealings.

It's also likely that your CSRs are doing some order upgrading or enhancement as well as occasional conversion of inquiries and complaints into sales. Customer service actually has a great deal in common with telemarketing as it is most commonly construed. In fact, customer service may in the long run be more effective than either outbound or inbound telemarketing in the conventional sense, because your reps have already established credibility with their customers and usually find above-average acceptance for their recommendations on purchase quantities, applications, and substitutions.

Perhaps customer service *is* telemarketing!

Principal Roadblocks to Effective Telemarketing

Buying decisions made as a result of telemarketing are similar in many respects to impulse buying, a purchase made as the result of a suggestion rather than as part of a formal buying plan. Like impulse buying, the success of telemarketing depends very heavily on good customer service: the ready availability of the service or product, the knowledgeability of the telemarketer, the right to return the product or obtain an adjustment on the service within a stated time, and, naturally, the assurance that what's being sold and the way it's made available to customers will live up to their expectations.

A potential roadblock to effective telemarketing can be a feeling by customers that those expectations won't be met, that there's something slightly unscrupulous about the whole business, and that if buyers are dissatisfied they may have problems getting a suitable adjustment or refund. These reservations are sometimes justified by the time lag between placement of an order and its delivery as well as the difficulty sometimes encountered in securing adjustments.

One reason for fulfillment problems is that telemarketing and order fulfillment are sometimes handled by distinct entities, sometimes separate companies, with the result that there's very little coordination between telemarketing activities, which are based on closing sales, and fulfillment operations, which are often based on least cost rather than on customer service standards.

By contrast, when telemarketing activities are performed by your customer service department, credibility has already been established with your customers and they have confidence that you will meet their expectations. The fact that you have already established a satisfactory working relationship with your customers makes it that much easier for you to sell. You *sell by making it easy for customers to buy.*

This chapter is based on the premise that you have developed a good customer service system that has won the confidence of your customers and assumes that, whatever form your telemarketing takes, it will be backed up by good customer service. For that reason you will have a certain telemarketing advantage over non-customer-service telemarketing operations, either in your own company or in competitive organizations.

A New Look at Telemarketing

Now that you have read the more or less conventional definitions of telemarketing, it's suggested that you take an entirely new look at both telemarketing and customer service and start thinking of the whole of customer service as a telemarketing activity. Here is a series of questions and answers to introduce that new look:

1. Do you answer the telephone at work? ☐ Yes ☐ No
   If yes, proceed to question 2. If no, go back to doing whatever it is you do.
2. Why do you answer the telephone? _____
   If you answered "because it's ringing," go back to question 1.
   If you answered "because it's a customer," go to question 3.
3. What are the three most important reasons for answering the phone?

   a. _____

   b. _____

   c. _____

Can you top these responses?

a. Because it's a customer calling to place an order, and we want to handle it so well that she will continue placing orders—more orders and bigger orders.
b. Because it's a customer calling about a problem or a complaint, and we want to solve that problem or resolve that complaint so quickly that he won't even think about going to another source.
c. Because it's a *potential* customer calling to ask about a service, product, or application, and we want to respond to that inquiry in such a way that she *becomes* a customer—for good.

Now you have a pretty good inkling of why customer service sounds suspiciously like telemarketing. You may want to copy the questions listed above and try them out on your reps.

Four Preliminary Steps in Handling Inbound Calls

Once you've established the rationale of "new look" telemarketing, you need to familiarize your reps with four preliminary steps that should be taken with every inbound call:

1. *Always have your objective in mind* before *answering the phone.* Don't ever answer the phone just because it's ringing. If your reason is nothing more than to project a positive image for your company or enthusiasm for your job of serving customers, that's good for openers. An upbeat, enthusiastic response lays an excellent foundation for a sale!
2. *Identify and qualify.* Establish firmly who the caller is, his or her relationship to your company and role in ordering. For example, is the caller an assistant calling to confirm a purchase order number or an engineer seeking specifications on precision ball bearings?
3. *Readjust objectives as appropriate: assign a value to the call.* Both the assistant and the engineer get a respectful, courteous response. The CSR readjusts the call objective and the priorities: the assistant's confirming call can be handled in a minute or two without rushing; the engineer, who is also a specifier, will get a response in depth.
4. *Select a strategy and decide on a script or approach.* The assistant will get a greeting, hear the purchase order number read back for verification, and receive an expression of thanks and appreciation. The engineer, on the other hand, will get the exact information she requested plus some well-scripted reasons why this product is best for the intended application. If indicated, the call may be transferred to a sales engineer, that is, a salesperson with an engineering background. Your standard procedures should indicate when and how to make such transfers. Scripting is further discussed in Appendix C, where sample scripts are provided.

Is This a Company I Would Like to Do Business With?

A key element in telemarketing in the customer service environment is the way the phone answerer is perceived by callers. This perception applies to switchboards and personnel in other departments as well as customer service reps, so you may want to try the following quiz on personnel outside as well as inside the department.

Phone Perception Quiz

Phrases such as the following are quite common in telephone conversations or transactions. Place a check mark in the appropriate box to indicate whether you do or do not use that particular phrase or one like it.

Phrase or Wording

1. "XYZ Company. This is Sharon Smith. How may I help you?"	☐ Yes	☐ No
2. "I'll be glad to help you with that."	☐ Yes	☐ No
3. "As I understand it, the thermostat clicks, but the furnace doesn't go on. Is that right?"	☐ Yes	☐ No
4. "I appreciate your calling that to my attention."	☐ Yes	☐ No
5. "You have every reason to be upset [angry]"	☐ Yes	☐ No
6. "When you called here before, who did you talk to?"	☐ Yes	☐ No
7. "I'll have [him/her] call you as soon as possible."	☐ Yes	☐ No
8. "He's not in right now. Would you like to leave a message?"	☐ Yes	☐ No
9. "You'll have to talk to Bob Smith in sales [credit, etc.]. Hold on, I'll transfer you."	☐ Yes	☐ No
10. "When did you place the order?"	☐ Yes	☐ No

As you've undoubtedly surmised, responses 1 through 5 represent responses that build customer confidence and project warmth. Responses 1 and 2 indicate helpfulness, whereas response 3 shows the phone answerer's concern for having the correct understanding. Response 4 is a nice way of giving status to the information, possibly a complaint, the caller gave you. It reinforces the caller's self-esteem, a very important point with calls that have negative overtones, where customers may expect a defensive response. Response 5 is a solid empathetic response to a complaint. It puts the phone answerer on the same side as the caller, rather than in an adversarial position, and makes it easier to reach a mutually agreeable solution.

At this point, you may be wondering what's wrong with the remaining five responses, which you've probably heard, and perhaps used, more than a few times in the past. Remember, we are not talking about what your rep *intends* by these statements, but rather what your caller *perceives* and how that affects the caller's predisposition to buy or not to buy from your company.

Response 6, "When you called here before, who did you talk to?" will be interpreted by some callers as meaning you personally don't want to talk to them (a very few will be disturbed by the grammar of *who* instead of *whom*). Your more perceptive customers will see it as a sign you don't have a very good information system—imagine calling an airline to change a reservation and being asked who took the original reservation! If there's a valid reason for knowing who handled the matter on the previous call, preface your response by saying, "I'll be glad to help you," and then, "or, do you happen to remember whom you spoke to before?" That way, your response stresses convenience to the customer rather than to yourself.

Response 7, "I'll have [him/her] call you as soon as possible," suggests that the call handler has authority over the person being called. If that's true, fine. Otherwise, the response should be "I'll *ask* [him/her] to call you back." The other problem with this response is the phrase "as soon as possible." This phrase is vague and indefinite. Better to say, "As soon as [he/she] returns — which should be about three o'clock — I'll ask [him/her] to call you right away. Of course if the call handler knows what the call is about, he or she should volunteer to take care of the matter (see below).

Response 8, "He's not in right now. Would you like to leave a message?" This is a very common response that accounts for a large number of callbacks that wouldn't have to be made if the call handler had the initiative to first ask "Is it something I could help you with? He's not in right now." Remember, a major thrust in customer service telemarketing is projecting the image of being easy to buy from, pleasant to deal with, and fast and efficient.

Response 9, "You'll have to talk to Bob Smith in sales. Hold on, I'll transfer you." is another case where the call handler comes across as not wanting to help the customer. First of all, the phrase "you'll have to" will be interpreted by some callers as either a command (which most people don't appreciate from service givers) or a typical "not my department" response.

Also, when a CSR says "You'll have to talk to Bob Smith," to some callers it will sound as if their call is being downgraded and the caller can expect an unpleasant experience. A far better response is; "Bob Smith in sales is the real expert on that, and I know he'll be glad to help you." This response implies that you are upgrading the call by giving it to the most qualified person. It also shows mutual respect, and customers like that. And the buildup will make it easier for Bob to establish credibility and authority with the customer.

Response 10, "When did you place the order?" is likely to be interpreted as a defensive maneuver, similar to "If you only placed the order last week there's no point my even looking it up!" Instead of answering a question with a question of your own, buffer your response by saying "I'll be glad to help you with that" and then follow with "Do you happen to know the date of the order?" or "Do you have the confirmation number on that order?"

As manager, you are likely to feel that these nuances in phone response are relatively trivial points in customer service operations where you establish your credentials as much by what you do as by what you say. A good point, but it overlooks one basic fact. Very often the principal competitors in a given industry may be so much alike that the only way customers can tell them apart is by the way they handle phone calls. And another important point: customer service operations and customer service phone skills aren't mutually exclusive.

You can have good operations and good phone skills, and the better your phone skills are, the more they enhance customers' perceptions of the company and its products or services. If you have any doubts, simply multiply the number of reps in your department by the number of calls they handle daily.

Number of CSRs	Average Calls per Day per Rep.	Total Calls per Day (Dept.)	Total Calls per Year (Dept.)*
10	70	700	175,000
10	90	900	225,000
10	110	1,100	275,000
20	70	1,400	350,000
20	90	1,800	450,000
20	110	2,200	550,000

*Based on 250 working days

This table gives you an excellent picture of the number of opportunities your reps have to influence the buying patterns of your customers simply by the way they handle calls. The explanations of telemarketing that follow assume that you are performing telemarketing within the context of these day-to-day operations, not setting up a separate department. There are a number of excellent books on that subject, some running over 500 pages.

Customer service telemarketing is the most efficient mode of personal selling, for five main reasons:

1. No time or effort is required to find out whom to contact and how to contact him. The customer calls you and saves you all that time and effort just by initiating the call.
2. No time is lost in qualifying the caller as a potential buyer. The customer has done so by calling you.
3. No warmup has to be undertaken to create interest. The customer is already interested, or she wouldn't have initiated the call.
4. No effort has to be made, as in outbound telemarketing, to penetrate the screen of switchboard operators or secretaries to reach the buying influence, who saves you all that by calling you.
5. No need for callbacks when the customer isn't there or is too busy to talk to your rep. Your customer made the time to call your company.

The essence of customer service is *the easier you make it for customers to buy, the easier it is to sell*. It's assumed that the previous exercises have convinced you of the importance of both having a service orientation and projecting one via every telephone contact you make, and convincing your management that your switchboard and everybody else who talks to customers, from guards to dispatchers and, particularly, to credit managers and vice presidents of finance need to do the same.

Given that, the following discussion ranges from the conventional to the unconventional in customer service telemarketing.

Order Enhancement or Upgrading

Order enhancement, the most common form of customer service telemarketing, has a number of variations:

▪ *Increasing order size*. This is usually a matter of suggesting the customer increase the order up to the next price break based on weight, quantity, units of shipment (palletloads, containerloads, or truckloads) or some similar measure. Some companies give reps incentives for achieving such upgrades but an inherent risk in pushing too hard for upgrades of this type is that you may end up "borrowing tomorrow's business," as one manager puts it, or, in the words of another, "selling returns."

However, there are instances where it may be practical to sell customers on the idea of doubling their orders but only ordering half as frequently, thus cutting order costs in half and providing savings in transportation and handling. In addition, when customers commit for longer periods of time, their vulnerability to the competition is reduced.

▪ *Buying a higher-priced version*. In consumer sales, this type of upgrading must not be based on bait-and-switch tactics, but this caution should not discourage legitimate attempts to sell a full-service contract, a deluxe model or whatever, rather than the economy or bare-bones version. Examples include extended warranties, collision damage waiver (CDW) and different insurance options offered by car-rental companies, lawnmowers with and without self-starters, and more. In industrial and commercial sales, order upgrades of this nature may actually benefit customers who have unknowingly selected a lower-priced service or product that is inappropriate for their needs and in the long run will cost them more than the higher-priced version.

This issue can be sensitive with field sales personnel who sometimes see no alternative but to make sales based on what the customer can afford rather than what the customer actually needs. But you should be aware that the situation exists, and attempts should be made to aid the customer by means of upgrades whenever possible. In one instance, a customer was dissuaded from buying a $2,000 piece of equipment and persuaded to buy a larger capacity trade-in for twice that price but with the features the customer needed. The strategy led to a long-term, mutually profitable relationship between vendor and customer.

▪ *Add-on sales*. A common example of add-on sales is found in the shoe industry, where customer service reps take shoe orders from customers then typically suggest add-ons of laces, shoe trees and other accessories, primarily minor items that field salespeople don't care to sell. Yet the reps earn a commission from the sales, and the add-ons are perceived as a benefit by customers. Add-on sales are also found in the book publishing industry, particularly in specialty areas such as law or religion, where CSRs frequently suggest related titles or series. This category also covers services in such areas as travel and banking—buying cancellation insurance for tour packages or overdraft insurance.

▪ *Specials*. While most add-on sales by CSRs involve products or services related to a specific customer's order, "specials"—which are also add-ons—are generally offered to everybody who phones in an order. For example, a caller who orders clothing from the Neiman-Marcus mail order division is told about the current special in perfume or a caller ordering a part for a forklift from a company in Illinois is told that the special of the week is a 10-pound can of grease.

Specials can be easy to sell, and they can also be used to dispose of slow-moving or obsolete stock. However, they must be good values in order to maintain the credibility of your specials program, and they can't interfere with sales of regular products.

Outbound Telemarketing Sales

Outbound telemarketing sales calls by CSRs are usually, though not always, made to existing customers, as in the examples that follow:

■ *Misdeliveries and/or refused shipments.* These are sometimes the same thing. For example, a frozen food processor overships by several palletloads to a retail chain. The cost of return transportation for the overage, combined with the perishability of the product, make it a candidate for telemarketing by CSRs who are familiar with other accounts in the area who will buy the product at a discount.

The same strategy is used when the wrong product is shipped or the right product is shipped to the wrong destination. Rather than argue the rights and wrongs, it's often more practical for the customer service department to telemarket the product to an alternative buyer at a discount, thus saving the expenses of backhaul transportation, rehandling, and inventory damage or shrinkage.

■ *Sales of seconds, overruns, and excess inventory.* This telemarketing mission sometimes falls to the customer service department by default. The regular sales force is usually reluctant to take on a secondary selling effort that would normally pay less than their primary sales effort aimed at high-volume, high-margin sales.

Customer service personnel have proved very successful in this area because of their knowledge of, and ties with, customers of all types. Telemarketing for them does not consist of "pushing" unwanted products on people but rather matching up products with customers for whom the combination of price and availability is right. And, based on experience, customers have trust that CSRs will get them a fair deal.

■ *New product/service introductions.* It is not uncommon for companies to use their CSRs to introduce new products to smaller customers who are seldom (and sometimes never) visited by field salespeople. The usual practice is to place several reps on outbound telemarketing calls exclusively for set periods, either during slack periods or for a specified time period, until the calling cycle is completed.

The new product introduction is usually supported by direct mail and other media advertising, so that this type of telemarketing is very similar to what reps do most of the time anyway: talk to their customers about their services or products and take orders for them.

Of course, there is nothing wrong with mentioning new products in the course of conventional inbound calls. This form of order upgrading may also be presented as a special introductory offer. However, your sales department may prefer targeting individual customers for specific purchase quotas rather than the trial order that might normally result from a conventional order upgrade.

If you use your reps for outbound telemarketing of any kind, including new product introductions, be sure that the calls are required, not optional, on the part of the reps. If you leave it to them to "make some calls when things aren't busy," you imply that telemarketing calls aren't very important, and you'll find that very few get made.

Telemarketing can be an excellent motivating factor for reps, particularly if you offer a bonus or incentives, not necessarily money. A number of companies award points that can be accumulated and traded for various catalog items, free dinners, and similar awards. What's important is that your reps enjoy some success, that is, actually make some sales. Otherwise, they will soon become discouraged and suffer loss of self-esteem. To avoid this, they should receive adequate training, be provided with appropriate scripts, and work from accurate customer/prospect lists with correct phone numbers.

Negotiating Alternatives

This very broad area of customer service telemarketing has two main objectives: (1) to keep customers from turning to other sources for services or products when their orders can't be filled according to original specifications and (2) to balance inventory by substituting slow-moving items for fast movers where practical. Sometimes it's necessary to offer the customer an incentive to accept the alternative. This incentive usually takes the form of a price discount or the substitution of a higher priced item without charging the higher price. Here are some examples:

▪ *Selling standby positions.* This incentive method applies primarily to airline seats or limited capacity educational, sporting, or entertainment events, but it may also be applied to a number of other areas such as processing time, manufacturing capacity, and maintenance and field service engineering. It's the service equivalent of entering a back order for a product currently out of stock.

There are two advantages to this waiting list approach for the vendor: (1) The customer who accepts the standby or waiting list offer is less likely to search out another source, and (2) if the service or product becomes available through a cancellation or other cause, the vendor doesn't have to go looking for a customer. There's already a prioritized waiting list of ready buyers. Note that in many instances, vendors do not maintain a first-come, first-served waiting list but instead set priorities in terms of account size, criticalness of need, or other criteria.

▪ *Direct substitution selling.* Although substitution telemarketing is generally thought of in connection with product substitutions, it's not uncommon in the case of such services as hotel and transportation accommodations, service contracts, delivery zones, and personal services.

The most common form of product substitution occurs in the case of minor variations in product feature. For example, "We don't have it in red, but we do have it in yellow or blue. Would you like to order one of those colors?" Or, "Model 0-112 was designed as an OEM part rather than a retrofit, so if you want to modify an existing machine you'll need to drill two one-eighth-inch holes in your baseplate and use three-inch spacers when you attach it. Your shop people can make the change in about an hour. I'd suggest you go ahead and order it rather than wait for the retrofit version." Another example is, "The metal version is backordered, but we have that particular gear in nylon, which might be better for an intermittent application like yours." And a final variation is, "We have it with a Velcro closure, but the zipper version is out of stock. The Velcro is very popular. Would you like to order that instead?"

Industrial, engineered, and scientific products often have critical standards relating to resistance, tensile strength, purity, water content, and the like. These standards often lend themselves to computerized substitution programs that list products by their critical standards. When an item is ordered but is not available, the order taker can punch up the critical standard and see a display of all other products that meet that critical standard. These are usually listed in such a way that the rep can quickly zero in on the substitutable item that most nearly resembles the item ordered by the customer. Items purchased by the government are often organized by *milspecs* (military specifications), which are also useful as a basis for computerized substitution programs.

▪ *Equivalency programs.* These are quite similar to substitution programs and usually involve a similar product that is offered under different brand names, as in the case of private label merchandise or commodity-type products. Equivalency programs often involve products that are essentially generic from the buyer's viewpoint: fasteners and many other hardware items, certain automotive replacement parts, and many other consumer and industrial items.

In a typical equivalency program, your reps (and your distributors' reps) would maintain equivalency lists enabling them to translate competitive part names or numbers into your part numbers. For example, a customer may call and ask, "Do you have a Superdry filter element for a Parsons dehumidifier?" Your rep would obtain the part number, or reference by name if the customer didn't know the part number, look it up on the equivalency list and respond, "That's the same as our part number A35497. How many would you like?"

Of course equivalency selling can be used against you by your competitors, so if you're in that type of market or have distributors who carry brands competitive to your own, it's essential that everybody who talks to customers have access to your equivalency data in just the same way they have access to substitutability information. And they must be trained in when and how to use it. Like substitution selling, equivalency selling lends itself well to computerization for both information and actually selling by means of scripts or prompts.

▪ *Alternative packs and packaging.* This reason for customer service telemarketing is very common and is used frequently with consumer goods that come in different sizes and packs. "We're backordered on twenty-pound bags, but I can give you two ten-pound bags at the same price, " and "We're backorderd on fiber drums, but I can give it to you in multiwall bags, " are just some of the variations that can be used in this version of substitution selling. The practice can also extend to packages versus bulk, liquid versus dry, concentrated versus diluted, clusterpacks versus singles, and more.

▪ *Alternative dimensions.* This alternative applies where products are sold by length or width. If a customer orders 40-foot lengths of pipe and none are available, the customer may be able to use two 20-foot lengths for each 40-foot length. The same could apply for lumber, paper on rolls, fabrics, sheet metal, and other materials that are typically cut into smaller sizes by buyers.

 ▪ *Discounted damage and errors.* This version of customer service telemarketing is used by companies that drop ship to customers direct from manufacturers rather than from their own warehouses or distribution centers. For example, an office furniture company shows a wide range of merchandise in its catalog, which is widely mailed to small businesses across the United States, but it does not carry any of the goods in stock. When customers call and order furniture items, the cataloger places orders to one or more manufacturers for the items and has them drop shipped to customers. A customer who orders several different items is likely to receive shipments from several sources. When customers receive the wrong items, or the items they receive are damaged in transit, the return process can be quite costly, complicated, and burdensome to the customer—sufficiently so, in some cases, to kill off thoughts of future purchases. To avoid this, the company has trained its customer service representatives to negotiate with customers to actually keep the damaged furniture in exchange for a reasonable discount to cover the cost of having repairs done locally. This agreement is usually agreeable to the buyer, because it avoids having to repack and reship the furniture. In many cases the damage is minor and can be easily repaired or, in some instances, concealed simply by the way the furniture is placed in the customer's office.

To show how buyer psychology can enter into customer service telemarketing, one important aspect of this company's approach is that it is designed to make the buyer look good to her boss. As noted, the customer base is largely small companies or offices. The purchases themselves are usually made by a secretary or office assistant with little experience in such matters. When furniture is damaged in transit, these personnel are concerned that they will appear inept to their bosses by not knowing how to repack and return the furniture. The negotiation procedure developed by the vendor is designed to provide a fair adjustment for the buyer, and to make her look good to her boss by virtue of having negotiated a good resolution and a favorable price or discount for the furniture.

Making buyers look good in their environment is fundamental in every aspect of customer service and should be particularly emphasized in telemarketing situations involving negotiations such as those described here.

 ▪ *Other negotiations.* These often relate to persuading customers not to cancel an order or back order, to accept partial shipments, to order through a wholesaler or agent rather than direct, or to accept new credit terms or alternative shipping arrangements such as FOB shipping point or freight charges collect.

Converting Complaints Into Orders

This relatively narrow area of customer service telemarketing gets a great deal of attention in various writings on customer service. In practice, only a few main types of complaints lend themselves to this kind of telemarketing:

▪ *Poor results from a service.* This customer complaint is generally that a service—maintenance, information, or whatever—is inadequate to that customer's needs. It often turns out that the customer underspecified in ordering the service initially or that the customer's needs have changed, and he needs a higher level of service at higher cost, for example, a 24-hour maintenance contract in place of a business-hours-only contract or an on-line information service instead of a once-a-week newsletter. Insurance policies with increased limits or added coverage are often excellent candidates for this kind of conversion.

Very often all that's needed is to point out the need for the expanded or upgraded service and then to offer to sign the customer up for it. It's sometimes helpful to offer a discount or credit or free trial period, and the script can be written to help the customer save face by citing another customer who had a similar problem, and how the upgraded service cured it.

▪ *Poor results from a product.* In this parallel situation the customer either underspecified the product in the first place or used it for applications for which it wasn't intended. Undercapacity and similar situations can often be converted to sales by demonstrating the correct application and offering a good trade-in or retrofit arrangement.

If the misapplication is the vendor's responsibility, that is, an incorrect application recommended by a salesperson, then it's usually in the company's best interest to make a generous adjustment to overcome the problem and keep the customer.

▪ *Customer error.* The most common example of this complaint is the customer who angrily calls the bank about a dishonored check, only to find that she is in fact overdrawn. The customer service rep who handles the call may use the occasion to sign the depositor up for overdraft insurance, which is actually a form of loan.

In some cases customers order in insufficient quantities, or with too little lead time, and complain because of late or short delivery. Such cases present opportunities for diplomatically recommending that customers order in larger quantities and increase their lead times to avoid recurrences. These suggestions normally lead to increased order size and lower unit costs for your own operations and are thus a valid application for customer service telemarketing. In short, telemarketing does not have to lead to a specific sale. If it reduces your costs and thereby increases your profit margins, it's still telemarketing—and effective telemarketing at that!

Free-vs.-Pay Special and Support Services

Some companies offer premium service at a higher rate, which can be an excellent source of added revenue as well as a help for customers who have last-minute emergencies. If you offer such services, make sure they actually contribute to profits, at least to the extent of recovering the fully distributed costs of providing those services. Customer service telemarketing is an excellent way to sell and control those premium services as described in the following:

▪ *Expedited manufacturing and/or delivery.* A survey of U.S. manufacturers by *Customer Service Newsletter* in the mid-1980s revealed that many companies offered expedited service to customers with emergency requirements but that only about one-third imposed a surcharge for providing such service. Of those who did charge for expedited service, 70 percent did so expressly as a deterrent to customers, that is, to discourage rush orders, below-minimum orders, fill-in orders, and the like. The remaining 30 percent of the companies in the surcharge-imposing group said the purpose of the surcharge was to recover the extra costs incurred. Several pointed out that the work was often performed on weekends so as not to interfere with regular commitments and that the charge was not so much a penalty as it was a guarantee that the work would be done.

The climate has changed considerably since then, and more and more companies are changing their pricing structures to accommodate and profit from customers who are willing to pay more to get more. As an example of this phenomenon, a traveler on a late-night red-eye flight from the West Coast to the East Coast recently observed that all seats in the first-class cabin were occupied, while the lower cost coach class cabin had entire rows unoccupied.

If you are going to offer expedited service at a surcharge—and the current thinking appears to favor it—you'll benefit from the experience of a custom converting (embossing, printing, die-cutting, and laminating) company, which found that over a period of time some 40 percent of its orders had come to be rush jobs, which were being charged a $100 premium for the priority service.

The $100 surcharge recovered only a portion of the added cost incurred by short-term scheduling, and it also degraded service to customers who scheduled their orders with longer lead times. The problem was solved by two changes in basic policy: (1) changing the surcharge from a flat $100 to a percentage of the total charge for the job, with a $100 minimum; and (2) a requirement that all rush jobs be shipped by premium transportation (air freight or dedicated, sole-use truck) at the customer's expense.

This discipline—and that's just what it was—not only reduced the troublesome rush orders significantly but also made those that remained profitable as well as manageable, with virtually zero interference with regular orders. So, if you do offer an expedited service of this type when customers call in with rush orders, be sure that it's making a profit contribution and not simply supporting customers' inefficient buying habits or reducing the quality of your service to others. And, of course, train your customer service reps in the proper telemarketing presentation of the service as well as its subsequent administration and monitoring!

▪ *Optional free-vs.-pay support service.* The proliferation of telephone support services in software, banking and financial services, equipment support, and dozens of other areas has created extremely high costs for companies that provide, as a number of software companies do, what amounts to unlimited free support. The more units of a product or service that are sold, the more support calls are generated and the more support capacity that has to be added in terms of people and phone lines.

As discussed in Chapter 13, it's often possible to upsell customers to a higher level of service. This in effect decongests the free service and not only covers the cost of the premium service but also results in a profit.

Converting Inquiries Into Sales

Inquiries that can be converted into sales are usually triggered by some form of advertising or sales promotion. The advertising may be a specific campaign promoting a particular product or service that prospective buyers hear or see in the various media or it may be a directory listing in a buyers' guide or yellow pages, which prospective customers turn to when they need a particular product or service. There are a number of different applications for customer service telemarketing, and it's quite possible that your CSRs will need training in several different approaches.

Direct Inquiry Conversion From Advertising Campaign, Deal, or Special Promotion. Perhaps the most widely practiced form of inquiry conversion is this type of direct inquiry. The company has advertised a specific product or service and has given the customer service department responsibility for taking orders for the service or product or answering inquiries in such a way that the caller will enter an order at that point.

In many cases, the ads have been keyed so that the company can determine which ads or which media pulled the most inquiries and which inquiries were most readily converted to sales. Sometimes the keys are visible: the caller is asked to read a code or department number from the ad; the term *priority code* is frequently used for this purpose while conveying a sense of prioritized response. Other keys may be more transparent: asking for a particular individual (usually a pen name) or calling a specified extension. In both instances, keeping accurate statistical records on call origins is an important part of the job and may require additional probing by the CSR.

Normally, the telemarketing approach on inquiries triggered by ad campaigns involves four techniques: (1) answering specific questions asked by the caller; (2) citing features and benefits of the product or service; (3) overcoming objections; and (4) closing the sale. These sales techniques are the most fundamental, but your reps will still need specific instruction, coaching, and practice in performing them.

Remember that many of your reps have been primarily reactive in their jobs, and the notion of steering a customer into making a purchase may be somewhat new and unsettling to them. Once you show them how easy it is and remind them that the sale is halfway made when the customer initiates the call, they will become adept at the process. Naturally, they need to be well indoctrinated in the specifics of the products or services being offered.

Direct Inquiry Conversion From Buying Guides. This process may be as basic as filling an order for a pizza from a customer who has called a local pizzeria advertised in the yellow pages. Or it may involve a call about parts, electronic components, machinery, security services, software, consulting—any kind of products or services that can be listed in one of the hundreds of different buying guides issued each year. As with ad-triggered inquiries, you will want to document the sources of these inquiries, but you may want to set criteria to distinguish between routine inquiries that can be readily converted by front-line personnel and those that may have to be referred elsewhere for a more comprehensive approach than is practical for the customer service department. This strategy is described next:

▪ *First-stage inquiry conversion.* This is generally practiced where the selling job may require special skills or knowledge, as in the case of high-tech or engineered products and specialized services. It often consists of developing basic information about the caller and then passing that information along to a field salesperson for follow-up. In some cases, inquiries may be referred to engineers to determine whether the customer's need can be met with existing technology.

In other instances, the primary function of customer service reps is to set up appointments for sales reps to call on customers or prospects who have indicated interest in a particular service or prospect. It should be clearly understood by CSRs that this responsibility is in no sense menial or trivial. Setting up an appointment for a salesperson isn't always easy, and it's often the most critical step in inquiry conversion on high-ticket items.

The same process may be used to set up appointments for customers to attend demonstrations of equipment, software applications, segments of training programs, open houses, and more. Some companies offer special training seminars for customers or prospective customers—this is fairly common in the real estate, franchise, and investment fields—where salespeople also attend and follow up with sales proposals to attendees. As with direct inquiry conversions, your reps may need training in the details of this specialized area that apply specifically to your type of business.

▪ *Lead screening and qualification.* One of the problems with inquiry-generating media like bingo cards and card decks is that they frequently generate too many inquiries from individuals or customers who are not serious prospects for the company's services or products—at least not serious enough to warrant a sales call—as well as inquirers who will never be prospects but are merely curious or have time on their hands, for example, prison inmates. In their raw form, such inquiries have practically zero credibility with field salespeople, who rarely follow up on leads that have not already been screened and qualified as genuine prospects for the company's services or products.

Where such media are used, it's often part of the customer service department's job to screen and qualify leads by first scanning the cards and then following up by phone to further qualify immediate prospects. Inquiries that are qualified as genuine hot prospects are turned over to the sales department and usually show a high conversion rate. If they don't, then it's incumbent on you as customer service manager to improve the qualification criteria based on feedback from salespeople in the field. Otherwise the leads you forward to them will lose their credibility and probably won't be acted on.

Inquiries that are screened out may include a category of secondary prospects who get a personalized response by mail and are added to the mailing list for further mailings and a category of nonprospects who receive a token response but are not placed on the mailing list.

In some cases, the customer service department may be involved in telephone follow-up of selected prospects to determine whether they require further information, would like to place an order, or are no longer in the market.

This activity may be performed on a fill-in or standby basis, but should be assigned for specific time frames rather than on a "when you have time" basis.

▪ *Lead generation from existing customers.* This application should be practiced more widely than it is, because it can generate substantial increased sales from existing customers without placing an undue burden on the customer service department. It's best illustrated by a program at the Callaghan Company, Deerfield, Illinois, a legal publishing company where CSRs are making an important contribution to the bottom line. Elvira Mazzoni, director, customer service, says that CSRs are trained to ask probing questions when customers call in with orders or inquiries.

After handling the customer's request, a rep says, "While I have you on the phone..." and use a special decision tree to lead into questions such as "Does anyone in your firm work in the field of [communications law, entertainment law, trusts, labor law]?" or, more simply, "What is your firm's area of expertise?" Reps also have a look-up list of legal terms that callers are likely to use and that often indicates additional titles that may be saleable to that particular caller. Between these two processes, CSRs turn up good sales leads, which are immediately passed along to sales reps for follow-up and entered into the sales lead database for further tracking. Every lead that is converted nets a $7.50 bonus for the CSR who generated it, plus $2.50 for a departmental pool. The conversion rate is a healthy 30 percent, which indicates that the program is more than paying for itself.

Imaginative Telemarketing Applications

Customer service telemarketing enjoys a unique advantage over conventional telemarketing because when the phone rings it is either somebody who is already a customer for the company's services or products or somebody who has prequalified himself as being interested in those services and products and therefore a better-than-average prospect.

But there are also instances where you may find excellent prospects almost purely by chance, for example when a competitor's angry customer calls *your* company's customer service department by mistake.

Most CSRs and their managers would breathe a sigh of relief when the angry caller turned out to have called the wrong number, but at Chemineer, Inc., the Dayton, Ohio, manufacturer of industrial mixing equipment, this error is seen as a golden marketing opportunity: an opportunity to find out what the competition's customers are dissatisfied with and an opportunity to make a significant sale for Chemineer.

In the manufacturer's aptly called conversion program, reps involve the wrong-number caller in a dialogue and ask probing questions about her problems with the competitive equipment that sparked the initial call. They then follow with a presentation of the benefits of Chemineer equipment and offer to take the competitive equipment in trade. And the strategy generates sales, even when the immediate result is only in the form of negative information about the competition. In the hands of an effective salesperson, that information may be all that's needed to close some significant sales.

Marketing Intelligence Applications

As the Callaghan Company and Chemineer examples suggest, normal customer service contacts often turn up extremely valuable marketing intelligence, which can often lead to substantial sales and profits. Again, customer service telemarketing enjoys this advantage over conventional telemarketing, which seldom allows for probing and developing information about one's customers as well as one's competitors.

Thus it's important that your reps be trained to identify key issues or topics that may be mentioned by customers and pass them along immediately to you for further evaluation. One of the most important of these is competitive pricing information, which should be given to your marketing people right away. Also news of competitive problems, which can often help a salesperson dissuade a particular customer from signing up with a competitor. (Note that knocking the competition is generally frowned on in selling, but it is perfectly acceptable to make product or service comparisons or to cite verifiable case histories.)

Your reps should also be on the lookout for references to proposed new plants, mergers, acquisitions, relocations, and the like, and of course to new product introductions by competitors as well as sales campaigns and special promotions or deals. Reports of customer dissatisfaction with your own products or services, policies or procedures, pricing, packaging or whatever, should be similarly passed along quickly to the appropriate people in your company. It's never safe to assume that your marketing people are aware of all these news items, and by informing them and others you increase your value to them and enhance your image as a member of the corporate strategy team. Which is where you belong!

14

Controlling Costs for Efficiency and Profitability

In the majority of companies today, the customer service department is generally considered a cost center, that is, it creates costs but not profits. This very narrow view creates an internal perception of the department as somewhat of a necessary evil. Much of the financial support you can expect from your management is likely to be aimed at reducing costs and improving productivity, with improvement in customer service itself often a secondary goal.

This isn't necessarily a disadvantage. One of the surest ways to attract management attention in any company is to devise a plan for reducing costs. A number of reducible costs incurred in customer service are the result of policies or outmoded practices that actually interfere with giving quality service in the first place. If you can combine cost reduction with service improvement, that's an excellent start toward recognizing the customer service department for its potential as a genuine profit center, a real money-maker for your company.

At the same time you must guard against the kinds of cost reduction—downsizing the department is a common example—that are sometimes undertaken solely to save money and almost always degrade the quality of your customer service. To prevent this sort of thing from happening and to become recognized as a positive element in the company's profit picture, you need a basic understanding of the principles of cost allocation and cost-benefit analysis. You also need to be familiar with the overall budgeting practices that affect how much you get—or don't get—for your departmental operations.

As manager, you need not be a cost accountant, but it wouldn't hurt to take a few courses in accounting and cost analysis. Chances are your company has an educational reimbursement program and would look kindly on your taking courses that will help it save money. If it sounds like heresy to recommend courses in finance in a book focused mainly on marketing, remember that financial-minded people in your own company often are the hardest people to sell on customer service improvement. Fight fire with fire: Meet them on their own ground with proposals and cost-justifications phrased in the language with which they are most comfortable.

Principal Cost Concepts in Customer Service

Customer service is often a complex activity with subtle cost interactions. As an example, one company was concerned with the cost of its overseas phone calls and provided all customer service reps in the international section with 3-minute timers and instructed them to keep their overseas calls to 3 minutes or less. The following month, there were no calls over 3 minutes in length, but the net phone bill was significantly higher because there were 25 percent more calls. It turned out that reps were keeping an eye on their 3-minute timers and as the time approached they were telling the overseas contact they were going to hang up and call back immediately in order not to violate the 3-minute rule, which resulted in more calls at a significantly higher *unit cost* per call. The policy was revised when management realized that the *incremental cost* of talking another minute or two was far less than the *fixed cost* of making an additional call to avoid violating the 3-minute rule.

Another company took the opposite course and required its reps to volunteer information not requested by customers making inquiries by phone. A study of call patterns had indicated that customers who had called previously often called back for additional information. The *fully distributed cost* of handling additional calls was far greater than the *variable cost* of calls that gave customers information they would be likely to call back about in addition to the specific data they asked for.

As you can see, there's more to customer service costs than meets the eye! Let's look at some of these cost concepts in the context of your customer service operations.

Fixed Costs

The most basic cost concept, fixed costs are often referred to as *G&A* (short for general and administrative) or simply as *overhead*. In cost reduction proposals, fixed costs may also be referred to as *nonreducible* costs to differentiate them from certain variable costs, which can be reduced and sometimes eliminated altogether.

Perhaps the best and most common definition of fixed costs is "whatever it costs to put the key in the door every morning," which is another way of saying that fixed costs are the sum of all the costs that you incur just by being open for business and that are not greatly affected by the amount of business that you actually do. The story is told that on its first day of business, Federal Express carried fewer than ten packages: the fixed expenses of having a fleet of aircraft, terminals, materials handling equipment, and a communications network required to transport those packages were in the millions.

In customer service, fixed costs generally include the costs of the space the department occupies; the furniture and all office equipment including computers and telecommunications; light, heat, and power; and a proportionate share of the company's overhead for security, insurance, taxes, administration, maintenance, and so forth. These costs occur every day you're open for business, and most of them occur even when you're not. Light, heat, and power will be used

somewhat less when you're closed, but otherwise your fixed costs go relent-
lessly on from day to day. One reason for management's ongoing concern with
the size of the department is that more people means higher fixed expenses just
to accommodate them. By some estimates, the fixed annual cost of one additional workstation in a customer service department can be double the annual
salary of the employee who uses that workstation.

Companies have different methods of arriving at fixed costs. Some simply
allocate them as a percentage of all other costs; 15 percent and 20 percent bases
for G&A are not uncommon. Chances are your company already has some such
basis, and if so your life will be a lot easier than if you try to calculate fixed
costs on your own. If fixed costs are calculated too low for your department, it
may be somewhat more vulnerable to downsizing. You may find it worthwhile
to make your own calculations of fixed expenses just to see if you agree with
the company's figures.

However, bear in mind that since fixed or overhead costs are usually a
constant, you can exclude them from many of your budgetary and other proposals. That is, the fixed costs of proposal A, proposal B, and proposal C are
not going to be significantly different from one another or from your present
fixed costs, so your cost comparisons of the three alternatives are made a lot
less complicated and potentially confusing if you omit them from the proposals
altogether.

One final question: What's the one situation where fixed costs become
variable? When you reach capacity, of course! Let's assume that in order to provide better service you are going to beef up your product inventories. To do so,
you are going to have to build more warehouse space to supplement your
present 100,000 square feet, which are bulging at the seams. You only need
several thousand square feet right now, but down the road you'll be needing
more, so you build an additional 25,000 square feet. Wow! Your fixed expenses
skyrocket way out of proportion to previous fixed expenses, because you're
only using one corner of this vast space but paying the fixed costs on all of it.

Fortunately, as long as your business keeps growing, that won't be a consideration for long. But, when you discuss issues of capacity utilization, fixed
expenses are a very important consideration. Let's assume that in their wisdom
your architects designed access doors to the new space with insufficient clearance to accommodate forklifts moving from the old section to the new — the
type of thing that happens an embarrassing number of times.

No problem! Just buy another forklift and use it solely in the new space.
Except that for the time being it's only going to be used several hours a day,
and your fixed costs — in this case they may be referred to as "costs of
ownership" — are going to be exceedingly high in proportion to the use you get
from the equipment. And they'll stay that way until there's enough to keep the
forklift busy for a full shift. Then, of course, you'll have to buy another forklift
and incur another increase in fixed costs, and so forth.* In short, fixed costs do
vary, but usually in fairly large steps rather than in the smaller increments that
are true of variable expenses such as overtime.

*If you are wondering what kind of operation this might be, assume it's a flow rack and
conveyor design, where forklifts are used mainly for receiving merchandise.

Variable Costs

Variable costs are the costs that vary with the amount of business you do. Labor costs are a major component. For example, after you put the key in the door and open it, you need somebody to run the place. The number of people you need varies with the amount of business and the nature of the transactions.

In a self-service supermarket, the amount of business the store does affects two main labor elements: cashiers, including baggers, and stock personnel who handle inventory. The two functions are sometimes interchangeable, so that an increase in store traffic may not bring about an immediate increase in variable costs; during slow periods checkstands can be closed and personnel assigned to restocking shelves. In a customer service department encountering peaks and valleys of telephone activity, personnel can be taken off phones to perform filing and other nonphone duties during slack periods. Yet at some point personnel will have to be added where business has increased, or laid off where it has decreased.

The labor cost problem is often acute in customer service operations because of the peak-and-valley situation. During a typical workday, for example, the number of incoming phone calls to be serviced can vary significantly from one 15-minute segment to the next. Many companies use temporaries, seasonal, or permanent part-time workers to handle their busiest periods. To do this properly in larger departments requires the kind of demand forecasting now available in most state-of-the-art ACD systems.

However, as pointed out in Chapter 10, some of the fluctuations in traffic can be leveled out simply by asking customers to call at different times, and overall call volume requiring live handling can often be reduced sharply by using alternative means of communication. In addition, some calls can be avoided altogether via proper scripting and/or customer education.

Labor costs in customer service aren't confined to the telephone, of course. Some companies have found it more cost-effective to have data entry performed off-line by a staff different from those who deal with customers via phone. They have found that data entry skills are much more readily available and less costly than the customer service and account management skills needed by their customer service reps, and their volume of business justifies having two separate groups.

Another variable cost that is frequently at issue is usage, which includes use of telephone time, computer time, outside services, postage, forms, stationery, and other supplies. Some of these can be quite large, others relatively small, depending on your kind of business. One use element you will want to look at is the proportion of inbound calls that represent revenue for the company versus those that do not.

Variable costs can also be influenced by company policy. One customer service department found that its policy on merchandise returns was incurring high administrative costs in authorizing returns and restocking the merchandise when it was returned. The solution was a basic change in policy: trust customers, and let them make returns for any reason without having to phone or write for approval. So the company did just that. Enclosing preapproved authorization forms and return labels with each shipment eliminated many phone calls and streamlined the entire process with a net savings of some $70,000 in variable costs and no increase in the number of returns.

A common example of this type of tradeoff is found in customer service departments that provide free parts or goodwill adjustments to customers in cases where the administrative costs of the paperwork involved would exceed any revenue that could be derived from the transaction itself. One company making small dollar amount refunds to consumers found that the administrative cost of writing checks—about $25 per check—often exceeded the amount of the check itself, so it adopted a policy of making refunds under that amount in postage stamps. This policy was acceptable to customers and in effect saved the company $25 in variable costs every time a refund was made for less than $25.

Incremental Costs

The concept of incremental costs has widespread application in customer service operations. It is particularly useful in computing price breaks and in offering different levels of customer service based on account volume. A common example is the cost of entering an order for services or products. There is a base cost of the *header* that is, account name and address, ship-to and bill-to information and so forth, that is common to all orders. Then there is the variable cost represented by the number of products or services that are being entered and accompanying descriptive data, discounts and extensions, plus any special instructions.

The cost of the header, or initiating the ordering process, is generally computed at anywhere from $3 or $4 up to $50 and more. It is essentially a fixed cost, although it differs in different companies. The variable cost tends to be quite small in comparison to the fixed cost. It is usually computed in *lines*, that is, separate products or services that are ordered.

As an example, the base cost of entering an order might be $25, and each additional line ordered might cost $1 to enter. In this instance, an order for twenty lines would cost the company $45 to process, whereas an order for twice the number of lines, that is, forty lines, would not cost twice as much to enter but only $65, reflecting a theoretical saving of $25 in order processing costs between the two orders.

The essence of incremental costs is: What would it cost us to produce one more unit of work once we've incurred our base costs? In the example we've used here, the incremental cost is $1 per line item, and it's basically the same as a variable cost, although it is often used in a different context.

For example, one company conducts basic customer research among telephone customers by a relatively convenient and low-cost method described in detail in Chapter 9. When the customer's inquiry has been handled or his order entered, the customer service rep asks the customer, "While I have you on the phone, may I ask you several questions for a survey we're conducting?" The data are gathered at very low cost because the customer is already on the line and identified as the proper person to contact for a particular category of information. This is the equivalent of the header or base cost. The two or three questions asked the customer can be entered directly into a real-time database at very small cost—incremental cost. The alternative of preparing a call list and initiating calls to sometimes-elusive customers, explaining the purpose of the call, and so forth—the equivalent of setting up the header on an order but more time-consuming—would be many times the small incremental costs incurred in the first or "opportunistic" approach.

Incremental costing can also apply in opportunistic situations such as: inquiry conversion, or upselling or cross-selling to customers who have called in to place an order. In the basic example, a caller inquires about product or service features and/or price; the customer service rep provides the wanted information, often from a prepared script, and then asks for the order. The cost of converting the inquiry is incremental in relation to the investment that's already been made in responding to the caller's inquiry. Upselling and cross-selling are typically add-on sales made after a customer has placed a regular order. They may involve related products or services or entirely unrelated ones. The actual techniques are discussed in detail in Chapter 13.

Unit Costs

Unit costs are quite likely to give you trouble because they underlie much of business accounting, not always to the benefit of customer service operations. Using the example of the two orders, one for twenty lines costing $45 to enter and the other for forty lines costing $65 to enter, if these orders are rendered in terms of unit costs they look like this:

Order 1. $45 ÷ 20 lines = $2.25 unit cost per line
Order 2. $65 ÷ 40 lines = $1.625 unit cost per line

Translated to a manufacturing environment where there is a fixed set-up cost of, say, $1,000, and a variable or incremental cost of $10 per unit produced, the picture looks like this:

A. Fixed cost $1,000 + variable cost 200 units @ $10 = $3,000, ÷ 20 units = unit cost of $15
B. Fixed cost $1,000 + variable cost 400 units @ $10 = $4,000, ÷ 40 units = unit cost of $10

This example could also be used to justify a pricing differential of as much as 50 percent depending on the quantity ordered.

In manufacturing, unit costing tends to dominate decisions on what to produce and when to produce it. Production-oriented managers like to schedule long runs and defer short runs until demand builds to the point where they're longer and more economical. This is fine from a unit cost viewpoint, which is what manufacturing and production planning people are typically rewarded for, but it can play havoc with customer service levels when demand exceeds forecast and customers have to wait until production decides it's economical to produce the items they ordered several months ago!

Production people often strongly resist any suggestions that they interrupt regularly scheduled production runs for emergency orders, even for your best customers. Your most effective solution for this problem is to improve forecasting to the extent that such emergencies rarely arise. Some customers, particularly in just-in-time situations, are likely to offer you the option of shared forecasting, which helps you avoid most emergency situations involving your preferred customers.

Another approach, and one that has wider application, is to push for change in the underlying rewards-and-penalties system whereby production people are rewarded for low unit costs and penalized for high ones, regardless of what the impact is on sales, customer service, and overall profits. This proposition is difficult to sell, but if management is genuinely interested in improving customer service, they'll never achieve that goal by rewarding production people for *not* providing service and penalizing them when they do.

This is not a reflection on production people or anybody else who is rewarded on unit-cost basis. It simply explains why customer service goals are often so difficult to meet because of the cost goals that are set by senior management.

An example of unit costing in the service industries was recently provided by a tree removal company, which quoted a price of $245 for removing one tree from a property, and $375 for removing two trees, reflecting a 23.5 percent differential in unit pricing, the difference between $245 per unit and $187.50 per unit. From a marketing point of view, the transaction was presented as the difference between $245 for one tree and only $130 additional for a second tree, a $115 saving, or almost 50 percent.

Of course it really wasn't a $115 saving, but rather half that—$57.50 overall—and represented a substantially enhanced profit opportunity for the tree removal company. The company calculated that its cost of sending a truck and two-person crew to the site was $100 and that its labor cost was roughly $50 per tree, so that its margin on the first tree was $95 and on the second tree an acceptable $80, since it would be increasing its overall gross margin from $95, or 38.8 percent, to $175, or a respectable 46.7 percent gross margin. The management of the company schedules single-tree jobs only in time slots where it has no multiple-tree assignments.

The same type of unit costing can be applied to almost any type of service situation where there is a significant initial cost and a smaller variable cost for providing additional units of service. The Federal Express and warehousing space examples would be relevant here.

Whatever your business, your management is not going to look kindly at any customer service offerings you propose that appear to incur high unit costs. A common example features a customer who buys a truckload of product per month at a truckload price. Occasionally, this customer runs short and orders a fill-in shipment of a palletload of merchandise, which he expects to get at the truckload rate. Your financial department feels that he should pay the palletload rate, which has a 25 percent higher unit cost in the price book. Since the customer picks up in his own truck, shipping costs are not an issue.

You tend to agree with the customer that he should be charged the truckload rate. How do you sell this idea to your financial department? Try incremental unit costing. If you sell twelve truckloads of forty pallets annually, with eight fill-in orders of one palletload each, what is the *real* unit cost of handling those eight palletloads spread across a total of 488 palletloads sold annually? It could conceivably increase unit costs by 10 cents per palletload, or $48.80 for the year's business, which is probably less than one hundredth of one percent of your total revenue from the account—a reasonable price to pay for the continued goodwill of a customer who has other sources he can turn to. The parallel in a service industry would be to waive surcharges or late payment charges assessed to major accounts.

Fully Distributed Costs

Fully distributed costs is a common term in almost any kind of business operations and is part of the process referred to as *loading* or *burdening*. In the case of a customer service call center, for example, the unit cost of a telephone call would comprise a proportionate share of all of the following elements:

Labor Costs

Manager
Supervisors
Phone reps
Administrative personnel
Taxes and fringes (38 percent of wages)
Time paid but not worked (productivity ratio)

Equipment Costs

Telephone system fixed costs
Telephone system variable costs
MIS costs
Fax, copying, and other equipment costs

Other Costs

Product sheets and catalogs
Miscellaneous computer and office supplies
G&A @ 20 percent

With this kind of loading, which is essential to determine the true cost of rendering service, the fully distributed cost of a customer service rep earning a modest $12 an hour answering inbound calls would be close to $65 an hour. If the rep handles nine calls an hour, which represents good productivity in most small and medium size industrial customer service departments, the fully distributed cost per call would be $7.22 per call. This cost varies with the number of calls handled and the relative productivity in your department. You can often arrive at the fully distributed cost by a much quicker route: Use the average cost method described next.

Average Costs

Average costs are similar to unit costs in that they are derived by dividing the total cost of performing a series of transactions by the total number of transactions. For example, if the total cost of running a customer service department is $500,000 a year and the department handles 10,000 orders, the average cost per order is $50. In the example of telephone costs cited above, it's reasonable to develop an hourly cost and then divide it by the average number of calls per hour to determine the average cost per call.

As long as the transactions being measured are relatively alike, averaging is an acceptable way of expressing costs. For example, in a reservations center where most calls are under 5 minutes in length and more complex calls are referred to a separate customer service center, the unit costs of one call are not going to differ markedly from another call. The mix of longer and shorter calls will be evenly distributed among workers so that a standard of handling 110–125 calls a day at an average cost of $5 to $6 per call is a reasonably accurate reflection of the true cost of handling those calls, and it's quite easy to arrive at.

But contrast the situation in a software or technical support center, where calls can range from a few minutes to an hour or more. Here, the term *average cost per call* has no meaning. There is no such thing as an average call, since one call may cost $5 to service and the next one $100 or more. The same would be true in deriving average order costs when some orders consist of one or two parts and others million-dollar units of capital equipment.

Variances of this type can hurt your chances of providing adequate service levels to your customers. For example, an average cost per order of $100 based on this range would require you to impose a minimum order size of $200 so you could at least break even on orders for one or two parts or a few supplies. What does this do to a customer who wants to order a single part listed at $37.50, and which is already perceived by that customer as overpriced?

Yet in a company selling goods from inventory, that is, standard items, there's relatively little difference in the cost of processing an order for $1,000 and processing another order for $10,000, since the main difference is in the quantities ordered and simply involves entering different numbers on the keyboard. Of course the costs of actually assembling and shipping the orders varies with the number of units ordered, but even then large orders are proportionately less expensive on a per-unit basis.

If yours is an order-oriented department and meets the standard of reasonable similarity of orders by type or size, don't worry because your department does other tasks in addition to handling orders. Almost all of that other activity—order status inquiries, technical or application questions, customer training, complaints, returns or exchanges—is triggered initially by order placement and is generally in proportion to the size of individual orders. In other words, the million-dollar order generates ten times as many of these other activities as the $100,000 order. If your department does work that has no relation to orders for goods or services, then the cost of performing those activities should be excluded from the averaging process.

Labor Costs at Varying Levels of Productivity

Many customer service departments operate at relatively low levels of productivity, not because personnel are poor workers, but because it's inherent in the nature of customer service: frequent interruptions and almost constant switching from one task to another, with all the slippages and inefficiencies that these interruptions entail.

The putting-out-fires syndrome characteristic of many customer service operations contributes to this inefficiency; it means disruption of economies of scale in performing routine tasks and concentration on exceptions handling, which by definition can seldom be done by means of standard (and reasonably efficient) procedures. Informal surveys of customer service managers in industries over several years produced estimates of productivity levels ranging from a low of 50 percent productivity to a high of 90 percent, although the average is much closer to the low figure than to the high one.

This means that if you have 80 percent productivity and have a fully distributed labor cost of, say, $50 an hour, you will need to allow for the 20 percent loss in productivity by multiplying your $50 hourly cost by an increase factor, or IF, of 1.25, making the true hourly cost $62.50. The IF is derived simply by dividing 100 percent by the actual level of productivity. Thus:

The IF for 90 percent productivity is 100 percent ÷ 90 percent = 1.11
The IF for 85 percent productivity is 100 percent ÷ 85 percent = 1.18
The IF for 80 percent productivity is 100 percent ÷ 80 percent = 1.25
The IF for 75 percent productivity is 100 percent ÷ 75 percent = 1.33
The IF for 70 percent productivity is 100 percent ÷ 70 percent = 1.43
The IF for 65 percent productivity is 100 percent ÷ 65 percent = 1.54
The IF for 60 percent productivity is 100 percent ÷ 60 percent = 1.67
The IF for 50 percent productivity is 100 percent ÷ 50 percent = 2.00

Allocated Costs

Many of the costs incurred in normal business operations are allocated to different departments, accounts, or activities. Some companies allocate costs of specific customer service activities to the customers for whom the activities were performed, in order to measure the relative profitability of different accounts based on the levels of service they may require. For example, by allocating costs among several major accounts, one customer service manager was able to determine that one major customer incurred customer service costs of 14 cents per dollar of sales, whereas another large customer incurred costs of only 8 cents per dollar of sales. Allocating costs in this fashion has enabled other firms to decide which customers to concentrate field selling efforts on and which to de-emphasize because of their limited profitability.

If you think that similar situations exist in your operations, you will want to collect data on the number of transactions handled and the average cost per transaction, as well as such items as average dollars per transaction, number of returns, exchanges, credits, or adjustments, support or technical assistance calls, and so forth. These data will also help you identify marginally profitable accounts that could be made more profitable through a process of customer education.

Fry Communications, Inc., a Mechanicsville, Pennsylvania, printing company, set up an account development team to salvage accounts of this type, ranging in actual size from $1,000 to $1 million, and bring them into the profit column. It experienced a 95 percent success rate, mainly by educating them in the technology as well as scheduling and other procedures. Allocating costs is an excellent way of demonstrating the profit contribution of customer service, but be sure to have your before-and-after costs lined up to make the proof convincing.

Standard, Imputed, or Assigned Costs

Standard, imputed, or assigned costs are calculated in much the same way as work standards, by means of a series of precise measurements of specific customer service operations and the costs associated with them, and then adopted as the standard costs to be assigned to those operations. In other words, specific operations are not repeatedly measured to determine individual or discrete costs. This approach is similar to the standard operating costs per mile allowed by the Internal Revenue Service as a deduction for business use of personal autos.

Whereas it would be possible to assign precise costs to individual transactions in handling phone calls on an ACD system or order entry on the basis of keystrokes and similar measures, in most cases it isn't worth the effort: The cost of calculating costs would normally outweigh any benefits from doing so.

Cost Tradeoffs

Cost tradeoffs usually occur in connection with calculations of total cost. For example, a high-tech company decides not to stock high-value parts at its fifty local branches. Instead, it centralizes all stocks of such parts in a single inventory stored at Memphis. When orders come in, the needed parts are shipped out by the next Federal Express flight at the highest priority rate. The relatively high cost of the Fedex service is offset by the even greater cost that would be incurred by maintaining safety stocks of the high value parts at fifty local branches. As a result, the total cost of the centralized operation is substantially lower than the total cost of decentralized stocking, while the levels of service are just about the same.

You will find many opportunities to use cost tradeoffs in supporting proposals for improvements in customer service. A number are illustrated in our list of forty-five cost reduction tips later in this chapter. But cost tradeoffs are not always easy to sell inside the organization. Since they are likely to cross departmental lines, the gain to one department is likely to be obtained at the expense of another. The marketing department that uses air freight to provide overnight service and gain a larger market share may run into resistance from the distribution department that has to pay the bill.

Another scenario might reveal that diverting the high-value products from the regular distribution chain would dilute the volume in the warehouses and in the company's private truck fleet, which in turn would reduce capacity utilization and reflect on the department's efficiency and raise unit transportation costs. Most businesses are structured into departments where each manager's accountability is to his or her department's budget or cost standards, not necessarily to overall savings or benefits. This is the reality you must deal with, not the team spirit you read so much about, and the more you know about costs and budgeting and how other departments are measured, the more effective you will be as customer service manager.

Financing Customer Service as a Corporate Strategy

From a financial viewpoint, improvements in customer service operations fall into two main categories: (1) low-cost and self-liquidating improvements, which can often be undertaken with little or no need for added corporate resources or budgeting; and (2) longer-term projects, which cost more and may require long-term investment, supported with proof of a significant payback.

Low-Cost and Self-Liquidating Improvements

■ *Improvements in procedures and reduction of red tape.* Many businesses simply write off customers' deductions and claims under a certain dollar limit because it's the most cost-effective way of dealing with them. The practice of multiple signoffs is costly in terms of managerial time and often costs more than the amounts they are signing off on. In another area, many companies have dispensed with order acknowledgments and have realized substantial savings just through eliminating paperwork and filing. Their customers have enjoyed similar benefits. One large chemical company eliminated acknowledgements and saved $100,000 and a proportionate sum for its customers.

■ *Improved diagnostics and problem-solving.* These important functions are increasingly performed by computer. One of the most common examples is computerized claims analysis and payout, which in some insurance companies is now being used to resolve some 95 percent of all claims. The advantages include speed, consistency, and extremely low labor costs. It was recently estimated that to duplicate the claims analysis and resolution output of the computer system used by Blue Cross of Georgia, which receives claims on-line directly from hospitals, clinics, and other health care providers, would require some 900 human claims analysts with terminals tied into a mainframe computer, if such a computer existed.

It is hard to find any area of diagnosis and problem-solving in business that isn't computer assisted to a greater or lesser degree. The advantage of using computers is not that they replace human beings but that they free human beings to do the kinds of complex problem-solving that only human beings can do and that computers cannot.

However you approach this facet of customer service, the underlying principle is the same: Using decision rules is the only way to assure fast, consistent diagnosis and solutions to common customer service problems. As a practical matter, many of those rules can be readily programmed into your computer system, as many probably are already.

An example in a customer service department might be a problem where a major customer, a public utility, has suffered an ice storm and requires an emergency shipment of replacement insulators and antirattle units in order to restore power to its community. The decision rules would be something like:

> Can we fill the customer's order completely?
> > If yes, pack and ship by overnight service today.
> > If no, can we make partial shipment?
> > If yes, make partial shipment and return to decision rules.
> > If no, are there substitutable items in stock?
> > If yes, pack and ship as necessary.
> > If no, is there product committed to others still on our docks?
> > If yes and suitable, divert to customer with emergency in accordance
> > > with company policy and back order original consignees.
> > If no, poll other customers for buyback options.

This process, which would take at best half a minute on a properly programmed MIS, could save as much as $1,000 or more in judgmental decision making at the managerial level. Decision rules of this type are often used to assure fast and correct response in product recalls, hazardous materials spills, threats, and other emergencies. They are also desirable in hundreds of routine situations that account for a great deal of time, stress, and expense in the department.

▪ *Error-avoidance procedures.* By some estimates, the process known as *rework*—correcting mistakes or repairing the damage caused by mistakes—can account for as much as 50 percent of the operating cost of a company. This proportion can be as high for banks and other service organizations as it is for manufacturers and retailers. A high proportion of these errors can be avoided by improvements in procedure and decision rules.

Errors originating outside the department are more difficult to deal with. A major source of errors is mis-specification by sales personnel and customers. Some departments minimize this problem by developing special formats and sequences for entering orders and then training salespeople and customers in their use.

Surprisingly, some companies do not permit customer service reps to read back telephone orders or cross-check product numbers with product descriptions. Their reasoning is that salespeople's time is too valuable to be spent listening to order readbacks on the telephone. Actually, there are faster and better and far more accurate ways of entering orders—automated or semiautomated methods that don't require participation by sales personnel.

What's the best way to initiate an error-avoidance program in customer service? If you're not already using statistical process control techniques, you will be soon, as their original manufacturing applications expand to include services of all kinds. In the meantime, you will want to develop some basic statistics on these four points:

1. Errors by type
2. Errors by number
3. Errors by cost
4. Errors by impact on customer

Your source for the first three sets of numbers will be mainly credits and deductions. Most error prevention programs don't go any further than this, but if you want to be realistic you need to know how errors affect customers. The best way to find out is to ask. Then set priorities based on the cost-savings potential for your company versus the value-added savings realized by reducing the errors that most seriously impact customers.

▪ *Rewriting manuals and instructions in user-friendly format.* As discussed in Chapter 10, much needless expense arises from handling telephone inquiries from customers who simply can't understand product or service instructions, policies, warranties, software manuals, and the like. You certainly want to tally calls by type in your department to determine whether such a communications problem exists between your company and its customers. And whatever literature or policy statements, instructions, or manuals you prepare in your own department should be reviewed by outsiders before you issue it in final form. The more technical your products or services, the more essential it is to have outside review to make sure your readers don't become bogged down in technical language or company jargon that forces them to call you for further explanation.

The potential for cost savings in this area is extremely high, since most of these calls are "nonmachinable" and need to be answered live, at a cost of $5 to $10 per call.

▪ *Redesign of invoices and forms for faster processing.* Invoices that are complex, difficult to interpret, or don't meet the customer's requirements cost U.S. companies millions of dollars annually in three main ways:

1. Delayed payment when invoices are set aside for later analysis, resulting in delayed cash flow and lost interest
2. Cost of responding to phone calls from customers asking for clarification of their bills or invoices
3. Cost of rectifying errors in billing or payment caused by invoice format or complexity, compounded by the fact that undercharges are likely to go unreported

Taken together, these costs can run into the thousands of dollars daily in a single company. Many managers mistakenly treat the symptom instead of the cause: They concentrate on increasing telephone productivity to handle the flood of calls rather than on correcting the poorly designed forms and invoices that caused that flood of calls.

▪ *Improved logistics.* The term *logistics* can be applied to the supply and distribution functions in manufacturing, wholesaling, and retailing, and it can also be applied to the dispensing of services, for example in hospitals, on highways, in queues at banks, airline ticket counters, and in hundreds of similar applications. Logistics improvements come about in both instances through improvements in system design, which balance efficient operations with needs and expectations of customers for reasonable levels of service.

Although the logistics of transportation and distribution are largely outside the scope of this book, if you are in the manufacturing business as customer service manager you will be working very closely with your logistics personnel. Numerous suggestions for improving logistics in a service environment, and in the department itself, were discussed in Chapter 11.

■ *Automatic reorder or inventory replenishment systems at customer sites.* Companies as diverse as Manville Corp. and International Minerals & Chemical Corp. long ago realized the benefit of educating customers in improved purchase planning, economic lot ordering, and practical inventory management and replenishment systems. Besides benefiting customers, these practices also reduce costs for the vendor company by systematizing customers' purchasing practices and eliminating expensive hand-to-mouth and last-minute crisis buying. As an added benefit, helping customers in these ways makes them less likely to be lured away by competitive offerings.

■ *Decision rules for automatic adjustments.* As discussed in detail in Chapter 8, decision rules ensure consistent decisions in repetitive situations, which in turn ensure consistent application of company policies on customer service. Decision rules are also an economic measure because they ensure that the correct, most cost-effective remedies are applied to each situation. They also speed up the resolution process and eliminate the delays that typically occur when multiple signoffs are required.

Applied to complaints, deductions, and other adjustments, decision rules typically trade off the administrative costs involved in investigating and resolving these issues against the costs of automatic payouts, which often cost less overall.

■ *Courtesy training.* This is a normal part of customer service training but its economic contribution is often underrated. For example, a certain number of complaints are the result of perceived discourtesies by service givers, but these must be handled like any other complaint, and the cost is seldom under $50. Courtesy training reduces the number of such complaints and, consequently, the cost of handling them. Moreover, lack of courtesy training often aggravates tense or difficult situations and frustrates service givers who don't know how to cope with them. The net result is increased stress, burnout, and high-cost turnover.

Several direct cost savings are inherent in courtesy training beyond the conventional wisdom that customers who are treated well tend to spend more money. Concrete proof of this was provided by the Miami Nice courtesy training program for cab drivers at the Miami, Florida, airport. The program grew out of concern that visitors' first contact with the area was often a negative one, which could well translate into shorter stays, reduced expenditures during their stay, negative word of mouth about the area as a vacation spot at a time when it was already suffering image problems, and decisions to hold business meetings and conferences elsewhere.

The first year after the Miami Nice program was undertaken, complaints against drivers dropped by 80 percent while their tips increased by 15 percent.

Figure 14-1. A typical corporate budget, with more than two-thirds of the budget already committed

Source: Customer Service Newsletter

The total economic contribution of the program is reflected in an 80 percent savings in complaint handling cost for the local administration and, on an average $30 a day of tips, a $4.50 daily increase totaling $22.50 weekly or $1,125 annually for each cab driver. And those numbers don't include the overall impact on the local economy of visitors who have enjoyed a better-than-average reception from their cabbies!

Improvements With Higher Investment Cost and Longer Payback

Improvements in this category are more likely to be treated as investments rather than out-of-pocket expenditures. Thus, as customer service manager and chief sponsor of such improvements you should be familiar with three management science techniques in particular:

1. *Forecasting.* Although your sales and marketing departments are already engaged in some forms of sales forecasting, these forecasts are often unreliable for operations planning purposes, and you would be well advised to generate your own forecasts.

Most forecasting is based on historical records, with allowances for growth and seasonal factors. Your concern is mainly with forecasting the volume of transactions your department is expected to handle and what you need in the way of systems and staffing to handle it. You need credible forecasts, and a beneficial side effect of developing such forecasts is that you'll find it much easier to get management attention in the future.

2. *Corporate budgeting or resource allocation practices.* Major improvements in customer service often require major investment or allocation of resources. And there are never enough resources to go around. Figure 14-1 shows a typical corporate budget, with well over two-thirds of the firm's resources already committed and very little left over for discretionary purposes. You are competing with

other department heads for your share so you had better have good numbers!

3. *Return on investment (ROI) and other cost justification measures.* Different companies use different approaches in evaluating their investments in personnel, equipment, and general improvement. See Figure 16-7 for a typical ROI projection for investment in training and monitoring customer service performance totaling $300,000 over a 5-year period. This type of cost justification is the most common and can be applied to any number of situations in customer service.

Following are the principal types of customer service improvements requiring higher investment cost and generally involving longer payback periods:

▪ *Improvements in absolute response time or reducing wait time.* These improvements apply to inbound phone calls, inquiries, service requests, order fulfillment, disbursements, and similar transactions. In this use *absolute* means that the process is already operating at maximum efficiency with existing personnel and systems, and that red tape, signoff practices, and restrictive policies have already been corrected. Given this, response time can be improved only by replacing the existing system and/or increasing staff, usually at considerable expense.

As an example, if average wait time on a call is one minute and the intent is to reduce it to 30 seconds, the only practical solution may be to replace the existing system at costs ranging up to $100,000 or more. Or, the solution may lie in supplementing the present system with an automated voice response unit (VRU) at greater initial cost but lower operating cost. A more complex situation might involve improving on-line response to inquiries, from a current 70 percent rate to a proposed 95 percent level. This improvement would probably require complete replacement of the company's information system and restructuring data flow methods throughout the organization, at a total cost possibly approaching several million dollars.

Investment alone, regardless of the amount, will seldom, if ever, bring about the desired improvement. Virtually every major investment in improved service requires a concurrent change in corporate culture, disciplines, and protocols. In the example of the upgraded information system, virtually every department in the company will have to convert its input procedures from its present batching methods to a real-time basis and to be held accountable for any time lapses or lags beyond 30 minutes. Together, the changes represent a major departure from tradition, a cultural change, for most of the parties involved and one that isn't easy for them to accept.

▪ *Increased availability of resources.* Including services or products, personnel, equipment, communications, upgraded systems and database, finished goods inventory, parts inventory, and more, this category of improvement is very closely related to improvements in speed of response, as illustrated above in connection with telephone and information systems.

Availability of resources is particularly critical in the response time involved in filling orders for services or products. For example, if a company wants to respond to requests for service on its copying equipment within 4 hours, it will have to hire more field engineers, provide more training, and furnish more automobiles, tools, and test equipment, and the added investment can be substantial.

Similarly, if a company wants to reduce turnaround time on orders for its products, the only way to do so is to increase inventories of those products. This, too, can be costly. To provide 100 percent 24-hour turnaround on all orders for stock items could easily require doubling the company's inventory investment. Most managements are unwilling to make this kind of investment, and yet it's important that they understand that it's often the only way to bring about the "excellent" customer service they're so interested in. They should also be aware of the high cost of *not* committing resources—that too many inventory shortages and stockouts will result in lost credibility, lost business, and lost customers.

This is particularly true in the case of parts inventories. The finest equipment in the world is only as good as the level of availability of the parts required to keep it running. A company that expects to sell more than one unit of equipment to a customer, whether that equipment be an automobile or a mainframe computer, will never do so unless it can provide a ready supply of parts. The Beloit Corporation in Beloit, Wisconsin, maintains parts inventories to support papermaking machinery that is sometimes as much as 100 years old. Manufacturers of farm equipment are in a similar position and recognize that not to support outdated farm equipment still in use would cause them a great loss of credibility in the tightly-knit agricultural communities they serve.

In some cases adding personnel is the only way to overcome major service deficiencies. A large West Coast company found that its performance in resolving claims and issuing credits had gotten so far behind due only to a lack of personnel that, in a futile attempt to catch up, many claims were being denied without any investigation. It isn't hard to imagine the impact of this practice on the company's customer relations. (For the record, it should be noted that this company already had a $500 automatic adjustment policy in place, but even this wasn't enough to offset the shortage of personnel working on claims.) The company belatedly hired the necessary personnel and eventually worked its way out of the hole it had dug for itself.

▪ *Providing extra services.* Examples of extra service include 24-hour emergency aid, customizing, special credit arrangements, training for customer personnel, consignment inventories, drop shipments, on-site personnel, and other exclusive-use or dedicated resources. Some of these services may be required by the nature of the business. For example, providing life-support equipment to hospitals requires exceptional levels of service, far beyond the kind of support required for home appliances, office equipment, automobiles, and machinery in general.

Sometimes the cost of exceptional service is included in the price of the product, and sometimes it's charged separately, as in a service contract. For example, several telephone companies offer a hot site or disaster recovery service to subscribers who are highly dependent on their incoming call centers. Subscribers who sign up for the program pay a monthly maintenance fee; if they suffer a fire or other disaster, within hours they can move into a fully equipped call center maintained by the telephone company for just such occasions and have all their calls diverted there for handling by their own people until their own call center is back in operation. They pay an added charge based on actual use.

By contrast, a manufacturer of high-tech farm equipment found that farmers did not object to paying a relatively high initial price for the equipment but strongly resisted paying reasonable field service costs for equipment maintenance. As a result, the manufacturer built extremely high reliability into the product and passed the cost along as part of the initial price. Field service charges were set at a ridiculously low $25 an hour, which was acceptable to farmers, but there were few calls for field service because the equipment was highly reliable.

Some companies provide extra services in order to give the company an advantage in a tight competitive situation where all companies provide basically the same service or products—a generic or price-parity market. The airline industry's frequent flyer programs are one example, the various checking options offered by the banking industry another. Currently, some supermarket chains are breaking from the cost-competitive mold by offering, at extra cost, phone shopping and home delivery.

In much the same way, fast-food outlets are beginning to accept credit cards and direct ordering by customers using pushbuttons. Although the costs of these extra services can't always be passed along to customers, in most cases the added volume of business is expected to pay back the investment. In the case of credit cards, for example, it's well established that customers tend to spend more money when using credit cards than when paying cash, which helps offset the service charges assessed by the credit card companies.

A whole array of so-called value-added customer services fall in this category, including:

Free management services for smaller customers
Free training for customers' equipment operators
Pharmacy computers that flag incompatibilities in prescriptions
Consolidation and overflow shipment allowances
Consignment shipping, field warehousing, special credit terms
Personalization and customization of surgical kits
Software programs, low-cost hardware, fax equipment for customers

These value-added services are effective as differentiators because they help reduce customers' costs, increase customers' productivity, improve customers' management information, and help customers make more money. They also tie customers more closely to the vendor company, thus fulfilling a major mission of customer service—keeping and cultivating customers.

Profit Contribution by Cost Reduction: Forty-Five Ways to Cut Customer Service Costs

Although the customer service department makes a continuing profit contribution through the customer retention process, as manager you should not overlook the many opportunities to further contribute through a systematic program of cost reduction.

What may appear at first glance to be relatively small savings are likely to be better understood and appreciated when they are first annualized and then stated in profit equivalents. For example, a savings of $10 a week annualized totals $520. As a profit equivalent, this $520 equals the profit on $10,400 in sales for a company in the 5 percent profit bracket. A $20-a-week savings would translate into $1,040 annually and would be the equivalent of the profit on $20,800 in sales.

Efficiency Improvement

Penny-pinching and cost reduction are not the same. As manager you are probably under great pressure to reduce expenditures, often just for the sake of saving money. Don't give in. As an alternative, select one or more of the following suggestions, which reduce costs not by withholding expenditures but by improving operating efficiency. Note that many of the following suggestions don't save money directly for the department but do reduce total cost for the company and thus reflect substantial profit contributions:

1. Write scripts to ensure optimum time use on standard telephone transactions or inquiries.
2. Reduce busy signals and call overload by informing customers of best times to call.
3. Minimize callbacks by providing complete information on first call.
4. Reduce information inquiries by improving literature clarity.
5. Eliminate acknowledgments where practical.
6. Reduce order status inquiries by improving reliability of promises.
7. Reduce field service and other appointment status inquiries by improving the dispatch system.
8. Identify error sources and cut error rates systematically, starting with the most costly.
9. Level department workload by scheduling customer call-ins by location, type of business, or other identifier.
10. Use facsimile to relieve phone traffic and enable batching of low-priority materials.
11. Encourage use of mail with longer lead times, thereby imposing a discipline of systematic ordering on customers.
12. Use a recorder for overflow calls.
13. Use voice response units (VRUs) for handling routine calls.
14. Use time on "hold" to provide information to customers that will shorten the talk time when the call is answered.
15. Use voicemail or recorders for after-hours calls.
16. Use voicemail to cut telephone tag and repetitive calls.
17. Call customers by appointment.
18. Cut red tape on adjustments.
19. Cut back on use of customer service department as message center for field sales personnel and others.
20. Set up a departmental quality circle with cost-reduction goals.

21. Develop computer-to-computer (EDI) transaction capability.
22. Develop priorities by customer class or channel.
23. Set productivity standards for most common, repetitive tasks.
24. Establish surcharges for special services.
25. Encourage use of self-service options by customers.

Cost Tradeoffs

Cost tradeoffs are situations where a change in customer service practices can save money or improve efficiency in other departments, resulting in a savings or a net gain for the company as a whole. Tradeoffs are based on the premise that each department can perform certain tasks more efficiently than other departments. When each department performs the tasks it is best suited to do, even though this may mean crossing jurisdictional lines, the result is that all departments involved function more efficiently and make a significant contribution to the bottom line. It is the cumulative or annualized savings that count, not just the one-time figures. Trade off costs with:

26. Sales, by handling more adjustments and administration in the customer service department so that sales personnel have more time for face-to-face selling.
27. Shipping or traffic, by giving customers incentives to consolidate their orders, resulting in lower handling and shipping costs.
28. Engineering and R&D, by cross-training customer service reps and enabling them to handle the most frequently asked questions without having to transfer calls to high-priced personnel.
29. Marketing, by increased involvement in promotion planning and new product intros, thereby increasing the likelihood of success in both.
30. Credit, by minimizing credit holds or shipment delays due to disputed invoices rather than actual credit problems.
31. Field engineering and similar services, by improving telephone diagnostics, user repair, and dispatch procedure.
32. Production, by educating customers in economic lot ordering with sufficient lead time. (The reciprocal would be discouraging hand-to-mouth buying practices by customers.)
33. Production, by persuading customers to use available machine capacity.
34. Warehousing, by minimizing change orders and rush shipments.
35. Warehousing, by improving customer pickup procedures.
36. Sales, by screening and qualifying leads so that sales personnel can concentrate on high-potential prospects.
37. Sales, by arranging demos and making appointments so that sales personnel can maximize face-to-face selling time.
38. Sales, by arranging local (destination) sales of refused or damaged shipments to avoid cost of return haulage.
39. Sales, by arranging sales of seconds and overruns, which are difficult for sales personnel to handle in the normal course of events.
40. Sales, by telemarketing inactive or marginal accounts.

41. Sales, by developing substitution programs for product in short supply.
42. Human resources, by rewriting job specs to conform with real job requirements and reduce costly turnover.
43. Finance, by improved forecasting of inventory and other resources required to meet customer needs.
44. Finance, by evaluating hardware and systems before buying, and selecting the most productive equipment for the customer service environment.
45. Management, by relieving senior managers of need to respond to inquiries and complaints, which can be handled more effectively, and at much lower cost, by properly empowered front-line customer service personnel.

Tradeoffs With Sales

Sales-related functions that can be performed more efficiently by customer service than by salespeople offer an excellent tradeoff opportunity. When customer service personnel take over these functions, which are often in the area of adjustments, return authorizations, and the like, salespeople can make more actual sales calls or, where appropriate, sell in greater depth by calling on more people at a given account. This can be quantified in two ways:

1. *Impute a dollar value to the added sales calls enabled.* For most companies, a sales call costs out at between $250 and $400. A salesperson making one more sales call per week at the lower rate ($250) or fifty per year would be increasing his or her productivity equal to $12,500 annually.

2. *Estimate actual sales results from this increased productivity.* Most companies have a standard hit rate (one hit or sale per so many calls) and an average dollar amount per sale. As an example, a chemical manufacturer with fifty field salespeople has a hit rate of one sale per every ten calls and an average sale of $40,000. If each salesperson makes fifty more calls per year, that averages out to five sales per salesperson, or $200,000 each per year. With fifty salespeople this total would be $10 million per year in added sales revenue.

Your selling costs, hit rate, and average sales per hit may vary, but you can hardly help but come out ahead. And you incur little if any added cost in the customer service department, since most administrative matters eventually end up there anyway. Removing salespeople from the administrative equation usually makes operations more efficient.

The Profit Contribution of Customer Service as a Marketing Strategy

The most significant financial contribution by the customer service department occurs when customer service is understood and used as a marketing strategy specifically aimed at retaining and "growing" customers. Like the ancient Chinese proverb that says that a trip of a thousand miles starts with a single step, the strategic goal of customer service starts with the servicing of a single account and continues with the cultivation of repeat business and account growth.

One of the most significant measures of customer service is the percentage of repeat business, the "renewal rate," from one year to another. This percentage is strongly influenced by the quality of customer service: the better the service, the higher the retention ratio and the lower the turnover rate. And, of course, accounts tend to grow in proportion to the quality of the service they receive.

Allowing for growth of individual accounts at a rate of 10 percent a year and account retention or renewal rates as shown, small increases in customer retention can generate substantial increases in net revenue over a period of time:

Renewal Rate	Revenue 1st Year	Total Revenue, 10 Years
70%	$1,000,000	$ 4,038,000
80%	$1,000,000	$ 6,012,000
90%	$1,000,000	$ 9,562,000
100%	$1,000,000	$15,940,000

You can use these statistics to demonstrate the payoff from a customer service strategy aimed specifically at increasing customer retention rates. Just rephrase them in this fashion:

A 10 percent increase in customer retention will generate a 50 percent increase in total revenues.

A 20 percent increase in customer retention will generate a 137 percent increase in total revenue.

A 30 percent increase in customer retention will generate a 295 percent increase in total revenue.

A detailed description of the account retention and revenue growth process appears with an accompanying chart showing year-by-year customer revenues in Appendix D. Data illustrating the reciprocal, that is, the cumulative effect of account losses, appear as Appendix E. Both approaches have proved to be effective tools in creating companywide awareness of customer service as an important, profit-oriented marketing strategy.

The best way to improve customer retention rates is to improve the quality of customer service while maintaining competitive pricing. This is often a question of fine-tuning customer service to be more responsive to specific customer needs and, in some cases, offering different types of service to different classes of customer. In addition, be ready to employ typical account-saving strategies such as:

- Effective handling or correction of a difficult situation that otherwise would have resulted in loss of the customer.
- Raising levels of service to meet competitive situations that would otherwise siphon off customers.

Figure 14-2. Profit contribution by account size, reflecting proportionately higher costs usually incurred in providing customer service to smaller accounts

Size of Account $/Year

	$1,000,000 and Over	$500,000– $999,999	$100,000– $499,999	$25,000– $99,999	Under $25,000
Net sales (average company in group)	$1,272,240	$636,120	$233,244	$45,590	$18,022
Less: short-term variables	342,000	173,736	69,996	23,138	12,170
Less: long-term variables	102,782	54,355	24,391	13,258	5,665
Net contribution to profit and overhead	$ 827,458	$408,029	$138,857	$ 9,194	$ 187
Percentage of net sales	57.69%	28.84%	10.58%	2.07%	.82%
Percentage of total contribution to profit and overhead	59.80%	29.49%	10.04%	.66%	.01%

Source: Customer Service Newsletter

- Offering angry customers credits, gift certificates, or vouchers as an enticement to patronize the firm at least one more time.
- When customers are disappointed with a particular product or service, offering them a different product or service in the company's line, thus keeping them as a customer of the company if not for the original service or product.
- Entering into a tie-in arrangement such as EDI, forecast sharing, or other partnership relationship, which creates a "most favored customer" status and makes it difficult for the customer to break away. These may also include credit arrangements, field warehousing, and consignment shipping.

The Final Measure of Customer Service Cost-Effectiveness

If you've applied as many of the cost reduction and profit contributing measures listed here as are applicable to your situation, you've already made a significant profit contribution. But there's still one major step to be taken: resource allocation by account value, which simply means gearing the level of service to the importance or profit potential of each class of accounts. Here's how it's done:

1. *Analyze profitability by account, channel, industry* (see Figure 14-2).
   - Identify target accounts, which include the top 20 percent of accounts,

Figure 14-3. Target accounts identified as part of a company's service strategy

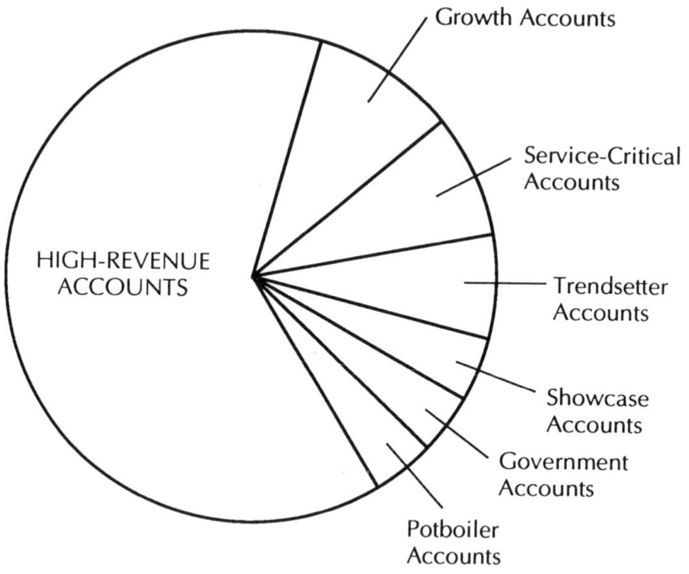

Source: Customer Service Newsletter

plus accounts with growth potential, accounts with high-service
needs, and sometimes a few "prestige" accounts to improve the company's visibility and status (see Figure 14-3).
- Stratify balance of accounts by dollar value into three or four additional groups.
- Include accounts that produce high dollar volume but small margins
in the top group as a matter of policy, but call them to management's
attention.

2. *Allocate resources by account value.*
- Analyze costs of servicing different classes of accounts, including
telephone support, labor, logistics, etc., using fully distributed costs
where applicable.
- Identify accounts or classes of accounts that are disproportionately
expensive to service in terms of revenues and profitability.
- Reallocate expenditures based on account value. This reallocation
may mean dropping some marginal accounts altogether, a strategy
known as demarketing that will become more common as market
segmentation becomes more intense.

You should not expect that your suggestions along these lines will be wel-
comed with open arms by management, and particularly by sales and marketing people who have traditionally been oriented to the acquisition rather than
the retention of customers. On the other hand, marketing people are rapidly

Figure 14-4. Simulation program showing impact of service levels on market share, in top graph after 900 sales and in lower graph after 7,500 sales

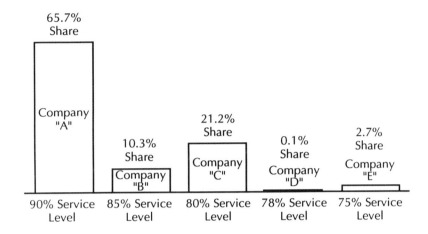

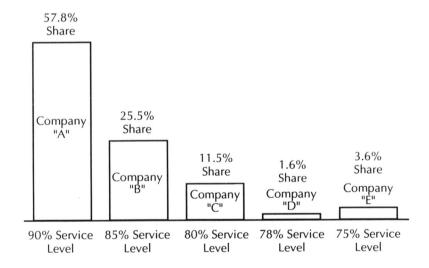

Note: Because of limitations of screen area, bar graphs are not necessarily proportionate.
Source: Chicago Consulting

becoming acclimated to the concept of highly targeted marketing and have already coined an expression to describe it: "hypertargeting." This connotes a high degree of customization of the marketing effort to different market components. That's essentially what you'll be undertaking with customer service, and logic as well as current marketing trends are on your side.

The management science known as computer simulation will also be of considerable help to you in developing cost-effective levels of customer service. Figure 14-4 illustrates one such program, which enables a user to test the effect of different service levels on market share. What's particularly significant is the showing that the highest service levels do not always deliver a proportionate market share, and in some instances, a lower service level produces a higher market share. For example, the top chart in Figure 14-4 suggests that, among the five competing companies in question, being number 2 in service may be less desirable than being number 3, and both charts suggest that being number 4 in service is much less desirable than being number 5.

These findings contradict the popular notion that high levels of customer service automatically generate high profit levels. This isn't always the case, and as manager your biggest challenge is to develop a truly cost-effective customer service system that ensures a return on your customer service investment proportionate to the time, effort, and resources you expend. Your next biggest challenge is to sell the program to your management.

Section IV

Hiring, Training, and Keeping the Best People

15

Perfect Customer Service Requires Hiring Perfect People

"The customer service rep's job is the most important job in the company!"

We heard this comment for the first time almost three decades ago from a senior manager sharing his experience with juniors just entering the field of customer service. In the intervening years, we have never seen anything to contradict that statement. The CSR's job is indeed the most important job in the company, because the CSR is the lifeline between the company and the people who keep it in business: its customers.

Few things will affect the success of your career as manager as much as the quality of the people you surround yourself with. But you will also find that finding and hiring the right people, and keeping them, is a complex, sensitive job that requires a great deal of your time and attention.

Yet that time and attention can be well spent. Even though reps come to you with CSR experience in other companies, much of it is of little relevance to the services, products, policies, or procedures of your company. So you must invest in training, and in some CSR jobs it can be as much as a year before your trainee is prepared to go it alone. If you can't keep that CSR for at least another year, you haven't recovered your initial investment in hiring and training him.

Turnover in CSR jobs is often a major problem and is often a major cause of poor service. It's popular to blame working conditions, low salaries, and job stress — the overall working environment — for the turnover, but the main cause of turnover is failure to hire the people most suited to the job.

This chapter discussed some of the steps to take *before* you start recruiting and interviewing and some of the precautions to take once you start interviewing. Chapters 16 and 17 deal with training, morale, and motivation, which are critical to avoiding and reducing turnover *after* the hiring process is complete.

12 Tips for Choosing the Right People

1. Set hiring goals by type. Reactive personnel will last on the job and will do fairly good work but will seldom grow beyond a certain point. Proactive workers will learn quickly, do a good job, meet challenges, and grow rapidly, but they may outgrow the job. You should probably figure on having a balance between the two diffferent types: reactives to maintain continuity, proactives to infuse new ideas and new vitality into the department.

2. Create the right environment. Proactives need challenges and career pathing that will keep them on the move. Job enrichment and other conventional motivators—plus security—will keep the reactives happy and productive. Where practical, dividing the department into account or product reams has excellent motivational possibilities for both types.

3. Compare choices with personnel department. Review and rank all resumes and ask personnel department to do the same. You're likely to find very little overlap, which will tell you why you need to be involved in the process and may suggest that personnel would benefit from some guidance from you.

4. Rewrite job descriptions: change titles. Most job descriptions don't do justice to the job or to the people who perform it. Remove reactive phrases and replace with proactive ones such as "initiates action," "analyzes data and pro-jects trends," "manages account relationships," and so forth. Replace traditional conventional titles such as customer service representative with account executive, applications specialist, technical analyst and the like.

5. Rewrite job specifications. A specification describes the individual skills, experience, and background that are required for the job. Current specs probably emphasize clerical skills and little else. Don't ignore these in rewriting but balance them by including such qualifications as good interpersonal skills, problemsolving ability, initiative, potential for growth and others.

6. Interview the top people of your choice. Avoid trying to sell them on the company; let them sell you on themselves. Conduct part of the interview over the telephone; if they can't sell themselves to you over the phone for a job they want, ask yourself how they're going to project an image of caring and competence to the customers they'll be assigned to.

7. Describe the job truthfully. Tell it like it is, and let the applicant know precisely what will be expected of him or her. Encourage informal meetings with your reps (with yourself absent) where job applicants can get an insider's view of what it's like working for you. If good people keep turning you down after such bull sessions, you may have a problem!

8. Hire people who want to be involved—and give them something to be involved in. Quality circles and other forms of participative management are excellent motivators and attract good people who will grow in the job and help you do the same.

9. Relieve stressful conditions. Identify the policies, procedures, and conditions that cause stress and can be improved. But remember that a certain amount of stress is inherent in the job, and in your interview try exerting some mild stress on the applicant by interviewing him or her two-on-one, i.e., yourself and a supervisor interviewing the applicant.

10. Provide immediate feedback, positive reinforcement. Particularly with new hires, make it a point to let them know when they're doing right and when they're not. Again, make sure people know precisely what's expected of them.

11. Let people know how they'll be measured. Comparative measures of performance are sometimes perceived as unfair, particularly if one job differs from another. Make sure that prospective hires not only understand your measurement system, but also are the kind of people who *want* a tangible measure of how well they're doing.

12. Be a leader. Be prepared to hire people to whom you can delegate, people who will put out their own fires while you plan and manage—and go to bat with them with your management.

Where to Begin

When you prepare to hire new personnel, you need two basic tools, without which, you will very likely put in a lot of effort and get poor results. Those two basic tools are:

1. *Job descriptions*. Job descriptions list the duties the worker will perform, the responsibilities, the reporting patterns, and so forth. Many customer service job descriptions are completely outdated because they do not reflect what the worker actually does in the customer service job in today's business environment. If this is the case in your department, one of the first steps you should take is to rewrite job descriptions to reflect what people actually do.

The best way to accomplish this is to have your reps rewrite their job descriptions as a team effort. This activity is an excellent motivator because it creates a sense of involvement. And it's possible that with those new job descriptions your human resources people can upgrade the jobs to a higher salary level. Figure 15-1 shows the results of one company's rewriting of a basic job description. Not only does the new description provide a more comprehensive picture of what the job involves but it changes the rep's title also.

Figure 15-1. Before and after: one company's rewriting of a basic customer service job description

Before Rewrite
Sales Order Clerk A

Typical Duties:

A. Processes order for material or merchandise received by mail, telephone or personally from customer or company employee.

- Canvasses customers by telephone and mail to ascertain needs.
- Edits orders received for price and nomenclature.
- Informs customer of receipt of order, prices, shipping date, delays, or additional information needed on order, using mail or telephone.
- Ascertains credit rating of customer.
- Records or files copy of orders received according to expected delivery date.
- May check inventory control and notify stock control departments of orders that would deplete stock.
- May initiate requisitions.
- May route orders to department for filling and follow-up on orders to ensure delivery by specified dates.

B. Performs any combination of equivalent or lower level work.

Education — Knowledge — Skills:

Ability to communicate orally and in writing; tact, courtesy, and ability to relate to people. A thorough knowledge of company products; ability to perform general office duties such as typing, filing, record keeping, and preparing reports. Knowledge is usually gained through high school commercial courses and on-the-job training.

Experience:

Six to 18 months' experience is usually required to perform on this level.

After Rewrite
Customer Services Representative
A

Typical Duties:

A. Provide optimum customer service as required to maintain and enhance existing business and to obtain new business. This requires that the Customer Service Representative take personal and complete responsibility for every order to ensure that the customer requirements are met from time of initial order receipt until the product is delivered, invoiced, and the customer is satisfied. This will include the following or some combination of the following:

- Assist the customer and/or sales representatives with any inquiry or problem concerning their orders. Provide prompt and efficient response and resolution to each inquiry. Such inquiries or problems could involve product quality, coordination of deliveries, availability of product, customer pricing and/or billing, etc.
- Maintain accurate customer account information, efficient billing of all orders, and maintenance of all required paperwork.
- Process all orders in an efficient and expedient manner as received by mail, telephone, or personally from customer or other company employees.
- Advise customers on market conditions that may affect their order and price breaks that will benefit them.
- Keep each respective sales representative knowledgeable of all activities associated with each customer account.
- Obtain current product pricing information from management; update product price lists and advise all concerned of all competitive price adjustments.
- Provide product technical information as required to respond to customer technical inquiries and to recommend alternative materials or products. Refer customer to appropriate qualified divisional personnel in response to sophisticated customer technical inquiries and/or problems.

B. Assist in the solicitation and sales of company products or services to new and existing customers. This function is primarily maintained through a telemarketing effort. It includes some

Source: Customer Service Newsletter

combination of the following:

- Identify potential customers through analysis of the market place; through gained knowledge and/or personal knowledge of the industry and product lines; by attendance at customer services seminars, in-house training seminars, sales meetings, plant tours, and trade shows, and by keeping knowledgeable of existing customer needs through various contacts and periodic personal visits to customer locations.
- Research inactive accounts and follow up directly with former customers or sales representatives with a goal of regaining lost business. This is conducted by phone and in conjunction with the sales representatives. In some instances it actually involves personal visits to customer locations.
- Analyze and confirm past order history of existing customers to identify high volume accounts. Follow up with the customers for the purpose of enhancing their current business. Enhanced contact is also periodically maintained with existing customers for the purpose of moving excessive inventories of certain products.

C. Coordinate inventory schedules and information concerning product availability.

- Maintain accurate and current product inventory information as this relates to current and anticipated customer order requirements. Function as the focal point between the customer and sales representative regarding this information.
- Monitor inventories to ensure customer and supplier product availability. Adjust shipping schedules as necessary and make recommendations concerning necessary adjustments to plant production schedules.

D. Maintain information concerning customer credit limitations. Follow up with all concerned regarding past due accounts.

- Maintain new customer credit information and communicate these to all concerned.
- Keep accounts up to date.

E. Provide customer service orientation/training of new sales representatives and new customer service representatives. Also provide senior guidance to various junior sales order clerks in their related job responsibilities.

F. Perform any combination of equivalent or lower level work.

Education — Knowledge — Skills:

Education at the college level or equivalent experience is required. Must possess the proven ability to converse well, both orally and in writing, with all customers at all levels of management. Should be tactful, courteous, and possess the ability to motivate others. Must possess a thorough knowledge and extensive technical knowledge of all company products. Should have a minimum of 3 years' experience or related experience as a sales order clerk and should possess the proven ability necessary to influence the sale of company products.

---

2. *Job specification.* Job specifications list the qualifications the individual must have in order to perform the job. Under equal employment laws the skills and qualifications you list must be relevant to the job and must be required of all candidates for that particular job.

You can specify such things as experience, education, levels of skill with computers, and specific clerical skills such as typing and filing, provided they are needed to perform the job. Your human resources people can give you valuable guidance on staying within the law, but you should write the actual job specification to ensure that you get the kind of people who will fill your department's real need, not somebody else's perception of what that need might be.

Should Titles Be Changed?

If you're going to rewrite job descriptions, consider changing job titles as well. There is some sentiment among managers that the title "customer service representative" has become so closely identified with a clerical job that the only way to escape the clerical image is to change the actual job title. Some possibilities for the CSR job title: account manager or specialist, customer representative, technical specialist, client service representative, sales service specialist, industry specialist, product specialist, and others. The word *specialist* seems to carry more weight and more of a sense of professionalism than *representative* and appears to be gaining in popularity.

Upgraded job titles are also an important morale factor, and, like revised job descriptions, have been a factor in improving salary levels in some companies. Remember that improving your reps' image throughout the company leads to greater cooperation from others and, as a result, moves you closer to that perfect customer service you're striving for.

Exempt or Nonexempt?

Although the status of customer service personnel, particularly in newer industries such as computers and software, has improved considerably in recent years, the majority are still classified as hourly or nonexempt workers, meaning that you're required to keep accurate time records and comply with the applicable wage and hour laws. If the job requires technical knowledge and involves certain degrees of responsibility and decision making, it may be classified as exempt or professional.

Except for very large customer service operations such as credit card companies, mail order, airlines, and the like, it seems likely that an increasing number of customer service representatives will in fact be classified as professional, or exempt. These will be career-oriented people, and some companies are recruiting inexperienced candidates with high promise in order to train them for professional-level customer service jobs.

If you are planning to do likewise, be aware that your new hires will probably be classified as nonexempt during the training period. In one instance, the Bureau of Labor Standards (BLS) ruled that trainees for professional-level customer service jobs were to be classified as nonexempt during their training period. In addition, the BLS ruled, they would not be permitted to take any company literature or manuals home during this period, because that would constitute homework, which in turn would be construed as uncompensated overtime under wage and hour laws. Your tax dollars at work!

Coping With the Scarcity of Good People

In recent years it has become increasingly difficult to find and keep qualified customer service personnel. A real and growing shortage of qualified personnel is a result of a combination of relatively low salaries, high stress conditions, and declining skills in the work force. These conditions are a real incentive to make the job more attractive, not only by paying more money (which is beginning to happen), but also by improving the working environment and providing top quality logistical support in information systems and communications.

In short, it's easier to make the job more attractive to capable people than to work with second-best people because nobody else will take the job under present conditions.

Personnel Sources

After talking with hundreds of customer service managers about the best places to find good people, I've come to the conclusion that there is no "best" source of qualified CSRs or CSR trainees. To put together a truly excellent department from scratch could take you a month of intensive recruitment in some areas, whereas in others you could achieve the same results in a week. The difference has to do with the available work force in a given area, which in turn is influenced by the other types of industry there, the cost of living, and the overall unemployment rate.

Try as many of the sources listed here as practical, and then concentrate on those that seem to give you the best results:

▪ *Personnel agencies* are still one of the best sources, provided they ascertain your needs, preferably by visiting your operation, and give you a guarantee, as most ethical agencies now do. Of course, your company should pay the fee. If an agency starts sending you "warm bodies," people who are clearly unsuited for the job, find another agency.

▪ *Temporary agencies* are also an excellent source, particularly where you have the opportunity to buy out the contract of any temps you'd like on a permanent basis. Another advantage of temps is that if they're unsuitable you can ask that they be replaced.

▪ *Physically challenged training facilities* are yet another source. There is an increasing trend to train physically disabled individuals in customer service operations at state-supported facilities, and they have proved to be extremely qualified for customer service jobs. New computer and communications equipment enables paraplegics and blind persons, as an example, to work well in conventional customer service jobs where high mobility is not a major prerequisite.

▪ *Permanent part-time employees* are an excellent resource for dealing with the surges and uneven work load characteristic of customer service. It's a significant portion of the work force, consisting of highly motivated individuals in three age groups: young parents, middle-age work force reentrants, and older retired persons. Most of these individuals prefer part-time work because it fits a particular lifestyle they have chosen. Permanent part-timers are stable and reliable, and research has shown them to be more productive than full-time workers, probably because of their strong motivation to keep that particular job. For the same reasons, they're generally not seeking promotion or careers, so turnover is relatively low.

Referrals from current employees can be an excellent form of recruitment. Many companies now offer premiums to employees who refer potential new hires to the company. This source is particularly good if the referrals are made by individuals who are familiar with customer service operations. A Midwestern high-tech company pays a cash premium for referrals to its customer support group and, in addition, holds an annual drawing for all who have participated. Prizes have included a new automobile, a Superbowl weekend, and a trip around the world. The company obviously values its customer support personnel!

Job posting is practiced by many companies as a matter of policy, and its success depends generally on the level of customer service jobs as compared to other jobs in the company. There is no consensus among the managers we've talked to. Some feel that job posting generates excellent prospects, while others feel that it simply delays and complicates the job of hiring qualified personnel.

Hiring from within (with or without job posting) has, according to some customer service managers, produced exceptional results recruiting personnel from other departments in the company. A dental equipment company in the Northwest found that some of its best reps came from the assembly line in the plant. As the customer service manager put it, "When a dealer called from New York City, they could always tell him which wires connected to which and how the whatchamacallit fit into the thingamajig!"

A large division of a major chemical company recruits many of its reps from the ranks of production supervisors at its many plants. In both of these companies, the customer service jobs offer a combination of better pay and more comfortable working conditions than the plant jobs, so the managers usually have a waiting list of well-qualified applicants and seldom have to go outside their companies.

In some instances, it may be the job status that appeals, rather than the pay or the work. For example, the network services manager of a Virginia company has hired a number of applicants for customer service job openings from among forklift operators and warehouse workers in the company's distribution center. She explains that they see the customer service jobs as career rather than monetary opportunities. She adds that their hands-on experience has made them excellent troubleshooters when there are problems with customer orders. They're measured against standards set for problem resolution and they're characterized in a single word: "fabulous!"

Job fairs have also been successful in recruiting customer service personnel in the view of a number of companies. One company reported good results with its own onsite job fair.

Vendors are yet another source. Your purchasing department may be able to steer you toward some outstanding customer service reps it has dealt with. One manager reported outstanding results with this approach, which he described as "hiring pre-vetted reps."

Advertising can be helpful, although customer service managers differ on its effectiveness. It's generally most effective when professionally prepared and placed in trade publications. Classified ads usually pull a great many responses but require a great deal of screening. The term *customer service representative* in an ad can be interpreted in a dozen or more different ways. Thus you should be very specific as to the skills and experience required. Of course, you must be able to prove that these skills are required for the job in order to comply with equal opportunity employment regulations.

Summer or vacation time interns such as college students, have been reported by managers as showing good potential. If they work out well, they're invited back the next year and may ultimately be offered permanent employment. One manager reports good results hiring school teachers during the summer months to fill in for customer service reps during their vacations. As a spinoff benefit, many companies find that the experience often overcomes the antibusiness bias some teachers hold and helps improve community relations with the companies that have employed them. And customer service jobs give them a chance to see the other side of business-customer relationships!

Your company's built-in appeal: If you are fortunate enough to work for *the* company to work for in your particular community, you will have to do very little recruiting. People will take entry-level jobs just to be working for the company, but often with every intention of transferring to another department as soon as the opportunity presents itself. With job posting, that could be almost any time. So, you must be just as careful in screening out overqualified candidates who are using your department as an entrée to the company as you are in screening out underqualified or clearly misqualified applicants.

Screening Job Applicants

In some companies, much of the screening and preliminary interviewing, including checking references and ensuring compliance with Equal Employment Opportunity (EEO) laws, is done by the personnel or human resources department. If such is the case in your company, you should make sure that human resources personnel actually spend some time in your department—perhaps even working at a terminal for a while—so that they'll see at firsthand what the job really requires in terms of ability to withstand its pressures as well as actual job skills.

If your human resources personnel don't have this kind of hands-on knowledge of your operations, they may be sending you the wrong kinds of people. The perception still exists in many companies that customer service is a clerical job requiring little initiative or aptitude. You don't want this kind of perception controlling the screening of applicants who will be holding down one of the most sensitive jobs in the organization.

Before you interview any of the candidates in person, one additional step should be taken: *interview each candidate by phone*. This is a virtual "must" for any individual who will be representing your department and your company by phone. If applicants don't come across well to you on the phone, they won't come across any better to your customers. Of course, people can be trained to improve their diction, grammar, speaking voice, and so forth, but the phone interview will give you an idea of just how much training will be required and whether you can afford the time and expense.

There are several variations on the telephone interview. A customer service manager in Dallas asks that applicants telephone her before sending in a resume. If an applicant doesn't introduce himself by name before starting the conversation—which this manager considers the mark of a pro—that candidate is usually written off immediately. Several other managers feel this may be a little too arbitrary, but acknowledge that if there's a large pool of qualified applicants it makes sense to apply rigorous standards.

A Wisconsin manager who conducts telephone interviews followed by personal interviews concludes the personal interview by asking applicants to send him a brief written summary of why they feel they're the right person for the job. He says this serves four purposes: (1) It shows how much attention applicants paid to the details of the job during the phone and personal interviews; (2) It's an indication of how well they can express themselves; (3) It provides insights into their self-esteem, which he feels is essential in a job that's so often laced with negatives; and—most importantly—(4) How soon and how well they respond is an almost infallible measure of their motivation.

Peer Evaluation Screening

Another approach to selecting personnel that is meeting with considerable success is called *peer evaluation*. As the phrase implies, it's simply a process of having applicants assessed by the people they'll be working with side by side. At the same time, applicants have an opportunity to experience the work environment and decide whether it's for them.

This approach is particularly useful where personnel must work under considerable pressure and where teamwork is critical. Even though you will conduct the final interview and make the final decision, you will find that your people will be very thorough in their assessment. They will probably consider some factors that didn't occur to you and will make good recommendations. And they will make sure that, once the new hires are on board, they'll get the best support and training. After all, your reps' own reputations are at stake!

Probationary Period and Other Conditions

Particularly with customer service personnel, there are good reasons to be very thorough in assessing both the skills and the job suitability of prospective reps. These individuals will be representing your company to its customers, and in fact will be entrusted with millions of dollars worth of business. They will also be working as part of a team, where one disruptive element can undermine the efforts and the morale of the entire group.

That's why most new hires in customer service are not considered permanent until they have completed a formal training program or have been on the job for 60 to 90 days. At the General Electric Lighting Division facility in Richmond, new hires undergo a rigorous, 8-week training period. It's understood that they may be let go at any time during that period if they're judged unsuited for the work.

One company manager advertises for temporary workers, usually specifying that it's for a 90-day period. At the end of that period a worker or workers who have done well are invited to become part of the permanent staff. This practice is similar to hiring temps through an agency and buying up their contracts if they work out well. It probably saves some money over working with a temp agency, but it also lacks some of the flexibility. With temps hired through an agency, you can try a different worker every day, if you choose. When you're interviewing and hiring yourself, you just don't have the time.

Whatever approach you take to hiring, make sure that the people you hire fully understand any conditions attached to their employment. Your human resource people will take care of most of this, but be sure your new hires are aware of any special circumstances such as the probationary period, having their calls monitored, working different shifts, or getting permission to go to the restroom. This last condition may seem a little far out, but in high-volume operations it's likely to be necessary in order to maintain service levels. And the best kind of relationships with your reps is one where there are no surprises, even about such seemingly minor items as trips to the restroom!

Using Tests

Although human resources departments often administer batteries of tests to job applicants as part of the initial screening routine, there's no indication that these do much more than weed out clear misfits. That is, they don't identify likely candidates for customer service as much as they identify noncandidates. Even then, results may be misleading. If human resources perceives customer service as a clerical job, they may screen out individuals with low-average clerical skills who have offsetting customer service skills such as poise, ability to think on their feet, stress resistance and more.

A few tests are designed specifically for rating individuals' aptitude for customer service jobs. These are generally developed by inventorying the skills and characteristics of individuals who have proved successful in the job. The problem is that customer service jobs differ so widely from one company to another (and sometimes even within the same company) that individuals who would be rated as "successful" customer service reps in some companies would be dismal flops in another. If tests of this type are used, be sure that they are not automatically used to screen candidates out until other qualifications have been assessed as well. For example, if a candidate scores low on the test yet has a record of 5 years' continuous employment in another customer service job and is leaving it only because the current employer is relocating to a distant city, you had better give more weight to the employment record than to the test score!

You should be on the lookout for several other problems associated with tests. First of all, tests that are not directly related to job skills may violate EEO laws by testing an individual's culture rather than his or her aptitude for the job. If you are going to disqualify someone from a CSR's job, do it because they're not suited to do the work, not because testing reveals they believe the world is flat! Second, remember that people who have taken a number of tests soon develop what's known as "test sophistication" and learn how to give the "right" answers that give them high scores. Third, permissible skill tests are likely to place undue emphasis on data entry, for example, rather than on data interpretation or problem solving. So, if your primary concern is hiring an applicant with judgmental skills, make sure that someone up the line isn't just sending you people with mechanical skills, which, of course, are much easier to test for.

Remember, too, that it's very difficult to replicate the stress that's created when a screen can't be entered or takes 10 or 15 seconds to come up or the system goes down altogether while an irate customer is on the line! In such cases a candidate with a cool temperament will serve you and his or her teammates and your customers a lot better than a hotshot data entry person!

Some customer service managers use a different type of test, role playing, to assess how well an applicant would function in a typical customer service situation. This approach gets mixed reviews from managers who have been surveyed. Some managers feel that it's a good measure provided that a standard format has been developed and people with appropriate skills administer the test. Others feel it is better to plunk applicants down in the middle of the real customer service environment and see how they react.

One manager asks candidates to allocate 4 hours of their time—for which he pays them—to try out on the job. Since it's a 24-hour operation, candidates can come at their convenience. Those who say they don't have the time are automatically screened out on the basis of low motivation. Similarly, the support manager in a software company invites candidates to sit at an offline terminal and work with the company's programs. This gives him the opportunity to assess their initiative and interest as well as their skills.

Again, whatever approach you use for screening, be sure to double-check that nobody with potential has been screened out just because they don't fit the CSR profile in your company. In a recent informal survey of thirty-five customer service managers attending a seminar, almost all said they would hire an individual who didn't know how to type or operate a terminal if that person was otherwise excellent for the job. Yet in many of those companies, that individual would never even have come to the manager's attention, let alone reach the interview.

Conducting the Interview

By the time you are interviewing candidates, they should have been thoroughly vetted by others in the organization. If you're lucky, you'll have the kind of problem every manager likes to have: making a choice between two or three extremely well qualified candidates.

Here are some basic dos and don'ts for conducting interviews that get results:

▪ *Let the applicant do most of the talking.* In hiring for a job where initiative, resourcefulness, and the ability to control conversations are important, you should give the applicant an opportunity to display his or her skills—or lack of them.

▪ *Don't oversell the job.* Unless you've been specifically trained in interviewing techniques, you will probably fall into a common managerial trap: selling the job, the department, and the company instead of evaluating the applicants you interview. The applicants should be selling themselves to you, because essentially they will have to do the same with customers: establish credibility, exhibit competence, and create confidence and mutual liking.

▪ *Ask open-ended questions.* These general-type questions basically cannot be answered yes or no or in just a few words. They force candidates to think and talk on their feet: "Tell me what you consider your most outstanding achievement in your previous (present) job." "Tell me what you liked most and least in that job." "Tell me what you consider your greatest strengths and your greatest weaknesses."

Avoid closed-ended questions, which can usually be answered with a yes or a no, or just a few words. These tend to signal the "correct" answer in advance. In addition, as your human resources people will tell you, some closed-end questions may violate EEO laws. For example, you can ask someone "Do you speak Spanish?" if it's relevant to the job, but you cannot ask "Did you learn to speak Spanish in the home?" However, if a candidate volunteers information in responding to an open-end question and without your having asked for it, there's no violation.

▪ *Avoid hypothetical questions.* Don't ask a job applicant "What would you do in a situation like this?" Such questions are too easy to answer. For a more realistic response, ask the candidate: "Tell me about the worst day in your life, the day when everything went wrong. What did you do?" It's very difficult to make up or fake an answer to a question of this type, and the response will give you a good clue to the individual's ability to handle difficult situations.

▪ *Videotape your interview.* Customer service managers are increasingly using videotape during job interviews because a videotape can:

- Refresh your memory after you've interviewed a string of candidates.
- Be circulated to others without their having to conduct their own interviews.
- Help decide among two or three closely matched candidates.
- Help review and improve your own performance as an interviewer.

Videotaping in this type of employment situation could be construed as an invasion of privacy as well as a violation of the spirit of EEO legislation, if not the letter. In the cases we are familiar with, that is not the intent. In fact, an important goal is to give all candidates equal exposure so that candidates interviewed early in the process are not overshadowed by those interviewed toward the end. There is some feeling that it puts undue stress on candidates, but in most cases you are hiring for a stressful job. An individual's reactions on camera may be more revealing than the accepted written tests designed to reveal a candidate's ability to withstand the stress of the job.

Of course, for a third party—an employment or executive search agency—to use videotape in such situations would be a very questionable practice, and quite possibly illegal.

▪ *Pick the right person—or none at all.* Granted that applicants may not be breaking down your doors applying for that job, don't take the best available candidate if he or she isn't what you really want. You'll do better going through the process a second time, possibly trying different sources or re-advertising the job. And you may decide to use temps for a while in order to avoid any long-term commitments.

What to Look for: Qualifications and Motivations

As you can see from Figures 15-2 and 15-3, it isn't too hard to work up a list of skills and personal characteristics to measure potential reps against. Obviously there are certain qualities that you would want in anybody applying for any job: reliability, honesty, ability to get along with others, motivation. In customer service you'll add interpersonal skills, resilience, problem-solving ability, ability to work under pressure, attention to detail, and excellent language skills.

Figure 15-2 shows how a major multiplant manufacturer views the relative importance of different personal traits and customer service skills in evaluating the job applicants for its centralized customer service department. Note that the least weight is given to mechanical and computer skills. Some managers require that applicants be able to type, whereas others say that if applicants are strong in other respects, they are willing to teach them whatever keyboard skills may be necessary. Figure 15-3, a checklist developed by Chicago Consulting, lists approximately forty-five "most wanted" characteristics in customer service representatives and enables scoring on a point basis. As indicated under rating guidelines, an average score of 5 would reflect an average candidate, although most companies would probably be more likely to hire in the 7 to 10 range.

Issues related to the individual's background, the truth of the statements on his or her application, checking references, sexual preference, drug testing, and the like should all be dealt with by your personnel or human resources department.

Beyond these issues and the qualities that relate to the specific job requirements in your customer service department, it's particularly important that you also consider the individual's motivations in applying for the job. Some motivations include:

▪ *Convenience and/or benefits.* Some people will apply for a particular job simply because it's convenient, for example, it's located close to where they live, or the spouse's job or the babysitter's, or you offer flextime or other conveniences. Offering benefits such as a day-care center or an elder care center can also be a factor.

These motivations are perfectly acceptable, particularly because the individual will normally be willing to work in noncareer positions just because of the benefits. In some cases, the employee wouldn't be able to work *without* the benefit, so there's also a strong bond of loyalty. The same can be said for the relatively few but growing cases where CSRs are set up to work at home, with direct phone and computer linkage to an ACD system at headquarters.

You can expect to see increasing numbers of these arrangements, because they have already proved an excellent way to attract people who might not otherwise be available. Benefits and convenience are not ironclad guarantees that an employee will stay with you, however. Your competitors can offer them, too, so you will want to take additional steps to ensure that good people stay and unsuitable ones don't get on board in the first place. Chapters 16 and 17 discuss people-keeping and turnover issues in depth.

▪ *Unemployed—needs a job.* Whereas some employers feel that people who are already working elsewhere are better job risks than candidates who are currently unemployed, candidates who are out of work for valid reasons such as

Figure 15-2. How a major multiplant manufacturer rates the relative importance of personal traits and customer skills in evaluating job applicants for its centralized customer service department

Personal Characteristic

Rating*

Dependability	10
Ability to handle stress	10
(Multiple tasks; setting priorities; meeting deadlines)	
Team player	9
Aggressiveness	9
(Takes initiative; self-motivated; works independently)	
Sense of urgency, punctuality	8
Flexibility	6
Interpersonal skills	6
Outgoing type, i.e., extrovert	4

Skills and Knowledge Requirements

Communication skills	10
(Telephone; oral, major; written, minor)	
Accuracy	10
Reading comprehension	9
Problem-solving ability	9
Arithmetical skill	8
Keyboard skills	5
Knowledge of computers and systems	4

*Where 1 = Needed, 5 = Medium Importance, 10 = Critical

Source: Customer Service Newsletter

plant closings or downsizings—and your human resources people should check such points—are highly motivated to get back to work and perform well. If they've held similar jobs in the past, you may be in luck and get an excellent worker.

But you must also want to try to screen out overqualified applicants who will take the job in order to have income while they're looking for the job they're *really* qualified to fill. If you both understand that it's short-term employment, that's fine. You'll get some good talent at relatively low cost, and in some cases the individual may work out so well you can induce him or her to stay.

But some candidates won't tell you that they have actually filed applications with school systems and government agencies, with the intention of giving notice and leaving your employ if and when the application is accepted. When this happens, there isn't much you can do but go through the hiring process once again—a little wiser and a little more alert to candidates who seem too good to be true.

Career-oriented. You really want to attract these kinds of people if you

Figure 15-3. Checklist of approximately forty-five "most wanted" characteristics among customer service representatives enabling scoring on a point basis

Customer Service Representative Requirements Evaluation Form

Rating	Explanation	Rating	Explanation
1	Unsatisfactory	6	Better Than Average
2	Very Poor	7	Good
3	Poor	8	Very Good
4	Below Average	9	Excellent
5	Average	10	Exceptional

Scoring Instructions: Skip any individual items that do not apply in your particular situation. Total all ratings entered. Divide this number by the total number of items scored in order to obtain the average score.

Personality Traits	Rating	Skills Knowledge and Experience	Rating
Intelligence:		Organizational skills:	
■ Common sense	____	■ Sets priorities	
■ Quick thinker	____	■ Plans/schedules time efficiently	____
■ Decision maker	____	■ Problem preventing and solving	
■ Requires minimal instruction	____	capabilities	____
Maturity		■ Knowledgeable about	
■ Independent	____	requirements of overall	
■ Resists internalizing		work flow	____
problems	____	■ Can visualize the end product	
■ Deals well with irate		from the productive steps	____
customers	____	Reading comprehension:	
Empathy:		■ Understanding	____
■ Relates well to customer	____	■ Insight	____
■ Relates well to company	____	■ Discrimination	____
Job Commitment:		Technical skills:	
■ Will (wants to) work		■ Can operate and is basically	
overtime as needed	____	familiar with computers	____
Flexibility:		■ Basic typing and composing	
■ Can deal with confusion		skills	____
■ Handles the unexpected well	____	■ Copies information with	
■ Can keep several tasks		a minimum of errors	____
going simultaneously	____	■ Spots own errors quickly	____
		■ Can reference manuals or	
		instruction guides easily	____

Source: Chicago Consulting

Communications Skills	Rating	*Skills Knowledge and Experience*	Rating
Listening:		Mechanical aptitude:	
■ Empathy	――	■ Undaunted by technical	
■ Comprehension	――	situations	――
■ Elicits needed information	――	■ Readily determines parts	
		of an assembly	――
Writing:			
■ Grammar	――	Mathematics comprehension:	
■ Composition	――	■ Does basic level	
		of math with the aid	
Speaking:		of machines	――
■ Phone voice	――		
■ Standard American accent		Knowledge of U.S. geography:	
and vocabulary	――	■ Can name and locate	
		(approximately) most	
Other:		states on map	――
■ Expresses spoken			
and written thoughts		*Education*	
clearly and logically	――	Some college or degree:	
■ Quick to gain rapport		■ Liberal arts, English, speech,	
with persons of varied		Marketing	――
backgrounds	――	■ Capable of having earned a	
■ Maintains a professional		degree	――
demeanor	――		

have career pathing in your organization. You will find them to be intelligent, innovative, and resourceful. And you will have to constantly provide them with new challenges and opportunities to exercise their talents.

But you'll have to reconcile yourself to the fact that under the best of conditions, you'll be lucky to hold on to them for as long as two years. But what a great two years it will be! You'll get a great deal out of them, and your department will be the better for it, quite likely the showcase of the company.

And don't overlook the fact that when your department is used as a training ground for sales trainees or management trainees, you can make your presence felt throughout the company and build some excellent interdepartmental bridges—many people will owe their careers to you, and they will have a far better understanding and appreciation of the company's customer service mission.

1. *Security-oriented.* If you have little to offer in the way of career pathing, then you will focus on workers characterized by stability, reliability, longevity in the job, and capability for maintaining continuity in customer relationships. For this, you want people who are more concerned with job security than with career advancement.

People with this motivation can serve you well but unimaginatively for as long as 20 and sometimes 30 years, and they build some excellent relationships with customers. But they also present some problems. They become very set in their ways, and whatever innovation takes place will be largely of your own doing. As each year goes by, you (or your successor, because they will probably outlast you!) will find it harder and harder to sell change to these workers. For mature companies with a well-established market niche, this kind of stability may be preferable to a department full of superstars who do a great job but leave you all too soon.

Job longevity and turnover can be influenced by factors completely outside the company: the local economy, demographics, living conditions, and more. For example, companies in semirural or rural areas seem generally to have lower turnover in their customer service departments than those in urban or highly industrialized areas.

Making the Offer

By the time you are ready to make the actual job offer to the top candidate, the individual selected has been made aware of all the conditions of the job and has indicated clearly that he or she wants that job and fully understands all conditions of the job, including shifts, overtime, and any "restroom clauses" or similar requirements. So you make the formal offer, preferably in writing, and set the date for him or her to start work.

What happens after that is detailed in Chapter 16 and 17. But, don't relax yet! There's one other little warning: *Don't notify the other finalists that the job has been filled!* Hold off on such notifications until your new hire is actually on the job. Things can happen in the week or two before he or she reports for work, and it is awkward to contact people you'd already turned down. Of course, candidates who are out of the running altogether should be notified immediately.

Terminating Unsuitable Employees

In spite of your best efforts to hire the right people, train them well, and provide them good incentives to perform well and productively, some people don't always work out for lots of reasons. As an occupation, customer service has become increasingly complex and demanding. It also varies considerably from company to company. People who do well in one work environment may have problems in another.

So, sooner or later, you'll have to terminate an employee because he or she can't meet the particular requirements of your department. As the saying goes, it never gets any easier. But you will feel better if you follow these steps, which relate only to terminations for poor performance, not for disciplinary reasons covered by company policies:

1. *Lay the groundwork.* At regular performance reviews, make it clear to the employee where he or she stands and that failure to improve to a specified level by a specific date will lead to discharge. That way, when the day comes, it won't be a surprise (it seldom is a surprise, in any event).

2. *Whenever possible, avoid firing for a specific incident or foulup.* There are usually several sides to most of these cases. If you fire somebody for what appears to be exercising excruciatingly bad judgment, or for something like excessive rudeness to a customer, make triply sure there aren't extenuating circumstances. In many such cases, the individual feels that he or she was acting in the best interests of the company and may appeal your firing. If the termination doesn't stick, you'll lose face and credibility with your people. Far better to build a case, as described in item 1.

Remember, too, that a data entry error of $1 million by one rep should normally not merit any greater discipline than a data entry error of $10 by another rep, if they were both caused by the same software deficiency. In fact, a $1 million error would more likely be blamed on you as manager for not having proper checks and balances in your system!

3. *Look into alternatives to firing.* See if the worker can be transferred laterally to another department where he or she can handle the work and make a positive contribution. But don't "dump." Also, some employees who are near retirement age may be willing to take a downgrading to a lesser position in order to stay on the job and qualify for their full pension.

4. *Terminate early in the week.* Don't wait until Friday; that allows emotions and bad feelings to fester over the weekend. Discharge early in the week, so that the employee can start looking for another job right away.

5. *Do it at a neutral site.* Not your office and not the employee's workstation. Pick an office that's temporarily vacant, make it brief, and then leave so the employee can compose him- or herself, call home, or whatever.

6. *Do it with dignity.* Some companies require terminated personnel to be escorted off the premises by a uniformed security guard, apparently to prevent sabotage or other forms of reprisal. This practice may be valid when disciplinary matters are involved, but in terminations for poor performance it is unnecessarily degrading on top of the emotional trauma of the firing itself. If it's a policy in your company, substitute yourself for the security guard if possible and walk your ex-employee to the parking lot or gate. You'll gain respect for doing it!

7. *Offer suggestions.* The personnel or human resources department will probably take over at this point, but before it does, make any suggestions that may help the employee find another job. Make it clear that because he or she didn't work out for you doesn't mean he or she won't work out some place else. Evidence indicates that as many as one-third of discharged employees actually end up getting better jobs!

8. *Do it now.* It's a painful process, and most of us wait much too long before firing someone. But delaying the process doesn't make it any easier and can easily create morale problems among other CSRs who recognize that this particular worker isn't doing his or her fair share. When you fire a worker who is clearly performing well below departmental standards, you're sending an important message to the remaining workforce that you're decisive as well as fair.

9. *Explain to other employees.* They won't be surprised. Employees who don't carry their own weight are a burden to the others, and your remaining workers will respect you for taking decisive action. That's one of the best reasons not to delay doing what you know you'll have to do sooner or later anyway.

The Importance of a Quality Relationship

Customer service people are involved in complex and important relationships unlike those of anybody else in the organization. They must represent the company equitably to its customers, and they must represent customers equitably to the company. They must work with all elements of the company to get results for their customers, and they must be able to maintain their motivation and self-esteem in the face of the pressures and sometimes abuse they are likely to get from all sides in the process. They must work closely with other members of the department, often under highly stressful conditions. And at the end of the work day, they have to go home to their families and take up their equally challenging roles there.

Because the front-line people who work for you are so important on so many counts, I have gone into great detail to help ensure that when you hire them, they are right for the job and the job is right for them.

Chapters 16 and 17 provide detailed guidance on getting those employees to work to their full potentials.

16

■ ■ ■
■ ■ ■
■ ■ ■

Effective Training for Excellent Customer Service

HELP WANTED. Individual of high intelligence and personal charm, capable of working under extreme pressure with frequent interruptions, resourceful and flexible, cheerful and even-tempered. The individual selected for this position must be completely trustworthy, as he/she will be entrusted with millions of dollars of the company's business, and must be able to represent customers' best interests with the company while remaining completely loyal to the company. Must be a self-starter with high initiative and an excellent team player. Must be willing to work long hours in a confined spaced under less-than-ideal conditions. Must be willing to work for low pay with little opportunity for advancement. Applicants must have a college degree and at least five years' experience as a customer service representative, preferably in a high-tech firm. A working knowledge of Vietnamese or Russian would be helpful. This is a nonexempt clerical position. Equal opportunity employer M/F. Apply Box 0000.

As this fictitious but only slightly exaggerated classified ad suggests, most companies expect a great deal from their front-line customer service reps, but beyond the usual benefits packages they don't always give a great deal in return. Formal training is often sketchy, and a general companywide perception of CSRs as low-grade clerical workers is compounded by a perception that they're also troublemakers, since they show up in other departments only when there's a customer service problem they can't handle. Mix these elements with the typical pressures of the customer service environment, and it's not hard to understand that problems of morale, stress, burnout, and turnover are virtually endemic to the customer service function in business.

In this chapter and the next you will find the distilled experience of several thousand managers to help you overcome those problems through systematic training, motivational enhancement, and elimination of the principal sources of stress and burnout in typical customer service operations. This chapter and Chapter 17 deal with the complex psychological issues that arise when people work in a job where there's typically much emphasis on productivity and yet seldom time to complete a job once it's begun a job where two of the major components of stress-uncertainty and constant interruptions—are inherent in the job; and a job that's almost completely lacking in one of the most important motivators: a sense of accomplishment.

Training Is a Great Motivator

If you want people to work well and with high levels of motivation in the challenging customer service environment, you as manager must set five basic conditions:

1. Your reps must know specifically what is expected of them in the job.
2. They have to know or be taught how to do the job correctly.
3. They must know how they will be measured. They must receive feedback, preferable positive feedback, that tells them how well they're meeting your expectations.
4. They must maintain high levels of self-esteem.

All of these are inherent features of any sound customer service training program, and you must be sure that your training program covers all these bases and doesn't just focus on job skills, for example. A checklist illustrating some of the factors involved in setting up an effective customer service call center is shown in Figure 16-1.

Training New Hires

If yours is a typical customer service department in an industrial business, or a customer service department of fewer than fifty persons in a consumer market, you very likely hire reps one or two at a time and start them off with a day or so of orientation. From that point on you train them mainly by assigning them to observe a senior rep for a few more day, perhaps as much as a week or two, supplemented with some interactive audio or videotapes and product training. They work under close supervision for a brief period, then they're on their own, learning as they go.

The reason there are relatively few formal training programs for new reps in industrial and smaller consumer operations usually relates to economies of scale. The feeling is that it doesn't pay for human resources or training people to develop and conduct a formal training program for one or two people at a time. This feeling is reinforced by the common perception that customer service is a clerical job and has a relatively low priority compared to sales training, production, and other labor-intensive jobs.

That doesn't mean you can't do a more than adequate job with the talent you already have in your department. For example, at the Du Pont medical imaging division in North Billerica, Massachusetts, newly hired CSRs "train their way through" the company's customer service manual, a chapter at a time, under the guidance of existing staff.

The manual replicates the environment and routines of the department, highlighting the other departments' reps regularly interface with and answering the questions they are asked most frequently. It also provides instruction in professional telephone service, gives details of key accounts and list sales reps the CSRs will be in contact with. (Appendix A includes a detailed outline of a customer service manual that could be adapted for this purpose.)

When new hires come on board at the Du Pont facility, a lead person gives them an in-depth overview of the job. The facility specializes in the sale of diagnostic drugs for the detection of cancer, tumors, and heart disease, and because of the nature of the business the orientation process takes several days.

After that, individual CSRs take over the training process, under the direction of the leader, with each member of the department responsible for teaching a specific section. This takes about two more weeks, and then it takes about another six months for the new reps to get up to speed with the business. Supervisor of Customer Service Richard Williamson explains that it can take as long as 9 to 12 months before a CSR is fully trained and comfortable in the job.

The Du Pont approach appears to have a high success rate, and it's very well received by the new hires, Williamson says. "It works because they're allowed to see the job in real life. They watch as CSRs apply different approaches to the job and are more able to develop their own methods of high-level performance." He adds that the new reps enjoy the opportunity to develop relationships with the different reps they work with as they go through the manual.

At Integron Corporation in Winston-Salem, North Carolina, Customer Service Manager Robin Yokley integrates the training process with the actual selection of personnel. "We sit applicants down beside a qualified CSR and plug them right into our phone lines," she says. "They wear headsets and listen to our CSRs and their customers. Watching them closely as they learn what their job will be like is much more enlightening than the actual interview."

Applicants who feel capable of handling the job are given in-depth training by supervisors. "These people must be knowledgeable in all phases of our company business—insurance—so they're taught, then quizzed, until we're confident that they can answer any question put to them by an agent or a customer. Usually, in four to six weeks, they're promoted to the trainee level."

Yokley adds that trainees then work alongside CSRs and after about six months are ready to work on their own. She says that the listen-and-learn format of the hiring interview has also reduced the turnover rate, although not as much as the company had hoped it would.

Startup or Relocation Training Opportunities

A different kind of training situation occurs when your company is either starting a new customer service department or centralizing or relocating an existing one or planning to staff it mainly with new hires. In such cases, you'll

Figure 16-1. Checklist of items for an effective customer service call center, involving the environment, training and monitoring, and personnel policies

- *People.* They are the most important element in any telephone operation. They need to be professionals and sound like professionals when customers call. It's sometimes hard to convince management that you need professionals, but it's vital to do so.

- *Screening before hiring.* Do a phone interview after reviewing applicants' resumes. They have to be able to think on their feet, and a spontaneous phone interview gives you an idea of how they will handle themselves.

- *Probation period.* Ninety days is recommended. Some new hires just don't work out, or they don't like the work, and you don't want to invest a lot of time and money needlessly.

- *Service/product training.* Keep your people current, but remember that there's no way to determine the training a person needs until you monitor him or her.

- *Interpersonal skills training.* This concerns how to deal with different types of customers and how to change one's personality to suit the caller who's irate, belligerent, or, on the other hand, easy-going.

- *Environment.* Part of the training process is showing personnel how to maintain their work environment in a professional way, starting with their workstation—anything to provide a pleasant and comfortable environment. Management must lead the way.

- *Dress code.* This is needed to develop a professional image as well as self-esteem. The way a person looks makes a difference in the phone image he or she projects.

- *Technology.* If you offer a service but can't access the information quickly, you're not adding anything to the company's effectiveness. Quick and efficient call routing and response are essential.

- *Monitoring.* This is the most important element of improving your customer service. But don't sell it as though you're the secret police. Say something like: "Hey, I'm going to help you develop; this will help your career!" There is really no other way than monitoring to determine quality of individual performance and to provide a basis for training.

- *Feedback.* Personnel need to be praised, patted on the back, encouraged and coached.

- *Quality and results.* Help your reps realize what they're doing. Instead of saying, "Oh, you took 100 calls today," say, "What did you do on those calls?" and "What was the outcome?"

- *Recognition.* It's very important to give recognition to individuals in front of their peers—certificates, awards, and the like.

Source: Customer Service Newsletter. Adapted from Eliah M. Kahn, GE Answer Center Consulting Services in Louisville, Kentucky

- *Job satisfaction.* Make your people realize how helpful they've been. Play back calls that demonstrate the point. There's a tremendous amount of satisfaction that comes from your people knowing they add value to a business.
- *Empowerment.* If you've got to have 10 layers of management signing off on every minor decision, what's the sense of having a customer service center?
- *Promoting.* This depends on the kind of business, but a lot of people don't realize that customer service people are great candidates to be promoted into sales. They have a lot of experience, they're professional, and customer service is really selling.

normally know far enough in advance that you can develop a recruitment plan and a training package to give your new hires before they go on-line.

An example of a relocation in Chapter 6 is General Electric's Lighting Division, which closed down twenty-two branch customer service operations in order to open a centralized national customer service center in Richmond, Virginia. In this move, GE transferred very few personnel and in effect started from scratch with 160 new customer service reps hired in the Richmond area.

The company's training department developed a special 8-week training program for this group, parts of it related to the state-of-the-art telecommunications and data terminal technology that made the centralized operation feasible. The 8-week training period was also a probationary period for the new hires, who could be terminated at any time during that period.

The GE case is one of those relatively rare instances where it's possible to keep an existing customer service operation running while a new, turnkey operation is being developed and phased in. However, since it's well within the bounds of possibility that you may find yourself involved in a departmental relocation of some kind, consider some of these opportunities:

- The opportunity to clean house and start from scratch. Heartless as they may sound, it may be the only practical way to raise your standards, rewrite job descriptions and specifications and improve the overall quality of your personnel.
- The opportunity to develop a customized training program of that all personnel apply policies and procedures uniformly and reflect the company's image and concern for customers in a uniform way.
- The opportunity to move up to state-of-the-art technology and train all personnel simultaneously, even to the extent of debugging the system as you go.
- The opportunity to set up a probationary period, and measure individual performances against norms for the group, screening out those who will adversely affect the quality of departmental performance.

New-Hire Training in Large Customer-Oriented Organizations

Most of the formal, full-scale training programs for new CSRs occur in very large organizations conducting a high volume of business by telephone or through personal contact, particularly where customer services is an integral part of the "product" being sold, or where customer service is seen as the main difference between companies that are otherwise very much alike.

Examples of customer service training designed to create product identity are most common among renowned organizations, such as Disney, which place a high premium on visible one-on-one customer service in their theme parks, as well as uniformity in projecting the Disney Look. The success of this approach is evident in the comments of visitors to the parks, who invariably comment about how well trained the personnel are rather than how good the service is. In fact, the service is sometimes poor judged by normal standards — for example, the waits of an hour or more at some attractions — but this appears to be largely offset by the perception of unusually well-trained personnel.

Most contact personnel at airlines go through similar training, essentially for the same reasons. Airline personnel usually receive specialized training in transactional analysis and similar approaches for keeping the goodwill and business of customers angered or upset by flight cancellations, overbookings, delays and so forth.

Public utilities and other organizations that deal with large segments of the public also fall in this general category. It's not unusual to find a two-tiered arrangement, where front-line personnel are trained to handle the 20 percent of subjects that account for 80 percent of the inbound calls, where a more highly trained group will deal with the 80 percent of subjects that account for 20 percent of the calls.

Warning! The excessive publicity that's being given to the training programs of such organizations as Disney, Federal Express, L. L. Bean, Marriott, and others has led some managements to believe that training of front-line personnel is the key to customer service success. This perception is likely to make it easier for you to get money for training purposes, but in reality training alone will do very little for the quality of your customer service unless it's fully supported by an excellent system, sound policies, practical standards, and a workable system of quality control.

No matter how well you train your reps in every aspect of their jobs, they're never going to be any better than the system and policies they have to work with. So, if you want your training to really count for something, work on the system, too!

Customer Service Training as a Continuous Process

Training new hires for customer service work is only a small part of the total training process. A much larger and more significant part of training takes place after this "basic training." This second-stage process is continuous and has these main elements:

- Setting standards of individual performance
- Measuring reps' performance against those standards
- Providing feedback and positive reinforcement; retraining where performance is substandard
- Providing cross-training with other disciplines
- Training in new skills and technologies
- Refresher training
- Familiarization programs or customer visitations
- Empowerment and participative management programs

Setting Standards of Individual Performance

Standards tell workers what's expected of them in both the quality and the quantity of their work. In customer service, work itself is the principal training medium, and these three types of work standards are the most commonly used:

1. Conventional work standards: so many units of work in a specified time frame.
2. Standards of accuracy: error rate no greater than a specified number per 1,000 transactions.
3. Standards of performance for customer service skills including dealing with customers, problem solving, follow-up and more. May be measured on a point scale (1–5 or 1–10) or on the basis of "exceeds standards," "meets standards," or "acceptable."

Chapter 7 discussed similar standards as measures of actual customer service quality. This chapter shows how they can be used in training reps in customer service skills.

Measuring performance against work and accuracy standards is usually a by-product of the system. The ACD system automatically generates data on number of calls, type, and length. The system of credits and/or actual sampling provide data on accuracy. Most managers make these statistics available to individuals, and in some departments they're posted as part of incentive programs.

Measuring performance against standards for customer service skills is more complex and can only be accomplished by direct observation of reps by a supervisor or trainer, or in some cases by customers themselves. The ratings are essential to the training process, and supervisors or trainers typically provide feedback one-on-one to the individual rep.

Whenever possible, feedback should be in the form of positive reinforcement—or, as one manager puts it, "Catch 'em doing things right." Substandard performance is usually dealt with by a discussion between supervisor/trainer and rep of how the particular problem might have been handled better. Observations usually become part of the individual's performance rating, and of course are not made known to co-workers.

Figure 16-2 is an example of how supervisors might rate several typical customer service skills.

Figure 16-2. Method for rating some typical customer service skills

1. Attitude Toward Customers

Measurement: Supervisor review, customer feedback (enthusiasm, empathy, confidence, tact, professionalism, voice projection/enunciation).

Performance standards: [*To be filled in by supervisor*]

Exceeds: Makes maximum effort to satisfy both internal and external customers. Always exhibits the above characteristics.

Meets: Works well with customers and makes an effort to see that customers are satisfied with service. Generally exhibits the above characteristics.

Acceptable: Behaves in acceptable manner with customers. Provides adequate customer service.

Review guidelines:
a. Supervisor reviews a minimum of 10 items per week. Surveys are mailed to each of the 10 customers.
b. Ratings are discussed monthly.
c. "Acceptable" rating applies to entry level grades only.

2. Accuracy of Information Provided to Customers

Measurement: Supervisor review (product/procedure knowledge displayed).

Performance standards: [*To be filled in by supervisor*]

Exceeds: Work always displays the highest degree of accuracy. Correct response is consistently given to the customer.

Meets: Responses are usually error-free. Understands the importance of accuracy.

Acceptable: Responses are sometimes inaccurate. Most mistakes are not critical.

Review guidelines:
a. Supervisor reviews a minimum of 10 items per week. Surveys are mailed to each of the 10 customers.
b. Ratings are discussed monthly.
c. "Acceptable" rating applies to entry level grades only.

3. Thoroughness and Timeliness

Measurement: Supervisor review, customer feedback (letters, callbacks, paperwork).

Performance standards: [*To be filled in by supervisor*]

Exceeds: Work related to customer inquiries is completed with the highest degree of accuracy. Commitments to customers are consistently achieved. Customers clearly understand responses.

Meets: Work related to customer inquiries is usually error free. Customer commitments are usually achieved. Customers generally understand responses.

| Acceptable: | Work related to customer inquiries is sometimes inaccurate. Commitments to customers are sometimes overlooked. Response to customers is sometimes unclear. |
| Review guidelines: | a. Supervisor reviews a minimum of 10 items per week. Surveys are mailed to each of the 10 customers.
 b. Ratings are discussed monthly.
 c. "Acceptable" rating applies to entry level grades only. |

4. Teamwork and Cooperation

Measurement:	Supervisor review
Performance standards:	[*To be filled in by supervisor*]
Exceeds:	Maintains a positive rapport with management and co-workers. Volunteers to provide assistance where the need is greatest. Consistently makes recommendations for improving the quality of service. Has a strong commitment to achieving departmental goals.
Meets:	Generally relates effectively to management and co-workers. Is willing to lend assistance to other areas when asked. Volunteers input on decisions impacting quality of service. Generally strives to achieve departmental goals.
Acceptable:	Generally relates effectively to management and co-workers. Lends assistance to others. Offers input when asked on decisions impacting quality of service. Is aware of departmental goals.
Review guidelines:	a. Ratings are discussed monthly. b. "Acceptable" rating applies to entry level grades only.

Telephone Quality Standards: Service Observation or Monitoring

Telephone monitoring or, as it's sometimes called, service observation, is one of the most valuable training tools available to you as a customer service manager. The capability is built into most telephone systems used in customer service applications, but it can also be accomplished with an inexpensive (under $10) accessory consisting of a suction cup attached to a conventional handset and connected via a jack to an ordinary tape recorder.

Like the customer service skills standards, telephone skills are best evaluated by direct observations of the interaction between reps and customers. This can be done live, by actually listening to conversations between reps and customers as they occur. Or, calls can be taped and reviewed at supervisors' convenience. Either way, it's essential to hear both sides of the conversation in order to properly assess how reps handle different types of calls. Many companies also survey customers after the fact, but this survey measures customers' perceptions, not the actual skills displayed by reps.

As you're probably aware, there may be some legal limitations on the manner in which you can monitor, depending on the laws of the state in which you're located. Here are the most common variations:

- In most states monitoring, including taping, is legal as long as one of the parties consents. Reps are advised that their consent to monitoring is a condition of employment.
- Monitoring is permitted as above, except that companies are required to place a star or other mark by their telephone book listings to indicate that calls are subject to monitoring.
- Calls may be monitored live, but not taped.
- Calls may be monitored or taped but require the consent of *both* parties. In Pennsylvania, a dual notification state, this is handled simply by adding the phrase "This call may be taped for training purposes" to the rep's standard greeting on inbound calls.

You naturally want to make sure your service observation or monitoring methods comply with the laws of your state, but try to make this determination *before* you involve your legal department. Being naturally cautious, it will likely find all kinds of reasons for *not* monitoring your customer service calls. As far as is known at this writing, no states specifically prohibit live monitoring of transactions between customers and companies. And taping is too important a training tool not to be used as fully as your state law permits.

From time to time, the issue of monitoring also surfaces as an ethical and/or labor relations issue, usually couched in pejorative and emotional verbiage such as "snooping," "invasion of privacy," and so forth. Since monitoring is essentially a training and quality control measure, it's hard to see what privacy issues or rights could possibly be involved when a customer calls a company on a business matter and a member of that company handles the call, while another member of that company monitors that call to ensure that it meets quality standards for handling such calls.

In fact, when monitoring is used for training and quality control purposes, it's in the public's best interest because it assures higher levels of service on the part of service givers.

In some situations monitoring may actually be required by law, for example, in securities or banking transactions where verbal instructions that affect the disposition of millions of dollars may be given in a minute or two. And taping of 911 and emergency calls is standard practice, both to cut down on false alarms (and save the taxpayers money) and to enable emergency workers to identify a calling location when a caller loses consciousness or the connections is cut.

If calls aren't already being monitored in your operation, you should plan to introduce monitoring at the earliest opportunity. To repeat: there is no other method of training in telephone use that even approaches monitoring in effectiveness.

You will probably meet some initial resistance to monitoring, particularly if your people have had no previous experience with it. It's extremely important that you make it clear that monitoring is *not* snooping and is *not* an invasion of privacy but is the proven way to help them enhance their skills and at the same time make their jobs easier by identifying system problems and areas of misunderstanding by customers that can be avoided by changing procedures or policies, rewriting instructions, and so forth.

Be sure to emphasize that monitoring is first and foremost a training tool and that it's the best way to ensure a fair and objective assessment of the skills they are acquiring. You should also emphasize that, while monitoring will be used to relate their skills in handling different types of phone calls, monitoring will be applied equally to all workers and will not be used for punitive reasons.

Of course there is no question of your right to monitor reps' performance on the phone, just as you would inspect the work of a machine tool operator, a typist, or an inventory or production planner. Explain that monitoring is a condition of employment, and have your reps sign statements that they understand this. Some companies post signs to this effect as well, just as a reminder.

Beyond these steps, make it clear that calls are subject to monitoring at all times, although supervisors are instructed to immediately disconnect from any personal calls they plug into. Even with this disclaimer, you'll find a sharp reduction in personal calls, which is as it should be. Some departments provide a separate, unmonitored line for personal calls as a courtesy to their reps, and it's seldom abused. In any event, you should probably not be too aggressive in limiting personal calls; if you have reasonable standards of quality and productivity, they will automatically limit how many nonbusiness calls anybody can handle.

Making Monitoring a Positive Experience

You may also add, as many managers do, that you will be developing training or demo tapes for future hires, based on the best performances observed during the monitoring process. This makes monitoring a positive rather than a negative experience and creates a strong incentive to perform well on the telephone at all times.

For example, you can compile a tape on "best" order taking procedures, best inquiry response, best software support, best complaint handling, best transfer and hold techniques, best dealing with foreign accents, best handling of emergency, best dispatch of field engineers, best technical explanation, and more. These are excellent for training and have an advantage over commercial or professional tapes because they feature your company's services or products, your company's customers, and your company's customer service reps as role models. Who could ask for anything more!

The Different Kinds of Monitoring

Monitoring can take several forms, and there are some tradeoffs between acceptability to your reps and the degree to which you actually control the monitoring:

▪ *Standard live monitoring or service observation.* This is used when it's important to hear the call as it's being handled rather than later on a tape. It's found in organizations where reps have the capability of signaling a supervisor to listen in on a particularly difficult or sensitive call and to intervene (come on-line) if he feels this is merited. Live monitoring is also useful for spot monitoring of an individual's performance and for timing the different segments of a call, that is, response, identification of self, response to inquiries, problem-solving and resolution, and close and sign-off. Live monitoring is adequate for rating CSRs' performance but isn't as effective as taping for actual training where you want to review specific transactions offline and in privacy with a rep.

▪ *Monitoring by taping plus supervisor review.* This is the most prevalent form of monitoring for training purposes. Supervisors can review and select specific conversations for review with individual CSRs. Tape segments can be played and replayed, discussed and analyzed without having to resort to memory or notes, as would be the case with live monitoring without taping. Tapes provide qualitative feedback that is so essential to training, and particularly to positive reinforcement.

▪ *Monitoring by self-taping plus supervisor review.* In this version, reps are asked to tape their own calls and then bring what they consider their best tapes to their supervisors for review. This method has the double advantage of emphasizing only positive performance, and at the same time gives the rep a sense of control, which eliminates virtually all the stress in the situation. It also has the same practical effect as a training medium as the monitoring approaches described above.

▪ *Monitoring by self-taping plus self-review.* Under this arrangement, reps agree to tape a certain number of calls and then review those calls on their own. The supervisor does not listen to the tapes unless a rep specifically requests it. Although this approach has the potential for abuse, it also reflects a high degree of mutual trust, which is essential to a sound working relationship. Managers who use this method feel that the added element of trust makes it a more effective medium than those in which supervisors are actively involved in the monitoring and review process.

Rating Methods

The usual method of rating telephone customer service skills is to employ a preprinted checklist of telephone skill or quality factors and to rate each rep according to a scale. Figures 16-3 and 16-4 show forms used by two different companies for this purpose. Even though the rating uses quantitative or number scores, you are still rating qualitative factors that can be subject to personal bias. Thus it's desirable that any given set of ratings be made by the same supervisor, so that whatever bias she has about how calls should be handled is applied equally to all reps. Also, the rating process should be rotated among supervisors or lead personnel as a further validation of scores.

When you are monitoring for rating purposes, everybody must be rated by the same standards and on a comparable mix of calls. Where reps' ratings become part of their permanent performance record, you may need to show that your measures are applied equally to all personnel so that no equal opportunity employment laws are violated.

How Much Monitoring?

It's generally not practical to monitor all calls, and it probably wouldn't improve the quality of your training significantly if you did — the size of the workload and the time off the phones to review the tapes would probably undermine rather than improve the quality of performance.

As one manager puts it, "When you have forty to forty-five reps on several shifts handling up to 4,000 calls in a 10-hour day, you have to consider the time factor in monitoring." He adds that this company's formula for monitoring is broken down by level of expertise:

New employees	20 calls per week
Intermediate personnel	8–12 calls per week
Top CSRs	2–4 calls per week

Another manager says that her supervisors monitor about 5 percent of each rep's calls. In a company where each handles sixty to seventy calls a day, this would average about sixteen or seventeen calls per week per rep but would not necessarily require that they all be taped.

Some Monitoring Spinoffs

Once monitoring is accepted as a basic element of the training program, it can be extended to some additional useful applications. At Norm Thompson, the Portland, Oregon, direct marketer of leisure and sporting attire and accessories, it's company policy that anybody in the company, from warehouse or maintenance worker on up, can monitor customer service transactions. This policy has proved an excellent way of building a corporate customer service culture as well as increased companywide understanding of the complexity of customer service operations and how they can be influenced by the performance of other departments.

At Federal Express, a showcase department of almost 300 reps in Memphis is equipped with a monitoring room where customers touring the facility can sit comfortably and monitor transactions between callers and Fedex personnel. The company feels that the monitoring room has excellent marketing value as a way of demonstrating the lengths to which the company goes to ensure quality service to its customers. And it's a highly visible incentive to employees to deliver a quality performance to prove that they're worthy of being showcased in that particular way!

The customer service manager of a replacement parts company in Chicago says that monitoring is a key element in training new reps. The company's product line is very broad and requires considerable expertise on the part of reps. Monitoring new reps closely helps them get up to speed quickly. She adds that trained reps are rarely monitored, and then only when they have a difficult or unruly customer on the phone, or a problem they don't know how to solve, and specifically ask the supervisor to listen in. "We'll plug into the call

Figure 16-3. Sample form for rating telephone skills

CSR Name _____   Code _____

Length of Call 1 _____   Length of Call 2 _____

Date _____ Call Type _____

— —

Call 1: Points Possible _____   Points Achieved _____   Rating _____ %

Call 2: Points Possible _____   Points Achieved _____   Rating _____ %

— —

	Call 1	Call 2	
1. Proper greetings (Unacceptable = 0; Acceptable = 10)	_____	_____	points
2. Effective probing (Poor = 0–2; Acceptable = 4, 6, 8; Excellent = 10)	_____	_____	points
3. Timely screen access (Unacceptable = 0; Acceptable = 5)	_____	_____	points
4. Adherence to script (Unacceptable = 0; Acceptable = 5)	_____	_____	points
5. Grammar and articulation (Poor = 0–2; Acceptable = 4, 6, 8; Excellent = 10)	_____	_____	points
6. Conversation control (Poor = 0, 3; Acceptable = 6, 9, 12; Excellent = 15)	_____	_____	points
7. Attentiveness to caller comments (Poor = 0, 2; Acceptable = 4, 6, 8; Excellent = 10)	_____	_____	points
8. Proper hold procedure (Unacceptable = 0; Acceptable = 10; Not applicable = N/A)	_____	_____	points
9. Diligence in acquiring pertinent information (Unacceptable = 0; Acceptable = 10; Not applicable = N/A)	_____	_____	points

Source: Customer Service Newsletter

	Call 1	Call 2	
10. Responsiveness (no pause or delays) (Poor = 0, 1; Acceptable = 2, 3, 4; Excellent = 5)	____	____	points
11. Courtesy and enthusiasm (Poor = 0, 3; Acceptable = 6, 9, 12; Excellent = 15)	____	____	points
12. Brevity and thoroughness (Unacceptable = 0; Acceptable = 10)	____	____	points
13. Proper closing (Unacceptable = 0; Acceptable = 10)	____	____	points
Total	____	____	

and pass them a note telling them how to proceed while the customer is still on the line," she says.

In some companies reps can SOS their supervisor and ask him to actually come on line to straighten out knotty situations. These are seen as positive, stress-relieving applications of monitoring and reinforce the point that there's very little resistance to monitoring once reps see it as a training and support mechanism that not only enables them to improve their skills but can also take much of the stress out of call handling.

The newest technology, adopted by Metropolitan Life Insurance Co. in mid-1990, supports this SOS capability with the ability to transfer from the rep's screen to the supervisor's, so that the supervisor can enter the discussion with a good knowledge of who the customer is and what the background of the situation is, and can do so without having to go the rep's workstation and go through a question-and-answer session before intervening. This same capability exists for transferring calls and data simultaneously in conventional transfers, for example, transferring a call to an applications specialist, a Spanish-speaking rep, or a claims clerk.

Quality Control and Training

Training is an essential component of any effective quality control program. Companies that say they can't afford the time or money to give their customer service reps (and managers) regular training sessions end up paying far more for the lack of training than they would have paid for the training itself.

High costs in customer turnover, rework, and other areas are typically

Figure 16-4. Evaluation form used to record observations made during individual CSR telephone calls

Monitoring Evaluation

Rep _____   Customer Name _____

Date _____   Customer Number _____

Type of call _____   State & Zip _____

		Points* (From 0 – 10)	Explanation
Technique	Answers telephone promptly and correctly.		
	Hold handled properly – no unnecessary gaps of silence.		
	Offers to help when customer asks for someone else.		
	Concludes properly.		
Getting/Giving Information	Media code probe.		
	Lets customer tell story in own way, without interruption; uses appropriate responses to encourage him or her to volunteer useful information.		
	Develops and explores unclear statements and pursues any customer indication of dissatisfaction.		
	Presents information and explanations clearly, concisely and in an easily understandable way — patiently continues to explain until clear.		
	Tactfully corrects misunderstandings or customer misstatements that could cause later misunderstanding.		
	Answers questions willingly and at time asked when more information needed form customer to answer; explains reason for questioning if appropriate. Verifies and spells back custom items.		
	Explains company policies and practice in such a way that reasons for them are clear.		
Overall Handling	Does everything reasonable to help and satisfy the customer — offers to look into the matter further when: 1. Unable to satisfy customer 2. Beyond authority. 3. Action beyond normal handling required.		
	Talks with customer and questions customers in a way demonstrating interest and attentiveness and keeping discussion "on track" — controls the call.		
	Conveys understanding, helpfulness, and concern if customer is inconvenienced by company.		
	Accepts responsibility for his or her mistakes without blaming others.		
Sales	Offers sales items to customers on contacts other than sales.		
	Does everything possible to generate or add to sales.		
	Uses good sales technique.		

*Where 0 = Poor, 5 = Average, 10 = Outstanding

Source: Customer Service Newsletter

incurred in service companies that have neither customer service training not measuring (monitoring) of performance. See Figure 16-5 for a graph of how lack of customer service training leads to poor service and high costs. Figure 16-6 shows the advantages of investing in training and monitoring. Over a 5-year period, this chart shows that training and monitoring costs raise total cost for the first several years, but as the improvement program pays off, customer turnover, rework, and other costs drop rapidly and provide substantial savings from that point on. Figure 16-7 converts the percentages in Figure 16-6 into a demonstration of the return on investment (ROI) that a $300,000 investment in training and monitoring over a 5–7 year period would be likely to generate.

As Figures 16-6 and 16-7 show, the investment in training raises total costs slightly, but by the end of the third year, substantial savings begin to accrue and continue from that point on. The key to this substantial ROI is the recognition by management that training and feedback are integral parts of any quality programs undertaken by the company. And its implicit that training can't be confined to the customer service department, but must also involve other departments that play key roles in the total customer service process.

Update Training

Update training usually refers to training administered in connection with new products or services, major changes in policies or procedures, special promotions or adoption of new technology in the department. Unfortunately, it's often one of the most neglected of all customer service training activities, and is one of the most complained-about problems that customer service reps have to deal with.

As customer service manager, you should make sure that you are informed well in advance of any upcoming plans or programs or changes that will affect customer service operations. But don't expect people to come running to you with the information. Others in the company may not even be aware of your need to know, and some are so preoccupied with their own roles that they don't realize how much customer service can contribute to or detract from the success of their particular project.

There are many "war stories" to illustrate this. Here are some of the most common ones:

▪ A major health care organization changed its credit and payment policies on short notice but failed to notify customer service or to provide any scripts or guidelines to equip customer service reps to deal with the flood of calls that was bound to result. The next effect was a serious rupture of customer relations at the beginning of its biggest selling season.

▪ A chemical manufacturer redesigned its invoices in an effort to maintain confidentiality on pricing. The new format confused customers and resulted in over 1,000 calls claiming errors in invoices and embarrassment and stress to the customer service reps who hadn't been informed of the changes and had been given no training in interpreting and explaining the new format to customers who called.

Figure 16-5. The high cost of poor customer service

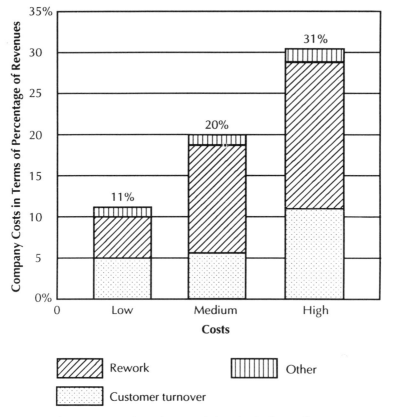

Source: "The Service Quality Advantage," Temple, Barker & Sloane, Inc., Lexington, Mass., 1987

There are hundreds of cases where customer service reps receive no notification or training in the details of special promotions, advertising campaigns, or special deals and ultimately learn about them from customers. These situations are extremely stressful and embarrassing for CSRs, who feel—with some justification—that their credibility with customers has been undermined through the simple thoughtlessness of the members of their companies.

These situations aren't universal; some companies provide outstanding training for customer service reps in anticipation of such situations. Here are some examples, which are highly recommended for adaptation in your own company:

■ *Abbott Laboratories*, North Chicago, Illinois. The customer service group responsible for supporting laboratory equipment at hospitals is represented by one of their members, a customer service rep, on the laboratory's new product development committee. This representation serves a dual education or training function. Because these CSRs have extensive knowledge about the primary users of this equipment—lab technicians at hospitals—through their daily contacts with them, these reps are exceptionally well-suited to advise equip-

Figure 16-6. Savings generated from an investment in ongoing training

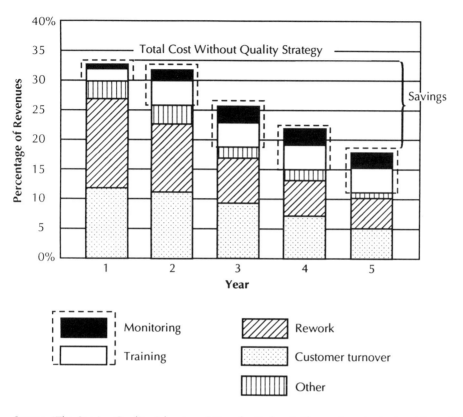

Source: "The Service Quality Advantage," Temple, Barker & Sloane, Inc., Lexington, Mass., 1987

Figure 16-7. Conventional ROI format used to justify investment in training by projecting payback over a 5-year period

Projected Return on Investment for a 5-Year Training and Monitoring Program						
Cost Element	Present	Year 1	Year 2	Year 3	Year 4	Year 5
Training	—	$ 20,000	$ 40,000	$ 40,000	$ 40,000	$ 40,000
Monitoring	—	10,000	20,000	30,000	30,000	30,000
Rework	$150,000	150,000	120,000	80,000	60,000	60,000
Customer turnover	135,000	120,000	110,000	90,000	70,000	50,000
Other	50,000	30,000	30,000	20,000	20,000	11,000
Total Cost	$335,000	$330,000	$320,000	$260,000	$220,000	$191,000
Savings	—	$ 45,000	$ 15,000	$ 75,000	$115,000	$144,000
ROI*		17%	25%	108%	164%	206%
*Savings ÷ Cost of Training and Monitoring						

Source: Customer Services Newsletter

ment designers, developers, and marketers as to which equipment features are user-friendly and which need to be revised to make the equipment more salable to hospital laboratories. At the same time, reps in the department are in on the ground floor of new product introduction and have ample time to be trained to support it when it enters the marketplace.

• *Fuller Brush Company,* Great Bend, Kansas. Commercial customer service reps at this well-known company hold monthly job training meetings, including sessions devoted to learning how to strip, clean, and apply floor wax at a commercial level. As CSR Bernie Nightengale described this experience, "It very definitely gave all of us an appreciation of people involved in floor care maintenance and gave us hands-on knowledge of our products that we could pass on to our customers when they called. And, it was fun!"

• *CP Rail,* Toronto, Ontario. CP Rail places a member of its customer service staff at a major customer site, and in return a member of the customer's expediting staff works at CP Rail offices. This training is excellent for both customer service personnel and their equivalents in customer organizations because of the "real world" understanding and empathy it creates on both sites.

• *Dow Corning Corp.,* Midland, Michigan. When this company's management decided to institute a major policy change — from delivered pricing to FOB origin, freight charges collect — the customer service manager was invited to submit a proposal, including budget and timetable, for preparing customers as well as CSRs for dealing with the policy. With ample lead time, specially prepared literature, and appropriate coaching of the customer service staff, what could have been a traumatic experience for the company and its distributor-customers was engineered with very little adverse reaction.

• *Marion Laboratories,* Kansas City, Missouri. At this pharmaceutical manufacturer, which has since merged with Merrell-Dow Corporation of Cincinnati, the customer service department was faced with the complex task of learning to read and interpret hundreds of product codes recently developed an ingenious self-training program involving flash cards, crossword puzzles, number search games, and more. Senior CSR Pauline Ash, CCSP (Certified Customer Service Professional), says, "With these tools, the challenge of learning that many product codes became a game that produced quick and positive results. It was amazing to realize the simplicity of a difficult assignment when we pooled our resources and transformed it into an accomplishment that made our learning process beneficial, easy, fun, and exciting." The program also illustrates the benefits of participative management, when CSRs are empowered (and encouraged) to participate in the management of the activities in which they themselves participate.

Refresher Training

By contrast with update training, refresher training is aimed at bolstering or enhancing existing customer service skills. As its name implies, refresher training reminds CSRs of some of the points they may have forgotten about correct customer service procedure. It's very important that your schedule include refresher training at frequent intervals. There are several ways to accomplish this training.

Passive Training. This consists mainly of audio- or videotapes, which reps can review either singly or in groups. The training is mainly passive in the sense that reps simply listen or view, without actually interacting with the programs in any way. Some managers arrange brown bag days and purchase a deli or pizza lunch for their reps, who view video training tapes as they eat. Some managers get extra mileage out of their tapes by opening the lunch meetings to members of other departments.

Audiotapes lend themselves to bilevel activity training — for example, listening to a training tape while driving to or from work, or while filing, checking invoices, or whatever. As one authority points out, portable tape players have become so inexpensive that a great deal of training can be assimilated by having players and tapes located at workstations, near copying or fax machines, at file cabinets, or other locations where individuals perform mainly manual tasks. One manager reported a plan to install tape players in the department's rest rooms!

The limitation of passive training is that trainees generally assimilate less when they simply sit and listen or look than if they are actually required to interact with the training. Yet this limitation can be an advantage for casual brown-bag-lunch training, where the size of the group is indeterminate, people may come and go at different times, and the situation doesn't lend itself to taking on a third activity, such as using a workbook or entering into a roundtable discussion while munching on a slice of pizza.

Many audio- and videotapes on customer service subjects are available and new ones are constantly being made. They vary considerably in quality, and it's recommended that you preview before buying or renting whenever possible. Be sure to look also at the interactive programs described next.

Interactive Audio/Video Training. There are some excellent interactive programs in which trainees perform specified tasks in response to program instructions: answering questions or entering data in workbooks, conducting brief roundtable discussions with other trainees, and in some cases role-playing with other reps on inside lines. Some of these programs are self-directed, while others may require a leader of facilitator, a role that often can be taken by a senior rep.

Interactive training can also be used for training in new skills or technologies, and there are computer programs and games that can be used for this purpose as well.

Live Refresher Training. There's a great deal of material that can be used for live training led by the manager or a supervisor or senior rep. Newsletter articles or questionnaires, sections of the training manual, and puzzles or computer games lend themselves well to such sessions.

Role-playing is a quick and easy form of live training. The most common method is to seat two reps back-to-back (so they won't give each other visual cues) in front of the group, and assign one a role as a customer and the other the role of CSR trying to deal with a complex problem involving the customer. When they finish their dialogue or transaction, ask others to critique the performance, then repeat the role-playing using other reps. You can either write out the roles beforehand, as some managers do, or simply discuss the material with the participants and audience and let your role-players take it from there. If you have telephones you can unplug and use for the exercise, so much the better. It creates a familiar and comfortable setting for everybody.

Outside Training. There is an almost infinite number of individuals and/or organizations who provide one-shot training programs ranging from a few hours to a half-day or two days. Their fees range from a few hundred dollars a day to as much as six or seven thousand dollars.

Although many of these programs tend to be generic, and sometimes more motivational than skills-oriented, they usually have a very positive and beneficial effect. Bringing in outside experts is a mark of recognition that reps appreciate because it tells them you care and are willing to go to bat to get budget for the event. Of course, you had better be sure that your outside expert is qualified and the program is relevant to their jobs. These training sessions are usually referred to as seminars and should be presented to reps as a benefit, not a chore.

Programs for training the customer service department as a smoothly functioning team face some unique problems. As a customer service manager in South Carolina pointed out, "They keep talking about teamwork and comparing us to a football team, knowing all the plays and supporting one another, and so forth. But a football team has a whole week to practice in—and we *never* have a chance to practice. We're in there playing for keeps all the time!"

His point is very well taken. It's not easy to get the entire department off the phones at the same time and into a group training session that simulates their actual work environment—that is, it involves all department members. Yet you should do so at least once a year, even if it means having a Saturday training session (see Figure 16-8) and paying overtime.

When you schedule such a seminar, plan to get the maximum mileage from it by following these simple suggestions:

- *Decide on the format.* Will it be two half-day sessions, with half your group in the morning and the other half in the afternoon, or two full-day sessions? Will it be a Saturday session comprising the entire group? Will you get temps in to help handle calls? Be sure to schedule the seminar when most of your people are available. And be sure that you are there personally to introduce speakers. *Don't* schedule the seminar during your own vacation; this sends a message that it's not that important an event. Do be present, or have a supervisor present, at the daily sessions to let people know that the seminar *is* important.

- *Publicize the seminar in advance.* Some seminar givers will provide you with miniposters or circulars you can pass around. For others you may have to make your own. Either way, a little advance buildup is important. Let it be known that the seminar is in recognition of their importance and good performance, and avoid any suggestions that it's being held because of their poor performance in the past.

Figure 16-8. Tips for Saturday seminars

Holding training sessions on a Saturday is often the most practical way to get all your people together at one time without having to worry about telephone coverage and other demands on their time. And although your people are usually paid for attending such sessions, they still have to give up some of their regular weekend activities. The following tips will help you maintain high levels of motivation and assure that your people get the most out of that training:

1. *Notify personnel as soon as the date has been set.* Even though attendance may be required, early notification will be seen as a courtesy. It will also encourage attendance by others—for example, managers from other departments, senior management people—who are invited but not required to participate.

2. *Present the Saturday session as an "event."* Make your people aware that the session reflects management's interest in them and that it's a rare opportunity to enhance their skills and enjoyment of their jobs.

3. *Circulate teasers on topics with personal appeal as part of the buildup.* Stress management, dealing with difficult people, self-realization, etc. always have considerable appeal.

4. *Hold the session off-site if possible.* This gives it more importance. But check out the facilities beforehand to make sure they're adequate and comfortable. Otherwise, the appeal of going to a new location will be wasted.

5. *Set an early starting time.* Starting your session at 7:00 or 7:30 A.M. is not too early, provided you have coffee and Danish ready when your people arrive.

6. *Encourage casual attire.* This will heighten the participative workshop environment and will make it easy for people to return to their normal weekend activities after the seminar—another courtesy on your part.

7. *Have a light lunch brought in and hold the lunch break to 30–45 minutes.* This will emphasize the fact that this is a fast-paced working session. Resist the temptation to have a fancy sit-down meal, which will put everybody to sleep!

8. *Schedule a team activity as the final item on the agenda.* This enables you to end on a high note and re-emphasizes the importance and value of the subject matter.

9. *End the seminar in midafternoon: no later than 2:30–3:00 P.M.* This will create a sense of accomplishment at how much ground your reps have covered professionally in such a short time. Keep them much longer, and you're likely to lose them!

10. *Follow up several days later with a thank-you note and questionnaire.* The questionnaire should focus on how your staff will use the information in the future, not on whether they "liked" the session. The thank-you note is because you know the way your CSRs treat customers reflects the way you yourself treat your CSRs.

Source: Consumer Service Newsletter

▪ *Hold the seminar offsite.* This has two purposes: (1) to keep the seminar from being interrupted by others in the company, calls for reps, and so forth; and (2) to let reps know they're important and you're going to see that they're comfortable and well fed. If you have people coming from out of town, you can hold the seminar in the hotel or motel where they're quartered. At one in-house seminar conducted by James River Corp. in Kalamazoo, Michigan, the local customer service department maintained a hospitality suite in the seminar hotel for CSRs from other plants.

▪ *Give the seminar status.* Kick off the seminar with a brief pep-talk by a member of senior management—the more senior the better. At the James River Corp. seminar mentioned above, each group's session was introduced by a top officer, and members of management observed at the different sessions. At the luncheon break, the seminar group was joined by a company officer. These presences gave the seminar significant status and at the same time reminded CSRs of their own importance to the company and its management. At an in-house seminar at Applause, Inc. in Woodland Hills, California, the company's president addressed both sessions of the seminar where he frankly and openly addressed customer service concerns. As at the James River Corp. seminar, the presence of a top officer had a strong positive effect on the seminar itself.

▪ *Check the logistics* carefully. Experience with more than 250 in-house seminars has taught me that the most serious problems arise from the simple failure of persons in charge to check out the facilities well in advance. This often results in meeting rooms that are too small, audio-visual equipment that is incorrect or absent, nonexistent coffee or refreshments, and so on. As manager, you should check out the meeting room yourself no later than the evening before the meeting, and somebody should be there at least an hour before it begins to ensure that:

The meeting is properly posted, so people can find it;
The room is arranged the way the speaker has requested;
The proper audio-visual equipment is in place and supported with spare bulbs, extension cords taped to the floor, markers for flipcharts, and so forth;
There are arrangements for coats if needed; and
the coffee and luncheon breaks are properly set up.

Don't take for granted that these things will happen just because somebody said they would! It can be very embarrassing to run into the kind of poor customer service some hotels are capable of at a seminar devoted to customer service excellence!

▪ Don't *ask your CSRs to rate the seminar.* Seminars are not entertainment but training. If you want to rate the seminar as training, tell reps beforehand that you are going to ask them some questions about it after it's over. Give them a questionnaire in the next day or so after the seminar asking them to list what they learned from the seminar that they were doing right, what could be improved, and how they expect to use the information they got over the next six months. These questions make them focus on the positive aspects of the seminar and the importance of incorporating what they learned in their future behavior. You get a good deal more mileage from the seminar than you do if you simply ask them whether they liked it.

In addition to annual and sometimes semiannual seminars, you should have at least one departmental meeting a week for informational purposes, even if it lasts only 10 or 15 minutes.

Some customer service managers have short daily meetings to brief reps on any unusual situations as well as to give them a chance to report any problems they encountered or solutions they engineered. Sometimes the main purpose of these daily meetings is to allow reps to let off steam. At Scott Worldwhite, CSRs have a brief mid-morning meeting in what they refer to as the "screaming room." Although they seldom actually scream, says customer service specialist Jeanne Bannon, the short get-together enables them to compare notes, sound off, and return to work with accumulated tensions cleared.

Normally, you want your daily meetings to be of the standard variety, which lets people know that they need to be brief and to the point and to confine their discussion to important matters of general concern.

One manager lists topics or problems raised by CSRs at meetings on a flip chart and then asks the group to decide which topic is the most important and of the greatest general concern. When this has been done, she closes the meeting and tells her reps that she will start working on the problem and report her progress at the next meeting. This is an excellent way not only to train personnel in prioritizing and decision making but also to create nonthreatening participative management situations that boost morale as well as actually improve operations.

Off-Job Training Opportunities

Don't overlook the opportunities for your reps to receive off-job training in your area. Most community colleges offer some forms of business management and marketing training applicable to customer service, and some have courses designed specifically for customer service personnel. Community colleges are always interested in developing courses for which there is a demand among local businesses, particularly if local managers like yourself are willing to instruct some sessions.

For example, Richard Holcombe, vice-president, sales service and distribution, at Woolrich, Inc., in Woolrich, Pennsylvania, has been teaching customer service courses at two community colleges for 5 years. His most recent course at this writing—a 5-week course entitled "Customer Service: The Selling of an Intangible"—focuses on communication skills, handling complaints, time and stress management, and customer service role-playing. The course has proved so popular with local businesses that at any given time there is a waiting list of as many as seventy-five people.

Initiating such a program or supporting an existing one is a matter of self-interest. If you volunteer to teach some or all of such a course, it will add considerably to your credentials, and it will earn you some added income as well.

Most companies have tuition refund or educational support programs for their personnel, and you should certainly encourage your reps to sign up for courses that will improve their skills, whether directly or indirectly. You might suggest that it looks good on their record when it's time for performance review and pay increases, and indeed it does!

You should also encourage your personnel to participate in the professional certification program sponsored by the International Customer Service Association (ICSA). Reps who take specified training and participate in extracurricular customer service activities receive points toward the designation CCSP, Certified Customer Service Professional. A number of customer service managers report that this program has been an excellent motivator and morale-builder for their reps that is reflected in improved performance.

If there's an ICSA chapter in your area—and more are springing up all the time—involve yourself in its activities and take your reps along to designated rep meetings and Rep Appreciation nights that ICSA chapters typically sponsor. The recognition that reps get at these events, as well as the practical information and exchange of ideas, will enhance their self-esteem, enthusiasm, and practical skills. Participation in chapter activities also garners points for you as manager at the management-level certification designation of CCSE (Certified Customer Service Executive).

Ouchless Feedback in Training Personnel

It's been stressed throughout this chapter that the training by feedback should focus whenever possible on the positive observations you've made rather than the negative. Juan Gutierrez, a widely experienced trainer of customer service personnel, makes these suggestions for ouchless feedback, which helps increase reps' productivity and professionalism without damaging their self-esteem:

- *Take the win-win approach.* Present your comments in a fair, honest, and respectful manner that reflects understanding of the employee's point of view.
- *Use the 90-10 rule.* 90 percent of the time your reps are probably working effectively; 10 percent of they time they aren't. Don't fall into the trap of focusing your feedback on the 10 percent. Focus on the 90 percent by saying "Here's how you can do this even better."
- *Communicate caring.* It's a customer service axiom that the way CSRs treat customers reflects the way those same CSRs are treated by their managers and supervisors. When giving performance feedback to your reps, express interest in seeing them excel in their work and make it clear that you're willing to work with them to strengthen areas where improvement is needed. Let them know you care. "People don't care how much you know until they know how much you care," says Juan.
- *Teach form first, and speed and accuracy will follow.* Reps must fully understand the mechanics of the job first, whether it's stuffing envelopes or reorganizing a database. Then coach them on their technique and as they practice

they're almost certain to improve. But they have to understand how the job is done before they start. (And stuffing envelopes isn't all that simple—the right way is about 100 percent more productive than any of the other ways!)

■ *It's not what you EXpect, it's what you INspect.* If you tell CSRs that courtesy is the number one priority but rate their performance by the number of calls they handle, productivity will increase but courtesy will go down. People naturally try to do their best in the areas they think are being inspected, so be sure that you inspect—and reward—quality as well as quantity. Otherwise you'll end up with a fixation among your reps that "it only counts if it's counted," which is another way of saying that if performance of a certain type is *not* measured or counted, then it's not important. You can't afford this perception!

■ *Catch them doing something right.* Don't limit yourself to a specific time for providing feedback. Make is spontaneous. When you notice a job well done, say so then and there.

Pie-Chart Analysis Solves Problems of Mutual Misperceptions

Juan Gutierrez's feedback tips raise the important issue of reps who misperceive or misprioritize tasks depending on what they think is important. The problem may also arise when you as manager assume that reps know your priorities when in fact they don't. A simple and effective way of ensuring that you're all on the same wavelength is to conduct a pie-chart analysis, preferably one-on-one, with each of your reps. If time doesn't permit individual conferences, a group session will do, as long as you make sure everybody participates:

> *Step 1.* List five or six principal customer service tasks on a sheet of paper or flip chart. Ask participants whether any other tasks should be added, and add any they nominate.
>
> *Step 2.* Give each participant a sheet of paper with a large circle, with a diameter of at least 5 inches drawn on it.
>
> *Step 3.* Instruct participants to section off their circles in pie-chart fashion, into wedges proportionate to the relative importance or priority of the different tasks you have listed.
>
> *Step 4.* Draw your own pie chart reflecting the priority or order of importance you attach to each of the activities.
>
> *Step 5.* Compare notes and discuss the reasons for any differences.
>
> *Step 6.* Reconcile differences and draw a new pie chart reflecting what everybody agrees are the real priorities.

Figure 16-9 illustrates pie-chart analysis with *A* representing a hypothetical sectioning by a CSR, *B* the manager's version, and *C* the final version agreed to by both sides.

Very often these differences in perceptions of priorities are significant. Reps are likely to perceive the importance of a particular task or activity on the

Figure 16-9. Pie-chart analysis contrasting priorities

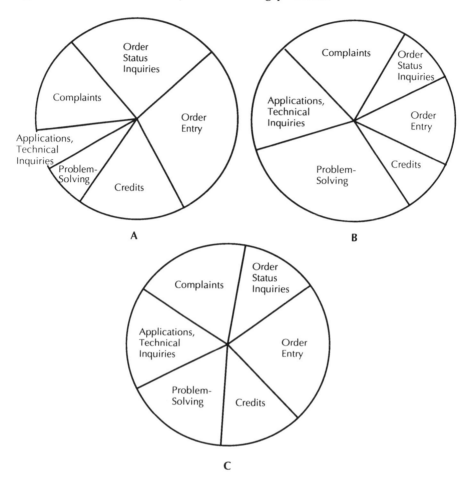

Source: Customer Service Newsletter

basis of the amount of time spent on it; how the activity is measured or not measured; and how much you as manager talk or don't talk about a particular activity. So, don't overlook the possibility that you may be sending misleading messages about what's important and what's not. A pie-chart analysis is an excellent way of finding out and an excellent training tool. I first saw this technique used by trainer/consultant Robert E. Tannehill.

Cross Training Programs

Cross training is a widely used term with several different meanings.

Familiarization With Other Departments or Activities

The most common type of cross training employed in customer service departments is familiarization with other departments or activities. It's somewhat of a misnomer to call it training, since the objective isn't to teach skills per se but rather to develop an understanding of how other departments function and to instill empathy for the difficulties they may encounter when customer service personnel ask them to help out with customer problems or emergencies.

Most cross training of this type is mainly observation. At Robbins & Myers, the Dayton, Ohio, manufacturer of progressive cavity pumps, a program called "Foreman for a Day" has proved an effective means of improving understanding between customer contact personnel (known as master schedulers) and plant production personnel. Once a month, one of the master schedulers spends a full day with a plant foreman and observes what he deals with during the day.

As Master Scheduling Manager Norm Shearer points out, these dealings cover a variety of issues:

> "The foreman has to deal with union problems, stipulations, require-
> ments, machine problems. The nature of the pump and the fact that we
> shoot rubber into it brings in a lot of production variables. If it's too
> humid, it won't set right. The consistency of the rubber varies, and
> sometimes there are problems with that. The schedulers get a first
> hand look at all the variables the foreman has to deal with. This
> helps them understand why their schedules weren't met and it also
> helps them make more realistic schedules in the future."

Ideally, cross training of this type is a two-way street: CSRs visit other departments to observe, and personnel of other departments spend time in the customer service department. At Robbins & Myers, foremen spend one day a month in the master scheduling department, observing as well as actually handling customer complaints and inquiries. "That way, they know what we go through," says Norm Shearer. "It makes them more responsive when we tell them we have a real angry customer and need their help!"

These exchanges don't have to be limited to a single day. At Cargill, Inc., Carpentersville, Illinois, cross training averages out at about one week per person per department. In addition to customer service reps, the program involves personnel from a number of other departments at this manufacturer of resins for the point industry. Other departments involved include sales, accounting, product development, paint lab, quality control, purchasing, invoicing, shipping, and receiving. Customer Service Supervisor Judy A. Sossong reports excellent results from the program, which has been in effect 3 years at this writing.

Where personnel exchanges aren't practical for reasons of distance between departments, workload, union rules, or whatever, an excellent alternative is to videotape activities in the various departments and then exchange videotapes. At a company where CSRs were constantly having confrontations with the shipping department, a tape showing what the shipping foreman had to go through just to expedite a shipment or put through a change-order was enough to virtually eliminate the causes of friction. In similar fashion, the customer service manager of a midwestern chemical manufacturer produced a tape on customer service operations and circulated it to field sales personnel. The result was vastly improved discipline on the part of field sales personnel in placing rush orders or requesting other emergency or immediate action from the customer service department.

Cross Training for Liaison Purposes

Although it's an overall objective of cross training to improve cooperation between departments, some companies use their cross training to develop certain reps as "liaison experts" to whom other reps may turn when they are having problems with another department. The peer recognition factor that results from designating certain individuals as "resident experts" is an excellent morale factor.

For example, at Woolrich, Inc., the apparel manufacturer referred to earlier in this chapter, two CSRs are sent into another department each month to observe and probe into its operations. Upon returning to the customer service department. This report is circulated throughout the customer service department. For the next year, these two reps are the "resident experts" on the particular department they visited. Next month, two other reps visit another department, and the pattern repeats itself throughout the year.

Woolrich Customer Service Supervisor Elaine Glimm observes that the program has been in effect more than 4 years and is "very successful." A point emphasized by Elaine Glimm and other managers who employ this kind of cross training is that it should always be aimed at a specific objective or result. As one manager puts it: "Don't just dump your people in another department and leave them to their own devices. Brief them beforehand on what you expect them to learn and require them to make a written report showing that they've done so."

Cross Training in Related Skills

Cross training in related skills is not as common as observation-type cross training, but it's quite useful in departments where there's a variable workload. One of the most common examples is cross training customer service reps in outbound telemarketing so that when inbound calls are light reps can immediately convert to proactive telemarketing. This requires that reps be trained, and also that there is a readily accessible support system already in place. Or, reps can be trained in customer survey techniques and interview designated customers during slack periods or as a special project.

The Customer Service Department as a General Training Ground

The customer service department is sometimes the basic training ground for newly hired sales trainees as well as management trainees. Their stay with you may be relatively short, but you should get them working with customers as well as your permanent staff as quickly as possible, for two reasons. First, they're probably talented people and you can get some good work out of them. Second, and equally important, as they move out of the customer service department and into other slots in the company, their understanding of the customer service mission and the problems the department faces daily will give you some very valuable intercompany support when you need new equipment, more personnel, or changes in policies or procedures to help you do your job better.

Internal Customers Programs

A serious flaw in the training and motivational programs of many companies is that, in their attempt to make everyone in the company sensitive to the needs of its customers, they completely overlook an even more critical point: that high levels of service to customers depend on high levels of service to so-called internal customers—other departments that depend on one another for certain actions so that the ultimate customer can be served. For example, the customer service department depending on the marketing department to provide pricing information so that an order for products or services can be filled and billed. Or, the production department in a printing company depending on the customer service department to get the OKed proofs from the customer, in turn enabling the job to be printed and completed in order to meet the commitment made to the customer by the field salesperson.

There are many such examples throughout business, yet relatively few companies have developed standards of interdepartmental accountability requiring individual departments to respond to their internal customers that the needs of external customers are met as the company intends them to be. And the customer service failures that occur are often blamed on the customer service department, rather than on the system that lets such failures happen. So, as customer service manager, you have a real stake in developing an internal customers program to overcome this problem.

A quality program at Haworth, Inc., the office systems manufacturer located in Holland, Michigan, provides a good example, known as the Haworth Quality Improvement Process, the program revolves around the concept of internal customers—each individual correctly meeting the needs of the next stage in the total process. It includes these steps:

1. *Identifying internal customers.* Each work unit identifies all the groups or individuals who are their customers as "very specific populations who have very specific needs."
2. *Prioritizing customers.* The work unit then prioritizes its top three customers—those without whom the work unit would no longer be needed.
3. *Identifying key work output.* This is the work which, if not completed, would force the unit's top three customers to shut down their operations.
4. *Defining the key work output in measurable terms.* This step consists basically of setting standards that the work unit believes reflect its customers' requirements.

5. *Verifying requirements.* This is the process of ascertaining that internal customers' requirement have in fact been correctly defined and, if not, adjusting the standards as necessary.

From this point on, the internal customer process focuses on improving each work unit's service to its internal customers. One hour per week is spent in quality improvement process meetings where work units are asked to contribute ideas for improving what they do in the other 39 hours of the week. Haworth executives say the program has been very well received by workers because of three main factors:

1. Workers have a clear understanding of who their internal customers are.
2. They're given clear methods for meeting those internal customer's needs.
3. They're given the opportunity to participate and contribute to the total process.

A Do-It-Yourself Internal Customers Program

You can conduct the following program within your own department or in company with other departments. All the main elements are quite· easy to work with:

1. *Identify internal customers.* Figure 16-10 illustrates a rating sheet in which workers are asked to identify their principal internal customers; list the principal tasks or services they render to those internal customers; rate their own performance in serving those internal customers; rate their own performance in serving those internal customers; and indicate what they could do to improve their performance on behalf of those internal customers.

2. *Identify internal vendors.* Now the shoe is on the other foot, and workers are given the rating sheet shown in Figure 16-11 to identify the departments that serve them in the company, their vendors so to speak, and to rate their performance in the same way they rated their own.

3. *Discuss the responses.* Ask participants to explain their responses to the group. Invite others to debate or defend their positions.

4. *Set standards.* Divide your group into small teams and assign each team the task of setting standards for one of the following company departments or activities: sales-marketing, credit, distribution warehousing, customer service, MIS, quality control, accounts receivable, field service engineering, management, and other departments as appropriate.

Bear in mind that this is a team exercise designed to create awareness of internal customers, not to rebuild the company from the ground up. So it should be enjoyable for the participants—it usually is—and perhaps broken up into two or three different time segments so as to maintain interest. Note that rating sheets can be given out and filled in beforehand, so that the internal customers/vendors portion of the program can focus on live discussions. You can conduct the exercise entirely with your own people if you wish, but it

Figure 16-10. Internal customer rating sheet

I am the Internal Customer of:	This is What I Depend on Them to Do For Me	How Well They Do (0 – 10)*	This is How They Can Improve Their Performance on My Behalf

*Where 0 = Poor, 5 = Average, 10 = Outstanding

Comments:

Source: Customer Service Newsletter

Figure 16-11. Internal vendor rating sheet

These Are My Internal Customers:	This is What They Depend on Me to Do For Them	How Well I Do (0–10)*	This is How I Can Improve My Performance on Their Behalf

*Where 0 = Poor, 5 = Average, 10 = Outstanding

Comments:

Source: Customer Service Newsletter

will be far more effective if you can involve other departments you interface with frequently. The concept of internal customers is becoming increasingly important in business management, and it's an excellent area for you to showcase your talents along with those of your reps!

The Role of Feedback in Improving Performance

In many industries and occupations, it's already practical to provide continuous feedback to workers so that they know how well they are doing and are encouraged by the feedback to improve their performance if necessary, or maintain it at existing levels if they are already meeting requirements.

Because that term *meeting requirements* is the essence of all quality programs, an increasing number of companies are now viewing continuous training via monitoring and feedback as a linked element in ongoing quality assurance programs such as statistical process control (SPC). Even in small customer service departments, we are beginning to see one supervisor whose primary responsibility is a joint one: training *and* quality assurance for the customer service subsystem or process.

This makes excellent sense, because it's clear that the continuous process approach to training is beneficial and motivational to workers and involves them in the quality process rather than making them victims of it. Quality assurance is of necessity a continuous process itself, and continuous, and continuous training fits perfectly into that process. It shifts the focus, as it should, from the "how many" of traditional productivity measures, to the "how good" of quality assurance.

Another very cogent reason for linking customer service training to the quality assurance process is that it makes the idea of cross-training and interdepartmental or internal customer programs more appealing to senior management and heads of other departments. By presenting such programs as a benefit to the entire organization, rather than just something that will benefit your own department, you'll see a greater degree of acceptance generally, as well as higher levels of enthusiasm for participating and generating a genuine sense of teamwork.

17

Keep Your Employees Motivated: How to Deal With Stress and Burnout

The topic of this chapter is an assignment that would intimidate most mortals, but it's all in a day's work for today's fired-up customer service manager, meaning you. Your training responsibilities as a department head and operating manager merge naturally into your leadership role in dealing with the "people problems" that are inherent in almost any occupation, but tend to be particularly pronounced in customer service.

Stress is a basic component of most customer service jobs. Stress comes in many different forms, and different people are stressed by different things. A number of books have been written about the medical and psychophysiological aspects of stress, but they are well beyond the scope of this book. This chapter is concerned with the kinds of stress most commonly associated with customer service work and with the ways you can minimize their impact on the work of your department. Some examples of the different kinds of stress situations that you may encounter, and the sometimes unexpected causes follow:

• *Warranty claims adjusters.* This job often falls in the same category as bill collector: People don't stand in line applying for the frequent openings that occur. In one company, the primary duty of these CSRs relates to paying, or not paying, extremely high dollar claims related to complex and expensive machinery. The job is well paid, and working conditions and benefits are excellent, with none of the typical pressures of the job that occur when phone calls are backed up and there aren't enough people to handle them.

Yet turnover at this company was extremely high, and CSRs stayed in their jobs barely long enough to recover the cost of training them. Raising salary levels had no appreciable effect, and it was generally assumed that the heavy dollar responsibilities of the job were creating high stress levels that led to burnout and turnover.

But, like many assumptions, this one turned out to be false. In fact, a simple change in these reps' benefits changed the turnover rate from 50 percent to practically zero. That change was not inexpensive, but in the end it cost far less than the turnover the company had been experiencing in these particular jobs—hiring and training costs that could easily run to $10,000 or more per hire.

The change that miraculously relieved turnover, believe it or not, consisted simply in giving these reps 5 weeks' vacation per year, one more week than the president of the company received. The cost to the company was essentially the cost of adding one person to the department to offset a total productivity loss for the department of about 1 man-year annually resulting from the additional vacation time. Unusual? Yes, but it worked.

The stress factor, it turned out, was not connected with the heavy responsibilities of the job, rather it resulted from the poor status of the job in the company, where it had been historically viewed as a basic clerical assignment. Once again, this demonstrated that low self-esteem is frequently a principal cause of stress. The perceived status conferred by the added vacation days eliminated the principal source of stress and the turnover problem practically overnight.

The key factor here was that the dollars involved made it practical to deal in a fairly radical way with one of the most common causes of stress in customer service, poor self-image. In the majority of companies, it would be very difficult to convince management of the value of this particular remedy, but it might be worth a try!

▪ *Interrupt-itis.* In another company with a stress-related turnover problem, the manager determined that a primary cause of stress and burnout (and hence turnover) was the constant stream of interruptions that made it difficult and sometimes impossible for reps to complete one task or transaction before having to take on another one, only to be interrupted again.

The manager decided to counter this problem by empowering reps to sign off the phone system at their discretion in order to complete any paperwork or research associated with the call just completed. The result was a slight slowdown in telephone response during the busiest periods of the day but a more than offsetting gain in productivity and a significant drop in turnover.

Other managers deal with the interrupt-itis problem by allocating half-hour, 1 hour, or sometimes half-day segments in which personnel are off the phones entirely to catch up on their research or paperwork. If you have such a program in place (and it's highly recommended that you do), you should make every effort not to violate it. It's one of the most effective antidotes to stress that you'll ever find.

The customer service manager at a well-known insurance company reported that she readjusted schedules so that reps now work 5 hours on the phones and 2 hours off to do their paperwork, but at staggered hours. The result, she says, has been a drop in employee turnover from 40 percent to less than 20 percent.

Although some companies place great emphasis on prompt response and minimum holds, remember that a high percentage of interrupt-itis stress is caused by flashing lights or various signals which tell reps there is a backup of calls they're expected to get to promptly.

▪ *The joys of stresslessness?* The customer service manager of a highly regarded direct marketing company complained that although she had virtually zero turnover and her customer service reps were the salt of the earth, they were also dull, unimaginative people who contributed hardly anything in the way of new ideas or suggestions for improvements in customer service operations.

Yet the price of hiring dynamic and innovative people was more than she and the company were willing to pay. The department was an excellent place to work in most respects: fair pay, a good class of customers, good support systems, an even workload, congenial co-workers and excellent fringes, but no opportunities for promotion inside or outside the customer service department. She said,

> So we ended up hiring people who wanted security and who are willing to put up with the stresses of the job in order to get that security. They have no problem "turning off" at five o'clock and coming back the next day for more of the same — a diet of stress that would send more ambitious people up the wall.

At this writing, average longevity in the job is rapidly approaching 15 years and only the manager is feeling stress.

▪ *Empowerment cuts turnover from 47 percent to 3 percent.* One company was able to cut turnover dramatically via a participative management program, which gave customer service reps a voice in interdepartmental matters involving new products and promotions as well as in the operations of their own department. This elevated the reps' self-esteem to the level that the common stress of being "left out" of things disappeared completed.

▪ *Colors cut stress.* A call center manager in Canada claimed to have achieved a "drastic" reduction in stress level by selecting burgundy and rose as the main colors in her department, although a close reading of the article suggests that the actual furniture including work-together quad-pods and ergonomic chairs that she chose may have been a factor, as well as the attention paid to that department when all other offices at the company use a corporate blue color scheme.

This example may be a version of the so-called Hawthorne effect in which productivity gains were noted at the Westinghouse Hawthorne Works in Cicero, Illinois, as the walls were progressively painted with different colors. Each time a new color was applied, productivity increased, and many theories developed about the most effective colors. Finally, engineers realized that the colors were not causing the increases in productivity but the attention itself that was being paid to the worker's environment. It made them feel they were important, and they responded accordingly.

Whether burgundy and rose reduce stress, there's an important point here: Pay attention to your reps and their environment. Remind them that they are important not just with words but with positive visible actions as well, and you'll be repaid many times over.

The Main Causes of Stress in Customer Service

Different occupations cause stress in different ways. In customer service, stress arises from these four main causes:

1. *Interruption or incompletion.* The more you can redesign jobs and workflow so that workers can complete tasks once they are begun, the more productivity you'll enjoy, and the less stress your people will suffer. And the quality of your service will improve accordingly.

2. *Lack of confidence or self-esteem.* Lack of confidence or self-esteem is related both to inadequate training and to the way the department and its workers are likely to be perceived by others in the company and, on occasion, by customers. It can be largely overcome by training, interdepartmental or internal customer team building and various kinds of empowerment including participative management.

3. *Lack of control.* This cause combines elements of the two above items and is usually the most pernicious of all causes. It is manifested by not being able to get things done, not being able to get others to cooperate, not being able to satisfy customers' needs, and not being able to assimilate and organize the workflow. This kind of stress is due in part to lack of authority to make even simple decisions; in part to not being consulted about procedures, policies, and the work environment; and in part to not knowing how to cope with stress.

Most experts on stress say that the first step in dealing with stress is to learn to accept conditions that are essentially unchangeable or over which the individual can't hope to have any control and to concentrate on those that she can control.

Psychologists have determined that the feeling or perception of control is more important than the reality. For example, flextime has proven to be a powerful distressor because of the symbolic control it gives the individual over his job. The same is true of participative management as well as broadening reps' authority to make decisions and to bend the rules when necessary.

4. *Leadership issues.* Could *you* be the cause of employee stress? Yes, it's possible. A survey of customer service reps identified the following "manager stress factors," listed in descending order of importance:

- *Poor communications from manager.* This factor has three main subsets: (1) not communicating necessary information before customers have it; (2) not communicating corporation information before reps get it through the grapevine; and (3) not providing feedback on the quality of reps' work.
- *Unwillingness to delegate; excessive supervision.* This is often coupled with disregard for a rep's ability or inability to do a job. One rep described "the manager who has a finger in every pie—who can't seem to let subordinates do a job on their own." Another described the manager's actions as "Micro-managing! An almost complete failure to delegate responsibility!"
- *Slow or no response on inquiries and requests.* This is typified by the rep who characterizes managers as "listening to problems and either doing nothing or saying they'll do something and then not doing anything." Another rep describes a stress-carrying manager who "takes two or three days to respond to questions raised by reps trying to serve customers better."
- *Changing priorities* Psychologists point out that unexpected change can be a major source of stress, and comments of reps seem to bear this out. Yet

this area is one where managers are normally right in doing what they do, regardless of whatever stress might result to reps. It's fundamental to the manager's job to change priorities when conditions warrant it and to lead her reps through such changes. Of course this implies that when changes are in the wind, managers notify their reps right away.

- *Perceived discourtesies by managers and supervisors.* This category of stress factors is self-explanatory, although a review of the examples provided by reps suggests thoughtlessness rather than deliberate discourtesy. Remember that perception is reality, and actions which to you may seem perfectly normal, such as closing your office door to handle a sensitive phone call, standing over a worker while he completes a phone call, or swearing, may come across to some reps as rank rudeness.
- *Leadership problems.* Wishy-washy behavior, failing to stand up for the department and blatant partiality are among the examples cited by reps. Although this cause was last on the reps' list, it's actually involved in most of the other stress factors. In times of change and uncertainty, lack of leadership by the manager would probably move quickly to the top of the stress list.

Developing High Morale and Motivation in the Customer Service Department

Customer service people see few tangible results of their work, and, as a result, suffer from a shortfall of the most important of all motivators: a sense of accomplishment. In order to develop high morale and motivation in your department, you need to take some specific action to compensate for this shortfall:

1. *Create a tangible identity for the department.* This is usually done via brochures introducing members of the department, photographic business cards or self-mailers, and writeups in external and internal house organs. Chapter 12 tells you how to get the maximum results from these media, inside the company as well as externally.

2. *Involve the department in a major project.* One example: development of companywide programs in observance of customer Service Week, which is observed the first week in October and has currently been proclaimed by the governors of more than half the states. If you're involved in activities of the International Customer Service Association (ISCA), as you should be, you are automatically informed about this event and have access to supporting materials and suggested activities.

Another and more far-reaching project would be to get your entire company involved in the Award of Excellence competition sponsored by ISCA, with a deadline for entries usually in June of each year, and announcement of winners at the organization's annual conference in the fall. There are two categories, one for manufacturing and the other for service. Competition is intense, but even if your company doesn't win, developing its entry and supporting it with customer service improvements creates pride, motivational intensity, and recognition for your reps that would be hard to duplicate in any other way.

3. *Demonstrate the dollars the department is responsible for.* One manager of a relatively small department finds it adds tangible value to the job when reps realize they each handle about $70 million annually for their company. In the usual proportion, this is five to fifty times as much revenue as the individual field sales person generates in sales in a typical year.

Activity reports can be helpful in this respect, for example, charts, graphs, or illustrations showing:

- Volume of product in car loads or truckloads or distribution center square footage reflected in departmental transactions
- Number of "years" reflected in total telephone calls handled
- Percentage of error-free transactions handled by the department
- Number of individuals helped or problems solved by the department
- Additional dollars contributed through order enhancement, substitution programs, reversals of cancellations, inquiry conversations, service upgrades, or add-ons

You can also involve your CSRs directly in these exercises. Debi Rauckhorst, customer service manager for Mactac/Morgan Adhesives in Stow, Ohio, asked her reps to answer this question after a particularly successful month: "What was *your* contribution to the company's making its sales plan this month?" After answering, reps selected prizes from a catalog, but what was significant was that they first had to express their contribution in tangible terms. This exercise is a good application of the principle that the best way to inform oneself is to organize one's thoughts to inform others.

4. *Rewrite job descriptions.* The how-to of this process was describe in Chapter 15. The rewrite should be performed by reps themselves, so they will be forced to think through their jobs and express them in tangible, logical terms. As the example in Chapter 15 suggests, the rewrite will be much longer than the original, but you want it that way to demonstrate the scope and complexity of the job to the individual as well as to your human resources people.

5. *Send customer service reps and other support people out into the field on customer visitations.* David Hain, customer service manager for ICI Films, Wilmington, Delaware, makes sure that this reps are well prepared before making such visits. Reps take a short seminar on making presentations and then submit a plan to him describing how they will conduct the visitation, what they will discuss, what information they will seek from the customer, and more. Upon returning, the rep is required to file a formal call report just as if she had made a regular sales call. Hain feels that by setting objectives and structuring their visitations in this way, reps get the most out of visits that might otherwise end up primarily as social calls—good for goodwill, but not nearly as constructive as they could be.

Linda M. McGuffie, Sales Service Manager of Macan Kraft, Inc., Macon, Georgia, reports that sending her reps out on customer visitations proved to be the long-sought solution to the burnout problem. Customer service manager Charlie Close at Union Carbide in Somerset, New Jersey, says that it's also helpful to send out departmental support people who seldom have direct contact with customers but nevertheless are an important element in customer service quality.

A variation on visitation is sending customer service reps to work display booths at trade shows and conferences. This assignment is an excellent way of meeting customers face-to-face and a great morale builder. R. A. Jones Co., Cincinnati, Ohio, has used its CSRs to survey customers visiting its booth on Jones' customer service vs. the competition. The plus here is that reps themselves receive high ratings for their efforts, even when service problems exist, so that the survey activity combines with the face-to-face meeting to improve reps' morale and sense of being recognized.

5. *Protect your reps.* Protecting your reps is inherent in your leadership role, but it can also be expressed in small ways in the course of normal operations. David Wiegman, manager of the customer service group at Phelps Dodge, Fort Wayne, Indiana allows himself to be the fall guy when there are customer service failures. When a problem is resolved in favor of the customer, he says, "I make sure that my customer service people take back the good news to customers. But when the customer is especially irate and the news is bad, I'll call the customer and deal with the problem."

Like other managers, Wiegman realizes that to reverse a policy decision made by a rep without consulting that rep would result in a loss of face for the rep, whereas if he discusses the issue with the rep and then authorizes her to bend the rules and change the policy, the rep should be the conduit of the good news. "I want my reps to look good in the customer's eyes," he explains.

6. *Recognize your reps.* Recognition can be one of the most powerful of all motivators, and it can range from simple "ouchless" feedback to an elaborate presentation of awards with audience and a master of ceremonies. A number of different ways of recognizing CSRs' contributions are described in the next section.

7. *Thank your reps.* Andrea Cervantes, customer service supervisor at Rainbird Manufacturing Co., Azusa, California, discovered that when she started saying "Good night, and thank you" to her reps individually, they developed greater enthusiasm and team spirit, so she kept right on saying it!

Recognition Roundup

As a practical matter, a series of small acts of recognition on the job are often more effective than a major ceremony taking place weeks or months after the fact. Some companies have comprehensive recognition programs, but for the most part customer service managers seem to prefer informal, spur-of-the-moment approaches to recognition such as the following:

▪ *Mercantile Bank,* St. Louis, Missouri. Vice-President Lorinda Selvo offers a form of recognition that's hard to beat: free housecleaning services for reps who perform in an outstanding way.

▪ *B. F. Goodrich,* Cleveland, Ohio. Customer Service Manager Susan J. Ficke says that when company executives call on key customers they often get glowing reports about the CSRs servicing their accounts. On their return, they make it a point to personally visit those reps, tell them the good things they've heard about them, and thank them for their efforts. It's a great motivator!

■ *Carefree General Aluminum Products,* Charlotte, Michigan. Customer Service/Order Processing Manager Dollie M. Beard tells about a valued customer service rep who decided she wanted out and gave notice. When customers as well as people inside the company almost unanimously told her how much she was valued and how much she would be missed, she changed her mind and decided to stay. A great incentive to start your recognition program *now*!

■ *Bianchi International*, Temecula, California. Customer Service Manager Karen Sasscer at the outdoor equipment company reports that three significant fringes— a weight room, a fitness room and a 1½ hour lunch period—have proven so attractive that her department has only had one position open in five years.

■ *Citicorp/Choice,* Towson, Maryland. Customer service reps at the financial services company periodically receive phantom phone calls from within the organization. If they handle the call correctly, a 6-foot, 7-inch Phantom of the Opera, complete with mask and costume suddenly appears and passes out checks of $25, $50 or $100.

■ *Siemens Life Support Systems*, Schaumburg, Illinois. For outstanding achievement by a customer service rep, Customer Service Manager Louise Haley awards a Ferris Beuhler Day, adapted from the motion picture about a high school students incredible adventures on a day he skipped school. The only requirement is that the rep use the day to have fun (no dental appointments) and make a 2-minute report at the next departmental meeting of how he spent the day.

■ *Whistler,* Westford, Massachusetts. Posting attaboy letters from satisfied customers isn't new, but Technical Supervisor Denise Wortman says Whistler has added a touch that gives such letters extra credibility. When a complimentary letter is received, it's forwarded to company President Charles Stott, who puts his comments on it and sends it back to be posted on the Wall of Fame in a high-visibility area.

■ *Pearle Distribution Center,* Dallas, Texas. Director of Distribution Service Virginia Herrin reports two recognition programs: (1) the Productivity Award, based on actual measured performance; and (2) the Most Helpful CSR Award, based on a survey of all Pearle customers. The winners' photos go up in the Ring of Honor, a permanent display at the facility. The Productivity Award winner receives a $100 cash award, while the Most Helpful winner receives a $150 award, a plaque, and a jacket with the title and year of the award. Although Pearle clearly favors quality customer service over actual productivity, Herrin reports that in two out of three years, the CSR who won the Productivity Award was also voted Most Helpful CSR.

■ *R. G. Barry Corp.,* Columbus, Ohio. Customer Service Manager Kathy May bought three punching bags and an 8-foot inflatable dinosaur suitable for kicking and punching to help reps through a particularly stressful period. The additions got a good workout, and members of other departments even appeared as guest punchers. A very popular purchase!

■ *Ashland Chemical*, Mississauga, Ontario. Each CSR is required to make two customer visitations per month, says Manager Customer Service Bob Craig. These visits are perceived in the company as a mark of prestige or a status symbol, and the department never lacks for job applicants from other departments. That's peer recognition, and it means a lot.

■ *Yale Security*, Charlotte, North Carolina. Ed Shimpack, manager of internal sales and distribution, observed that attaboy compliments were increasingly being made over the telephone, so he instituted a policy of writing down complimentary customer comments and posting them on the departmental bulletin board so everybody would see them in hard copy form. His comment: "The reps love it!"

■ *Boehringer-Manneheim Diagnostics*, Indianapolis, Indiana. Some form of recognition activity takes place every month, says Customer Service Supervisor Diane Smith, and birthdays and anniversaries aren't overlooked, either. Reps takes turns being Event Coordinator of the Month for the program and they're very inventive. It's an excellent way of accruing continuity and departmental involvement, worth adapting for your own department!

■ *Serviceland, Inc.*, Rolling Meadow, Illinois. Proving that recognition doesn't have to be any big thing, Service Manager Jerry Wereminski says that his reps spend most of their time in the field working from different locations and seldom meet one another face-to-face. What they want more than anything else is just a social evening together to compare notes and hoist a few. So he arranges a night out for them and hires vans to pick them up and deliver them home afterward. A safe social evening!

■ *OCLC*, Columbus, Ohio. Customer Service Manager Rick Hodge at the library database organization cites job features that recognize the special nature of computer oriented personnel: alternating months on flextime, a gaming area with computer games where they can get away from it all, and on-site biofeedback.

■ *O'Brien International*, Redmond, Washington. Stress levels sometimes run high at this rapidly-growing manufacturer of skis and water sports equipment, but Director of Human Resources Sue Wade has found a cure. Periodically, she has a professional masseuse come into the department to soothe those nerves and relax those muscles.

As you can see, the opportunities for recognizing your reps are almost limitless and programs can be undertaken for little or no money and without elaborate preparations. As with many other activities in the customer service department, the more you involve your reps the better results you're likely to get. As a first step, you may want to form a committee of reps and decide on procedure — the Boehringer-Mannheim format just described is suggested as a good model. Do a little brainstorming and you'll be pleasantly surprised at all the innovative ways you'll uncover for recognizing those people who so richly deserve it.

Customer Service Department Incentive Programs

Recognition programs and incentive programs have a great deal in common. Many recognition programs are incentive programs as well because they have essentially the same goal. That goal, to put it bluntly, is to get more and better work out of the department at less cost.

Money is not the only motivator in the workplace, and sometimes it is rather an ineffective one. Instead, psychological factors related to job satisfaction such as sense of accomplishment, recognition, the working environment, and the nature of the work itself are often more effective in stimulating better output from workers, and more of it.

The most common incentive in business today, however, is the sales commission, whereby salespeople are given a percentage of the sales they make as commission in order to motivate them to make more and bigger sales. As customer service manager, you sometimes see the downside of this arrangement, when, in order to gain their commission, salespeople sell products or services that aren't available or make commitments that your department can't keep—an idea to remember when you consider the appropriateness of giving your own reps a commission for add-ons or order upgrades.

Yet incentives have their place in customer service department operations, and they normally fall into two main categories:

1. *Production-oriented programs* designed primarily to increase production while maintaining quality and accuracy and, as a side benefit to improve quality and accuracy without decreasing production. From a corporate viewpoint, increases in customer service department productivity contribute to greater profitability via cost reductions as well as avoiding the rework costs discussed in Chapter 14.
2. *Morale and motivation-oriented programs* often indirectly aimed at productivity via improved job satisfaction, higher attendance, greater involvement of reps in corporate goals, reduced stress, and turnover. On a broader scale, they also relate to increased sales and profits through building better and longer-lasting relationships with customers and greater continuity in handling their accounts.

Basic Requirements of a Customer Service Incentive Program

As customer service manager, you will probably be better off developing your own incentive program working with your reps than if you buy an outside package program, because the customer service environment is quite different from most others and a program developed outside the department is likely to be a poor fit.

If your company has an overall incentive program that is well conceived, well managed, and well funded, by all means make sure that your reps are included and measured fairly. The principles discussed here are based on the premise that your particular program originates in your department and that you have a limited or in some cases nonexistent, budget to support it. Here are the minimum requirements for such a program:

1. *Clear objectives and understanding of purpose.* These are critical. Everybody concerned must be in complete agreement as to what the program is supposed to do. As examples:

- *Productivity.* Reward output directly such as number of calls handled, orders written and so on.
- *Quality.* Reward performance to quality standards, for example, lowest error rate, most inquiries handled on-line, and so on.
- *Morale and motivation.* Create higher improved job satisfaction, reduced stress, and turnover.

2. *Acceptability to workers and management.* Obviously your program must be consistent with company policies and the rewards shouldn't be so spectacular as to create interdepartmental ill-will (envy is all right, but in moderate doses!). But beyond that your CSRs have to buy into the program from the very beginning, particularly on these key issues:

- *Credibility and fairness.* The program can't discriminate against some CSRs because their jobs are more complex or difficult, nor can it favor others whose jobs are easier or more routine.
- *Relevance.* The best way to ensure that reps will buy into and support an incentive program is to involve them in designing the program and determining what to reward and how to reward it. Peer-based programs are working effectively for a number of customer service departments.

3. *Program administratability.* Scorekeeping on an incentive program can be a full-time job, and there's always the danger that emergencies and sudden surges in business will interfere with administering the program, which in turn will quickly undermine its credibility as well as its effectiveness. So, your program should incorporate these features:

- *Reliable and consistent measures.* Agreement beforehand as to how performance will be measured and whether allowances will be made for experience, complexity of individual jobs, vacations, sick leave and so forth. To the extent possible, select measures that can be generated automatically as a byproduct of the work itself.
- *Event- or time-orientation.* Some programs provide an incentive for performing specific acts regardless of when they are performed, for example, upgrading orders. Others reward performance over a period of time, for example, the fewest errors in a week, the greatest improvement in a month. Both approaches are effective; you may want to suggest to your reps that they be alternated from time to time.
- *Continuity.* Incentive programs don't have to go on forever, but they should have sufficient continuity to achieve credibility. They shouldn't be interrupted because of the press of business, although it's certainly all right to build gaps or intervals into the original plan to allow in advance for such events.
- *Flexibility.* Programs should be updated at least once a year and preferably more often. Of course your reps should be involved in such updatings and revisions as they were at the outset.

Production-Oriented Customer Service Incentive Programs

There are five main types of production-oriented customer service incentive programs for you and your reps to consider:

1. *Simple output.* In this type of program, everybody does the same work and is measured against the same standards. A hotel or airline reservation system is a good example. Although individual calls may vary in length and complexity, over time the ACD system ensures that everybody gets the same mix of calls. Incentives based on output must naturally include standards for accuracy, quality, and courtesy to ensure that reps aren't making their numbers via shortcuts or discourtesies to customers.

2. *Weighted output.* Where there's a significant division of labor or specialization within the department, you need to allow for the fact that some tasks are more difficult and complex than others. This is usually done through a process of "weighting," whereby handling a call relating to export-import matters may be worth three times as many scoring points as handling a routine call about order status or service or product availability. This is explained in more detail in Figure 17-1.

3. *Randomized incentives.* A pitfall of some incentive programs is that the prizes are always won by the same people, the superstars, which tends to discourage others in the department. One way to counter this is to set a specific standard, for example, ninety phone calls a day, or an error rate below one-half of one percent, and then conduct a drawing for everyone who meets or exceeds the standard. The drawing is so arranged that everybody wins a prize, but the value of the prize is determined by the random drawing, not by the individual's actual score. So-called scratch cards like those used in lotteries are being used increasingly in this type of program. One application is described later under Typical Incentive Programs.

4. *Team programs.* These are appropriate to situations where your department is organized by teams or work units and also in cases where you want to involve people in other departments as part of a team. Team programs are particularly suited to multilocational operations, for example, where there are customer service people as well as warehouse workers, inventory personnel, and so forth at a number of different distribution centers. Note that in such cases your measures must allow for differences in the size and volume of the different operations.

5. *Profit-sharing programs.* There are several versions of profit-sharing programs. In one, the customer service department is automatically allotted a percentage of monthly sales, which is then divided among reps. Some managers feel that the best way to divide this commission is on the basis of attendance: For example, if the commission is $1,000 and the department worked a total of 1,000 hours, each rep gets $1 of commission for each hour she worked. This is an incentive to show up for work, and it's a truism that if people report to work more work gets done. Some managers feel that the commission should be divided equally among all departmental members, but it can be argued that at this point it's no longer an incentive but a fringe benefit. There are also profit-sharing programs related to order upgrading, providing sales leads, and telemarketing.

Morale and Motivation-Oriented Incentive Programs

Morale and motivation-oriented incentive programs often overlap with recognition programs because they are concerned primarily with job satisfaction, which

Figure 17-1. The right and wrong ways to measure productivity

Right	*Wrong*
Analyze claims by type. Weight and credit productivity of claims agents accordingly: Simple claim 100% Moderately complex claim 150% Extremely complex claim 200%	Measure claims agents' productivity by number and accuracy of checks issued.
Count mixed-type phone calls by type and length and measure against a standard for each.	Count number of phone calls handled only.
Rate call volume for handling uniform or standardized calls against courtesy standards, adherence to script content, call-backs and transfers.	Count number of phone calls handled only.
Weight number of orders handled or lines entered by accuracy, dollar volume, and add-ons or substitutions accepted by customer.	Rate productivity by number of orders or lines entered.
Rate field engineers by type of repair, diagnostics, mean time between failures, callbacks and other criteria. Allow for travel, waiting time, or availability of equipment.	Rate field engineers by number of assignments completed.
Rate classified ad takers by dollar volume, mix of standard vs. display ads, etc.	Rate ad-takers by number of agate lines or ads taken.

Source: Customer Service Newsletter

presumably in turn leads to improved productivity. There is also considerable overlap with some forms of training programs, as you'll note in the following list:

1. *Career pathing.* This is a built-in incentive for companies that want to hire and retain top quality personnel for their customer service activities. Many college graduates won't consider jobs where there isn't a clear career path within the department as well as beyond it. People who seek career paths are highly motivated and productive and tend to stay that way. However, career pathing isn't practical in all situations, and different incentives must be developed.

2. *Informal, fun-type programs—de-stressors.* This is the most prevalent type of incentive program in customer service, and it's particularly well suited to departments that don't have career pathing or other opportunities for growth

or advancement. A number of the recognition programs described under Recognition Roundup fall into this category. They're fun, they keep people interested and coming to work, and greater job satisfaction and continuity result.

3. *Job enrichment.* This is a practical alternative where career pathing isn't suitable because of department size or function. Job enrichment means basically making the job more interesting by broadening its scope and giving individuals more responsibility. It can also involve developing specialization within the department, or in departments that have export-import specialists, claims specialists, foreign language experts and the like. Job enrichment provides a strong incentive in the form of status among peers.

4. *Customer visitations and trade show participation.* Many companies have found these to be excellent incentives, as mentioned earlier in this chapter. Managers almost invariably comment that CSRs see such excursions as rewards, even though the company itself is usually the main beneficiary.

5. *Training.* Cross training and internal customer programs as well as straight skills training will be perceived as rewards if they are presented that way, and they certainly shouldn't be presented as chores!

Typical Incentive Programs

Customer service department incentive programs are limited only by the imagination, or the sense of humor, of the people responsible for their development. Here are some examples:

▪ *Alpha Wire Corporation,* Elizabeth, New Jersey. Lottery-type scratch cards have proved an excellent randomized incentive to reps to persuade customers to accept substitutes when the items they order aren't available. Inside Sales Manager Theresa Williams says that the cards, printed in denominations of $5, $10, $25, and $50, are awarded on the average of one a day or five a week. Unlike a conventional lottery, there are no nonwinners, and the cost is more than offset by the value of keeping the customer plus moving inventory that's currently in the warehouse. But Williams warns that scratch cards are suited for conventional order enhancement or upgrading programs where their use simply results in "borrowing tomorrow's business," and not keeping business form going to a customer or balancing out the inventory by selling slow-moving stock.

▪ *Port Authority of New York and New Jersey.* An incentive program that rewards people for not taking their sick leave has had excellent results for the Tenant Service Unit of the Port Authority, according to Supervisor Ed Monteverde. "In mid-November," he says, "our employees receive a check for the days allowed them for sick leave that they didn't use. If they didn't use any, they receive $400. If they used some, they receive less." He points out that the job itself is a tough one, involving fielding calls from 800 tenants with some 45,000 employees in the World Trade Center and arranging maintenance work through 1,300 contractor employees, all unionized. Almost half his employees qualified for the full $400 checks, Monteverde says. He feels that the timing of the awards is particularly critical: "We give them the checks right before Thanksgiving." He says that his unit spends a month or so finding the right person for the demanding job, and it pays off. "Our people *want* to come into work!"

■ *Esselte Pendaflex/METO Division*, Garden City, New York. The Customer service manager instituted a Pot o'Gold incentive program on a simple premise: Whenever the ACD system shows a service level exceeding 85 percent of all calls answered by the third ring, graded sums are paid into the Pot o'Gold account for equal distribution among CSRs each quarter. The greater the margin over 85 percent, the larger the deposit. When the program was instituted, the service level was 81 percent. It rose almost immediately to 90 percent and has stayed there ever since. Scores are posted daily, and checked by CSRs with interested every morning, an indication of the program's sustained staying power.

■ *Customized Transportation, Inc.,* Kansas City, Missouri. Plant Manager Dave Lamolinara reports than an error reduction program developed with worker involvement is now producing 99.997 percent error-free performance. He attributes the program's success to worker involvement plus the quick feedback and positive reinforcement of prompt monthly payments.

■ *Foot-Joy, Inc.,* Brockton, Massachusetts. Customer Service Supervisor Debra Suvalle O'Keefe developed an Iceberg incentive program designed to reward CSRs for eliminating recurring problems altogether rather than simply fixing the tip of the iceberg and then having the problem recur later. When somebody breaks up an iceberg altogether by coming up with a new procedure or permanent solution, they are awarded an Igloo cooler selected to accompany the iceberg theme. O'Keefe finds the program to be an effective way of rewarding individual initiative in a very specific way.

■ *Gibraltar Bank*, Dallas, Texas. The twenty-six reps in the customer service department elected a six-member committee to design its incentive program. The committee established an Employee of the Month award based on these criteria: attendance and punctuality, percentage of calls answered, percentage of research completed. The award consist of a trophy that rotates each month. The winner's photo is placed on display and his or her name is engraved on a plaque. Penny Rohde, Vice-President Customer Service, says that the program has combined with career pathing to substantially reduce turnover at the bank.

■ *McDonnell Douglas* Payment Systems, Irvine, California. Like the Gibraltar program, this Employee of the Month program was developed by a committee of reps, in this case representing the three shifts at the round-the-clock facility. The reward: a small trophy, a day off with pay, and the winner's name placed on a perpetual plaque on display in the department. The award is based on seven criteria:

1. Handling the most incoming calls
2. Showing the most improvement
3. Attendance
4. Absenteeism/tardiness
5. Best phone manner

6. Best product/technical knowledge
7. Most assistance to teammates

■ *Sonesta Hotels International,* Cambridge, Massachusetts. Vice-President of Human Resources Jacqueline Sonnabend is an avid board game fan. From this interest, and with the help of some 800 suggestions from hotel employees at all levels, she devised an ingenious board game based on solutions to the numerous customer service situations that arise in a hotel chain. The game was used in a tournament played by employees through the chain, with appropriate prizes, and generated high interest and measurably improved performance as reported by guests. Sonnablend stresses that programs of this type should be fun for all participants and that prizes or awards should not be too generous less they result in excessive competitiveness among workers.

■ *Hartford Insurance Group,* Southington, Connecticut. Customers who contacted the customer service department were subsequently contacted and asked to rate the service they received. Reps who received the highest ratings received gift certificate awards ranging up to $100. Assistant Customer Service Manager John DeMeo explains that the reps were consulted beforehand and approved the method of selecting winners based on highest overall scores. Some 8,000 questionnaires were sent out and about 4,000 returned, an extremely high rate of response, which gave the program great credibility and provided valuable information about service quality in general. Reps' names were not used on the questionnaires but rather sources codes by which the Hartford could identify the individual who handles the customer's call.

■ *Xidex Corporation,* Sunnyvale, California. It's just about the simplest kind of incentive program, and it works like a charm: a night on the town in return for an error-free month. Marketing Services Director Gary Lewis built the program around the department's three most costly types of errors: wrong product shipped; wrong destination; and pricing errors creating excessive paperwork. Lewis says he selected the night on the town award because it represents positive reinforcement whereas a cash award would simply be used to pay a bill. "We wanted CSRs to have a nice evening out so they'd remember they got it for doing such a good job." He says that errors started to drop even before the program got under way and that some months have had as many as three winners—a small price to pay for significant error reduction.

It may surprise you to find that so many of the best training and incentive programs are relatively narrow in scope and modest in their rewards. But these managers show tremendous concern for their reps, recognizing them as individuals and involving them in decisions that affect them, in such a way that the reps recognize the importance of the roles they plan and do their utmost to perform them to the very best of their ability.

Section V

Customer Service and Your Future

18

Managing Yourself and Your Customer Service Career

Customer service management promises to be *the* career of the decade and certainly one that will give its professional managers a fair shot at the executive suite. The path will not be easy, however, and nothing will be handed to you on a silver platter.

This chapter poses some searching questions about what you are doing and plan to do next and how to meet some of the major challenges you'll be facing. The commentary on those questions was born of more than a quarter of a century of experience working with successful and not-so-successful managers in the customer service field.

Together, the questions and commentary are designed to help you shape your customer service management career and draw up plans for action that you can start implementing immediately. The chapter ends with some predictions about the type of company you will be working in and, quite possibly, leading into the twenty-first century with the combination of your personal skills and talents and the information you have gained here.

As a career-oriented manager in charge of an increasingly important function, you'll be faced with a number of alternative choices, the most important of which are set forth below.

To Be *Replaceable* and Not to Be *Indispensable*

Between your own experience and what you've read in this book, you probably know a good deal more about customer service than anybody else in your organization. And that's good. Your department will be better managed for it, and your company will profit by it. But you can't afford to let it stop there. You need to use your knowledge and skills to build a strong line of succession. Because the last thing in the world you want is to be so good in your job that you're irreplaceable and indispensable. As a manager you should have already identified and started training your successor and your successor's successor. If you don't do so soon, you will have foreclosed your own chances of being promoted to a senior management position because there won't be anybody to fill the position you would have to vacate for such a promotion. Furthermore, managers who don't have strong seconds-in-command tend to be looked on as poor senior management material.

Beware in particular of becoming trapped in the "putting out fires" syndrome so common in customer service. Don't permit yourself to be the only person who can untangle knotty problems and solve recurring crises. Follow the lead of Vic Byrd, service parts manager at the Electronic Systems Division of Cincinnati Milacrons, Inc., Lebanon, Ohio. Each year, he sets a goal of delegating 20 percent of his tasks by year's end. Besides escaping the firefighting syndrome, he says, "I'm able to add 20 percent new responsibilities and grow in my job."

Before you move on to the next set of alternatives, answer the following questions thoughtfully and thoroughly for your own benefit. Write your answers on a separate sheet of paper that you can use as a self-management tool in the weeks and months ahead:

1. Have you identified your own successor? If you haven't and you were required to choose someone today, who would it be?
2. What do you need to do to get that person ready to fill your shoes?
3. Who would replace the person you'd choose to replace you?
4. If you don't have career pathing in the customer service department to facilitate this kind of succession, what must you do so that in your organization customer service becomes a true career that attracts people who *are* capable of replacing you?

To Be *the Yeast of a Corporate Culture* and Not to Be *the Frosting on the Cake*

There's about a 90 percent chance that if you want customer service to happen in your company, it is largely up to you to make it happen. If you can answer the following three questions with a strong affirmative, you qualify as that hard-working yeast rather than the decorative frosting:

1. Does your department have a customer service mission statement? Does your company have one? If not, have you already started planning in that direction?
2. Have you surveyed other departments for their definitions of the role of customer service and then published their responses for the record?
3. Does your department provide training to other departments as well as to your own personnel on how to provide good customer service for internal as well as external customers?

To Be *the Target* and Not to Be *the Marksman*

Getting other departments to subscribe wholeheartedly to the customer service mission is not always easy. Very often, they have been given highly specific agenda by management that make it difficult for them to help you serve customers as well as you would like. Bearing in mind that in many companies it's not unusual for customer service personnel to be regarded as "troublemakers" because they're always showing up with problems, it's often far more fruitful to ask other departments how you can help them than it is to take potshots at them for not helping you.

The four questions that follow suggest some of the ways you can develop a good working relationship by letting yourself and your department be the target:

1. Have you identified your department's significant internal customers and what they expect from you and your department?
2. Have you instituted a systematic program to solicit feedback from those internal customers, to set yourself up as a target for their criticism if necessary?
3. Have you determined what aspects of your performance are most significant to them?
4. Do you make it a point to shield or protect them from unreasonable customer demands by negotiating alternative arrangements with customers whenever possible? And do you make it a point to tell them that you've done so?

To Be a *Giver of Recognition* and Not to Be a *Seeker of Recognition*

The best way for the customer service department to gain recognition is to give it—to make sure that other departments, and individuals in those departments, are fully acknowledged for their contribution to customer service goals. Here are three good questions to ask yourself to determine how well you are gaining by giving:

1. Do you have a systematic way of identifying and publishing positive examples of good customer service, including behind-the-scenes contributions from all departments in the company, not just your own?
2. In your company, are there individual incentives to employees for doing their part to ensure that high levels of customer service are maintained? If not, what can you do to set up such a program?
3. Meanwhile, without a formal program, what can you personally do to recognize and reinforce this desirable customer-oriented behavior, regardless of where it occurs in the organization?

To Be *a Standard Setter* and Not to Be *a "Settee"*

Management has the ultimate responsibility for standards because it controls the resources necessary to meet those standards, as well as the accountability of all those involved in the total effort that results in customer service. But as customer service manager it's incumbent on you to actually develop and quantify standards that meet management's strategic goals and equally to make sure that they're attainable standards and that management has legislated adequate resources as well as interdepartmental accountability.

These four questions will help you determine how well you are doing in this respect:

1. Have you developed and submitted standards—tough but practical—against which you wish to have your department measured?
2. Are there existing standards for the quality of customer service that customers actually receive? Are they based on objective knowledge of customers' needs and wants?
3. If no such standards now exist, what will you do to see that they are in place within the next 12 months and preferably sooner?
4. Are there internal standards and response requirements for other departments on whose performance your own department's performance depends? If not, how will you establish such standards?

To Be *a Willing Measurer* and Not to Be *a Reluctant Measuree*

As one manager put it, "I would much rather be put in charge of a customer service department that's in a real mess than be handed one that's in apple-pie order with everything functioning smoothly." Her reason, she said was that when I take over a department that's in a mess, I have a chance to show management how good I am. If I take over one that's already in good shape, somebody else will have already gotten the credit!"

She's right, of course, and as manager one of the reasons you want performance standards for your department as well as overall customers service is that you need tangible, quantified measures to demonstrate your own value as well as your department's to the company.

These four questions will help you explore this important area:

1. Have you insisted on your department's being measured in hard numbers?
2. What measures have you insisted on? Do they favor you, or are they unassailably objective?
3. Do you report measurement data regularly to those being measured as well as to management?
4. Apart from company measures, do you measure yourself as a manager and discuss the outcomes with your boss or a mentor?

To Be *a Planner for the Unexpected* and Not to Be *an Expecter of the Expected*

It's been said that Murphy's Law was written for the customer service profession: "If anything can go wrong, it will." It's also been pointed out that developing contingency plans to deal with emergencies, disasters, and other unpredictable events is an activity you don't need to get permission for, and you will often get a great deal of credit for developing such plans, even though they may never need to be implemented.

The heart of contingency planning is writing decision rules based on criteria that are often referred to as *trigger points*. When you know that two feet of snow are being forecast, the decision rule tells you who will be driving the four-wheel drives and picking up which critical workers at what times. When you know that a strike may be possible within a certain time frame, decisions rules tell you when to contact customers, what to tell them, what alternatives to prepare, and so forth. Of course you have standing plans for hurricanes, fires, power outages, and the like.

But you also have very basic contingency plans relating to nonavailability of service or product, threats of legal action, toxic spills, product recalls, and more. Here again, decision rules are absolutely essential. The following three questions are not quite as easy to answer as you might think:

1. What specific decision rules still need to be written for your department in order to minimize the need for ad hoc decisions whenever anything out of the ordinary happens?
2. What contingencies do not as yet have contingency plans in place?
3. What are the smallest and largest contingencies for which you will plan?

To Be *a Respecter of the Bottom Line* and Not to Be *a Slave of the Bottom Line*

You know for certain that customer service is definitely not the cost adding function some managers still think it is. You know for certain that it is a value adding activity, and this book has subjected you to a barrage of information about the economics of customer service. Are you ready to put that knowledge to work?

Here are five questions to key in on, although you should probably supply another six or eight questions on your own:

1. Is your department's current performance being measured in any way in terms of its contribution to the bottom line? If not, how will you set about applying such measurements?
2. Do you have a system to document and quantify the value of tradeoffs between customer service and other departments? (As one example, contributing to increased sales call productivity and increases sales by field salespersons.)

3. Can you institute a system to demonstrate cost reduction in resolving deductions, claims, and complaints? Do you know how to convert those savings into profit equivalents for your company? As part of this, how would you plan to measure an account's purchasing patterns after complaint resolution?
4. Do you regularly measure profit contribution by class of account, based on revenues and service requirements by account class?
5. Have you developed a system to demonstrate account growth and tied it to a proposed account retention strategy aimed at the potentially most profitable sectors of your customer base?

To Be *an Investor for the Future* and Not a *Penny-Saver for Today*

As you know, not all investments in customer service pay off right away, although some do. One of the problems you as manager have to deal with is striking a balance between measures that show near-term savings and those that contribute significantly to your goals of profit improvement and market share growth, but not immediately.

This balance isn't always easy to sell to a management that lives on month-end reports, but it's helpful to remember that the Japanese got as far ahead as they did in both quality and productivity by setting goals as far as 10 years out instead of living in the shadow of the *Wall Street Journal* and concentrating on the current quarter.

So, here are three questions to help you measure that balance:

1. Does your department's budget for new technology offer genuine near-term savings measurable in reduced costs and improved productivity, faster turnaround, fewer errors, and other measurable benefits?
2. Have you been able to establish the point with your management that customer service is essentially *asset management,* that you are managing the company's most valuable asset, its customers, and that to do so certain long-term investments are needed for both protecting and nurturing these assets?
3. What other areas have you identified for investing your department's resources to add long-term profits to the company? (Don't overlook personnel issues, which are going to become increasingly more sensitive, complex, and expensive in the future.)

To Be *a Manager of Change* and Not to Be *a Victim of Change*

The history of customer service in the last quarter century has seen a sharp division between customer service managers who have initiated change, fought for it, and succeeded in implementing it and customer service managers who have allowed change to be imposed on them, and have had to live with inadequate systems, poor telecommunications, and somebody else's idea of what customer service ought to be.

For many people, change is difficult to accept. It's no easier for managers than it is for line workers, and it's sometimes more difficult because managers have developed a power base and perceived benefits from the status quo that are threatened by change. Don't feel badly, dear reader, if you feel an occasional tremor or resistance to change: Plenty of things still are best left as they are, like turkey on Thanksgiving and the eagle as the national bird, not the other way around.

But don't forget that successful customers service management is the management of change: keeping tuned in to the changing needs of customers and the sweeping changes in systems and technology that every month bring about profound changes in the way customer service operations are conducted.

Yet if management of change requires accepting innovation and being willing to try it, it also means not getting carried away with all the bells and whistles that characterize some of the new technology packages. The ultimate measure of the pros and cons of change for customer service managers is: *Does it make it easier for customers to do business with us and at a price they are willing to pay?*

With those guidelines in mind, here are your three final questions:

1. Do you subscribe to publications and news sources and attend seminars and conferences to keep abreast of ideas and changes in ways of providing customers service that can be applied to improving your own operations? Do you maintain an open attitude toward applications from industries unlike your own, knowing that some of the best ideas originate this way? Do you keep a constant eagle eye on the competition and make sure that your reps pass along to you any customer comments or feedback about the competition?
2. Have you already prepared a list of changes you wish to implement to improve your department's performance or your company's market position? Have you figured out how you're going to sell these changes to others, including your own customer service personnel?
3. Are you part of an active group in the company involved in identifying trends and upcoming changes? If no such group exists, how are you going to bring one into being?

By the time you have worked your way through to instituting all the positive practices implicit in these questions, you will be well-fitted for a senior management role and leading your company into the twenty-first century business environment described in Chapter 19.

19

■■■
■■■
■■■

Preparing for a
Very Different Future in
Customer Service Management

The dramatic changes in the business world in the last decade will almost certainly be eclipsed by those of the decade ahead. But the changes in technology that we keep hearing about will almost certainly be dwarfed by changes in the way business is done.

Many of these changes will affect you as customer service manager. This chapter reviews what I feel will be the most significant trends that you should be watching now and accommodating in your forward planning.

Personnel: New Deployments, New Incentives

The shortage of competent customer service people will continue into the foreseeable future. If the generally poor caliber of public education does not improve, there is every likelihood that companies like yours will be setting up their own private schools and recruiting workers whom they will teach how to read, write, reason, and express themselves clearly, as well as perform the various operations associated with customer service. Some companies have already started pilot programs: It seems inevitable that in time many companies will be forced into it.

You will also be hiring people to work at home, using terminals connected to a mainframe terminal and phone lines connected to a central ACD system, as a number of companies have already started doing. Look for the development of modular offices, which can be moved into an employee's home complete with all the proper gadgetry, terminals, workstations, telecommunications, and other amenities, all ready to plug in and function in a matter of hours. Your reps will be accessible to you via closed-circuit television so that you can hold meetings and provide training from your office. Transmission quality will be so good that your joint "telepresence" will be almost like the real thing.

Such arrangements will be highly valued, and if your company doesn't lend itself to "remote reps" — and many won't — you will have to offer benefits almost as good simply to attract suitable personnel. Day-care and elder-care centers would be one such benefit; the four-day workweek — four days of nine or ten hours each — is another which is already in place in some firms, and one that we think is very close at hand in many more.

One facet of the personnel situation that in time will work in your favor is that the customer service job will ultimately be upgraded to the point where it will be one of the most highly paid line jobs in the organization and will have one of the best working environments. Figure 19-1 is a checklist you can use to rate your current situation and to set goals for improving that environment. Customer service reps will be recognized as consultants, technical specialists, and account managers and will have considerably more status in the company than at present.

New Measures of Performance

The decade 1980–1990 was characterized by explosive growth in the use of the telephone for customer service. As 800 numbers came into almost universal use, increasing emphasis was placed on call center productivity, and the proliferation of ACD systems made measuring individual productivity relatively easy. Yet, by mid-1990, some very large call centers had abandoned the practice of measuring performance by counting the number of calls an individual rep handled within a given time frame. I expect this trend to continue.

It seems most likely that the emphasis on the quality of phone contacts will continue and even increase, as more and more routine calls will be handled — by the customer's choice — by one of several forms of user-friendly automation. The function of CSRs will be recognized more clearly as that of consultant or advisor to customers so that the primary measure of performance will be how well reps maintain their account relationships, not how many contacts they make in a day.

If you are thinking that this sounds a little like never-never land, one of the major breakthroughs of the decade — which you will almost certainly be reading about shortly — will be the development of practical techniques to effectively measure the impact of customer service on company profits. As one facet of this measurement, individual performance will lend itself to evaluation and improvement by methods that will make today's subjectively-biased live monitoring or performance reviews seem crude by comparison.

In the area of overall service measurement, one benefit of the new techniques will be to greatly simplify the question of how much to spend on customer service and when to stop spending, or the exact point at which the law of diminishing returns sets in for a given market, service, or product. Today's management science approach of simulation, which is not widely accepted in customer service circles in any event, will be superseded by more credible and understandable techniques.

In the area of adjustments, where some companies have gingerly adopted no-fault policies within what are often ridiculously low limits, for example, a

(text continues on page 356)

Figure 19-1. People-keeping checklist

Instructions: Place a check mark (✔) in the column whose heading most nearly approximates the situation or environment in your own company. The more check marks you have in the "Now Have" and "Can Do" columns, the more likely you are to have an environment that not only attracts good people but also keeps them from making lateral moves to other companies. Too many check marks in the "No Way" column suggests that you try anyway or that you share this issue with your management.

	Have Now	Can Do	No Way	Don't Know — Will Try
The Company and the Environment				
1. Are there unusual benefits that other companies don't offer — such as day-care center, free travel, etc.?				
2. Do the physical surroundings of the department stand out in terms of appearance as well as perceived status in the company.				
3. Are systems state-of-the-art and genuinely user-friendly?				
The People				
1. Is the management seen as a leader and not just a "promoted rep"?				
2. Is the manager seen as being fully accepted by other managers?				
3. Does the manager delegate sufficiently and become involved in day-to-day operations only when absolutely necessary?				
4. Are there tangible evidences of what the manager has done for his/her people?				
5. Are supervisors respected and perceived as capable and fair?				
6. Are co-workers generally helpful and congenial?				
The Job and the Work				
1. Is the work organized in such a way as to be interesting to the worker?				

Source: Customer Service Newsletter

	Have Now	Can Do	No Way	Don't Know— Will Try
2. Is the workload evenly distributed?				
3. Is there proper and regular training?				
4. Are there opportunities for cross training and specialization?				

Measures of Performance

1. Are measures of performance fair and perceived as fair?
2. Are productivity measures weighted according to the difficulty and complexity of the task?
3. Are there incentives and/or rewards for high levels of performance?

Involvement and Motivation

1. Do CSRs know the job is important, and is this reflected in the way they are treated by others in the company?
2. Do they participate in quality circles, peer interviewing of job candidates, or similar participatory activities?
3. Is flextime used in the department?
4. Are CSRs able to see the result of their work so that it doesn't appear to be nothing but a string of negatives?
5. Do they receive appropriate recognition in the department and from sales, top management, and other departments?
6. Do they feel good about themselves in a way they would not find possible in another company?

$50 limit when a more realistic one would be $500, within the next few years you will see no-fault limits set on a case-by-case basis according to the value the company places on the account.

Most of these changes will come about, not because of any remarkable developments in computer technology, but because senior management has already begun to recognize the value of tracking the results of customer service in the same way that the company tracks the results of other investments or commitments of its resources.

Customer Service as Corporate Strategy

We have referred to customer service as a corporate strategy in other chapters of this book, but at this point the number of companies that have accepted this concept and have designated customer service as a profit center, are far out-numbered by those who still consider customer service to be "operations" or "after-sales service" and classify it as a cost center.

This will obviously change as a matter of survival, as marketing becomes much less of a mass-oriented activity and much more of what's now called "hypertargeting": zeroing in on very specifically delineated markets with very specific service offerings. This will be far more sophisticated than the differen-tiations some companies practice today. A manufacturer that today provides different levels of service to original equipment manufacturers will, in the future, be expected to develop a number of highly customized programs with value-added features and will be glad to do so in order to get the business.

An important part of this evolution will be driven by rising costs of sell-ing. These days it is rarely practical to engage in saturation marketing, and companies must concentrate on potential customers who are genuine prospects and not just "suspects." Mass marketing will become even less profitable in the future. As a few companies are now doing, the processes of segmentation and stratification employed in customer acquisition will be applied equally in something we'll call *managing customer retention*.

The hardest part of this trend for senior management and particularly top sales management, to digest is the concept of demarketing. Demarketing in its most common use simply means dropping customers that the company cannot profitably service, or customers whose cost of servicing diverts resources from fully servicing other, more profitable customers and exposes such accounts to greater risk from the competition. But demarketing can also mean reducing service to unprofitable accounts to levels commensurate with their contribution to profit and overhead.

If companies seriously intend to engage in hypertargeted marketing—and it appears that survival will require them to—their managements will have to recognize that demarketing accounts that don't fit is an essential component of hypertargeting, just as it is of niche marketing.

As customer service manager you will necessarily be involved in the demarketing process, for better or for worse, and it's strongly suggested that you anticipate that day by deciding how you're going to stratify and segment your accounts by cost of service versus contribution to profit and overhead. This process is not easy and you can't expect the highest levels of cooperation, but a good start would be to make friends with the financial department and interest it in the notion of developing return on investment data on an account-by-account (or account class by account class) basis.

Whatever you do, don't say "It'll never happen here!" Because if your prediction is correct, you'll probably become unemployed shortly thereafter. So, you have a pretty strong stake in *making* it happen.

The Twenty-First Century Environment

You can interpret the word *environment* in both its meanings: the physical environment, which is a major public issue, and the business, social, and political environment in which your company will be doing business.

For one of the certainties of the next few years is that businesses are going to be held to increasingly stringent levels of social and public responsibility regarding the environment, health, civil rights and workers' rights, family life, cultural and religious identity, and more.

Again, this is not so very far out, and many of the elements are already in place. Some companies have recognized new opportunities. A major paper company delivers the finished product to customers and in the same trucks backhauls their trash for recycling—and makes money in both directions. A manufacturer of masonry paint has developed a profitable sideline of legally disposing of customer's returns of the semi-toxic product—at their expense, and gladly paid.

Both of these applications happen to be in the customer service area, and that's probably prophetic. You will be increasingly involved in such matters, particularly if you are in the manufacturing business, but also if you are in any of a number of service businesses: just look at what concern with smoking and health has done to the hospitality and travel industries!

Overall, participating in socially conscious and responsible businesses will be a pleasant but sometimes trying experience. But you will also be making the world a better place in which to live and work following a hundred or so years of deterioration. And because you'll be directly involved in so many of the customer service innovations that will be part of this important evolution, you'll be participating in important and worthwhile work, and having a good time doing it.

Appendix A

A Model Manual for Customer Service Policies and Procedures

The manual outline reproduced on the following pages has been the basis for full-scale customer service manuals for a number of U.S. and Canadian companies. It was designed for a loose-leaf format and employs a decimal numbering system for individual sections and entries. This arrangement permits updating of entries anywhere in the manual without requiring extensive reprinting of pages or sections.

Note that the index pages at the beginning of the manual should show the date the policy or procedure was entered in the manual, as well as the date for automatic review and updating if necessary. Of course intermediate updates should be entered as the occasion arises. Their entry and review dates should be entered as well, particularly if any of the changes are short-term or seasonal.

If you do not already have a manual, you may want to involve your reps in preparing one. It's suggested that you have them do so a section at a time, and use this outline or a version of it so that they won't overlook any important points. Depending on your type of business, you may want to use a different format and topic headings.

The actual policies and procedures that go under those headings are of course up to you, your reps, and your management. Because you want the manual to be used regularly in order to ensure consistency in dealings with customers, the more you involve your reps in creating the actual language of the manual, the more likely it is to see that kind of use.

File No.	Subject	Date Published	Future Review
	Customer Service Manual: Index		
1.00.00	Organizations and Reporting Relationships	9/91*	Annually†
1.01.00	Company organization chart		Annually
1.01.01	Corporate officers		Annually
1.01.02	Department heads		Annually
1.02.00	Corporate customer service organization		Annually
1.02.01	Organization chart		Annually
1.02.02	Responsibilities — position		Annually
1.02.03	Responsibilities — territory (account)		Annually
1.02.04	Field organization		Annually
1.03.00	Plants, products, and shipping locations		Annually
1.04.00	Branch offices (sales)		Annually
1.05.00	Authorized brokers		Monthly
2.00.00	Customer Service Policy and Terms of Sale		Annually
2.01.00	Terms of sale		Monthly
2.01.01	Conflicts between purchase order and terms of sale		Monthly
2.02.00	New customers: procedures for handling		Annually
2.03.00	Credit limits, existing customers		Weekly
2.04.00	Special attention orders		Annually
2.05.00	Quality complaints		Annually
2.05.01	Product applications		Annually
2.05.02	Product hazards		Monthly
2.06.00	Service complaints		Annually
2.07.00	Returns of material		Annually
2.07.01	Refusal to accept delivery		Annually
2.08.00	Customer pickup		Annually
2.08.01	Backhaul allowances		Annually
2.09.00	Unauthorized deductions by customer; chargebacks		Annually
2.10.00	Allotment/allocation of products in short supply		Annually
2.10.01	Barter offers by customers		Annually
2.11.00	Change orders and cancellations		Annually
2.12.00	Transportation — General		Annually
2.12.01	Prepaid shipments		Annually
2.12.02	Collect shipments		Annually
2.12.03	Customer routing orders		Annually

*This date applies to all items in the index.
† Interim changes in personnel, policies, and procedures will be reported in special supplements to this manual.

5.00.00	Communications and Customer Contacts	Annually
5.01.00	Responsibilities, customer service, and sales	Annually
5.01.01	Orders	Annually
5.01.02	Reorders	Annually
5.01.03	Inquiries—Prospect/Product	Annually
5.01.04	Inquiries—Order status	Annually
5.01.05	Complaints	Annually
5.01.06	Other communications	Annually
5.02.00	Communications methods and channels	Annually
5.02.01	Telex: procedure	Annually
5.02.02	800 numbers	Annually
5.02.03	Voicemail and interactive systems	Annually
5.02.04	Correspondence	Annually
5.02.05	Inquiry and response forms	Annually
5.02.06	Form and guide letters	Annually
5.02.07	Other communications media (fax, EDI, etc.)	Annually
5.03.00	Policy of prompt response	Annually
5.03.01	"Right of Appeal"	Annually
5.04.00	Authority for shipping and delivery promises	Annually
5.05.00	Other communications	Annually
5.05.01	Sample internal report forms	Annually
6.00.00	Other Policies and Procedures	Annually
6.01.00	Minimum orders	Annually
6.02.00	Back orders	Annually
6.03.00	Deletions and substitutions	Annually
6.04.00	Standard lead time by product line	Annually
6.05.00	Time deliveries	Annually
6.06.00	Special orders and variances	Annually
6.07.00	Consolidation rules and cutoffs	Annually
6.08.00	Maintenance of customer file	Annually
6.08.01	Customer "profile" files	Annually
6.09.00	Other	Annually

(Appendix continues)

2.01.00   Terms of sale

2.01.01   Conflicts between purchase order and terms of sale

2.02.00   New customers: procedures for handling

2.03.00   Credit limits, existing customers

2.04.00   Special attention orders

2.05.00   Quality complaints

2.05.01   Product applications

2.05.02   Product hazards

2.06.00   Service complaints

2.07.00   Returns of material

2.07.01   Refusal to accept delivery

2.08.00   Customer pickup

2.08.01   Backhaul allowances

4.01.01   *Sales adjustments.* The most common type of credit. Includes billing errors, incorrect price, quantity or extension, also errors in order assembly and shipping. A sales adjustment credit does not usually represent a loss to the company (other than administrative expense) since in most cases it is issued to correct an overbilling or similar situation.

4.01.02   *Returns.* Credit for goods for which a customer has been billed but which have been returned. Typical reasons are customer overstock or error in ordering. Shipping error by the seller would not be included, however, since in most cases the customer would be returning goods for which he had not been billed which had been shipped in place of those for which he had been billed.

4.01.03   *Allowances.* These are generally prescribed by Sales or Marketing to cover special situations.

4.01.04   *Transportation—freight adjustments.* Carried as a separate type of credit to avoid confusion with marketing allowances. Includes loss and damage claims, reimbursement for overcharges, etc.

4.01.05   *Tax expense reimbursement.*

4.01.06   *Price concession.* For example, where retroactive pricing has been authorized. Note that correcting an invoice to published price falls under the heading of sales adjustment credits, whereas correcting an invoice to an authorized, but lower than published price, is price concession.

4.01.07   *Cancellation and rebilling.* In unusual situations, where a shipment originally consigned to one customer but refused by him is delivered to another customer nearby to avoid cost of returning to the shipping point. The original customer's invoice is cancelled and a new invoice is issued to the second purchaser. (Note that a price concession might also be involved, as an inducement to the second buyer, although in some instances the shipment might be sold to the second buyer, with the approval of the first, to overcome or avoid a plant shutdown for lack of product.)

4.01.08   *Quality.* Issued where product fails to meet a specific standard and authorization is given to invoice for a lesser amount.

4.02.00   Authority

4.03.00   Procedure

4.04.00   Maintenance of credits file

4.05.00   Effect of credits: salesmen's compensation, inventory records, sometimes the customer's credit record. Extreme care required.

4.06.00   Analysis of reasons for credits

4.07.00   Sample credit forms

5.00.00   Communications and Customer Contacts

5.01.00   Responsibilities, customer service, and sales

5.01.01   Orders

5.01.02   Reorders

5.01.03   Inquiries — Prospect/Product

5.01.04   Inquiries — Order status

5.01.05   Complaints

5.01.06   Other communications

6.00.00   Other Policies and Procedures

6.01.00   Minimum orders

6.02.00   Back orders

6.03.00   Deletions and substitutions

6.04.00   Standard lead time by product line

6.05.00   Time deliveries

6.06.00   Special orders and variances

6.07.00   Consolidation rules and cutoffs

6.08.00   Maintenance of customer file

6.08.01   Customer "profile" files

6.09.00   Other

Appendix B

Key Customer Service Documentation: Forms, Logs, and Surveys

Competitive Rating Survey. This form measures the company versus its competitors and asks customers to rate the relative importance of each service feature measure. This approach will show how to restructure customer service, if necessary, to surpass the competition as well as to rectify unmet customer needs.

Customer Satisfaction Survey

Please rate our service versus that of our competition on a 0 – 10 basis on each of the customer service features listed below, and at the same time indicate the relative importance (0 – 10) of that feature in your daily operations.

Service Feature	Importance (0 – 10)	Our Company	Our Competition
Accessibility of CSR			
Ability of CSR to get things done			
Delivery on short lead time			
Consistent lead time			
Case or line fill			
Complete order fill			
Unit load and pallet exchange program			
Clarity of invoices			
Issuance of credits			
Acknowledgments			
Order status information			
Emergency response			
Accuracy			
Other _____			
Other _____			
Overall rating			

0 = not at all; 10 = completely

Source: Customer Service Newsletter

Rating the Customer Service Environment.   This Corporate Culture Scorecard helps identify a company's strengths and weaknesses in respect to creating a climate that is conducive to sound customer service practices as part of the company's profit strategy.

Customer Service Corporate Culture SCORECARD

PLUSES—Rate each question on a 0-to-10 scale, with 0 representing "not at all" and 10 "completely."

SCORE

1. Does the company have a formal statement of customer service philosophy that is backed by management and known by all employees? _____

2. Does the company have specific standards of customer service performance reflecting that philosophy? _____

3. Is there an explicit system of interdepartmental accountability designed to ensure that those standards are met? _____

4. Is customer service recognized and used as a specific strategy integral to marketing, with specific input by the customer service manager? _____

5. Is there a specific complaint handling strategy with formal decision rules and automatic adjustment policies that intentionally favor the customer? _____

6. Is the customer service manager directly involved in forecasting and planning? _____

7. Are there sufficient inducements—salary, working environment, career pathing—to attract and retain professional-caliber personnel? _____

8. Are personnel provided with the proper tools—systems, communications equipment and similar resources—to do their jobs properly and professionally? _____

9. In their jobs, do CSRs regularly make visits to customers? _____

10. Is there a formal training program for CSRs including cross-training in other skills and disciplines? _____

Source: Customer Service Newsletter

SCORE

11. Does the company trust its CSRs to the extent that matters of high importance can be handled efficiently at relatively low levels?

_____

12. Do CSRs participate in quality circles or similar participative management activities, and are they actively involved in implementation of recommendations that are adopted?

_____

13. Are there formal, meaningful incentive programs and/or profit-sharing for CSRs?

_____

14. Are there ongoing companywide management communications and participative programs relating to the customer service mission?

_____

15. Are the managers and supervisors actively training their successors with the knowledge and approval of management?

_____

MINUSES — Rate each question on a negative 0-to-10 scale, with 0 representing "not at all" and 10 representing "completely."

SCORE

1. Customer service is considered to be a purely clerical function, and job specifications and pay scales are set accordingly.

_____

2. It is considered a "promotion" for the customer service manager when he/she leaves the customer service department and becomes a field sales representative.

_____

3. Customer service is regarded by management as a cost-adding function, and there is great concern with productivity in the form of numbers of calls handled and orders entered, etc., but little concern with actual service quality.

_____

4. The people in the customer service department are widely regarded as "troublemakers" by other departments in the company.

_____

5. The burnout period in the customer service department is less than two years.

_____

6. Unrealistic or impossible commitments are regularly made to customers by sales without consultation with customer service.

   SCORE
   _____

7. Credits and/or refunds in all amounts must be signed by at least two persons.
   _____

8. A high percentage (25% or more) of calls are non-revenue, i.e., customers calling about delays, errors, back-orders, and similar problems.
   _____

9. The customer service manager's principal occupation is crisis management.
   _____

10. The customer service manager is looking for another job.
    _____

Scoring Your Company. Calculate your company's score by adding up all your plus scores and then subtracting the total of your minus scores. If you scored 10 on each of the plus questions and zero on the minus questions your company would rate a perfect 150 score. A score of 75 or over normally signifies that progress is being made toward a true corporate customer service culture, but you can't afford to relax the effort. Under 75, there's work to be done — a great deal of it.

Pinpointing Customer Service Shortfalls.   Because öf the complexity of customer service operations, it's sometimes difficult to pinpoint subtle problem areas. Use this checklist to identify areas that are currently below par and may be undermining the customer service effort. In each of the fifty instances listed, check off whether the quality of performance is poor, fair, good, or excellent. Ratings are analyzed at the end of the list.

A Checklist of Customer Service Features

	Poor	Fair	Good	Excellent
1. The product or service itself—design, suitability, convenience, quality, pricing	☐	☐	☐	☐
2. Information about the product or service; availability, accuracy, understanding, completeness	☐	☐	☐	☐
3. Helpfulness in selecting proper application	☐	☐	☐	☐
4. Ease of placing orders and making purchases	☐	☐	☐	☐
5. Perceived attitude of personnel and "comfort level" of buyer	☐	☐	☐	☐
6. Policies: relevance and strategic value or disbenefit	☐	☐	☐	☐
7. Policies: how communicated and how perceived	☐	☐	☐	☐
8. Economics: customer service costs versus investments	☐	☐	☐	☐
9. Organization of the firm relative to CS responsibility, centralized, decentralized, reporting patterns, etc.	☐	☐	☐	☐
10. Organization of the department: account, territory, etc.	☐	☐	☐	☐
11. Specific responsibilities and authority of the department	☐	☐	☐	☐
12. Departmental personnel: training, compensation	☐	☐	☐	☐
13. Communications policies: direct, via sales, other	☐	☐	☐	☐
14. Communications channels: direct, switchboard, etc.	☐	☐	☐	☐
15. Communications hardware and software, customer options	☐	☐	☐	☐
16. Computer systems: on-line, real time, etc.	☐	☐	☐	☐
17. Departmental procedures	☐	☐	☐	☐

Source: Customer Service Newsletter

	Poor	Fair	Good	Excellent
18. Interdepartmental communication response standards	☐	☐	☐	☐
19. Interdepartmental performance standards, e.g., production, shipping, engineering, credit, sales, MIS, etc.	☐	☐	☐	☐
20. Planning and control systems, MRP, DRP or other	☐	☐	☐	☐
21. Procurement standards for resale parts, goods, or services	☐	☐	☐	☐
22. Performance standards for customer service personnel	☐	☐	☐	☐
23. Customer service standards	☐	☐	☐	☐
24. Availability of resources to meet standards	☐	☐	☐	☐
25. Response and performance, measured against standards, including statistical process control	☐	☐	☐	☐
26. Support of field personnel by customer service	☐	☐	☐	☐
27. Problem resolution: returns, exchanges, complaints	☐	☐	☐	☐
28. Handling of credits and deductions	☐	☐	☐	☐
29. Customer support	☐	☐	☐	☐
30. Customer education: literature, training programs	☐	☐	☐	☐
31. Customer communications: early warning of problems	☐	☐	☐	☐
32. Customer communications: policy and procedural changes, informational and goodwill matters	☐	☐	☐	☐
33. Order enhancement, substitutions, etc.	☐	☐	☐	☐
34. Telemarketing, including inquiry conversion, lead qualification, setting up demos or appointments, etc.	☐	☐	☐	☐
35. Maintenance and refinement of customer database for marketing as well as customer service use	☐	☐	☐	☐
36. Product recall or field revision or retrofit programs	☐	☐	☐	☐
37. Contingency plans for strikes, shortages, etc.	☐	☐	☐	☐
38. Disaster recovery programs for major events	☐	☐	☐	☐

	Poor	Fair	Good	Excellent
39. Compensation, mitigation, or protection for customers damaged or inconvenienced by customer service failures	☐	☐	☐	☐
40. Customer research or feedback on actual performance	☐	☐	☐	☐
41. Customer research on performance vs. competitors	☐	☐	☐	☐
42. Customer research on perception of service quality after actual contact	☐	☐	☐	☐
43. Recognition programs, departmental and company-wide	☐	☐	☐	☐
44. Suggestion systems, quality circles and other participative management programs	☐	☐	☐	☐
45. System for recovering customer feedback to customer service personnel and communicating internally to proper levels	☐	☐	☐	☐
46. Participation in industry affairs related to customer service	☐	☐	☐	☐
47. Cross-training at all levels	☐	☐	☐	☐
48. Attitudes of customer service personnel and others toward their jobs, understanding of relevance	☐	☐	☐	☐
49. Measurable economic contribution by the company's customer service performance	☐	☐	☐	☐
50. Suitability of customer service program for entry in an Awards of Excellence program	☐	☐	☐	☐

Rating Your Company. Give yourself two points for each time you rated your performance "good" or "excellent." Then add up the points. A total score of 90–100 would be Superior; 80–89, Excellent; 70–79, Above Average; 60–69, Average. Anything below 60 is a real cause for concern.

Logs as Basis for Activity Reports. The logs shown here and on the next page enable compilation of output or transaction data as a basis for generating activity reports. Note that calls are classified by each rep by type and number and will be compiled later into a report reflecting total departmental activity for the time period.

Daily Customer Service Representative's Log

Date: _____   Person: _____

	Tally	Number
Calls Received		
Nature of Call:		
Place an Order		
Expedite		
Price Inquiry		
Availability Inquiry		
Order Status Inquiry		
Field Sales Assistance Request		
Catalog/Price List Request		
Return Merchandise		
Distributor Refund		
Technical Information		
Discuss a Problem		
Other _____		
Disposition		
Handled Completely		
Internal Transfer		
External Transfer		
Callback Required		

Source: Chicago Consulting, 8 S. Michigan Avenue, Chicago, Ill. 60603.

Daily Credit Activity Log. This log is essentially an exceptions report that will show what *didn't* go right, both by the type of problem and by the number of times the problem arose.

Daily Credit Activity Log

Date: _____   Person: _____

Reason for Credit	Tally	Number
Memos (per line item):		
Shipped Wrong Item		
Item Billed — Not Received		
Duplicate Shipment		
Duplicate Invoice		
Previously Cancelled		
Took Too Long		
Did Not Order		
Customer Refused		
Customer Moved		
Defective Material		
Warranty		
Stock Adjustment		
Other _____		
Adjustments (per line item):		
Price Error		
Freight Misapplied		
Total		

Source: Chicago Consulting, 8 S. Michigan Avenue, Chicago, Ill. 60603.

Companywide Service Level Report.   This form enables the manager to compare service levels at different locations handling different volumes of orders as well as different product mix. The form uses ratios rather than simple output data, which would slant findings in favor of larger, high-volume locations.

Customer Service Center Measures

Month of: _____

	Location No. 1	Location No. 2	Location No. 3	Location No. 4	Location No. 5
% Calls Blocked					
% Calls Abandoned					
Orders per Call					
Credit Lines Issued per Line Received					
% Orders Shipped Complete First Time					
Average Days to Ship					
Shipments Made per Order Received					
Orders on Credit Hold					
Orders Held for Stock Availability					
Unshipped Orders With Availability					
Unfilled Plant Orders					
Average Plant Lead Time					
Stock Outage %					

Source: Chicago Consulting, 8 S. Michigan Avenue, Chicago, Ill. 60603.

Follow-up Survey. Formats such as these are useful in following up on field service calls, where a field service engineer or technical rep has gone to a customer location (home or business) to repair on-site equipment or an appliance. Surveys of this type generally obtain a high response rate because of their immediacy and relevance to the customer.

Quality of Service Survey

Please rate the service quality you recently received from us. Consider all visits required for this particular problem. Please indicate your answers by circling the appropriate response for each question. Return postage has been provided for your convenience. Thank you!

1. When you called for service/repair were you able to get through on the first call without getting a busy signal or being asked to wait?   *Yes*   *No*

2. When you called, were you placed on hold by our representative?   *Yes*   *No*

3. Was the person you talked with on the phone courteous?   *Yes*   *No*

4. Did the person you talked with seem knowledgeable and competent?   *Yes*   *No*

5. Overall, how would you rate our Customer Service Representative?
         Excellent   *Good*   *Fair*   *Poor*

6. Was your installation/repair completed on the scheduled date?   *Yes*   *No*

7. Was the technician courteous?   *Yes*   *No*

8. Did the technician seem to be knowledgeable and competent about your appliance?   *Yes*   *No*

9. Did the technician explain what was done to fix your problem?   *Yes*   *No*

10. How many trips were needed to complete the service/repair?   *1*   *2*   *3*   *4*   *5*

Source: Customer Service Newsletter

11. Overall, how would you rate our technician?

> *Excellent   Good   Fair   Poor*

12. If a part was needed to complete the repair, was the part:

> a. *Available on Service Truck*
> b. *Brought Back Later by a Technician*

13. If a part was ordered, how many days did it take for you to get the part?

> *Same   1 to 4   5 to 9   More Than*
> *Day   Days   Days   9 Days*

14. Considering all these questions, how satisfied are you with the overall service you received?

> *VERY   VERY*
> *SATISFIED   SATISFIED   DISSATISFIED   DISSATISFIED*

15. Please add any comments you have about the service you received.

_____

_____

_____

_____

Performance Report. This report measures a bank's performance against its own goals as well as against the competition. It shows a composite of measures employed by the Bank of Boston Cash Management Division reflecting the unit's performance (Actual) on eighteen service features, as compared to its own goals (Target) and to competitive cash management performance (Standard). The bank purposely chose goals higher than industry standards, on the premise that above-average service is a strong selling point in a business where services are essentially generic.

Cash Management Division Quality Objectives

Actual Volume of: 534,128

Product Deliverable	Measurement	Target*	Standard†	Actual	Current Performance
Lockbox					
1. Encoding	% items encoded accurately	99.965% (187/mo.)	99.956% (236/mo.)	99.963%	Standard exceeded
2. Data transmission	% transmissions on time & accurate	99.8% (2/mo.)	99.3% (9/mo.)	100%	Target exceeded
3. Boston transmissions	% deposit data transmissions to BOSTONET on time & accurate	95%	90%	95%	Target met
4. Timely mailing	% remittance packages mailed out on time	100%	99.8% (48/mo.)	100%	Target exceeded

*Target: A realistic obtainment goal that separates one's products from those of the rest of the marketplace. "The best in the business."
†Standard: The minimal level of acceptable performance. This is normally set from industry market research.

Source: Bank of Boston

Product Deliverable	Measurement	Target	Standard	Actual	Current Performance
Lockbox (continued)					
5. Accurate mailing	% mailed to correct address	99.979% (5/mo.)	99.958% (10/mo.)	99.983%	Target exceeded
6. Midnight mailroom holdover	# of trays of mail unprocessed	0 trays/month	10 trays/month	0	Target exceeded
7. Missing photocopies	% photos undelivered	0.05% (267/mo.)	0.08% (427/mo.)	0.04%	Target exceeded
8. Live checks	# of live checks returned for # of customers	2 checks ea. for 2 customers No repeat	2 checks ea. for 6 customers No repeat	0 check 0 cust.	Target exceeded
9. Desk errors	% items processed accurately	99.9925% (43/mo.)	99.990% (54/mo.)	99.9934%	Target exceeded
10. Deposit reporting	% reports on time and accurate	95%	90%	96%	Target exceeded
Check Paying					
1. Statement rendering (machine & manual)	Time required to render 100%	5 business days	6 business days	4	Target exceeded

Product Deliverable	Measurement	Target	Standard	Actual	Current Performance
Check Paying *(continued)*					
2. Timely statements & sorts—nonend of month	Time required to render 100%	1 business day	2 business days	<u>1</u>	<u>Target met</u>
3. Timely sorts—end of month	Time required to render 100%	5 business days	6 business days	<u>5</u>	<u>Target met</u>
4. Stop payments	# of checks paid over stops; confirm to customer	0	1	<u>1</u>	<u>Standard met</u>
Account Management					
Timely officer changes and account groupings	Time required to process	2 business days	3 business days	<u>2</u>	<u>Target met</u>
Account Analysis					
Timely statements rendered	Time required to deliver to relationship officers	12 business days from month end	15 business days from month end	<u>10</u>	<u>Target exceeded</u>

Product Deliverable	Measurement	Target	Standard	Actual	Current Performance
Reconciliation (Boston)					
1. Timely paid lists	Business days from end of month to send out (100%)	3 days	4 days	3	Target met
2. Timely paid tapes	Business days from end of month to send out (100%)	3 days	4 days	3	Target met
3. Timely microfilm	Business days from end of month to send out (100%)	10 days	12 days	10	Target met
4. Timely full reconciliations	Business days from receipt of good input to send out (100%)	10 days	12 days	12*	Standard met

*Full Reconciliation Distribution

1 – 5 days	86 accounts
6 – 10 days	136 accounts
11 – 12 days	49 accounts
13+ days	0 accounts

Self-mailer Survey Incorporating Reply Card.   This self-mailer survey from Braceland Brothers, Inc., is short and to the point—and as easy to send as it is to fill out and return. Printed in two colors on a letter size cover-weight stock, the Philadelphia printing company's survey is folded into three panels, one of which is used for the customer's address so that no envelope is required. The questionnaire occupies the bottom panel, with business reply indicia on the back and a perforation at the top of the panel, so that it can be easily detached and mailed back to the company.

Braceland Brothers Inc.
YOUR INFORMATION PRINTER

Dear Customer,

Thank you for your continued support. We value your relationship which is so necessary to our business.

In order to improve our service to you, we strive to learn and understand your requirements. Perhaps you could help us in this regard by completing the attached survey. This information will be invaluable to us and help us to be a better service organization.

We wish that you will be completely candid in your responses and provide any additional comments concerning your needs.

Thank you for your cooperation.

Sincerely,

Michael McGrail

Michael McGrail
Director, Sales & Marketing

7625 SUFFOLK AVENUE, PHILADELPHIA, PENNSYLVANIA 19153 ☐ 215-492-0200 ☐ FAX 215-492-8538

CUSTOMER _____   PUBLICATION _____
JOB NUMBER _____

PLEASE CHECK APPROPRIATE BOX

	EXCELLENT	GOOD	FAIR	POOR
Sales Representatives	☐	☐	☐	☐
Pricing	☐	☐	☐	☐
Customer Service Representatives	☐	☐	☐	☐
Printing	☐	☐	☐	☐
Binding	☐	☐	☐	☐
Delivery Time	☐	☐	☐	☐
Overall Performance	☐	☐	☐	☐

Comments _____
_____

Source: Braceland Brothers, Inc.

Business Reply Cards (BRCs). On the following page are three BRCs. The first one, labeled **A**, is the type used as a follow-up to complaints and inquiries concerning a company's products. The BRC labeled **B** is actually a questionnaire concerning shipping data. It is a good example of maximum use of a small space. The card is marked to the attention of the receiving department manager and is identified as an "Important Request." One side of the foldover card is used for the vendor's message to the customer, which reaffirms the company's customer service goals while explaining the purpose and importance of the questionnaire itself. On the reverse, response from the customer is solicited on nine specific points, using a mixture of yes-no, rating, and specific fact questions. In addition, sufficient space is left for comments by the customer. BRCs are especially effective for gathering shipping data, since the concise format doesn't infringe too much on the customer's time and can be filled out when the necessary documentation is readily at hand. The BRC labeled **C** is inserted in the shipment itself. It is adapted from one used as a quality control device by a frozen foods manufacturer. It requests specific information on the temperature of the product at the time of receipt by the customer.

A

Dear Customer:

We recently handled the matter you reported to us about _____

_____ and now we would appreciate hearing from you again. Your responses to the following questions will greatly assist us in measuring our service.

1. Did you receive a reply as promptly as you felt you should? ☐ Yes   ☐ No
   Comments _____
2. Was the explanation understandable to you?   ☐ Yes   ☐ No
   Comments _____
3. Did the letter give a complete explanation?   ☐ Yes   ☐ No
   Comments _____
4. If you returned the product, was a replacement (refund) sent? ☐ Yes   ☐ No
   Comments _____
5. If this was a follow-up from earlier correspondence, was this prompt enough and the information complete?   ☐ Yes   ☐ No
   Comments _____
6. Is there anything else we should know about? _____

B

Your order number or date _____

Arrival date (requested _____) actual _____

Was appointment (if applicable) scheduled as requested?   ☐ Yes   ☐ No

Was appointment (if applicable) kept?   ☐ Yes   ☐ No   ☐ Not req'd.

If requested, was merchandise segregated?   ☐ Yes   ☐ No   ☐ Not req'd.

What was condition of merchandise?   ☐ Excellent   ☐ Good   ☐ Fair   ☐ Poor

Any shortage on shipment?   ☐ Yes   ☐ No

Delivering carrier name _____

Shipper's No./Release No. _____

Additional comments _____

TO RETURN THIS CARD — REVERSE FOLD, STAPLE AND MAIL

C

PLANT TO COMPLETE	B/L NO.	CAR – TRUCK NO.	TRL. NO.	DATE SHIPPED
	CONSIGNEE AND DESTINATION			
	ROUTE		PRODUCT TEMP AT TIME OF LOADING	
CUSTOMER TO COMPLETE	ARRIVAL DATE		ARRIVAL TIME	
	PRODUCT TEMP AT TIME OF UNLOADING TOP		BOTTOM	OUTSIDE AIR TEMP
	HOW WAS TEMP DETERMINED? ☐ CASES PIERCED ☐ BETWEEN CASES		IS LOAD FROZEN SOLID? ☐ YES ☐ NO	
	SIGNED			

Source: Customer Service Newsletter

Bounceback Survey With Phone Response Option. Although it has the appearance of a conventional self-contained mail survey with a detachable card, this bounceback survey gives the customer the added option of phoning in a response to one of the two numbers. The survey is mailed out as a follow-up to a delivery or similar service problem and is considered an important step in maintaining service quality as well as subscriber loyalty in a highly competitive market. Note that phone responses can either be handled live or channeled directly to telephone answering equipment with message recorders for 24-hour availability.

NEWSDAY DELIVERY SERVICE

HOW ARE WE DOING?

We at Newsday pride ourselves in making sure
that you have perfect delivery service.

.....But our records show that you had a
recent service problem.
Was it solved to your satisfaction?

We want to hear from you. Please fill out the
postage paid card and let us know

HOW WE'RE DOING

Thank you for helping us make Newsday
The top paper on Long Island

If you prefer, call Penny at one of the following numbers:

• Eastern Suffolk **(516) 360-3434**   • Nassau/Western Suffolk **(516) 454-2000**

- -

Name _____

Address _____ Apt.# _____

Town _____ Zip _____ Phone _____

Type of Delivery: ☐ **Daily**   ☐ **Sunday**   ☐ **Daily & Sunday**   Yes   No

Did you receive a replacement paper?   ☐   ☐

Were you contacted by a Newsday representative?   ☐   ☐

Are you satisfied with delivery now?   ☐   ☐ (Please Explain)

Comments _____

_____

Source: Newsday, Inc.

Testing Customer Acceptance of Standards. The form shown here was used by Pearle Vision Centers' distribution center to inform customers of service standards the organization had developed and to test their degree of acceptance or nonacceptance. A survey of this type is an excellent way of introducing service improvements and at the same time finding out if further refinements are needed. Standards were set by a group combining front-line and management personnel in order to ensure practicality of standards as well as accountability for meeting them operationally.

Dear Pearle Customer,

On June 21, 1988, the Distribution Center established a panel, consisting of 13 members of our hourly and management personnel to look at our internal service levels and procedures. Our purpose - to improve our overall service to our customers. The panel has completed the first draft of service goals. It is now our plan to share these service assumptions with you, to ensure they will meet your needs and expectations.

Once the goals have been approved by you, we will publish a quarterly report on how we are measuring up to our objectives, a "quarterly report card." These service enhancements are listed below by distribution department.

Please check the appropriate box and if checking the "will not meet my needs box," please list what goals we should use.

Thank you in advance for your help with this survey; its purpose is to help us service you better.

	Will Meet My Needs	**Will Not Meet Needs**
I. Customer Service		
A. Order Shortages (items you were billed for but did not receive) Replacements will be shipped the same day.	_____	_____
B. Incoming Calls will be answered by a Customer Service Representative in less than one minute. (Goal .90 minutes)	_____	_____
C. Customer Concerns will be responded to within same day.	_____	_____
II. Credits		
A. Exchange Order Returns will be credited to customer's account within three days of receipt.	_____	_____
B. Return Product Quality Returned goods will be inspected for defects upon receipt. We will maintain a quality goal of 99.90%.	_____	_____

Source: Pearle Vision Centers' Distribution Center

	Will Meet My Needs	Will Not Meet Needs
III. Order Filling		
A. All orders received daily will be shipped daily.	_____	_____
B. Order filling accuracy - We will meet a 99.65% accuracy goal, or only 35 errors per 10,000 orders.	_____	_____
C. Packaging - Special care will be taken in packing to ensure the safe arrival of the products. We will maintain a quality goal of 99.90% safe arrival.		
IV. Fixed Assets		
A. Incoming calls/orders/inquiries will be resolved same day received or customer will be notified.	_____	_____
B. Tracers - Lost in transit concerns will be reported back to customer (same day we hear from carriers).	_____	_____
V. Special Services		
A. Special order frames will be placed with vendor same day received.	_____	_____
B. If special order frame has not been received within two weeks, clerks will call vendor and customer to check current status.	_____	_____

These are the service areas the panel identified. We need your help to determine:

A. If our goals will meet *your* needs.

B. If there are other areas/goals you would like us to set. Please use the attached sheet to write any additional needs.

Survey Combining Customer Service and Logistics Ratings.   The survey on the next page mailed by The Pinkerton Tobacco Company, Owensboro, Kentucky, asks customers to rate customer service versus competition and includes questions about suitability of invoices and desirability of customer pickups with backhaul allowances. The survey also includes an open-end question soliciting suggestions for improvement. Printed on one side of a sheet, the survey is short and to the point and was mailed out with a brief covering letter (shown below) and postage-paid envelope.

The Pinkerton Tobacco Company
Post Office Box 986
Owensboro, Kentucky 42302
(502) 685-7200

Dear Customer:

   The Pinkerton Tobacco Company is constantly striving to provide you with the very best customer service in the tobacco industry. We believe that in meeting the needs of the customer we are contributing to the success of your company as well as ours.

   For this reason, we are asking for your assistance by telling us exactly how you feel about the service you have been receiving. We are truly interested in looking for ways to improve our current service levels to you. Please feel free to make any suggestions or comments you feel would enable us to accomplish this.

   We ask that you complete the enclosed questionnaire and return it to us. A preaddressed postage-paid envelope has been provided for your convenience. I thank you for your help in providing us with this information. I assure you that your comments will receive our utmost attention and action.

                    Sincerely,

                    D. R. Modlinski
                    Distribution & Customer Service Mgr.
                    Pinkerton Tobacco Company

Source: The Pinkerton Tobacco Company

Customer Service/Distribution Service Survey

		YES	NO
1.	Are the customer sales associates pleasant, courteous, and helpful when you are placing an order or inquiring about an order?	☐	☐
2.	Are your calls answered promptly whenever you call into the customer service department?	☐	☐
3.	Are you pleased with the selected carrier that is now delivering your freight from our company?	☐	☐

If no, what carrier would you prefer us to use? _____

_____

		YES	NO
4.	Would you be interested in picking up your order at one of our distribution centers if you were offered a backhaul allowance?	☐	☐

If yes, whom should we contact? _____

		YES	NO
5.	Does our current invoice provide you with the information you need for your records?	☐	☐

If no, what would you like to see changed? _____

_____

6. How would you rate The Pinkerton Tobacco's customer service as compared to other tobacco companies that you are currently doing business with?

☐ **THE BEST**   ☐ **EQUAL TO**
☐ **BETTER THAN**   ☐ **WORSE THAN**

7. If you could select one specific change within the area of customer service and distribution in the way that we are currently doing business, what would that one change be?

_____

_____

_____

Company Name _____

Address _____

City & State _____

Your Name _____

Telephone _____

Appendix C

Sample Scripts for Telemarketing

Presenting the Service or Product

Here are some responses to basic, specific inquiries by customers:

"I'll be glad to help you, Ms. Franklin. Our new RD-2 rheostat is 20 percent smaller and 10 percent lighter than anything else on the market. It normally cuts installation costs anywhere from 10 to 15 percent. What sort of application do you have in mind?"

(Immediate benefit and interest-gathering statement; early involvement of customer)

"Mr. Coleman, we specialize in fast on-site and walk-in service on PCs and peripherals. We come to you or you can come to us, whichever you prefer. And you don't have to sign a service contract, if you don't want to—but you can save 25 percent if you do. If you'll tell me what equipment you currently have, I can punch it up and give you a quote right now."

(Concise description of service, benefits; early involvement of customer)

"It's a charming location on a cul-de-sac, and what a great place to raise a family! Larry Jennings is handling that home, and he'll be delighted to tell you about it in detail."

(Enthusiasm for property by phone answerer gives credibility, prepares for salesperson's offer to show)

"I'd recommend you start with our Telephone Dynamics training program, Ms. Fletcher. It's an excellent audio program you can run on any audio cassette player, and it's ideal for self-training or for small groups. It comes with workbooks and quizzes, and it can be worked on during the day without taking people off the phone. They can take the training right at their desks, and you can actually *see* and *hear* their improvement!"

(Concise description, cites benefits, addresses a common objection, that is, the need to take personnel off phones for training)

"Mr. Parks, I'm going to let you talk to John Guiness, our applications engineer. He's tops in the field and has all that information at his fingertips. He'll be happy to help you."

(Phone answerer who can't handle technical call builds up person to whom call will be transferred, establishes early credibility. Recommended when calls are distributed by switchboard or similar system.)

Answering General Inquiries

Not all inquiries have to do with a specific service or product, for example:

Caller:	This is David Hickman of Albertson and Brown in Los Angeles. I need some information about your filtration systems.
Inquiry Handler:	I'll be glad to help you with that, Mr. Hickman. Is your company in the process chemicals business?
Caller:	No. We're consultants to municipalities with public waterworks systems.
Inquiry Handler:	Then you'd be interested mainly in water treatment applications?
Caller:	That's right, but just a general sort of idea of what you have.
Inquiry Handler:	I have just what you need: our booklet on water treatment applications plus our applications bulletins with case histories about specific installations. I'll get these off to you today. And I'll ask Ms. Wolfe in our Burbank office to contact you later on to see if you need any additional information or applications data. Thank you very much for your interest, Mr. Hickman.

(Note that callers do not always state a precise interest or need, and it is the call handler's responsibility to narrow it down to a specific area. In this example, the call handler could also have made a transition to setting up an appointment, arranging a demo, or providing names and addresses of specific installations in the Los Angeles area.)

Always strive to get the caller's name and address, phone and fax numbers, and add to mailing or follow-up list as appropriate!

Shortcutting Inquiries to Make a Sale

In the following dialogue, note that the call handler doesn't go through an extensive dialogue but almost immediately narrows down the inquiry to a specific request for the business:

Caller:	Do you have limousine service from Silver Spring to Washington Dulles Airport?
Inquiry Handler:	Yes we do. What time is your flight?
Caller:	At four in the afternoon.
Inquiry Handler:	I'd suggest you take our 2:30 P.M. limousine from either the Sheraton or the Holiday Inn. Would you like me to make a reservation for you while we still have space?

Presenting Features and Benefits

Customers who are knowledgeable about products and services are naturally interested in learning about specific features of those products or services, but what *sells* them is the actual *benefits* that those features provide. So, it's essential when making a presentation and describing product or service features you always make a quick "so that" transition to the benefits that result from those features:

Feature	Benefit
Our distribution center is right at Memphis International Airport	*so that* we can take your order as late as midnight and still get it to you by the next morning.
It has a large tank	*so that* you can travel 400 miles without filling up.
It comes in fifteen colors	*so that* you can use either complementary or contrasting hues.
The policy is based on a low risk group	*so that* you save 20 percent on your premium costs.

Note, too, that features and benefits can be used as a means of closing the sale, that is, showing the caller the benefits of placing an order now:

Feature	Benefit
I'd suggest you place your order now	*so that* you can be sure of getting the exact colors you want.
Why don't you let me sign you up now	*so that* you can save that $300 initiation fee?
Our special offer is still in effect	*so that* you can save 20 percent on a full year's service contract if you sign up now.

Under the right circumstances, you can also use *non*benefits:

Feature	Nonbenefits
I'd suggest you let me show you the property today	*so that* it won't be gone before you get a chance to see what a great buy it is.
Let me sign you up now	*so that* you won't be without coverage if something happens.
I'm afraid if you don't order today	we may not be able to give you the full range of colors we have right now.

Answering Objections

Even though customers have expressed an interest in a service or a product, and everything about it seems suited to their needs and pocketbooks, they will almost always express some objection before making a buying decision. This is natural; most of us don't like to make decisions on the spot, and we're likely to stall or defer our decision on the grounds of "thinking it over." The only problem is that if we don't make the sale now we may never make it. So, objections need to be responded to quickly and positively. Here are some examples:

Need or Suitability Objection

Customer: I'm not in the market right now.

Telemarketer: [Defines the objection] You feel you wouldn't have any use for the PB-200 unit at the present time, you're satisfied with your present equipment, right?

Customer:	That's right.
Telemarketer:	If I could show you where the PB-200 could increase your revenues by at least 20 percent without increasing your operating costs by a penny, then would you be interested?

Price Objection

Customer:	Well, it's not just that I wouldn't be interested. The price is more than I can afford right now.
Telemarketer:	[Redefines the objection] You feel that in today's economy it's just too much money to be spending, right?
Customer:	That's right.
Telemarketer:	If I could show you how to finance this almost 100 percent out of earnings, then would you be willing to consider buying it?

Postponement Objection

Customer:	Well, perhaps, but I need time to think it over.
Telemarketer:	[Restates objection] It's not something you want to jump into feet first, right?
Customer:	You said it.
Telemarketer:	I couldn't agree with you more. It's a big decision. So while we're on the phone, let's go over the proposal point by point so we can clear up issues that you aren't quite sure about.

Note the importance of always restating the objection and securing the customer's agreement. This step is the first in converting the negative—the objection—to a positive. You both agree that this is the objection. And **never** make light of it or belittle it!

Objections can also be used as a stepping stone to a close:

"Our projections show us that spot-buying of the product down the road will cost you 10 to 15 percent more than if you place a blanket order now so we can give you the volume discount."

"I'm authorized to offer you a 15 percent discount now if you'll order a minimum of 2 months service."

Specific Objection

Specific objections are legitimate concerns and should always be treated with respect and understanding. Here are some typical responses you might use in such cases:

"That's an excellent point, Mr. Kirby. It shows that you've had a lot of experience in this business. Fortunately, corrosion isn't a problem with the PB-200. The Navy has had several hundred in deck-mounted use for almost 20 years without a single problem!"

"I agree that our price seems high next to the competition, Ms. Jackson, but you're not just buying the product. You're buying *service*—next day delivery on 95 percent of the items in the catalog, even on hard-to-find items. And if you let us take care of your fastener needs as well, we'll be so close in price you'll hardly know the difference!"

Hidden Buying Signals

Objections are sometimes hidden buying signals; answer them and you can make the sale. Here are some examples:

Customer:	I don't know where I'd put it; I'm crowded for office space as it is.
Telemarketer:	Ms. Paine, 50 percent of our installations are in offices smaller than yours. Many of our customers wall-mount the units and actually prefer them that way.
Customer:	It's a lot of money to be spending at one time. I'm not sure I could swing it.
Telemarketer:	Mr. Lobdell, we can put it on a lease basis, which would cut your immediate cash outlay to less than $2,000.

Visible Buying Signals and Closes

The most visible buying signals are likely to be in the form of questions:

- "What's your current lead time?"
- "When would my coverage begin?"
- "How soon would I qualify for————?"
- "Do you have a 220-volt unit?"
- "What's your policy on returns?"
- "What kind of warranty does it carry?"

- "What kind of quantity discount do you offer?"
- "Do you accept open account orders?"

Direct Close

A direct close is when you ask directly for the order or authorization:

"Why not let me enter your order now so you'll receive the goods before the holiday rush?"

"Can I put you down for a palletload?"

"With your warranty expiring next week, you'll want major component coverage at the very least. Can I put through a 12-month service contract for you today so you'll be sure of having that protection when you need it?"

"Can I make an appointment for Mr. Wright to review your present coverage so you'll be sure you're adequately covered on those increased property values?"

Note that in the final example you're not closing as such, but making an appointment for a salesman to visit the customer. This approach can also be used for setting up a demonstration as an intermediate step in making the sale or, in some cases, to send a sample where selling over the phone isn't practical:

"Mr. Sumner, if I send you a trial can of the X-2 additive, would you be willing to try it out on your next job? Would a gallon be enough?

"Ms. Jacobi, I'm going to send you a demo disk for your PC compatible. All I ask is that you work with it for 15 to 20 minutes and then just mail me back the questionnaire that's enclosed with it. No need to return the demo disk. You might want to pass it along to some of your associates in the distribution department."

The Assumptive Close

In using this close, you make it clear to the customer that you have *assumed* that he or she is going to buy, and all that's left is to work out the details. Here are some examples:

"I think you'll be glad you ordered our product line, Ms. Van Iver. If you can give me your ship-to address we can have a starter order of two dozen cases to you by Monday."

"You'll never regret having this kind of protection for your family. Let me have the correct spelling of your spouse's name and your children so we can start your coverage right away."

"That unit is really going to make money for you! Right now I need to get some financial data from you so we can push the lease through and set up delivery for next week."

Contained Choice or Alternative Close

This close also assumes the customer is going to buy and confirms it by presenting the customer with two alternatives, commonly referred to as a "contained choice." Here are some examples:

"I'm sure you'll want to start your training program right away. Which format would you prefer, 16 mm or VHS?"

"You can't get better coverage at any price. Would you prefer it with the $250 deductible or would you rather save on your premiums and have me write it up with a $500 deductible?

"Mr. Hugo will be glad to review the policies with you to recommend where you should increase the coverage to keep pace with inflation and increases in construction costs. Would you rather he called you in the morning, or would the afternoon be preferable?"

The "Desperation" or Negotiated Close

Don't overlook the possibility that the customer really wants to buy but can't articulate objections that need to be overcome. If other attempts to close have failed, try this one:

"Ms. Richmond, you've indicated a real interest in purchasing this product [service]. Let me ask you frankly: what would it take on my part for you to agree to a trial order?"

This approach could very well uncover hitherto unvoiced objections, which you can treat conventionally in leading to a firm close.

Converting Complaints into Sales

1. Defuse the situation:
   a. Accept and acknowledge the customer's feelings. Keep your cool.
   b. Look for feelings or statements you can agree with. Don't argue.
   c. Reflect the customer's concern. Give status to the complaint: "That *is* serious. I can see why you're upset [angry]!"

2. Get the facts:

   a. Qualify the complainer. Be sure you're talking to the right person—the individual who can accept your offer of a solution or compromise.
   b. Restate your understanding of the problem to be sure you have identified the real cause of concern.
   c. Determine the customer's real need. Sometimes the customer just needs attention and expressions of sincere regret on your part.

3. Resolve the complaint:

   a. Offer to adjust by asking the customer: "What would you like us to do? What do you feel would be fair?" Very often it's easily done.
   b. Offer specific alternatives or adjustments: "If we deducted $25 from the price, would you be able to get it repaired locally?"
   c. *If possible avoid saying "no" in resolving a complaint. Remember that the objective of complaint handling is KEEPING THE CUSTOMER.*
   d. Always ask the customer for another chance.

4. Use the complaint as a stepping-stone to a sale:

   a. "You know, Mr. Stone, since you've had this problem, I have an idea how it can be avoided in the future...."
   b. "Mr. Semco, American Chemical had the same problem last year, and I think you'll be interested in how they solved it."

Then, on to your presentation, discussion of features and benefits, answers to objections, and, of course, your close.

Appendix D

Managing the Million-Dollar Asset

Historically, businesses have viewed customer service operations as a cost-adding activity that subtracts from rather than adds to the bottom line. Companies frequently refer to customer service as "after-sales service," creating a perception that customer service is mainly a reactive function concerned with sales that have already been made, and with little relationship to future sales. Thus, many managements scrutinize customer service operations for cost-reduction opportunities rather than for ways in which customer service can contribute to increased revenues and market share.

Throughout the 1980s, this casual view of customer service resulted in relatively high customer turnover rates in many companies, reflecting the many customers who decided to try another vendor after they had received indifferent service from the original vendor once they have made their purchases. But it was also a time of economic expansion, with great emphasis on capturing new markets via the introduction of new products and services, Yet, with the cost of acquiring a new customer estimated at five times the cost of keeping an existing one, profit margins became increasingly thin—and still efforts to cut after-sales customer service costs continued.

It was a mixed blessing when U.S. businesses, which were in the habit of measuring results by the quarter and sometimes by the month, realized that they were being squeezed out of world markets by Japanese and German companies, which had been investing for the long haul in their customer relationships, and were profiting at the expense of U.S. companies by doing so. While U.S. managements were not blind to the value of repeat business—customer retention—very few were ready to quantify their customers as assets, or to recognize their customer service efforts as *asset management*. Overseas competition forced them to do so, and by the end of the decade there were signs that the concept of "customer value" would probably supersede the focus on

Figure A-1. Increased revenues that can result over time from improved customer service

Year	Revenues @ 70% Retention Rate	Revenues @ 80% Retention Rate	Revenues @ 90% Retention Rate	Revenues @ 100% Retention Rate
1	$1,000,000	$1,000,000	$1,000,000	$ 1,000,000
2	770,000	880,000	990,000	1,100,000
3	593,000	774,000	980,000	1,210,000
4	466,000	681,000	970,000	1,331,000
5	352,000	600,000	961,000	1,464,100
6	270,000	528,000	951,000	1,610,510
7	208,000	464,000	941,000	1,771,561
8	160,000	409,000	932,000	1,948,717
9	124,000	360,000	923,000	2,143,589
10	95,000	316,000	914,000	2,357,948
Totals	$4,038,000	$6,012,000	$9,562,000	$15,937,425

Note: Figures are based on 10% account growth annually.

excellence, quality, and customer satisfaction that dominated so much of management thinking during the 1980s.*

Figure A-1 represents the first known publication of data representing the customer base as assets, and reflecting the revenue enhancement that can result from improving the management of those assets. In this context, improved asset management is most often equated with improvements in customer service in any one of literally hundreds of ways, with the net result of retaining customers by ensuring that they have little incentive to deal with others.

An earlier version of this figure was published in the July, 1986, issue of

---

*For serious students of customer value issues, a 1991 book, *Competing Globally Through Customer Value,* edited by Michael J. Stahl and Gregory J. Bounds (Quorum Books), addresses the subject of customer value strategy. The contributions in the book are mainly from faculty members at the Colleges of Business Administration and Engineering, University of Tennessee. There are also case histories and descriptions of applications at companies such as Bechtel, Xerox, Procter & Gamble, Georgia-Pacific, and Warner-Lambert. Subtitled *The Management of Strategic Suprasystems,* the book offers practical examples of customer value determination, human resources management for competitive capability, marketing in a value-oriented company, and designing services to meet customer expectations. The editors credit the University of Tennessee's Institutes for Productivity Through Quality for having provided "a living laboratory for many of the coauthors of the book to develop, test, and validate their ideas."

For customer service managers who expect to engage in serious dialogue with their own managements on future directions in customer service management, this book is an excellent reference and resource.

Customer Service Newsletter, under the heading, "How customer loyalty goes to the bottom line." The version shown here, which was introduced several years later, is the first to portray customer service as asset management. It has had considerable impact in that respect.

On the basis of American Management Association data, a company with a 70 percent customer retention rate is typical of most U.S. companies, and an annual account growth of 10 percent among existing or retained customers is a reasonable expectation. The data in the figure have been calculated on this basis and reflec the increases in ten-year revenues that can be anticipated from improvements in customer service that will increase customer retention as shown.

Starting with a group of customers representing $1 million in sales during the first year, Figure A-1 shows these totals after ten years:

70% customer retention rate	$4,038,000
80% customer retention rate	$6,012,000
90% customer retention rate	$9,562,000
100% customer retention rate	$15,937,425

This can be phrased as follows. Using the ten-year revenues from a 70 percent customer retention rate:

A 10 percent increase in retention will increase revenues by 49 percent.
A 20 percent increase in retention will increase revenues by 137 percent.
A 30 percent increase in retention will increase revenues by 295 percent.

This approach to customer service as asset management does not mean that managers should attempt to reach the 100 percent retention level, because it's highly likely that the cost of providing that level of service would outweigh the returns.

What it does suggest, however, is that as customer service manager you will want to test different levels of customer retention—and the cost of the service features required to attain those levels—and then set service levels at the optimum point, when the asset return over a comparable period will be most favorable in terms of the cost of attaining it.

In 1991, senior managers are beginning to think along these lines. As a customer service manager, you are looking at a very powerful tool for convincing them that *expenditures for customer service improvements are not an expense but an* investment *that can vastly improve revenues for them as it has for their competitors across the seas—and will soon be doing for their competitors here at home.*

Appendix E

The Deadly Game
of Losing Customers

The article that appears here first appeared in 1988 and has had wide circulation since that time as an outstanding example of the losses companies can suffer through customer alienation. It is particularly, but not exclusively, applicable to multilocational retail establishments such as service stations, fast-food outlets, chain stores, banks, and similar operations.

In many such operations the loss of as many as 1,000 customers a day, spread across different locations, would go largely unnoticed. Cash customers making a single purchase and never returning would be equally difficult to track, but, as the article indicates, could represent significant lost business to the companies in question.

Although the number of "lost" customers is not as impressive in industrial or business-to-business situations, the amount of lost business is often substantially greater than in consumer or retail situations. For example, one major chemical producer has a single account that purchases $1 billion worth of product annually and is obviously considered a very sensitive account that cannot afford to be alienated in any way! Many other industries have comparable situations, where 20 percent of the customers provide 80 percent of the business, and the loss of a single account can represent a significant loss of profits as well as market share.

The Deadly Game of Losing Customers

In markets where most businesses are national, and where most business is repeat business, the loss of a single customer at a single location reflects a far more serious and costly problem than the numbers or the circumstances suggest.

By WARREN BLANDING

TWICE a week, the little old lady pushed her shopping cart through the aisles of the supermarket, spending about $25 on each occasion. One day, a competitive chain opened an outlet across the street, and she decided to try it . . . and never again shopped at the first store.

Not a very consequential happening—or was it?

Because the real cost of this loss of a customer is not just the dollars-and-cents involved in her particular case— about $50 a week, or $2,600 a year—but of how many times a customer is lost for *any* reason throughout all the stores operated by the chain, and what it adds up in total revenue lost or foregone.

In our example, the chain in question operates 70 stores, and it calculates that it loses about two regular customers a week at each location. This is a very small percentage, but it averages out at a loss of 20 customers a day systemwide.

Not a very big deal, right?

Not unless you consider an annual revenue loss of almost $19 million a year a big deal.

That's right, $19 million or, to be precise, $18,980,000. Here's how it's calculated. The daily loss of 20 customers throughout the system means that the chain loses a total of 365 x 20=7,300 customers a year, each spending $2,600 annually. And 7,300 x $2,600= $18,980,000.

What's wrong with this picture?

Two things: 1. It's generally not the little old ladies who switch sources, but rather the more affluent buyers who have more alternatives available to them; and 2. The weekly expenditures are more nearly in the range of $150-$200 for these affluent buyers. If the chain's customer loss is in this sector, the loss of 7,300 customers each spending $150 weekly or $7,800 a year would total $56.9 million annually.

So, You're Not in the Supermarket Business?

Glad you mentioned that! Because we used the example only to demonstrate the impact of customer loss in a very *conservative* way. For many firms, the weekly expenditures per customer are much larger and the consequences of customer loss much more devastating. Consider the range of commercial and industrial as well as consumer businesses where this is true:

Travel:	Hotels, airlines, rental cars, etc.
Manufacturing:	All classes, but especially generic
Equipment:	Lease or purchase
Services:	Insurance, banking, transportation, communications services, cable TV, etc.

In a number of these categories, expenditures in the thousands of dollars weekly are not uncommon, but as we've shown even expenditures in the hundreds can mount up to substantial sums—particularly when they show up on the minus side.

For example, a health care company handles about 7,000 orders a week averaging about $100 per order. Virtually all of these represent weekly orders from the same customers. The company has a 2% complaint ratio resulting from order errors, but it has no way of knowing how many errors actually occur that customers detect but don't complain about.

This means that 140 customers a week—again, 20 a day—may have occasion to go elsewhere. If we accept the usual figure that only about 20% of customers with a problem actually complain about it, then there may be another 560 customers (the non-complaining 80%) out there who *didn't* complain, but who are building up reasons to go elsewhere.

We don't know, of course, the customer loss ratio that this company can trace to its error rate. What we do know is that the potential in dollars is highly significant, particularly because the firm operates in an extremely competitive field where error rate is a significant factor in vendor selection.

Customer Turnover Ratios

What we also know is that the American Management Associations claims that 65% of next year's business will come from this year's customers, which implies a typical customer turnover ratio of 35% annually—a figure that is probably on the high side for industrial companies. However, if we assume that our health care company with roughly 7,000 customers each spending $5,200 a year has a 20% turnover each year, it will lose 1,400 customers a year and $7.3 million in total revenue.

What doesn't show here, of course, is the acquisition cost of actually replacing these lost customers. Figures vary from industry to industry, but it's generally accepted that it costs five times as much to get a new customer as it

does to service an existing one. In competitive markets, four or five sales calls at $250 per call would normally be required to acquire a new account. So, there's another $140,000 in costs to take into account.

Figuring Your Potential Loss

Companies with a larger company base and larger per-customer expenditures would have correspondingly larger loss potentials. In retail and consumer markets where customer bases may be in the millions, even the loss of $5-a-week customers can add up quickly into significant amounts.

The accompanying chart was drawn up to cover companies of all types and sizes, and is based on customer-per-day losses to facilitate calculations by firms which

Your Annual Revenue Loss is...

If you lose	SPENDING $5 WEEKLY	SPENDING $10 WEEKLY	SPENDING $50 WEEKLY	SPENDING $100 WEEKLY	SPENDING $200 WEEKLY	SPENDING $300 WEEKLY
1 customer a day	$94,900	$189,800	$949,000	$1,898,000	$3,796,000	$5,694,000
2 customers a day	189,800	379,600	1,898,000	3,796,000	7,592,000	11,388,000
5 customers a day	474,500	949,000	4,745,000	9,490,000	18,980,000	28,470,000
10 customers a day	949,000	1,898,000	9,490,000	18,980,000	37,960,000	56,940,000
20 customers a day	1,898,000	3,796,000	18,980,000	37,960,000	75,920,000	113,880,000
50 customers a day	4,745,000	9,490,000	47,450,000	94,900,000	189,800,000	284,700,000
100 customers a day	9,490,000	18,980,000	94,900,000	189,800,000	379,600,000	569,400,000

operate on a seven-day week. To calculate customer loss on a five-day week, simply divide total annual turnover by 365, and interpolate on the chart as necessary. For example, for the health care company cited in the article, the daily customer loss would be 3.84 customers. Take the figure for a loss of one customer a day at $100 weekly—$1.898 million—and multiply it by 3.84 to get a total of approximately $7.3 million, which tallies with our previous calculations.

Of course you don't need to use the chart to calculate actual losses after the fact. What it does is to enable you to *project potential losses* before you actually incur them—*and* to demonstrate the magnitude of the total loss potential when even small amounts are involved. Because even though you may sell to a relatively small customer base—distributors, for example—they in turn may reflect thousands and perhaps hundreds of thousands of customers down the line.

Controlling Customer Loss

Obviously a certain amount of customer loss is unavoidable and can't be controlled. In the retail sector, people die or move away or change in economic status or buying needs or habits. In the commercial and industrial sector, technologies change, mergers and acquisitions take place, new buyers come into the purchasing department, and so forth. Yet the most widely quoted statistics say that these "uncontrollables" account for less than one-third of all customer losses. The other two-thirds plus falls into the customer service category.

Customer service itself falls into two "controllable" categories.

The first and most important is obviously the quality of the service itself and its relevance to customer needs; if customers aren't getting the service they need and want, some will complain and some will simply go elsewhere without giving the vendor the opportunity to correct problems or improve service. If the vendor is unresponsive to those who *do* complain, they, too, will leave—although if their complaints are handled positively they will not only remain as customers but will also become bigger and better customers.

The second controllable, and certainly an important one, is what's usually called *a perceived attitude of indifference* on the part of the vendor employee. This is probably more of a factor in retail or consumer-type contacts, where it's cited as the cause of more than two-thirds of all customer exits, but it's far from unimportant in business-to-business contacts.

What's more, most companies now acknowledge that the issue of employee attitude is more often the company's responsibility than the individual's. Lack of training, stressful job conditions, poor systems, unrealistic policies, and frustration at repeated customer service failures beyond the individual's control—all these go to shape what the customer sees simply as "attitude."

And if in fact the vendor is overall difficult to deal with for whatever reason, this, too, is seen as part of the attitude problem and is usually verbalized simply as "They just don't give a damn."

Third and Fourth Party Influences

The issue of customer perception is further influenced by other entities in the distribution channel: distributors, wholesalers, retailers, truckers, brokers, agents, etc.—and the people who work for them, down to the distributor's CSR, the delivery truck driver or the clerk in the retail store.

Not all of these can be controlled, of course, but the levels of service they themselves receive will ultimately influence the service they give and to that extent the ultimate customer's perception of attitude further down the line. It may also be possible to provide some forms of training or incentives to distributors' buyers as well as CSRs to assure smooth and timely service to their customers. Third parties who are creating problems can be monitored and replaced if necessary. And of course there are many opportunities to improve both performance and perceived attitude right at home.

The Message: Increase Budgets!

Now that the real costs of customer loss can be so graphically demonstrated, management may be somewhat more willing to increase budgets in three critical areas:

1. Customer service system improvement. This is a critical area for companies which are losing market share through inability to perform. In some cases, they simply may not have an accurate reading on customers' service needs. This suggests that they're like a good many other companies which conduct little or no customer research directed specifically at customer perception and acceptance of existing customer service levels. Or, they may be investing their primary resources in customer acquisition— advertising and sales promotion, for example—and not enough in customer retention via the customer service department, technical support, inventories, communications and computer systems and the like. Either way, the figures cited here should be ample justification for not only deciding what needs to be done, but also for doing it.

2. Training personnel. There are no comprehensive figures for the number of customers who are mishandled either in person or on the telephone, but the number is substantial. One analysis of 5,000 calls to Yellow Pages advertisers showed that about 40% were in fact mishandled in one or more ways. Virtually all of these mishandlings were the clear result of inadequate training, or none at all.

It's safe to say that the average consumer receives at least one turnoff a day from untrained service personnel. Some of these represent the customer's only contact with the vendor: for example, the cashier in a self-service gasoline station, the customer service rep in a public utility, the teller in a bank, etc. A professional buyer may receive even more turnoffs.

Either way, some of these cus-tomers will eventually leave—and of course many of those who called to inquire won't even *become* customers. A look at the chart suggests that the costly consequences in both instances are well worth the relatively modest investment in training personnel how to deal with customers as human beings.

3. Informing, educating and training customers. This is a broad area with a number of individual subsets:

a. Training customers in the proper use of the product to reduce customer frustration and/or strain on the vendor's technical support personnel from uninformed customers.

b. Training customer personnel in inventory management, economic order quantities and other aspects of their business which will make the relationship work better for both sides.

c. Maintaining a high level of clear written, printed and spoken information and instructions to customers. Unfortunately, in many companies, instruction booklets, policy statements and bulletins are never reviewed outside the company for clarity or comprehension—rather, they're reviewed inside the company by people who already know what they're *supposed* to mean but lack the objectivity to judge whether they really do. The result is often miscommunication or misunderstanding, and excessive callbacks from customers for clarification . . . and more opportunities for turnoffs.

Conclusion: A Deadly Game Indeed

The numbers we have cited here are real. Whether your customer base is one hundred or one million, loss of market share is serious business. Automation, computerization and self-service have reduced person-to-person communications to minutes and sometimes seconds. This circumstance provides the best of arguments for making sure that the systems themselves are excellent, and the people who back them up even more so. ∎

Index